D1765482

SPAS, WELLS, & PLEASURE-GARDENS *of* LONDON

First published 2010
by Historical Publications Ltd
32 Ellington Street, London N7 8PL
(Tel: 020 7607 1628)

ISBN 978-1-905286-34-8
British Library Cataloguing-in-Publication Data
A catalogue record for this book is available from the British Library

Typeset in Palatino by Historical Publications Ltd
Reproduction by Tintern Graphics
Printed in China by South China Printing Company

SPAS, WELLS, & PLEASURE-GARDENS *of* LONDON

JAMES STEVENS CURL

BY THE SAME AUTHOR

Victorian Architecture: Diversity & Invention
(Reading: Spire Books Ltd., 2007).

A Dictionary of Architecture and Landscape Architecture
(Oxford: Oxford University Press, 2006).

The Egyptian Revival: Ancient Egypt and the Inspiration for Design Motifs in the West
(London & New York: Routledge, Taylor & Francis Group, 2005).

Piety Proclaimed. An Introduction to Places of Worship in Victorian England
(London: Historical Publications Ltd., 2002).

Kensal Green Cemetery. The Origins & Development of the General Cemetery of All Souls, Kensal Green, London, 1824-2001 (Edited)
(Chichester: Phillimore & Co. Ltd., 2001).

The Honourable The Irish Society 1608-2000 and the Plantation of Ulster. The City of London and the Colonisation of County Londonderry in the Province of Ulster in Ireland. A History and Critique
(Chichester: Phillimore & Co., Ltd., 2000).

The Victorian Celebration of Death
(Thrupp, Stroud: Sutton Publishing Ltd., 2000, 2004).

The Art and Architecture of Freemasonry. An Introductory Study
(London: B.T. Batsford Ltd., 1991, 2002, and Woodstock & New York: The Overlook Press, 1993, 2002 – winner of the Sir Banister Fletcher Award for the Best Book of the Year, 1992).

The Londonderry Plantation 1609-1914. The History, Architecture, and Planning of the Estates of the City of London and its Livery Companies in Ulster
(Chichester: Phillimore & Co. Ltd., 1986).

The Life and Work of Henry Roberts (1803-76), Architect. The Evangelical Conscience and the Campaign for Model Housing and Healthy Nations
(Chichester: Phillimore & Co. Ltd., 1983).

for

ALMA MAGDALENA

whose arrangement

of eggshells

enlivened a dark Winter

late afternoon

in London Town

'In sweet water there is a pleasure ungrudged by anyone'.
(Est in aqua dulci non invidiosa voluptas)
PUBLIUS OVIDIUS NASO (43BC-AD17)
Epistulæ ex Ponto **ii** vii 73

'The migration and egress of Metals and Minerals is obvious enough in the investigation of Mineral Spaws or Springs'.
WILLIAM PRYCE (*c*.1725-90)
Mineralogia Cornubiensis:
A Treatise on Minerals, Mines and Mining
(London: J Phillips for the Author 1778) 8

'From the midst of the fountains of pleasure
something bitter rises that torments us even among the very flowers'.
(Medio de fonte leporum
Surgit amari aliquid, quod in ipsis floribus angat)
TITUS LUCRETIUS CARUS (*c*.94-55BC).
De rerum natura **iv** l. 1133

SUBSCRIBERS TO THIS VOLUME

Regina Akel
Mr James Alexander
Nicholas Allen riba
The Late John Armstrong
Dr Mark K Askey
Mr & Mrs Anthony Ballantine
Dr G M Barnes
The Revd Canon Dr Jonathan Barry
Elizabeth Elsie Beggs
Terence Bendixson
Stephen Benson
David & Gladys Bigger
Dr Roger Bowdler
Dr G K Brandwood
Ian C Bristow
Timothy Brittain-Catlin
Eleanor Brown
Anthony Burrell
Dr Donald Buttress
Clive William Callard frics
Anthony R Cartwright
Brian Joseph Carty
Katy Cigno
Mr Neville C W Clarke
Antony Clayton
Diane Clements
Mrs Carolyn Cocke for Julius & Alice
Peter Collins
Derek Connell
Tim & Chris Cookson
Robert M Cooper
Sir Patrick Cormack, fsa, mp
Mary Cosh
Giovanna Lucia Costantini
Andrew Cowser
A J Crockart
Brian Cudby
Jack Dawson
Sir Donnell Deeny
David Dell
Patrick Roy Dennison
Professor Adrian K Dixon
Patricia & Tom Douglas
Mrs Inge Drew
Mrs Patricia Drummond
Patrick Duerden and Rosalind Stoddart
Viscount Dunluce
Martin Durne
John Earl
Lisbeth Ehlers
Dr Harold Elwood
John Fairleigh
Robyn Hand Firth
R J Flanagan
Dr & Mrs Enrico Flossmann
Dr Andreas Förderer
Mr Roger France
Jennifer M Freeman
Robert Freidus
Friends of Southampton Old Cemetery
Alan Frost
The Late John G Fryman
David Garnett
David Gaylard
Mr Meir Gillad
James Gilliland
Gerald Glover
Joscelyn Godwin
James Grimshaw
Keith Haines
Mag Claudia M Hamernik
John Harris
T O Haunch
R H Hayward
Cedric Helsby-Proffit
Roy Hidson dip arch fcilip
Adrian J Hill
Desmond & Margaret Hodges
Daniel Holden
J St Brioc Hooper
Mr and Mrs Bertrand R Hudnall II
Dawn Humm
Laurence Hunt
Livia Augusta Hurley
Ralph Hyde
Donald Insall
Mr & Mrs Richard Jay
Ian Johnson
Dr John M Kirk
Colin & Karen Latimer
John Law
Imre & Janet Leader
Dr Julian W S Litten
Jane McClure
Denis F McCoy
Dr Patrick M McCoy
Jill McIvor
R J McKinstry
Harvey Macmillan, Edinburgh
Terry McMullan
Ian & Antoinette McNicol
Naomi May
Elizabeth Meehan
H A Meek
Margaret M Miles
Paul Millar riba
The Late Brian Millar
Stratton Mills
Jeffrey Morgan & Patricia Craig
Simon Morris
Robert Moulder
Timothy Mowl
Jeremy Musson
Timothy Neville-Lee
Patrick Odling-Smee
Sir Michael Oliver
Anne Olney
Clarissa Campbell Orr
Hippolyte O'Toole
Christopher Parsons BSc dip bldg cons (rics) fca
Mrs Jean Pateman mbe
Jonathan Peacock, Co. Durham
John and Terry Pearson
Hugh Petter
David B Pettigrew
Denis Piggot
Albert Pinching
Dr Andrew Pink
Professor Jack Pinkerton
Alan Powers
Margaret Reed
W N B Richardson, dl
Daniel Rigby
Mike Rigby
Joseph & Ruth Robotham
Alan Russell
Nikos A Salingaros
Colin Sanderson
David M V Short
Alan J Skilton
Ronnie Smartt
Barry Smith
Brian D Smith
David H Smith
Gavin Stamp
Mary McKinney Stevenson
Professor Peter Swallow
Donald Henry Sykes
The Revd Anthony Symondson sj
Christopher Tarratt
Dave Taylor
Michael Taylor
Sue Taylor
John H Terroni
Linda Tilbury
Trevor Todd
Denis Tuohy
John E Vigar ma fsa scot frsa
Henry Vivian-Neal
Peter M Wakelam
Professor Emeritus David M Walker
Robert Wall
Professor David Watkin
Geoff Watts
Dr Philip Whitbourn, obe
Jenny Whitby
Vivienne Whyte
Mr & Mrs Adam Wilkinson
Jonathan Willers & Claire Foss
Martin Williams & Gillian Darby
Mr & Mrs Hal Wilson
Patricia Wilson
Mrs Primrose Wilson
John Woodman
Ron Woollacott, mbe
Robin Wyatt
David Wylde, architect riba riai
Michael C Wylie (Belfast)

CONTENTS

LIST OF ILLUSTRATIONS

Sources of illustrations are given in italics within parentheses at the end of each caption. The following abbreviations have been used:

BAG	Bagnigge Wells
BM	British Museum
Ce	Collage
CL	City of London
CLSA	Camden Local Studies & Archives
CLSLAS	Croydon Local Studies Library & Archives Services
EDG	Edgware
GA	Gloucestershire Archives
GAGCL	Guildhall Art Gallery, City of London
GB	Geremy Butler
GL	Guildhall Library
HP	Historical Publications Ltd
ILHC	Islington Local History Centre, Finsbury Library, London Borough of Islington Library and Cultural Services
JSC	James Stevens Curl
LMA	London Metropolitan Archives, City of London
MBC	Mayson Beeton Collection
MoL	Museum of London
NC	Norman Collection
New	New River Head
NMR	National Monuments Record, reproduced by permission of English Heritage
NOB	Noble Collection
PCA	Permanent Collection Accession
P&D	Prints & Drawings
PEN	Pennant's London
PR	Print
RBKC	Royal Borough of Kensington and Chelsea Library Services
SAD	Sadler's Wells
SAT	Satires
SC	Special Collections
TILUO	The Taylor Institution Library, University of Oxford
WAK	Wakefield Collection
WCA	Westminster City Archives

Illustrations from books in the Author's Collection are acknowledged by author (date) and page-number – details of publications are fully set out in the Select Bibliography.

The front-cover picture is of a scene at *Bagnigge Wells*, published by Henry Haukins in 1779. It is contained within a volume entitled *Bagnigge Wells: a poem in which are pourtrayed the most eminent files-de-joye*. Originally a mezzotint, the illustration has been modern hand-coloured for the present publishers by Kevin Robinson. It is reproduced by kind permission of Guildhall Library, City of London. *(Ref. A.5.2. no. 13)*.

The back-cover picture is of *The St Helena Tavern and Tea-Gardens*, Rotherhithe, shown in a watercolour by 'R.B.' dated 7 June 1839. Reproduced by kind permission of London Metropolitan Archives (see Plate 135 for reference).

PREFACE AND ACKNOWLEDGEMENTS

'Presumption or Meanness, are but too often the only articles to be discovered in a Preface'.
GEORGE CRABBE (1754-1832): *Preface* to *Inebriety, a Poem: in Three Parts* (Ipswich: C. Punchard 1775) i.

'I finde...occasion...to use a certaine Forewarnyng and Præface'.
JOHN DEE (1527-1609): *Mathematicall Præface* to Euclid's *Elements of Geometrie* (London: John Daye 1570) 2.

Some have held that a Preface is the 'most important part' of a book: 'even reviewers', one wit observed, 'read a preface'[1]. Others have lauded Prefaces: William Congreve (1670-1729), for example, said of John Dryden (1631-1700) that, if he had 'written nothing but his Prefaces', this would have 'intituled' him 'to the preference and distinction of excelling in his kind'[2]. Jonathan Swift (1667-1745), however, advised

'Read all the Prefaces of Dryden,
For these our critics much confide in,
(Tho' merely writ at first for filling
To raise the volume's price, a shilling)[3],

but the Preface of the present work is intended neither for reviewers nor for purposes of padding.

As for the Acknowledgements, they are only inadequate courtesies extended to those who have been kind enough to help a scribbler, now, alas!, in his eighth decade, by answering queries, assisting with photographs and other material, and generously providing support of one kind or another. Like the Psalmist[4], the Author acknowledges his many faults, and his omissions and offences are ever before him, but it is doubtful if even hyssop would purge his manifold shortcomings and defects, let alone the aperient waters described in the following pages.

This book had its genesis many years ago. Reading about, and getting to know, London, it was impossible not to notice how important was water, not just the River Thames, but its many tributaries, and, above all, the fact that water-supplies were of fundamental significance for the city, just as they were for every human settlement, but in London's case they were on a very large scale from the very beginning. Studies that led to works such as *The Victorian Celebration of Death*[5] and *Victorian Architecture: Diversity & Invention*[6] involved reading massive tomes such as the various *Reports* of Edwin Chadwick (1800-90) and the polemics of George Alfred 'Graveyard' Walker (1807-84) from which it was clear that catastrophes such as the cholera epidemics which started in 1831 were closely connected with water-supply and the whole vexed question of urban hygiene[7] (including disposal of the dead). Further voracious reading led to the realisation that there was far more to London's water-supplies than was at first apparent: quite apart from the logistics of getting the liquid to places where it was needed, in a state fit for human consumption, there was a whole world of entertainment, recreation, fun, and even curative aspects, that spawned enormous numbers of Pleasure-Gardens offering numerous variations, attractions, claims, and facilities, not all of them concerned with health or medication.

From tentative, yet eager, explorations of London in the 1950s and '60s certain ideas developed that led to publication of early articles on London's cemeteries and burial-grounds, certain themes relating to London's Victorian built fabric, and then the almost forgotten Spas of London[8]. From the first, Michael Wright (1936-2006) encouraged the writing of such articles, first in the *Journal of the Royal Institute of British Architects*, and then in *Country Life* (of which he was Deputy Editor and then Editor for a number of years): to his memory acknowledgement is made with gratitude, not only for his support, but for friendship that led to investigations of parts of London and the development of ideas for further research and writings.

During the period 1970-73, when the Author was Architectural Editor of the *Survey of London*[9], a great amount of material was gathered, friendships made, and many valuable contacts forged. Of enormous help was Ralph Hyde, at one time Keeper of Prints and Maps at Guildhall Library, City of London: not only did he draw attention to much interesting material, but hinted at various obscure avenues that merited a probe. So to Ralph Hyde sincere thanks are given. His successors in Prints and Maps, John Fisher, and especially Jeremy Smith, have rendered very considerable assistance in later years, the latter having been closely involved with the present book, so is warmly thanked for his patience, expertise, and very welcome suggestions.

Others who deserve grateful mention are Ruth Barriskill, Senior Assistant Librarian, Guildhall Library, City of London; Chris Bennett, Senior Borough Archivist, Croydon Local Studies Library and Archives Service, who was very accommodating concerning material on *Beulah Spa*; Nikki Braunton of the Images Collection, Museum of London; Geremy Butler, who once again speedily photographed documents; a friend and former colleague, John Earl, who very kindly made material available from his own collection; Lucas Elkin, of Cambridge University Library, who gave sterling help in tracking down obscure material; Helen English, who helped in many ways; Paul Evans, Development Archivist, Gloucestershire Archives; Auriol Griffith-Jones, who compiled the Index; John Harris, who offered kindly advice; Astrid James, who pointed to certain useful volumes dealing with the history of medicine; Ian Johnson, who was always encouraging and supportive; Professor E. J. Kenney, for clearing up various matters; Rory Lalwan, Senior Archives Assistant, City of Westminster Archives Centre; Josie Lister, Printed Book Researcher, Imaging Services, Bodleian Library, University of Oxford; Norma McCaw (a fellow-member of The Art Workers' Guild), who generously passed on various papers she had collected over the years; Denis McCoy, who once joined in explorations of parts of London (especially Clerkenwell) and shared his thoughts on changes that had occurred since the eighteenth century; Richard Ovenden, Keeper of Special Collections and Associate Director, Bodleian Library, University of Oxford; Margaret Reed, of Starword, who typed the book from assorted notebooks and disreputable scraps of paper; John Richardson, who quickly saw the point and agreed to publish a book after a good dinner at the Reform Club; Philip Temple, of the *Survey of London* who edited the two splendid volumes[10] on Clerkenwell; and last, but by no means least, George Stevens Curl, who read the first two published articles on 'Taking the Waters' in *Country Life*, and suggested that a book might one day emerge.

London has had plenty written about it, and on the subject of London's Wells and the places of entertainment often associated with them there is no shortage of literature, as a glance at the Select Bibliography of the present modest volume will demonstrate. Indeed, it is a daunting subject, and has been approached by several scholars, some of whom were involved in Hydropathy, Naturopathy, and of course, Balnealogy[11]. So why a book on the topic now? First of all, earlier publications had a paucity of illustrated matter, and in the case of certain establishments, a thinness of coverage that required filling out, as well as a correction of certain factual matters. It seemed appropriate to look at the whole subject again, to attempt to repair *lacunæ*, to illustrate where possible and appropriate, and to gather as much material as possible within the parameters set by the publishers. This book, therefore, is the result.

In the late 1960s and early 1970s, careful and

systematic perambulations of whole London Parishes (especially those of Clerkenwell, Islington, and Stepney), armed with maps from various periods, a camera, and a notebook, proved both fascinating yet at the same time depressing, so much had been lost: these forays frequently led to the writing of articles that were subsequently published.

At that time, in Clerkenwell, where once there had been so many Wells, 'Spaws', and Pleasure-Gardens (as well as lots of pretty open country), hardly anything of those places seemed to survive, except the occasional name (*Sadler's Wells* was one example, and the *London Spa* public-house another, but the last in 2009 was no longer extant). Such perceptions induced gloomths, exacerbated when reflecting on the fate of the eighteenth-century *London Spaw* and the subsequent history of the area, including the appalling Spa Fields burial-ground[12]: such places seemed to be infinitely remote and difficult to imagine in the context of the urban fabric as it was then. Plunges into melancholy suggested a break, and the *Empress of Russia* (another hostelry no longer extant) provided hospitality. As fine ale was consumed and blue pipe-smoke rose (a pleasurable combination, that, like the Spas and Pleasure-Grounds of London, has passed into the realms of the fabulous), the genesis of a book began, amœba-like, to form, and the conversation ranged far and wide as ideas were aired and eagerly, humorously, and pleasurably explored. Before Old Age crept up, unperceived, or it became impossible to call back days long gone (it was said, quoting that felicitous son[13] of Bordeaux, who, like claret, never palls), it was determined that a volume on lost Spas should be planned, and it was obvious that material for such a project should be gathered without delay. That must have been in 1969, and very soon certain writings started to take shape.

Shortly after this agreeable session, a battered copy of a volume on London's Spas and Wells was discovered and purchased in a dusty antiquarian bookshop (another delight that becomes rarer with each passing year): cleaned up, de-foxed, and re-bound[14], it was read and joined a collection that contained many works on London and the Home Counties, including *London*[15] by the under-rated[16] Charles Knight (1791-1873), *Old and New London*[17] by Walter Thornbury (1828-76) and Edward Walford (1823-07), and *Curiosities of London*[18] by John Timbs (1801-75), all of which had been collected over the years from friendly, old-fashioned bookshops such as Hugh Greer's treasure-house, Blackwell's Antiquarian Department in Oxford, and numerous other places that used to be found in almost every Cathedral-City in England, but are, alas!, like many a fine pub, no more. Then, in Long Melford in Suffolk, an excellent copy of Foord's book[19] gleamed from the shelves, almost drawing attention to itself; in Sedbergh a fine copy of the Wroths'[20] scholarly and invaluable study was purchased; in Crewkerne, a clean set of volumes by William Hone (1780-1842) was spotted; and in Fisher & Sperr's marvellous bookshop in Highgate a good copy of his great work on Clerkenwell by William John Pinks (1829-60) was bought. Their acquisition re-awakened a dormant project that had once been encouraged by the urgings of a father, now long dead, and outlined during laughter-filled gatherings in London pubs, giving shape to an idea that at one time seemed almost ungraspable, ephemeral, and too difficult to develop into a coherent and manageable form.

One remark above all changed everything: an old friend, Tom Braun[21], came out with it when suggesting that the material on Spas that had appeared under Michael Wright's aegis in *Country Life*[22] deserved to be hugely expanded, developed and augmented to become a book. Tom would often quote some felicitous phrase when making a cogent point, and urged

Vive memor leti: fugit hora[23]

during the Perne Feast at Peterhouse, Cambridge, only a short time before his shocking and premature death. It was Tom's encouragement which provided the catalyst: a book, illustrated, treating of a vanished phenomenon was proposed, toasted, and foolishly promised. What follows is the very late result of what was decided then, and would never have been completed without the promptings of friends and of a father who have gone the way of all that passes. Their appreciation and encouragement played no small part in the birth of this book, and to their shades be gratitude and acknowledgement of kindnesses and support: without their backing there would have been no such volume at all.

First drafts concentrated on establishments that were supposedly Spas, or where there were Wells, but it soon became clear that several 'Spas' were of the spurious variety, and only came into being when Taverns or Pleasure-Gardens needed some further attractions to draw in custom. Further work revealed that there was a great deal of copying that went on, and that if one place having a Garden put on shows, concerts, or novelties, others followed suit, and if 'medicinal' waters existed or could be found, so much the better. Thus Spas, Wells, Pleasure-Gardens, Taverns with outdoor attractions, and even public-houses with some sort of outdoor areas were often blurred as types, so the finished volume includes Spas, spurious Spas, Wells, Pleasure-Gardens, and other establishments that had attributes in common. And the most important feature they shared was a Garden: some were large and had many *fabriques*, water-features, plantations, and facilities, and some were very small, fitted out with minimal trellis-work, arbours, alcoves, and the like. So Gardens were the common denominator, and, being ephemeral, are difficult to recapture without recourse to drawings, paintings, engravings, and other illustrations. One has to will one's self into a Garden of the imagination, to find there, within the 'sequestered close', where bloom the 'hyacinth and rose', ...'beside the modest stock', the flaunting 'flaming hollyhock', and there, too,

> 'without a pang, one sees
> Ranks, conditions, and degrees'[24],

which might well describe a London Pleasure-Garden, when the spectators could see and be seen, partaking of all the delights on offer.

It is hoped, therefore, that the completed book will prove to be moderately entertaining, for it was fun (at times) to research and write, even though its gestation was long and sporadic and its final form only achieved after a great deal of investigation, daunting marathons of reading, and many hours buried in books, papers, libraries, and archives[25].

James Stevens Curl
Oxford, London, Cambridge, and
Holywood, County Down

1970-2009

References: Preface and Acknowledgements

1 Philip Guedalla (1889-1944): *Conversation with a Caller* in *The Missing Muse and Other Essays* (London: Hodder & Stoughton 1929) viii.

2 *See The Complete Works of William Congreve* MONTAGUE SUMMERS (*Ed.*) **iv** which includes *The Preface to Dryden* (London: Nonesuch Press 1923).

3 Jonathan Swift (1733): *On Poetry: A Rapsody* (Dublin & London: sold by J. Huggerson) l.251.

4 *Psalms* **li** 3.

5 Curl (2004).

6 Curl (2007).

7 Which might be described as the potty-training of Urban Man.

8 Curl (1971*a*, 1971*b*, 1976*a*, 1976*b*, 1979).

9 *See*, for example, Sheppard (*Ed.*) (1973).

10 Saint (*Gen. Ed.*) (2008*a* & *b*).

11 Bynum & Porter (*Eds.*) (1987, 1993). Acknowledgements to Astrid James for this and other medical items listed in the Select Bibliography.

12 Curl (2004) 113, 115, 117, 129-31, 133, 136, 178.

13 Decimus Magnus Ausonius (*c.*AD 310-95): *Epigrammata* **xxxiv** 3-4.

14 This was Sunderland (1915).

15 Knight (*Ed.*) (1878).

16 Until the appearance of Gray (2006). *See* also *ODNB* **xxxi** (2004) 893-7.

17 Thornbury & Walford (1879-85).

18 Timbs (1867).

19 Foord (1910).

20 Wroth & Wroth (1896).

21 Thomas Felix Rudolf Gerhard Braun (1935-2008), Oxford Don, Classicist, humorist, scholar, gentleman, and wit.

22 Curl (1971*a*, 1971*b*, 1976*a*, 1976*b*).

23 Live mindful of Death: the hour flies (Aulus Persius Flaccus [AD 34-62]: *Satires* **v** 153).

24 Henry Austin Dobson (1840-1921): *A Garden Song* (1885) in *The Complete Poetical Works of Austin Dobson* (London: Humphrey Milford at Oxford University Press 1923) 178.

25 Especially Guildhall Library, City of London.

CHAPTER I

WATER, SAINTS, GEOLOGY, CONDUITS, AND CURES

Introduction; Some Definitions; A Religious Dimension; A Geological Explanation; Conduits; Medicine and Water

'Then was there 3. principall Fountaines, or wels in the other Suburbs, to wit *Holy well*, *Clements* well, and *Clarkes* well. Neare unto this last named fountaine, were divers other wels, to wit, *Skinners* well, *Fags* well, *Tode* well, *Loders* well, and *Radwell*'.
JOHN STOW (1524/5-1605): *A Survey of London* **i** (London: John Windet, 1603) 11.
Reprinted in the Edn. annotated by CHARLES LETHBRIDGE KINGSFORD (1862-1926): (Oxford: Clarendon Press, 1908).

'He has yet past cure of Physick, spaw, or any diet, a primitive pox in his bones'.
FRANCIS BEAUMONT (1584-1616) & JOHN FLETCHER (1579-1625): *The Scornfull Ladie.: A Comedie* (London: T. Jones 1630, first printed 1616) **iii** 1.

INTRODUCTION: SOME DEFINITIONS

To begin at the beginning, it would be sensible to define a few terms. *Spa* (variously *Spaw*, *Spau*, *Spawe*) is the name of a town in the Province of Liège (Luik) in Belgium, lying in the valley of the Wayai (which river is here joined by the Picherotte), long renowned for its several Springs from which flow chalybeate and other waters. The most celebrated Mineral-Springs are the *Pouhon* (strongly impregnated with carbonic acid and iron) and the *Géronstère*, but there are others, including the *Tonnelet*, *Sauvenière*, *Barisart*, and *Groesbeck*. Long known for relieving arthritis, rheumatism, and heart-disease, Spa-water is still bottled and exported in large quantities by the Spa-Monopole Company, and indeed the place was fashionable from the beginning of the eighteenth century. Its name was introduced into the English language as a generic term for 'Mineral-Spring' and 'Watering-Place'[1].

Apparently the Mineral-Springs of Spa were known from the fourteenth century (and probably long before then), and the fashionable status of the place in the nineteenth century is suggested by the *Route de Balmoral*, *Boulevard des Anglais*, *Hôtel Palais St-James*, *Grand-Hôtel Britannique*, *Hôtel Balmoral*, Golf-Course, and English (i.e. Anglican) Church. From 4 August 1914 Spa was occupied by the Germans, and became a place of convalescence for thousands of sick and wounded soldiers: in 1918 it housed the General Headquarters of the German Imperial Army, the *Château Le Neubois* being used by Kaiser Wilhelm II (reigned 1888-1918 as King of Prussia and German Emperor) as his residence[2].

Certainly the word *Spa* was in use in sixteenth-century England: Edmund Spenser (*c*.1552-99), in *The Faerie Queene* (1590), referred to 'the german Spau'[3], and William Camden (1551-1623) mentioned going to 'drinke the waters of the Spaw' in 1619[4]. In a generalised sense, *Spa* was in use as early as 1610, and meant a Mineral-Spring or Well: William Mather (*fl.* 1657-1708) wrote of the 'abundance of Medicinal-Waters... particularly those of the Spaws of Yorkshire'[5], and Beaumont & Fletcher mentioned 'spaw' with this meaning in 1610[6].

So a *Spa* was a medicinal Spring or Well (or a Spring or Well with supposedly beneficial waters), and the word was also given to a town, locality, or resort possessing a Mineral-Spring or Springs. A person taking the waters could be said to be on a *spa-diet*, or was a *spa-drinker*, and a source of water was a *spa-fountain*, situated in a *spa-house* where *spa-water* could be consumed. To *spa* or *spaa* was to subject someone to spa-treatment, or to frequent or visit a Spa or Spas: a person staying at a resort where waters could be taken was said to be *spaaing*.

A *Spring* was the source or head of a Well, Stream, or River; the supply of water forming such a source, and such usage was known in the ninth century. It is also a flow of water rising or issuing naturally from the ground, or one found by boring; a flow of water possessing special properties, especially of a medicinal nature, usually given with appropriate adjectives, such as *chalybeate*, *hot*, *mineral*, *thermal*, *warm*, and so on. The word also means a place or locality having such springs which persons might visit in search of health or pleasure.

A *Well* is a Spring of waters rising to the surface of the earth, forming a small pool, a Spring of water supposed to have healing properties, sometimes associated with supernatural healing, and sometimes possessing medicinal qualities; a place where there are medicinal Springs, so a Watering-Place or a Spa; a fountain supplied from a Spring, a structure over a Spring to facilitate the obtaining of water; a drinking-fountain; a vertical excavation, usually a cylinder lined with masonry, sunk to such a depth as to penetrate a water-bearing stratum; and a source or origin from which water springs.

Chalybeat(*e*) is anything impregnated with iron, applied in this context to Mineral-Waters and Springs (*chalybite* is a synonym of *Siderite*, or native carbonate of iron). *Mineral-Water* is water found naturally impregnated with some mineral substances, but the term has also been applied to artificial imitations of natural Mineral-Waters, e.g. soda-water (water containing a solution of sodium bicarbonate or charged under pressure with carbon dioxide [carbonic acid gas], so strongly effervescent) or Seltzer-Water (effervescent Mineral-Water containing sodium chloride and small quantities of sodium, calcium, and magnesium carbonates), the natural version of which occurs at Niederselters in Hesse Nassau, Germany, formerly within the Electorate of Trier.

Waters such as Selters or Seltzer were known in the British Isles in the eighteenth century. Richard Brinsley Sheridan (1751-1816) said of a woman that 'she was such a hand at making foreign-waters! – for Seltzer, Pyrmont[7], Islington, or Chalybeate, she never had her equal'[8]. Now this is interesting, because two famous German Mineral-Waters are mentioned with 'Islington', which refers to a London Spa, and the more general 'chalybeate', which could be from many places. This suggests that a Spa north of London had acquired a certain fame by 1775, when Sheridan wrote *St Patrick's Day*.

Other waters were sulphurous, used as laxatives, and there were numerous Mineral-Waters containing various elements in many combinations that were recommended for one ailment or another. Diederick Wessel Linden (*fl*.1745-68), for example, in his extravagant claims for the 'extraordinary mineral-water' of the 'Shadwell-Spaw', in 'Sun-Tavern-Fields, Shadwell, near London', held the waters would prevail over 'Palsy, Rheumatism, and Gout; the Yaws, Venereal Distempers, Gleets, and Fluor Albus[9]; the Leprosy, King's Evil, Scurvy, and Consumption; the Dropsy, Jaundice, Fistulas, and Ulcers; Fluxes, and Inward-Bleedings; Broken Constitutions by Intemperance, or otherwise; the Diabetes, Sore-Eyes, Catarrhs, and other Defluxions of Humours, &c.'[10]. Indeed, it would appear that virtually no 'Distemper' was safe from the effects of these powerful waters, and it was a characteristic of eighteenth-century puffs for Wells and Spas that an absurdly ambitious number of cures could be expected by persons who drank the waters.

A RELIGIOUS DIMENSION

Water, Wells, Springs, and Fountains have long been associated with deities, religious figures, and healing properties. In particular, there were those who caused Springs to gush forth, including St Clement (Pope and Martyr, d. *c*.100)[11], and the Blessed Virgin Mary (First Century)[12] Herself is particularly associated with Fountains and Springs, especially of the healing kind[13], a connection shared with her great forerunner, Queen Isis. *Fons Signatus* (The Fountain Sealed) is a Marian Attribute that also has Isiac associations[14], and there are many other connections with supposedly Christian Saints and pre-Christian Deities. One Christian Saint especially connected with water in England is St Chad of Lichfield (d. 672), where a Well was named after him, and there was another Chad's Well in London. Sabine Baring-Gould (1834-1924) tells us that 'from the miracles alleged to have been wrought by mixing a little dust from his shrine with water, he got the character' of Patron Saint 'of medicinal springs'[15]. St Chad was wont to stand naked in the water of the Lichfield Well to pray: its location was actually at Stowe, to the east of the town (about fifty yards from where St Chad's Church stands today, approximately half a mile to the east of the Cathedral). According to the Antiquary John Leland (*c*.1506-52), a stone at the bottom of the Well was the place where the Saint stood. 'At this stone St Chadd had his oratory in the tyme of Wulpher, Kinge of the Merches'[16]. Although Wells such as that of St Chad at Lichfield were places to which 'devotees of the Romish religion resorted'[17], old customs died hard, and there were numerous Springs and Wells in sundry locations that remained in favour long after the Break with Rome in the sixteenth century, and with several of these the name of St Chad was connected. At Chadshunt[18], for example, there was an Oratory and Well called after him, and the priest-in-charge received as much as £16 a year from the offerings of pilgrims who gathered there. 'Chadwell[19] — one source of the New River — is, perhaps, a corruption for S. Chad's Well'[20]. There are other English Chadwells: one in Leicestershire north-east of Melton Mowbray; one in Shropshire north-east of Telford; a Chadwell End in Bedfordshire due north of Bedford; a Chadwell Heath due west of Romford in what is now Barking and Dagenham, Greater London; and Chadwell St Mary, north of Tilbury and east of Thurrock in Essex. There is also a Chadbury north of Evesham in Worcestershire, and there are numerous English place-names that allude to the Saint in one way or another.

One of the legends of St Chad tells of an episode when he was praying *by a fountain* near his cell: a hart 'with quivering limbs and panting breath, leaped into the cooling stream'[21]. Pitying its distress, the Saint concealed the animal from a hunter[22], for the hart bathing in the fountain foreshadowed the Sacrament of Baptism. As the Bible states:

> 'Like as the hart desireth the water-brooks;
> So longeth my soul after thee, O God.
> My soul is athirst for God, yea, even for the living God'[23].

Mention may also be made of the obscure St Gofor *or* Govor (unknown date), Patron of Llanover, Monmouthshire, where there were nine Springs close to each other, called St Gofor's Well or Wells[24]. For some reason shrouded in time there was a Spring known as *St Gover's Well* in Kensington Gardens[25]: the name may have been given quite late, by Sir Benjamin Hall (1802-67 – created Baron Llanover in 1859)[26], who was (1855-8) Chief Commissioner of Works during whose term of office 'considerable improvements were made in the London parks'[27], but the reputation of this Well for medicinal qualities would appear to be somewhat overstated, for by the 1880s the water was polluted with 'organic matter'[28].

There was indeed a *St Chad's Well* in London itself, near Battle Bridge (now called King's Cross), and its site is recalled by St Chad's Place, which was a small street on the east side of Gray's Inn Road lying between the Metropolitan Railway's King's Cross Station and what were then the Home and Colonial Schools (demolished). William John Pinks (1829-60) recorded that the 'miraculous water' was 'aperient, and was some years ago quaffed by the bilious and other invalids, who flocked thither in crowds, to drink at the cost of sixpence, what people of these latter days, by the "ingenious chemist's art", can make as effectual as Chad's virtues "at the small price of one halfpenny"'[29]. By 'aperient', of course' is meant 'laxative', for the water contained sodium and magnesium sulphates as well as a small amount of iron held in solution by carbonic acid: it was heated in a large cauldron and drawn off into glasses, a pint being considered 'actively purgative, mildly tonic, and powerfully diuretic'. Claims were made that the water was beneficial in cases of 'liver disorders, dropsy, and scrofula'[30].

A. D. Sinclair, M.D., who contributed several articles to the *Royal Encyclopedia*[31] on Chemistry, Medicine, and Comparative Anatomy, was the author of an undated handbill entitled

HEALTH
RESTORED AND PRESERVED
BY DRINKING THE
BATTLE BRIDGE WATERS,
(COMMONLY CALLED ST. CHAD'S WELLS,)
Being formerly dedicated to St. Chad, first Bishop of Lichfield.

Although undated, it appears to hail from the first part of the nineteenth century, and was printed by Isaac Pesman, a Jewish printer and stationer, who flourished in the first three decades of the century, and had premises at 15 Lamb Street, Spitalfields[32].

Sinclair analysed the waters, and found them 'impregnated with a small quantity of purging or sea salts, together with a small portion of iron held in solution by fixed air'. He had 'investigated the virtues & properties of most of the medical Waters in great Britain', and had 'no hesitation in pronouncing St. Chad's Wells Waters equal, if not superior to any of them'. The waters were 'nearest allied to Cheltenham', and Sinclair believed they would 'be found of the greatest service in Glandular and Visceral Obstructions, and in Bilious and Scrofulous Complaints'. In early stages of 'Dropsy' and in 'many of the most distressing Scorbutic Eruptions & Ulcerations on the Skin' the waters were of service, as they sweetened and purified the blood 'by their cathartic, diuretic, and antiseptic qualities'. For 'Chronic and Acute Rheumatism, Nervous Afflictions, Stone, Gravel, Indigestions, and all Complaints of the Liver' they were beneficial, and they could remove 'Head-Aches and seminal weaknesses' without the 'use of Medicine!'. As to their 'vermifuge[33] or anthelmintic[34] powers', evidence was displayed 'in the Pump Room, as worms several yards in length' had been 'brought away by drinking the Waters', and might 'be seen there'. Sinclair went on to state that the 'medicinal qualities and power of these valuable Waters' were too numerous 'to be mentioned in an advertisement, and many interesting cases of cures' were 'gathered' and could be 'perused on the premises'. He 'seriously' recommended the waters 'to all those labouring under obstinate and long-standing disorders, in preference to three-fourths of the drugs in the shops'[35].

Subscriptions were a pound annually, ten shillings quarterly, five shillings monthly, two shillings a week, or sixpence per person per day (except on Sundays, when the price was reduced to four pence). The waters were sold at a shilling a gallon, or three pence a quart, and the 'Entrance to the Wells' was advertised as being 'at the upper-end of Gray's-Inn-Lane Road, near King's Cross'.

St Chad's Well in London can therefore be considered as one of the very few Holy Wells which not only produced water with medicinal qualities, but became popular as a Spa, once various additions had been made to the site. It was probably known long before it evolved into a Spa: Alfred Stanley Foord (1844-1934) claimed it was 'a mineral spring of great antiquity'[36] suggested by the 'fact that, in conformity with the custom of the early ages, when each Spring had its tutelary Saint, this Well was consecrated to St Chad'[37]. Around the middle of the eighteenth century 'the Well was in considerable repute, at least in the neighbourhood, and is said to have been visited in the morning by hundreds of people who paid threepence for the privilege of drinking. A hamper of two dozen bottles could be bought for £1[38]. At that time the gardens attached to the Well were extensive, and abounded with fruit trees, shrubs, and flowers'[39].

These Gardens were indeed large, reaching 'a considerable way down Gray's Inn Lane'[40], and the planting appears to have been fairly typical of eighteenth-century London Spas, but it was not until the second half of the eighteenth century that 'laudatory notices began to appear in the newspapers'[41]. In the 1760s great numbers of persons came to drink the waters, and in 1772 the opening of the Season that Spring 'upwards of a thousand persons drank' there[42]. The Well was mentioned with four other London Wells in *The Macaroni and Theatrical Magazine* in 1773[43], and for the remainder of the century *St Chad's Well* seems to have enjoyed a respectable reputation when it was run by a Mr Salter (one of the owners of the establishment), but unfortunately the medicinal properties of the waters did not run to mental health, and Salter became deranged: he was found drowned in a pond in the Gardens in 1798[44].

By 1809 the Spa was 'much resorted to by the lower classes of tradespeople on Sundays'[45], although it was still frequented by certain enthusiasts, including the notoriously brusque and egregiously rude surgeon, John Abernethy (1764-1831)[46], the Judge, Sir Alan Chambré (1739-1823)[47], the comedian, Joseph Shepherd Munden (1758-1832 – who visited the Well three times a week for a period, possibly in an attempt to ameliorate the effects of the Demon Drink)[48], and Alexander Mensall (*fl.*1775-1825), for fifty years proprietor of the Gordon House Academy, Kentish Town, who took his constipated pupils to the Well once a week in order to save on medical bills[49].

However, by 1825 the place had gone into decline, the trees stood 'as if made not to vegetate..., and nameless weeds' straggled 'weakly upon unlimited borders'[50]. Apparently the grounds had been laid out formally in the manner of a Dutch landscape garden, and a painted sign announced 'Health Restored and Preserved'. A low pump-house with dwelling was tended by the 'Lady of the Well', an 'ancient, ailing female in a black bonnet, a clean coloured cotton gown, and a check apron'[51]. A drawing of the Pump-Room of about 1830 shows a relatively humble building of rustic appearance, clap-boarded and stuccoed, set in rural surroundings *(Plate 1)*. The Well (complete with a rebuilt Pump-House of 1832) was sold by another Salter in 1837 to a William Lucas, who issued numerous hand-bills and pamphlets, praising the waters and their slightly bitter taste, and attempting to revive the fortunes of the place. One such handbill dated 29 October 1840 and entitled *Treatise on the Characteristic Virtues of the Saint Chad's Well's Aperient and Alternative Springs*, described the Spring as having 'many Virtues' and as 'an universal medicine' capable of giving

Plate 1: Buildings at *St Chad's Well*, Battle Bridge, based on an original sketch of *c.*1830 *(From Foord [1910] opposite p. 74: Collection JSC).*

> 'speedy and sure relief from indigestion and its train, habitual costiveness[52], the extensive range of liver complaints, dropsy[53] in its early stages, glandular obstructions, and that bane of life, scrofula[54]; for eruptions on the face and skin its almost immediate efficacy needs but a trial. The evidence of the frequenters of the pump-room is the strongest testimony that can be offered the suffering part of the community. Pamphlets may be had at the pump-room, in which is set forth more fully the healing properties of this medical spring. The pump-room and gardens are tastefully arranged, and fitted up with attention to the convenience, &c., of the invalid, the latter offering a pleasant walk for visitors... An elegant pump and pump-room have lately been erected at considerable expense, affording, in comparison with former times, excellent accommodation for visitors. The water when freshly drawn is perfectly clear and pellucid, and sparkles when poured into a glass; to the taste it is slightly bitter, not sufficiently so as to render it disagreeable, indeed persons often think it so palatable as to take it at the table for a common beverage...'[55].

With all the skin-complaints, 'eruptions', and so on, one might be excused for hazarding the suggestion that, if the waters had been used for regular bathing, some of these complaints might have been avoided. Worms and other parasites suggest appalling hygiene, inadequately cooked food, and a general lack of attention given to elementary cleanliness.

'A Ground-Plan of St Chads Well 1830'

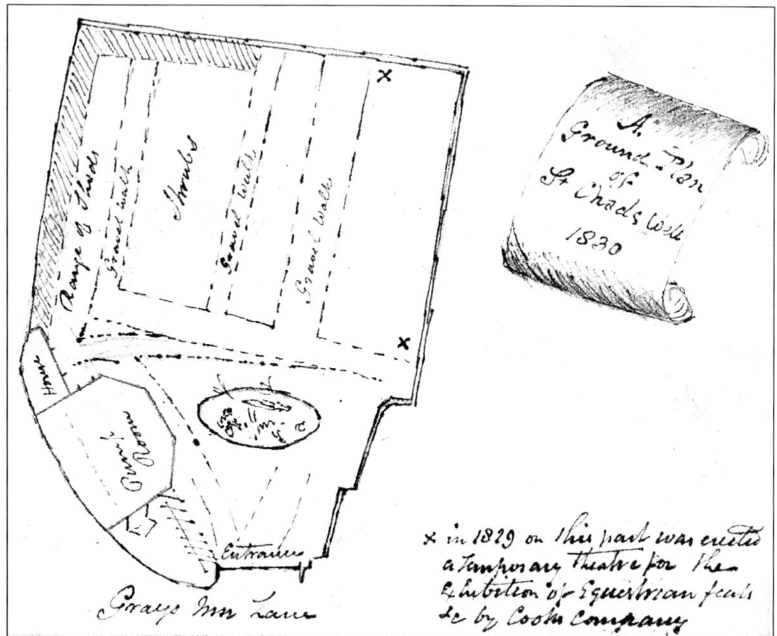

Plate 2: 'A Ground Plan of St Chads Well 1830': the rectangle on which the two X's have been marked was the site of a 'temporary theatre' for the 'Exhibition of Equestrian feats' by the Circus of Cooke, featuring the horsemanship of James Ryan *(LMA SC/GL/NOB/C/001/1-12).*

survives in the London Metropolitan Archives : it shows the entrance in 'Gray's Inn Lane', the Pump-Room, areas planted with shrubs, gravel walks, and the small dwelling-house next to the Pump-Room. One rectangular area, formerly planted, marked with XX, had a temporary theatre erected on it in 1829 for 'the Exhibition of Equestrian feats &c. by Cooks Company'[56] *(Plate 2)*, but a handwritten note in the same collection referred to the place being 'tolerably spacious and laid out in walks and arbours with a pump room for drinking and afterwards promenading', and that 'in 1829 on the ground a circus was erected by Ryan the riding master for his exhibitions of horsemanship'[57]. Presumably the last was James Ryan (*c*.1799-1875), the circus proprietor and great rival of the equestrian Andrew Ducrow (1793-1842), and 'Cook' must have been Thomas Taplin Cooke (1782-1866), whose second son, William Cooke (1807/8-86) went on to manage Astley's Amphitheatre[58].

In 1833 nearly the whole of the grounds of *St Chad's Wells* or *Well* became a timber-yard, but the Well remained for some time, and the waters could still be drunk in the 1840s, although 'all vestiges of the gardens' were obliterated. Apparently the 'old well house' was pulled down and a new one erected: presumably this was the Pump-Room, which was still there in 1860[59] but was demolished when the Metropolitan Railway was constructed in that decade. It seems that *St Chad's Well* 'endured longer than most of the other mineral springs in the neighbourhood, and, in contradistinction to some of the other spas, always remained respectable, as befitting its holy origin'[60]. Nevertheless, no traces of this Spa may be found today[61].

Opinions are divided concerning the so-called *Shadwell-Spaw*, mentioned above, puffed by D. W. Linden[62], but only used for a short period for drinking and bathing. Sunderland considered it of 'slight importance'[63], but Daniel Lysons (1762-1834) referred to Shadwell as 'formerly called Chadwelle' which 'took its name, as is supposed, from a spring dedicated to St Chad'[64], believed to have been where the Church of St Paul[65], Shadwell (Tower Hamlets), now stands, or perhaps somewhere near the churchyard wall. There was a large and impressive Roman Baths complex at Shadwell, where there was also what appears to have been a grand mausoleum and cemetery, so the place has been inhabited since Antiquity. It appears that land at 'Shadewell' was conveyed during the reign (1216-72) of King Henry III (b. 1207), which suggests that any connection with St Chad is probably spurious[66]. However, the name clearly refers to some kind of water-source, which may (or may not) have been associated with the Saint[67], but when the Mineral-Spring was found *c*.1745 in Vine Tavern or Sun Tavern Fields by a Walter Berry, somewhat improbable benefits were alleged concerning the restorative and curative properties of its waters[68]. But, although the water was said to be of some use for antiscorbutic purposes (that is, the treatment of scurvy, a disease caused by lack of Vitamin C), and for the treatment of skin-diseases, its ferocity proved too strong for internal consumption, so salts were extracted from the water, and these were used in the preparation of a liquor to enable calico-printers (of which there were many in Stratford and Bow) to fix their colours[69]. The location of the 'Spaw' at Shadwell was commemorated by Sun Tavern Gap, a lane off Cable Street, but, as the area has been altered so drastically, it is difficult to visualise anything like a Spaw today.

Septimus Philip Sunderland (1860-1950) suggested that some of the 'mineral wells' which had very short careers (such as *Shadwell Spaw*) 'may have originated in the endeavour of the people of old London to obtain a supply of water for domestic purposes...'. Shafts were 'occasionally sunk in the London Clay' in attempts 'to procure water, but without success, because there is no free water in clay. No water being found, some of the shafts were filled up, but others were simply covered up and were forgotten. Surface water sometimes found its way into these old shafts and accumulated, dissolving from the clay some of its constituents, such as lime, sulphur, magnesia, and iron: thus the water became strongly mineralized. When, sometimes after the lapse of years, the well shafts were reopened by accident, the water found therein would be erroneously thought to indicate the presence of a spring'[70].

However, in the case of the 'Shadwell-Spaw' it is difficult now to establish what exactly Walter Berry found: true, there once *were* Roman Baths in the vicinity, but the waters sound as though they were heavily polluted, and so the 'Spaw' was probably of what Sunderland (with good reason) called the 'spurious' kind.

A GEOLOGICAL EXPLANATION

As will become apparent in this book, there were several groups of Spas and Wells in London which require some slight investigation to point out why they existed. The distribution of water-bearing strata affects the occurrence of Springs: thus such distribution influenced early settlements and the distribution of population until technological advances in the nineteenth century greatly increased the possibilities of providing water for many areas not previously known for such supplies[71].

The geological strata of South-East England can be crudely divided into *permeable* and *impermeable* beds: the former will have dry surfaces, but they yield supplies of water from Wells and Springs; the latter are traversed by streams, and are often soggy through water seeping from overlying permeable beds, but, although saturated, they do not, as a rule, yield supplies of water. Permeable beds include Valley Gravels, Glacial Sands, Plateau Gravels, Chalks, and so on, while impermeable beds would include Alluvium, Boulder Clay, the heavy, gluey, London Clay, Woolwich and Reading Clays, Weald Clays, and so on.

The Valley Gravels yielded water-supplies for early human settlements, and these became the nuclei of villages such as Chelsea, Clapham, Ealing, Hackney, Islington, and Mitcham, which can be classified as Gravel Villages. By the time the railways arrived in the period roughly from the reign of William IV until the Great Exhibition (1830-51), London had expanded as far as the very edges of the Gravel Terrace (that included Holborn and Paddington, but the London Clay to the north was not heavily populated because water-supplies were poor[72]. The railway-termini, therefore, were at approximately what can be described as the edges of the built-up parts of London, roughly corresponding with the edges of the Gravel Terrace. The mass-production of cast-iron water-pipes led to the urbanisation of those parts of London to be built on London Clay.

Geological expositions can be tedious, but, as briefly as possible, to avoid such tedium, in London the Terrace Gravels rest for the most part on London Clay, thus water was thrown out from the Gravel in numerous Springs and Wells which occurred mainly at or near the edges of the Terraces and where they were cut into by Valleys such as those of the Tybourne and Westbourne. 'Some of them are commemorated' in place-names, 'such as Bridewell, Clerkenwell, and Shacklewell[73] ... Medicinal properties, laxative or chalybeate, were attributed to some, and Spas and Pleasure-Grounds were laid out at Bagnigge Wells, Sadler's Wells, Islington Spa'[74], and elsewhere. Apparently the River Fleet was called

'River of Wells'[75] from the number of Springs in the valley.

It seems that London was amply supplied with water from these Springs and from shallow Wells in the gravel, over which pumps were erected. But, through encroachment by buildings and raising of ground-levels, the fresh waters became polluted, and, as the population increased, sweet water had to be obtained from further away. Even in the thirteenth century a conduit system was introduced, and water was brought into London by means of elm or lead pipes[76]. Springs in the Tybourne Valley at Marylebone were piped thus, as were those of the Westbourne at Paddington. In the sixteenth century water was brought from Hampstead, and at the beginning of the seventeenth century the channel for the New River was cut (1604-13) to supply London with water from springs in Hertfordshire, a massive undertaking essential for the development of the metropolis. In 1605 the City of London sponsored and obtained an Act of Parliament[77] which permitted the construction of a channel to bring water from the Springs of Amwell and Chadwell near Ware to the north side of the City, and a further Act[78] clarifying rights was obtained in the following year. The guiding light in this venture was Hugh Myddelton (*c.*1556-1631)[79], supported by his elder brother, Sir Thomas Myddelton (*c.*1549-1631)[80], Lord Mayor of London in 1613, one of the first members of the Court of Assistants of 'The Society of the Governor and Assistants, London, of the New Plantation of Ulster, within the Realm of Ireland', a cumbersome title later shortened to 'The Honourable The Irish Society' (the overseeing body in charge of the City of London's estates in Ulster)[81], founder-member of the East India Company, and from 1609 involved in the Virginia Company and its efforts to colonise North America. The New River was ceremoniously opened in 1613, and by 1618 the New River Company was supplying Hertfordshire water to over 1,000 houses within the capital from the New River Head situated high in the fields of rural Clerkenwell (the site is contained within what is now Rosebery Avenue, Myddelton Passage, Hardwick Street, and Amwell Street[82]).

However, the New River was not the first such attempt to supply clean, wholesome water to London: other conduits were constructed by the City Corporation after an Act of 1543[83], bringing water from Hackney, Hampstead, and Muswell Hill.

Plateau Gravels that rest on London Clay are small reservoirs of water and were the sites of early villages such as Chipping Barnet and Totteridge. The Bagshot Sand of Hampstead and Highgate had many Springs at its southern margin, whence streams flowed over the London Clay. The Highgate and Hampstead Ponds were fed by such Springs, providing the head-waters of the Holebourne. *Shepherd's Well*, Hampstead[84], was the source of the Tybourne, and the Westbourne rose near Cannon Hill, West Hampstead. The medicinal Springs of Hampstead were of the chalybeate kind, like much of the water from the Bagshot Sand. London Clay is very retentive, and what supplies of water it may yield, along lines of septaria[85] or otherwise, are heavily charged with mineral matter, chiefly iron salts and sulphates from the decomposition of pyrite[86] in the clay, and the waters were once thought to be beneficial. 'Epsom Salts', for example, take their name from the minerals in a Spring on Epsom Common, and there were formerly Spas there and at Beulah Hill, Streatham, and Sydenham[87].

For the purposes of this book it will be sufficient to note that London was supplied with numerous sources of water, and many of these became prized for their mineral content *(Plate 3)*. The most important sources of water for Londoners in the past were the streams that issued from the uplands of Hampstead and Highgate: the largest of those was the Holebourne, otherwise known as the Fleet[88]. It seems to have been the 'Hole' that gave its name to 'Black Mary's Hole' at *Bagnigge Wells* and *Hockley-in-the-Hole*, for more of which see the following Chapters. The Holebourne became the Fleet as it approached the Thames, and (like the Walbrook) was navigable for a short distance upstream. The 'Entrance to the Fleet River' is shown in a delightful oil-painting which must date from the middle of the eighteenth century *(Plate 4)*, but from our point of view the Fleet (or Holebourne, or 'The River of Wells'), was immensely significant, not for navigation, but because it fed numerous Springs and Wells[89].

However, the Fleet silted up every few years, and became a source of continual expense for the City of London. It was also virtually an open sewer when it reached the built-up area, and was called the Fleet Ditch in the eighteenth century and long before that. It grew from two distinct sources: from Hampstead and Highgate Ponds, the two streams joining a little above the Regent's Canal, flowing past Battle Bridge and then between Gray's Inn and King's Cross Roads, then past Clerkenwell Green, and was joined by another stream that rose near what is now Russell Square. Flowing south towards Farringdon Road, it ran through the low lands called Whitefriars, and joined the Thames west of the present Blackfriars Bridge[90]. Even by Georgian times, however, the Fleet was intolerably polluted, and in due course was degraded to become a sewer and largely covered in.

Foord outlined the courses of the Holebourne, Tybourne, Westbourne, and Serpentine[91]. The geological structure of the basin in which London developed ensured that the settlements grew where water-supplies could be obtained, but these (for the most part) shallow sources were easily contaminated. Soakage from cess-pits, stables, byres, industries, slaughterhouses, and, of course, burial-grounds, made the water in many Wells deadly to humans. One only has to recall the large number of pumps that were sited in or near churchyards to realise that these water-supplies must have been extremely dangerous, and almost invariably contaminated[92].

CONDUITS

Although the whole business of water-borne disease was not understood until well into the nineteenth century, clean water-supplies were long thought desirable, and so water was brought into populous areas from great distances by means of conduits. The word 'conduit' in this context has two meanings: it alludes to an artificial channel or pipe for the conveyance of water, so can be an *aqueduct* or a canal; and it is a structure from which water is distributed or issues, perhaps as a fountain. In the latter meaning the structure is really best described as a *conduit-house*, and the term *conduit-head* is applied to a pond, pool, or reservoir fed by the conduit from some distant source. Stow put it rather elegantly when he wrote that the 'fresh waters that were in and about' the 'Citie, being in processe of time by incrochment for buildings and heighthnings of grounds utterly decayed, and the number of Citizens mightily increased', the population was obliged 'to seeke sweete waters abroad'[93], so that in 1236 water was conveyed by pipes from the Springs in the Manor of Tyburn.

This process was repeated, and in due course there were several conduit-heads or *bosses* (meaning a water-spout projecting from a structure of a sculptured figure, sometimes of grotesque gor-bellied[94] appearance) set up in various thoroughfares, all on the western side of the Walbrook (or Wallbrook), the eastern parts of the City being supplied by Wells, although later in the Middle Ages conduit-houses were built there too, as Wells became polluted (examples were Bishopsgate [*c*.1513], London Wall [*c*.1538], and Aldgate [*c*.1535 – with water drawn from heads in fields near Dalston]). On great days, such as Coronations, Feasts, or other celebrations, conduit-houses could run with wine (which was arranged at 'the Conduit of Chepe' in 1273-4)[95].

Conduit-houses could be of considerable magnificence[96]. The 'Great Conduit in Chepe' (which required regular maintenance, cleaning, and repair) was situated at the Poultry end of Cheapside, and was a long stone crenellated building enclosing a huge lead-lined cistern, begun in 1245 and rebuilt and enlarged in 1479[97]. This Great Conduit in Cheapside had 'as crystal stoon', water that 'Ranne like Welles of paradys', a 'holsome lykour, ffull Riche and of greate prys', and in 1432 when King Henry returned from France, was 'by miracle... turned into wyne'[98]. One of London's most prominent conduit-houses was built in 1282 in Cornhill, originally as a lock-up for unruly persons, and in 1401 it was converted into a conduit-house. Called 'the Tun', it appears to have been polygonal on plan, and is shown in an engraving published by the firm of Josiah Boydell (1752-1817) in 1818 *(Plate 5)*. About three-quarters of a mile to the north-west, the Charterhouse had its own water-supply laid on from Islington: this originated in a Spring in a meadow called Overmead, later identified by the *White Conduit House* which will be mentioned below.

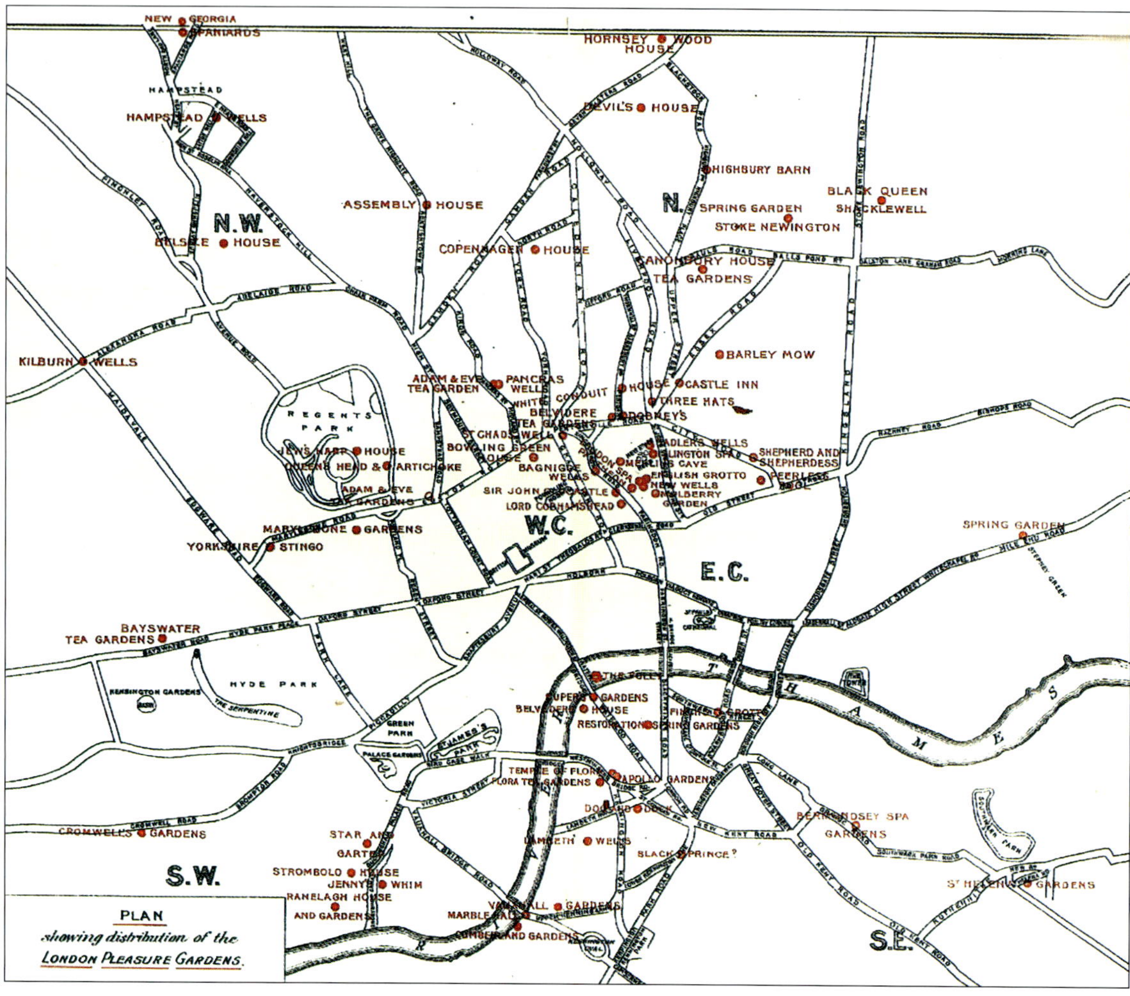

Plate 3: Plan showing the distribution of the Pleasure-Gardens of London, including Wells and Spas *(From Wroth & Wroth [1896]12-13: Collection JSC).*

So conduit-houses of the mediaeval period could be rather grand, and later ones could be architecturally of some distinction too: examples outside London include the Carfax Conduit, Oxford (1616-17), designed by John Clarke (*c*.1585-1624, removed as an eye-catcher or *fabrique* to the park at Nuneham Courtenay, Oxfordshire, in 1787), Hobson's Conduit, Cambridge (1614 – which was supplied with water from Nine Wells near Trumpington at the same time as London was supplied with water from the New River), and the vast fountain in the Great Court, Trinity College, Cambridge (1601-5, rebuilt by Robert Grumbold [1639-1720] in 1715-16).

Cardinal Thomas Wolsey (1470/1-1530) caused a conduit to be constructed between Kingston Hill and Coombe Hill to the new Palace of Hampton Court, and three of the conduit-houses survive, as well as one intermediate inspection-point[99]. In the sixteenth century the philanthropic gesture of William Lamb in providing fresh water is recalled in 'Lamb's Conduit Street', the sign of the celebrated public-house there (*The Lamb*) being a rebus on the name. Conduit Street in Westminster is another reminder of ancient water-supplies laid on for public benefit. There were many conduit-houses in London, and a few survive, including a handsome eighteenth-century example in Greenwich Park, probably by Nicholas Hawksmoor (*c*.1662-1736), who was Clerk of the

Plate 4: 'Entrance to the Fleet River' of *c.*1765, from an oil-painting, School of Samuel Scott (1702-72) *(GAGCL/PCA 46/Ce10048).*

Plate 5: *Cornhill, London, as it appeared about the year 1630 With the celebrated Water-Conduit called the Tun. Part of the Original Bourse or Royal Exchange, &c.* An engraving by Bartholomew Howlett (1767-1827) published by Boydell & Co. in 1818 *(LMA SC/GL/PR/COR/Ce1829/cat.no.q3697125).*

Works at Greenwich Hospital 1698-1735[100]. Foord wrote extensively about conduits and conduit-houses, and his work may still be read with benefit[101].

MEDICINE AND WATER

A revival of ancient medical doctrines drew attention to the fact that the benefits of bathing and of water had been recognised in Antiquity. During the sixteenth century, for example, educated persons sought medicinal baths, among them Michel de Montaigne (1533-92), for example. Soon several ancient baths were revived, and new facilities constructed for visitors[102]. The discovery of a Spring could bring potential riches if the waters could be exploited for health-giving benefits (real or imagined)[103]. In England, by the eighteenth century, many Spas had become fashionable as resorts (e.g. Bath), and many public baths were provided late in the seventeenth century, several acquiring reputations for loucheness[104]. From the late-sixteenth and early-seventeenth centuries, the development of Iatrochemistry (the application of Chemistry to Medical Theory pioneered by Franciscus Sylvius [1614-72] of Leiden) led to a growing interest in the 'taking of the waters', and Iatrochemical Practitioners sought specific treatments for specific conditions, and thus explored the medicinal properties of certain waters. From the latter part of the sixteenth century, it became common for waters to be subjected to chemical analysis in order to puff the medicinal properties of one source or another. Waters were bottled and marketed, and some entrepreneurs such as Nehemiah Grew (1641-1712) extracted the 'salts' which were then sold as cures.

An important student of Baths and Spas was Sir John Floyer (1649-1734), who denounced strong drink, tobacco, hot baths, warm beds, blazing fires, consumption of tea and coffee, lack of exercise, 'passion of the mind', youthful marriage, 'too much venery' (which he claimed injured the eyesight and digestion, as well as breeding 'wind and crudities'), and much else, leading to 'weakness of spirits... in the hysterical and hypochondrical'. Morality became associated with Hygiene, and many took up the notion that bracing cold baths, cold air, and so on hardened the constitution and gave protection from illness: thus such ideas, sometimes associated with the Victorian period, were current long before.

The belief that the drinking of Spa-water was beneficial, of course, was spread as communications improved, and ships and railways brought celebrated European Spas and Baths within the reach of an increasing number of persons: Aix-les-Bains, Baden-Baden, Bad Ischl, Karlsbad, Marienbad, and Wiesbaden were just some fashionable Spas which offered their clientèles an attractive range of diversions, including decent accommodation and food, music, casinos, promenades, and so on, in addition to the cures obtained by imbibing the waters and bathing in them. The system evolved by Vincent Priessnitz (1799-1851), which included plenty of exercise, a special diet, and the use of cold water, became known as Hydrotherapy (essentially the treatment of ailments by the external use of water, but often associated with the drinking of certain mineral-waters), and led to the establishment of various 'Hydros' as treatment-centres in places such as Malvern (where James Manby Gully [1808-83] and James Wilson [1807-67] set up hydropathic cures). A variant was *Kneippism* or *Kneipping*, evolved by Fr. Sebastian Kneipp (1821-97), a Bavarian Priest, a special feature of which was walking barefoot through dewy grass for curing headaches and constipation.

Thus, from the sixteenth century there was a growing interest in 'taking the waters', either drinking them or bathing in them, or both. The peculiarities of London's geology led to numerous Springs, Streams, and Wells being exploited, some as Spas, many of which were claimed to have Mineral-Waters with beneficial properties, capable of curing or alleviating the symptoms of an impressive number of 'distempers'. Several establishments acquired pretty Gardens, buildings for entertainment (music, food, theatrical performances, etc.), and other attractions, but the bases for their existence lay in the waters provided in their grounds. However, as there is a considerable overlap between the facilities provided by 'Spas', 'Wells', and other establishments, including Gardens attached to pubs, boundaries were often blurred, and several places that were not strictly Spas or Wells have been included in what follows.

These Spas and Wells fall into several distinct groups, of which perhaps the most interesting was what we might term the 'Clerkenwell Group'. Beyond that Group, to the North, was what can be called the North London Group, including the vanished Spa of St Pancras. There were also Groups in St Marylebone (Mary-le-Bourne), Hampstead, Chelsea, and the East, as well as an impressive number South of the River. The next Chapter will attempt to describe some of those Spas and Wells that once flourished as part of the Clerkenwell Group.

Chapter I References: Water, Saints, Geology, Conduits, and Cures

1 Karl Baedeker (1931): *Belgium and Luxembourg* (Leipzig: Karl Baedeker) 320.

2 On 9 November 1918 he left *Le Neubois* for Amerongen in The Netherlands (where he arrived on 10 November), bringing an end to the German Empire and Kingdom of Prussia.

3 **i** xi 30.

4 Gardiner (*Ed.*) (1865-8) 200.

5 Mather (1727) 390.

6 *See* quote at the beginning of this Chapter.

7 From Bad Pyrmont in Hameln-Pyrmont, Niedersachsen (Lower Saxony), the Mineral-Waters of which (*Bad Pyrmonter Mineralwasser*) are celebrated.

8 Sheridan (1789) 1 **i**.

9 Leucorrhoea (abnormal mucous or mucopurulent discharge from the lining-membrane of the female genital organs, vulgarly known as 'The Whites').

10 Linden (1749) title-page.

11 Baring-Gould **xiv** (1914) 506-8; Farmer (1992) 102-3; Jameson **ii** (1848) 149.

12 Jameson (1907) *passim.*

13 Witt (1971).

14 For these matters *see* Curl (2005) *passim*, and Witt (1971) *passim.*

15 Baring-Gould **iii** (1914) 32; Farmer (1992) 94-5.

16 Leland **iv** (1744-5) 11. Wulphere (d. 675) was King of the Mercians. *See ODNB* **lx** (2004) 550-1.

17 Pinks (1880) 504.

18 A parish in Warwickshire, in the Hundred of 'Kington', some nine miles south-south-east of Warwick, and two miles north of what is now Kineton.

19 In Hertfordshire, two miles west of Great Amwell.

20 Baring-Gould **iii** (1914) 32-33.

21 *Ibid.* 35.

22 Wulfade, supposedly son of the King, no less.

23 Psalm **xlii** v. 1 & 2 in *The Book of Common Prayer* given as 'As the hart panteth after the water brooks, so panteth my soul after thee, O God. My soul thirsteth for God, for the living God' in the Authorised Version of *The Holy Bible.*

24 Baring-Gould **xvi** (1914) 220.

25 Davies (1939) 156.

26 The famous bell, 'Big Ben' in the clock-tower of the Palace of Westminster, was named after him (1858).

27 *ODNB* **xxiv** (2004) 596.

28 Foord (1910) 171, opposite which is a photograph of the Well. *See* also Sunderland (1915) 28.

29 Pinks (1880) 504.

30 Sunderland (1915) 77.

31 Hall (1789-91).

32 Sheppard (*Gen. Ed.*) (1957) 30, 43, 55-6, 61, 97-8, 108, 127, 134-6, 183.

33 Ability to expel worms.

34 Destroying or expelling intestinal worms.

35 LMA SC/GL/NOB/C/001/12-003/2.

36 Foord (1910) 74.

37 *Ibid.* 75. Foord was an illustrator of scientific papers and secretary of a mining company. His book is decently produced, but its contents are largely derivative.

38 Which seems very expensive.

39 Wroth & Wroth (1896) 72.

40 Foord (1910) 75.

41 *Ibid.*

42 *Ibid.*

43 Williams *et al.* (1772-3) (January 1773) 162.

44 *The Courier* (18 July 1798). *See* also Wroth & Wroth (1896) 72.

45 Foord (1910) 76.

46 *ODNB* **i** (2004) 99-101.

47 *Ibid.* **x** (2004) 1009.

48 *Ibid.* **xxxix** (2004) 753-5.

49 Wroth & Wroth (1896) 73. Mensall is given as 'Measall' in Boulton **i** (1901) 66.

50 Hone **i** (1835) 323.

51 *Ibid.*, quoted verbatim in Wroth & Wroth (1896) 73.

52 Constipation.

53 Morbid accumulation of fluid in any part of the body, but often associated with heart-failure or diseased kidneys.

54 Tuberculosis, but especially chronic enlargement and degeneration of the lymphatic glands, also called *King's Evil* and *Struma.*

55 Quoted also in Pinks (1880) 506.

56 LMA SC/GL/NOB/C/001/12-003/2.

57 *Ibid.*

58 *ODNB* **xiii** (2004) 174-5.

59 Coull (1861) 22.

60 Sunderland (1915) 77. *See* also *Gentleman's Magazine* **ii** (1813) 557.

61 For further particulars *see* Ashton (1889) 49; Clinch (1890) *passim*; Cromwell (1835) 156 ff; Hone **i** (1835) 322 ff; Hughson **vi** (1805-9) 366; Kearsley (1791) on 'Battlebridge'; Lambert **iv** (1806) 295; Lysons **iii** (1792-6) 381; Palmer (1870) 75; Pinks (1880) 90, 504-6, 558, 561; Roffe (1865) 13; Thornbury & Walford **ii** (1879-85) 278; Wroth & Wroth (1896) 72-4.

62 Linden (1749).

63 Sunderland (1915) 91.

64 Lysons **iii** (1792-6) 382.

65 St Paul's (1817-21), designed by John Walters (1782-1821).

66 Hardy & Page (*Eds.*) **i** (1892) 16.

67 *See* Lysons **iii** (1795) 383-90; Noordhouck **v** (1773) 769-72.

68 Linden (1749) *passim*, but especially the title-page.

69 Foord (1910) 122.

70 Sunderland (1915) 65-66. Sunderland's book has a similar content to that of Foord. Sunderland himself was a medical man with an interest in Balneology and Climatology who published papers on *Gonorrhœal Rheumatism in Women* (1898), *Pelvic Pain in Women from Impacted Ureteral Calculi* (1900), and *Uterine Hæmorrhage as Affected by the Climate of Altitudes* (1898). *See Transactions of the American Clinical and Climatological Association* **lxiii** (1952) lix-lxi.

71 Davies (1939) 155.

72 *Ibid.* 155-6.

73 Situated in Hackney.

74 Davies (1939) 156.

75 *Ibid.*

76 Stow (1633) described these matters.

77 3 Ja. I *c.* 18.

78 4 Ja. I. *c.* 12,

79 Created a Baronet 1622.

80 Knighted 1603.

81 *See* Curl (2000) 46-8 and *passim.*

82 *See* Saint (*Gen Ed.*) (2008*b*) 165-184.

83 35 Hen. VIII *c.* 10

84 *See* Baines (*Ed.*) (1890) 205 ff.

85 Concretionary nodules of hard carbonate of lime, called *septaria*, found in the London Clay.

86 Iron disulphide. The term is also extended to a larger class of mineral sulphides and arsenides.

87 Davies (1939) 158.

88 *See* Stow (1908 edn.) **i** 11, 14-15; **ii** 271-2.

89 Waller (1875), but *see* also Foord (1910) Ch. II.

90 Waller (1875). *See* Timbs (1867) 346-8.

91 Foord (1910) Ch. II.

92 *See* especially Woodward (1906) for a description of the soils and subsoils of London.

93 Stow **i** (1908) 16.

94 With a corpulent, swollen, protruding stomach.

95 Foord (1910) 253.

96 Davies (1911-13) and *see* Davies's paper (1907) cited in the Select Bibliography.

97 Stow **ii** (1908) 331 and Foord (1910) 255. See also Davies (1911-13).

98 Kingsford (*Ed.*) (1905) prints this material complete.

99 Cherry & Pevsner (1983) 315.

100 *Ibid.* 265.

101 Foord (1910) Pt III Chas I, II, III. *See* also Davies (1911-13).

102 *See* Hembry (1990) 4-38; Porter (*Ed.*) (1990) 23-47.

103 Grimmelshausen (1962) 333, 338-9.

104 Bynum & Porter (*Eds.*) **ii** (1993) 952-3.

PART I

SPAS, WELLS, AND PLEASURE-GARDENS NORTH OF THE THAMES

'Dr Timothy Bright....[1] first gave the name of the *English Spaw* unto this Fountaine about thirty Yeares since, or more'.
EDMUND DEANE (*c*.1582-1640): *Spadarene Anglica: Or, the English Spaw-Fountaine* etc. (London: John Grismond 1626).

'The first inst. we arrived att the nasty Spaw, and have now begun to drinke the horid sulfer watter'(1665).
FRANCES PARTHENOPE, LADY VERNEY (1819-90) & MARGARET MARIA WILLIAMS-HAY, LADY VERNEY (1844-1930): *Memoirs of the Verney Family during the Civil War* (London: Longmans, Green, 1907).

CHAPTER II

THE CLERKENWELL GROUP I

Introduction; Islington Spa; Decline and Fall

'These once beautiful tea-gardens... were formerly in high repute. In 1733 their Royal Highnesses the Princesses Amelia and Caroline[2] frequented them in the summer time for the purpose of drinking the waters. They have furnished a subject for pamphlets, poems, plays, songs, and medicinal treatises, by Ned Ward[3], George Colman the older (*sic*)[4], Bickham[5], Dr Hugh Smith[6], &c. Nothing now remains of them but the original chalybeate spring, which is still preserved in an obscure nook, amidst a poverty-stricken and squallid rookery of misery and vice.'

GEORGE DANIEL (1789-1864): *Merrie England in the Olden Time* (London: Richard Bentley 1842) **i** 31.

INTRODUCTION

The anonymous author of *A Sunday Ramble*[7] claimed to have visited all the best-known Pleasure-Gardens near London in the 1770s, but such a feat would have been tiring for any normal mortal for the simple reason that there were so many of them. Some, it is true, were large establishments (like *Bagnigge Wells*), but others were little more than small Gardens attached to Taverns. In that part of London lying between Clerkenwell and Islington, where the New River Head lay in the centre of a series of open fields, many Springs and Wells abounded, and several sites were exploited by entrepreneurs for the alleged medicinal properties of the waters, but additional attractions in the forms of Long-Rooms, Gardens planted with trees and shrubs, arbours, musical and dramatic performances, food, drink, acrobats, tumblers, dancers, and so on made certain establishments such as *Sadler's Wells*, the *Islington Spa*, and *Bagnigge Wells* famous for a time. *St Chad's Well* has already been mentioned, but other places, such as the *Peerless Pool*, Old Street, offered scope for bathing and fishing, while the *Cold Bath*, Clerkenwell, was specifically a medical establishment, unlike many other London Baths, sometimes called *Bagnios*, which doubled as brothels or as places of illicit intrigues *(Plate 6)*.

A fine view (*c.*1740) of London from Islington by Thomas Bowles (*c.*1689-1767) shows the City of London, its skyline dominated by church-steeples and by the great cupola of St Paul's Cathedral. The foreground shows the rural character of the area with which we are concerned *(Plate 7)*. Some idea of the density of Gardens, Taverns, bowling-greens, Wells, Spas, and Baths in this small part of London may be gained by the plan *(Plate 8)* produced for Volume **xlvii** of the *Survey of London*. This and the following Chapters will attempt to describe some of these places, even though many of them have only survived as memories, legends, or place-names.

ISLINGTON SPA

This once-famous place of resort was situated opposite the New River Head, Clerkenwell, and has been confused with *Sadler's Wells*, but the two establishments were quite separate *(Plates 9 & 10)*. Referred to as 'the sweet gardens and arbours of pleasure' in an advertisement of 1684[8], it would appear that a chalybeate Spring was discovered in the grounds at some time in 1684 or just before, and the place was mentioned in the *London Gazette*[9] as having been purchased by a Mr John Langley, Merchant, of London: at first it was called 'Islington Wells', but by 1690, because the water was supposed to resemble in composition that of the celebrated *Tunbridge*

Plate 6: *Catching an Elephant.* Drawn by Thomas Rowlandson (1757-1827), this incisive caricature was published by Thomas Tegg (1776-1846) at a Shilling. It shows two young women displaying their charms to a corpulent old man (obviously given to Drink) outside an establishment advertising itself as 'Warm Bath' and offering 'Restorative Drops', capable of 'restoring to Youth and Vigour' any 'Old Age Debility': the episode is taking place in 'Bagnio Court' *(Collection JSC).*

Wells, in Kent, it became known as 'New Tunbridge' or 'New Tunbridge Wells'. Around 1754 it began to assume the designation of 'Islington Spa', but the allusion to *Tunbridge Wells* was never dropped altogether.

The Gardens, well shaded with lime-trees and provisioned with pretty arbours, were open two or three days a week from April or May until August. The price of admission was threepence, although the poor were admitted *gratis* provided they could bring with them a certificate furnished by a known apothecary or physician[10]. A coffee-house provided refreshment, and there was also a 'raffling shop'[11] and a room for dancing, so there must have been provision for a few musicians there, probably only a few not particularly accomplished fiddlers, as contemporary doggerel made plain:

'The Musick plays, and 'tis such musick
As quickly will make you or me sick;
But they to give the thing a grace
Had got three trebles and a basse,
With which (as Apes are often seen
To imitate the acts of men)
So vainly these pretend to play
Some lessons in the Opera.
'Twas now about the hour of Ten,
Precisely just the minute when
To Wells the Hackney coaches trot
As fast as wasps to honey pot'[12].

The author of this poetic gem claimed to have spent some six hours observing the company wasting time in 'what was neither work or play' before taking leave of a 'place of empty boyish prattle' in order to crack a bottle with a friend[13].

Surprisingly, admission could be gained as early as seven in the morning, but most people did not arrive until two or three hours later, and by eleven the Gardens were filled with an *outwardly* fashionable throng. However, as with many places of public resort of the period, the company was mixed: High and Low, Virtue and Vice, Fashion and its Opposite, all were represented. But a physician was also in attendance at the Well in order to advise those who sought to take the waters.

Nevertheless, the main attraction of *New Tunbridge Wells* was the promenade, where beaux could strut and ogle the powdered ladies (who, were known to discuss each other's appearance with their friends):

'Lord! Madam, did you e'er behold
(Says one) a dress so very old?
Sure that commode was made, i'faith,
In days of Queen Elizabeth;
Or else it was esteemed the fashion
At Charles the Second's coronation:
The lady, by her mantua's[14] forebody,
Sure takes a pride to dress like nobody'[15].

By the end of the seventeenth century we

Plate 7: *The North Prospect of LONDON taken from the Bowling Green at Islington* (probably around the middle of the eighteenth century) drawn and engraved by Thomas Bowles. In the foreground is the Upper Pond of the New River system (which now lies under Claremont Square), and the New River Head is clearly shown to the left of the windmill-tower. To the left of the Head and its handsome Water-House the trees of the Gardens of *Islington Spa* may be made out, and to the left again the trees of the Gardens of *Sadler's Wells* are visible. Above these trees on the extreme left is the obelisk-spire of the church of

St Luke, Old Street, designed by Nicholas Hawksmoor (*c*.1662-1736) with John James (*c*.1672-1746), built 1727-33, near the *Peerless Pool*. Immediately to the right of the top of the windmill-tower is the *London Spaw* with its Gardens, and along the path to the right of the *Spaw* is the substantial façade of the *Dog and Duck* set in its spacious grounds: that path is now Exmouth Market. The building and Gardens set in the Fields to the right of the windmill-tower is *Merlin's Cave* and the path running past the *Cave* is now Amwell Street *(Collection HP/5917)*.

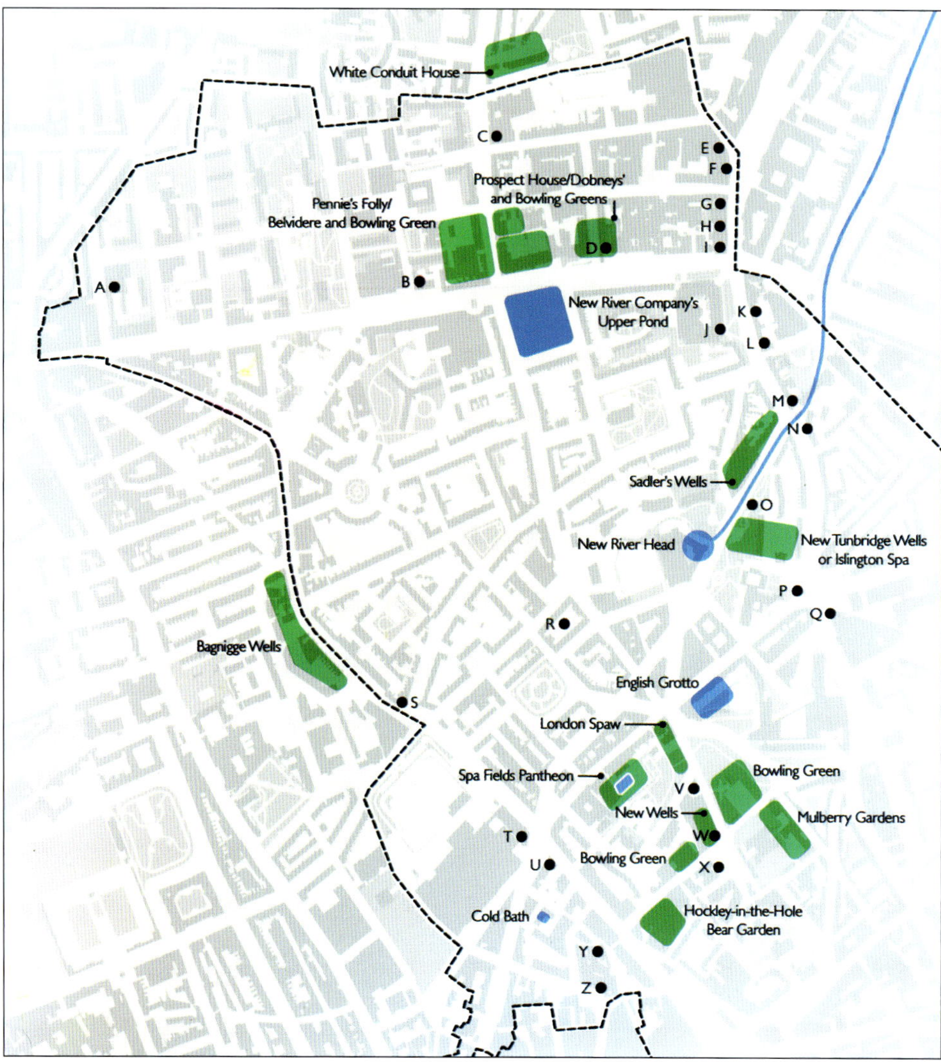

Plate 8: *Pleasure-Gardens, Spas,* inns, ponds, and Taverns in and around Northern Clerkenwell and Pentonville in the late eighteenth century overlaid on an Ordnance Survey Map. *Islington Spa, Sadler's Wells,* and *Bagnigge Wells* are shown as being large establishments. The New River, New River Head, and New River Company's Upper Pond are marked, as are the *Cold Bath* and *English Grotto.* The key is given below:

A	Prince of Wales	N	Empress of Russia
B	Crown	O	Sir Hugh Myddelton's Head
C	Salmon and Compasses	P	Coach and Horses
D	Penton Arms	Q	Lord Cobhams/Adam and Eve
E	Pied Bull	R	Merlin's Cave
F	Three Hats	S	Bull in the Pound
G	White Lion	T	Sir John Oldcastle's
H	Peacock	U	Cobham's Head
I	Angel	V	Red Lion
J	New Inn	W	Mason's Arms/John of Jerusalem
K	Old Red Lion	X	Cherry Tree
L	Crown and Woolpack	Y	Pickled Egg
M	Clown of the Wells	Z	Coach and Horses

(From Saint [Gen. Ed] [*2008b*] *3: by kind permission of English Heritage).*

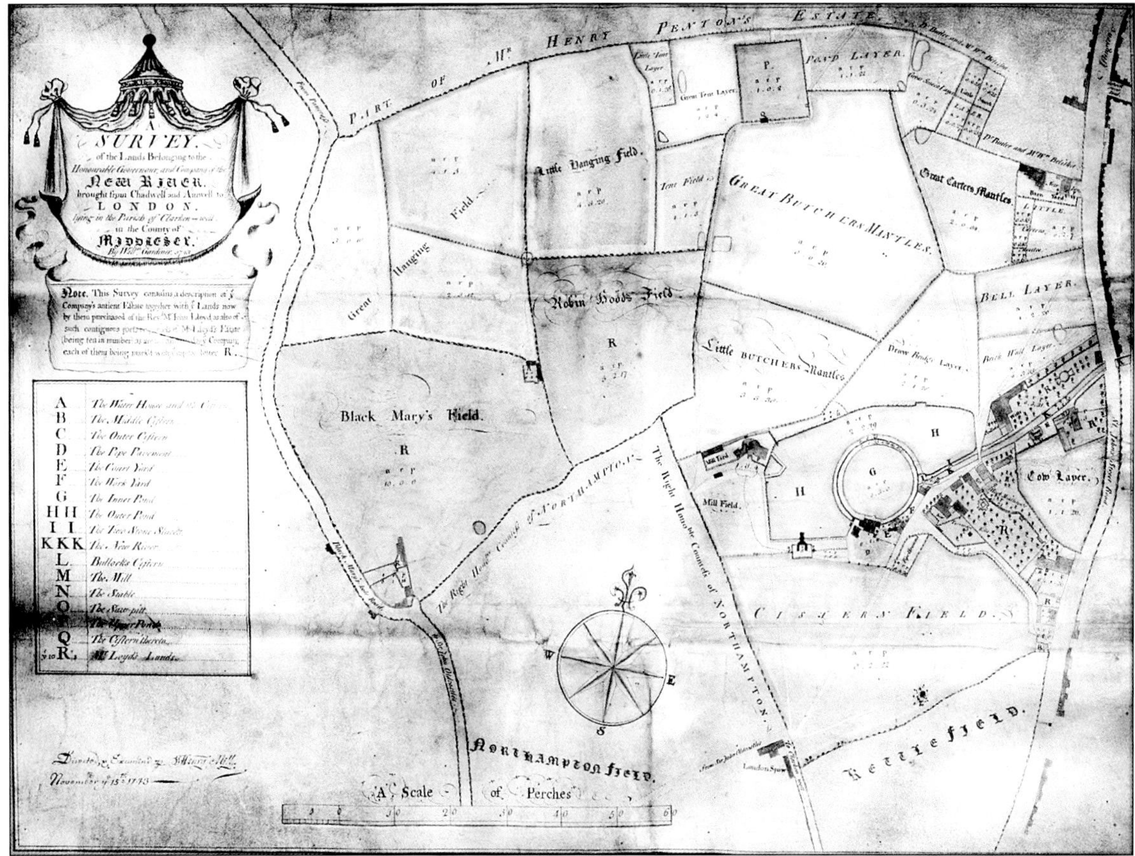

Plate 9: *A Survey of the Lands Belonging to the Honourable Governour, and Company of the NEW RIVER, brought from Chadwell and Amwell to LONDON, lying in the Parish of Clerken-well in the County of MIDDLESEX* by William Gardiner (*fl.* 1725-52), dated 1743, Directed and Examined by Henry Mill (1683-1770), Surveyor (a collateral descendant of Sir Hugh Myddelton), Engineer to the New River Company from 1720. Mill's assistant was Robert Mylne (1733-1811), who became Surveyor to the Company in 1767. The Survey shows the circular New River Head fed by the New River, which was bridged by the Islington Road (now St John Street). The planted area north of the New River and east of the Outer Pond (H) is *Sadler's Wells*, and that south of the New River due east of the circular Inner Pond (G) is *Islington Spa*. The road running north-south on the left (Black Mary's Hole Road) later became King's Cross and Farringdon Roads, *Bagnigge Wells* being to the west of the bend in that route *(LMA Acc/1953/C/1339).*

learn that entry to the Gardens was through a gate where 'abundance of rabble peept in'[16]. The walks

> 'Where lime trees were placed at a regular distance,
> And *scrapers*[17] were giving their woful [*sic*] assistance'[18]

seem to have been extensive.

As for the beau, Ned Ward said

> 'That he looked (as a body may modestly speak it)
> Like a Calf with a bald Face peeping out of a Thicket
> His locks drudg his coat, with such filthiness harbours,
> Tho' made of Black Cloth 'tis as white as a Barber's;
> His *Sword* I may say to my best of belief,
> Was as long as a spit for a Sir-loin of Beef,
> Being graced with a Ribbon of *Scarlet* or *Blue*,

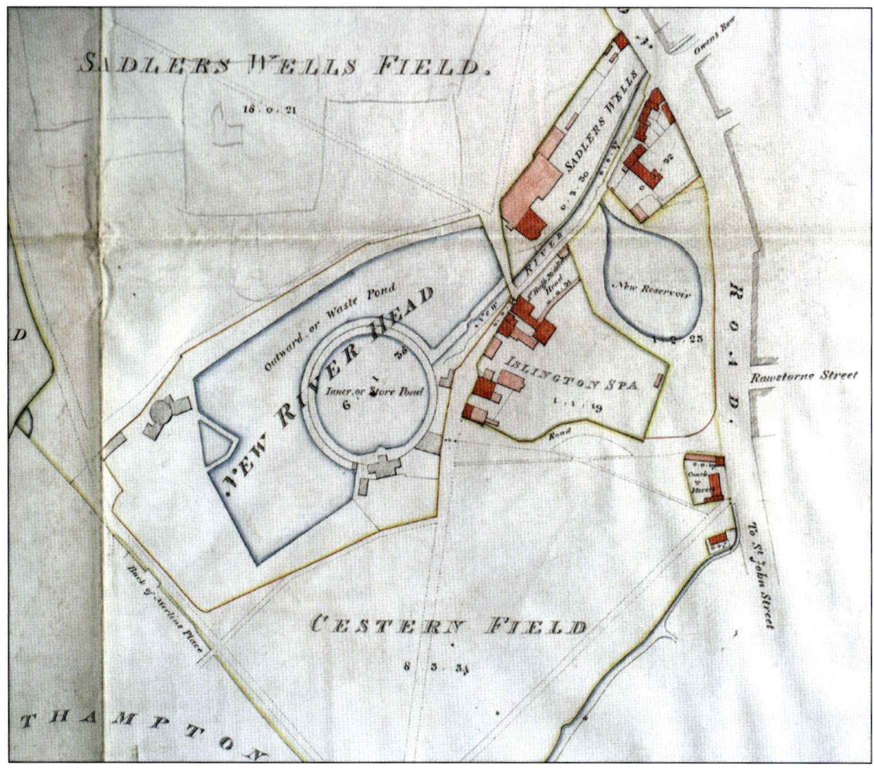

Plate 10: The New River Head with Inner and Outer Ponds, showing the extent of the grounds of *Sadler's Wells* and *Islington Spa*. The north-south road is St John Street leading to Islington Road. North-east of *Islington Spa* is the *Sir Hugh Myddelton's Head* Tavern with its Gardens. The long building extending south-east from the walk by the New River into the Gardens of *Islington Spa* contained the rooms for gambling, dancing, and drinking coffee. Plan of 1807 by Henry Leroux (*fl.* early nineteenth century) *(GA D3549/38/3/2 p.22).*

That hung from the hilt to the heel of his shoe.
Thus proud, as a Turkey cock spreading his plumes,
He stalks thro' the walks, so enrich'd with perfumes'[19]

.

The Gardens were magnets for persons

'of plebean fashion,
Who hither come for recreation,
In Arbours closely shaded o'er
With climbing shrubs and Sycamore,
In mighty state themselves regale
With fly plumb cakes and windy ale'[20].

In such secluded 'Arbours' amorous dalliances could take place, but for

'Others who cheap pleasures choose
To *Coffee-house* to read the news
Retire, and there devoutly prate
Of Luxemburgh and Catinat'[21].

Smoking could be enjoyed in the coffee-house, and speculation at 'Raffling' or the Royal Oak Lottery: the former was often suspiciously marred by the use of 'loaded' or 'cogged' dice; and the latter (set up in the reign of Charles II) was so open to fraud that Lotteries had to be suppressed in 1698[22]. At *Islington Wells*, therefore, it was a common sight to

'See the gamesters all frown, and the Lot'ry man smile,
Some scratching their ears, others biting their nails'[23].

In another room one might observe

'a parcel of Grave Paralitical Heads,
Sit sipping of coffee and poring on paper;
And some smoaking silently around a wax taper;
Whilst others at *Gammon* grown peevish with age,
Were wrangling for Pen'worths of tea made of sage'[24].

Islington Wells was the subject of several works by the hacks of Grub Street, including one dedicated to those who

> 'With their presence do honour famed
> Islington Wells'.

There, we are told

> 'Lawyers, Divines, Civilians, and Quakers,
> The Tradesman and his lovely spouse,
> Th'enamoured Youth and's dear Queen
> Blouze,
> Taylors and other trades which rack
> Invention to adorn the back,
> Go there to make their observation
> Upon the dresses of the nation,
> Of either sex whole droves together,
> To see and to be seen, flock thither
> To drink, and not to drink the water'[25].

During the early years of the eighteenth century *Islington Wells* appears to have gone into decline (or at least out of fashion), and by 1714 was being described as a deserted place, where

> 'Its ancient drooping Trees unprun'd
> appear'd;
> No Ladies to be seen; no Fiddles heard'[26].

Henri Misson, in 1698, said of the place that one could drink waters that did one 'neither Good nor Harm', provided one did not take too much of them. He noted that there was Gaming, Walking, and Dancing, and that a man could spend an hour there 'agreeably enough', but that *Islington Wells* was 'not much flock'd to by People of Quality'[27].

Its fortunes revived about thirty years later, and became a fashionable resort of the *Beau Monde*, said to have been due to the endorsement of the efficacy of the waters by Lady Mary Wortley Montagu (1689-1762) who, nevertheless, complained that they gave her a headache and prevented her from writing[28]. The *Gentleman's Magazine* credited Lady Mary with the notion that natural Mineral-Waters were the best, perhaps only, remedies for certain conditions, and so English watering-places became 'receptacles to which shoals of people rush'[29].

By the 1730s *Islington Wells* attracted many persons, some of Quality, and was patronised by the two Royal Princesses referred to earlier (an event greeted by a salute of twenty-one guns)[30], so Society flocked to 'New Tunbridge Wells': the place also received the *Imprimatur* of Richard 'Beau' Nash (1674-1761), Arbiter of Taste and Manners. The year before the Princesses graced the *Wells* with their presences, 'Lady Sunderland' was one of the many aristocrats who went 'constantly to Islington Wells' where she met 'abundance of good company'. The waters were said to be 'rising in fame, and already pretend to vie with Tunbridge. If they are so good it will be very convenient to all Londoners to have a remedy so near at hand'[31]. It was not all High Society, however, for Richard Temple (1675-1749), 1st Viscount Cobham from 1718, the creator of the Gardens at Stowe, Buckinghamshire, was relieved of a valuable 'gold repeating watch' when visiting the Wells one morning in 1733 when there were 'at least 1600 persons who paid for drinking' there, 'besides many others who were only spectators'[32].

An attractive view of the so-called 'New Tunbridge Wells' from across the New River Company's Outer Pond in 1730 shows an idyllic scene, with the *Sir Hugh Myddelton's Head* Tavern on the left and the extensive Gardens and buildings of *Islington Spa* on the right *(Plate 11)*. Something of the rural character of the surroundings may be gained from some of these views, which offer a painful contrast with much of what may be found there today. Another drawing by the same artist, entitled 'a View of ye New River Head and Water Mill at Islington near London', shows Sadler's Music-House (*left*) and the *Sir Hugh Myddelton's Head* Tavern and *Islington Spa* across the Outer Pond of the New River Head *(Plate 12)*.

In 1733, too, was published *The Charms of Dishabille*[33], *or New Tunbridge Wells at Islington*, a song by 'Mr Lockman' with illustration and engravings *(Plates 13 & 14)* by George Bickham Junior (*c*.1704-71) which appeared in *The Musical Entertainer*[34]. The words are recorded here (*left on p. 41*), but another version entitled *Ridotto al'Fresco*, or *New-Tunbridge-Wells* is shown on the *right*:

Plate 11: *Islington Spa (right)* among the trees seen from across the Outer Pond at New River Head, 1730. On the *left* is the *Sir Hugh Myddelton's Head* Tavern. From a drawing attributed to Bernard Lens (1682-1740) *(MoL 53.30/2).*

Plate 12: 'a View of y[e] New River Head and Water Mill at Islington near London' of 1730 showing *Sadler's Music-House* in its walled grounds *(left)*, while across the Outer Pond the *Sir Hugh Myddelton's Head* Tavern and *Islington Spa* may be seen. The building in the circular pool is the Water-House, and between it and the trees of *Islington Spa* is St Paul's Cathedral. Drawing by Bernard Lens *(BM/1853/0409.44-P&DB698).*

Whence comes it that the shining Great,
To Titles born & awful State,
Thus condescend thus check their Wills,
And scud away to Tunbridge Wells,
To mix with vulgar Beaux & Belles?
The Sages your fam'd Glasses raise
Survey this Meteors dazling [*sic*] Blaze,
And say, portends it Good or Ill?

Soon as *Aurora* gilds the Skies,
With brighter Charms the Ladies rise,
To dart forth Beams that save or kill.
No Homage at the Toilette paid,
(Their lovely Features unsurvey'd)
Sweet *Negligence* her Influence lend,
And all the Artless Graces blends,
That form the tempting Dishabille.

Behold the Walks, a checquer'd Shade,
In the gay Pride[35] of Green array'd;
How bright the Sun! the Air how still!
In wild Confusion there we view,
Red Ribbons groop'd with Aprons blew;
Scrapes[36], Curtzies, Nods, Winks, Smiles & Frowns.
Lords, Milkmaids, Dutchesses and Clowns,
In all their various Dishabille.

Thus, in the famous Age of Gold,
(Not quite romantic tho' so old)
Mankind were merely *Jack & Gill*.
On flow'ry Banks, by murm'ring Streams,
They tatl'd, walk'd, had pleasing Dreams,
But dress'd indeed, like awkward Folks;
Not Steeple Hats[37], Surtouts[38], short Cloaks;
Fig-leaves the only Dishabille'[39].

Whence comes it that the splendid great,
To titles born, and awful state,
Thus condescend, thus check their will,
And shape to *Islington* their way,
To mix with those of vulgar clay?
Astronomers your glasses raise,
Survey this meteor's dazling [*sic*] blaze,
And say, Portends it good or ill?

Soon as *Aurora* gilds the skies,
With brighter charms the ladies rise,
To dart forth beams that save or kill.
No homage at the toilette paid,
Their thousand beauties unsurvey'd,
Sweet *negligence* assistance lends.
And all the artless graces blends
That form the tempting dishabille.

Behold the walks (a chequer'd shade)
In all the pride of green array'd:
How bright the sun! the air how still!
In wild confusion there we view,
Red ribbons group'd with aprons blue.
Curtsies, scrapes, nods, winks, smiles and frowns.
Lords, milk-maids, dutchesses and clowns,
All in their various dishabille. &c.

No alternative version seems to exist.

The presence of so many fashionable Persons of Quality, however, also attracted the shadier sorts of character including

'light fingered knaves, who pockets drill,
Wits, captains, politicians, trulls[40],
Sots, devotees, pimps, poets, gulls'[41].

The resort was laid out around a central basin surrounded by a balustrade, and maps of the area show a variety of buildings catering for those seeking refreshments, those who wished to gamble, and those who liked to dance. In its earliest manifestations it was anything but exclusive:

'The Jilts[42] with their Cullies[43] by this time were Prancing
Within a large Shed, built on purpose for Dancing;
Which stunk so of Sweat, Pocky[44] Breaths, and Perfume,
That my Mistress and I soon avoided the Room'[45].

The upsurge of fortune appears to have owed something to the lease of 'New Tunbridge Wells' to William Young in 1712 for 21 years, a common eighteenth-century term, which suggests an earlier lease of 1691. Young's house appears to have been of brick, with four rooms on each floor, and a brew-house adjoining it. The coffee-house, dancing-room, lottery-room, and hazard-room (where dice were thrown) were all in one building (of brick and timber) probably erected in 1691: these rooms were distributed over two floors, and the upper floor became known as the Long-Room.

When Young died the *Wells* entered the doldrums, and when his widow died the lease was assigned to Robert Dowley, a City Merchant-Tailor, who obtained a new lease in 1732, and it

Plate 13: *Islington Spa* in 1733 engraved by George Bickham, Jr.; plate entitled *The Charms of Dishabille*, or, *New Tunbridge Wells at Islington (Collection JSC).*

Plate 14: Detail showing *Islington Spa* in 1733 by George Bickham, Jr.: the Well is surrounded by a balustrade *(right)* around which spectators are gathered. Some of the Spa buildings to the north are depicted. Between the trees to the left of the balustrade walks the 'Tunbridge Knight' with his hawk on his right wrist *(Collection JSC).*

is from that time that the place was vastly improved with lodgings, breakfast-rooms, and an elaborate entrance with the name of the establishment framed within a cartouche. The main buildings were grouped along a path to the north of the site which was entered from a path along the New River, and the Well with balustrade around it was sited south-east of the Long-Room building[46].

It was then that the Royal Princesses began to frequent the place[47] that was managed for Dowley by Mr and Mrs Reason. The 'Dishabille' referred to in Lockman's poem[48] refers to the affected 'rusticity' the place encouraged, which we might call 'dressing-down': indeed, the upper classes seem to have begun to enjoy the thrills of 'slumming' with the crowds who could be found there, often with more than a hint of the disreputable about them:

> 'What strange confus'd Variety is there;
> The Lord, the Knight, the Cit[49], the Rich, the
> Poor,
> The gentle Lady, and the brazen Whore;
> All sorts together jumbled crowd each
> Walk[50]'.

Apart from the inverted snobbery of 'Dishabille', the gardens of *Islington Wells* were frequented by numerous eccentrics, including the Tunbridge Knight, one Martin, who wore a yellow cockade and carried a hawk on his fist which he called 'Royal Jack'[51] *(Plates 14 & 15)*. Another visitor was the physician, John Misaubin (1673-1734), famous for his patent pills, and widely regarded as a quack. His arrogance, supposedly 'affected foreign ways', and methods of practice led to his being ridiculed by Henry Fielding (1707-54) in *Tom Jones* (1749)[52], and portrayed by William Hogarth (1697-1764) in *A Harlot's Progress*, painted in the early 1730s, then published by subscription as a series of engravings in April 1732[53]. The figure of the Doctor in *A Harlot's Progress* (the Harlot in question being 'Moll Hackabout') was based on Misaubin[54].

In 1750 new attempts were made to revive *New Tunbridge Wells*: it was advertised as a place where 'the strictest care is, and always will be taken, to preserve the most perfect decorum, and no person of a bad or exceptional character will

Plate 15: *New Tunbridge Wells near Islington* showing *Islington Spa* in the mid-eighteenth century. On the left is the 'Tunbridge Knight' with cockade and hawk named 'Royal Jack'. Above is the allegorical figure of Caprice, with a weather-vane on her helmet, signifying sudden changes of mind without motive. Her bubble-blowing and steeds emphasise her whimsical nature, encapsulating the atmosphere of the Spa *(LMA SC/GL/NOR/TEA & MUSIC vol. 9 p.39).*

be admitted to the ball room'. Tickets for the ball and public breakfast were 1*s*.6*d*. each. By 1751 the 'Gardens, &c.', had been 'much enlarg'd and beautified', and the 'Season for drinking the Chalybeate Waters' was announced: 'Proper Musick' was to be provided for those 'Gentlemen and Ladies who chuse Dancing', and 'no persons of ill repute, or of exceptionable or improper characters', would, on any account, be admitted[55]. However, by 1754, *New Tunbridge Wells* had become known as *Islington Spa* where 'Mineral and Chalybeate waters... in full perfection' could be consumed, breakfasts enjoyed, walks taken, and 'convenient and pleasant lodgings' were provided for 'such as chuse to reside on the spot'.

By 1755 the 'extraordinary efficacy of the Chalybeat Mineral Waters' of *Islington Spa* was trumpeted: it was said that, since the Spring had been restored to its original purity, the waters were useful 'in the cure of the Jaundice, Nervous, and other Weaknesses, Fluxes of Blood of every kind, Gravel, &c.', as well as offering 'Great Relief' in cases of 'wandering and irregular Gout', 'weaknesses and stiffness of the Joints', and other afflictions associated with Gout. Puffs became more extravagant, and by 1760, after 'the Rooms and Gardens' had been 'repaired and beautified at a great expense', the 'Waters' were confidently proclaimed as 'particularly useful' because of their restorative powers in 'all cases of Weakness or decay, in all Nervous disorders, in the Green Sickness[56], and in all kinds of Obstructions, in Palsies, Numbness, Convulsions, Asthmas, Hysterics, Vapours, Dropsies, and Swellings of the Legs; Rheumatism, Scurvy, Jaundice, and all disorders of the Liver; King's Evils[57], lost Appetite, Want of Digestion, Gravel, Gout, Strangury[58], and in Numbers of other Disorders wherein either Restorative or Deobstruent[59] Medicines are required or serviceable; and in wandering gout repeated experience has shown that two glasses of this water are sufficient to dispel the Disease from the Stomach into the Extreme parts'. The waters were claimed to have the 'same Virtue and Efficacy' as those of *Tunbridge Wells* in Kent, and compared with those of 'the German spa'. Ladies and Gentlemen could 'depend on having their best Teas, Coffee, and Chocolate, with due Attendance and the most civil and obliging treatment'. All 'bad and improper company' was discouraged by the absence of 'other liquors'[60]. Thus, from around 1750 to 1770, *Islington Spa* attracted those who wished to drink the 'Waters' or enjoy the other facilities. One young lady wrote home in June 1753 that the Spa was 'a very pretty Romantick place', and that the water was 'very much like Bath water, but makes one vastly cold and Hungary'[61].

Dr Richard Russell (sometimes given as Russel [1687-1759]), advocate of bathing in sea-water and drinking of Mineral-Waters, analysed the water of *Islington Spa* in *c.*1733, and found it had a taste of iron, but (unless diluted with other water) was apt to make the drinker somewhat giddy and sleepy, a phenomenon recorded by Lady Mary Wortley Montagu, who, however, claimed that she had derived benefit from her visits to the place[62].

Islington Spa appears to have been more popular as a Tea-Garden, sought for the company to be had and for the entertainment provided as much as for the supposed curative benefits conferred by the waters. By 1770, one Holland[63] owned the Spa, but although he took out a new lease in 1771 and spent money renovating the 'tea-garden', his establishment could no longer attract higher classes of visitors than 'publicans and tradesmen'. His efforts could not have been helped by *The Spleen; or, Islington Spa*, a farce by George Colman the Elder (1732-94) first given in 1776. In this work, 'Mrs Rubrick' commends the elegancies of the Spa to her friend, 'Mrs Tabitha' in glowing terms:

> 'The Spa grows as genteel as Tunbridge,
> Brighthelmstone, Southampton, or Margate.
> Live in the most sociable way on earth –
> all the Company acquainted with each other.
> Walks, balls, raffles, and subscriptions.
> Mrs Jenkins, of the Three Blue Balls; Mrs Rummer and family, from the King's Arms; and several other people of condition, to be there this season!
> And then Eliza's wedding, you know, was owing to the Spa.
> Oh, the watering-places are the only places to get young women lovers or husbands'[64].

Such low respectability would not have improved the fortunes of the Spa, and in 1777 Holland was bankrupted. The lease, which had some years to run, was sold to a John Howard in 1778, who embellished the Gardens with a bowling-green, and promoted them as a 'minor Vauxhall'... 'pleasurably disposed in a very agreeable style'. Attempts were made during Lent to raise the Tone by means of astronomical lectures with demonstrations involving an Orrery[65], and the band was enriched by the addition of French Horns[66].

In the 1780s the success of *Islington Spa* was temporarily revived. In particular, the virtues of the waters were again praised, so much so that one commentator felt that the Kentish Spa of *Tunbridge Wells* would be 'entirely deserted the ensuing season'[67] . In 1788 *Islington Spa* was hailed as a 'charming spot of beautiful rusticity' with 'the greatest reputation' for curing a 'variety of disorders'. Sir John Hawkins (1719-89), music-scholar and lawyer, took the waters there, but in May 1789, feeling unwell, he repaired to the Spa for his cure, then complained of a pain in the head and died shortly afterwards. Whether his death was 'owing to the mineral spring being taken when the blood was in an improper state to receive its salubrious effect, or whether it was the sudden visitation of Providence, the sight of the human mind is incompetent to discover'[68]. Now although Lady Mary Wortley Montagu and others had also experienced unpleasant side-effects after drinking the waters, Hawkins's death cannot have done the Spa much good, despite the fact that his passing was recorded as the result of a 'paralytic affliction' (which probably meant a stroke)[69].

DECLINE AND FALL

Thereafter, efforts to revive the faded glories of the Spa proved to be in vain. Forrester, previously of *Sadler's Wells*, reorganised the gardens 'in a stile of superior elegance' in 1806-8, but this failed to attract the punters, so the ground landlords, the Lloyd Baker family, granted a lease for 99 years, mindful of the potential for development. Samuel Bingham took up the lease and commenced building around the Spa Gardens. The entrance to the Gardens was moved from the side facing the New River (renamed Eliza Place) to the south, facing Spa Road (which later became Lloyd's Row). Nevertheless, the Gardens in the first decade of the nineteenth century were described as 'really very beautiful, particularly at the entrance. Pedestals and vases are grouped with taste under some extremely picturesque trees, whose foliage [is] seen to much advantage from the neighbouring fields'[70]. In around 1810 the greater part of the coffee-house was demolished, and then a three-storey stuccoed house for the proprietor was erected beside the new entrance: at the top of the façade was an inscription:

ISLINGTON SPA
OR NEW
TUNBRIDGE WELLS

(Plate 16)

The Gardens were further reduced in size by the formation of Charlotte (later Thomas) Street, and around 1815 Bingham decided to end all musical performances and dancing, concentrating on the Gardens only. However, this formula failed to attract custom, and, under a Mr Hardy and a surgeon called Molloy, the Spa was re-opened in 1826 with the Well enclosed in a new grotto. The remaining part of the building where the orchestra played was pulled down in 1827[71], and the much-reduced Gardens contained statues and inscriptions recording the virtues of the waters. Thomas Coull (*fl*.1825-61), in 1828, recorded that the water had a slightly saline taste and was cloudy, but by that time the Well was only producing very little[72].

Plate 16: *Islington Spa* or *New Tunbridge Wells* in 1863. The entrance to what remained of the Spa was to the right of the three-storey stuccoed house *(From Pinks [1880] 405: Collection JSC).*

Plate 17: Early twentieth-century photograph from Green Terrace looking towards Lloyds Row (formerly Spa Road) and showing the stucco-fronted house of the proprietor of *Islington Spa*. The entrance to the Spa was to the right of the house, but in the 1840s Spa Cottages were built over the remaining parts of the Gardens, so the alley gave access to those Cottages which, from the very beginning, were cheaply built and overcrowded: they were badly damaged in the 1939-45 war and were demolished to make way for the Spa Green Estate *(GA D3549, 38/6/6)*.

Plate 18: The remains of the grotto at *Islington Spa* in an 'obscure nook', from *The Illustrated London News* (20 August 1859) *(LMA SC/GL/NOB/C/001/12-003/2)*.

Finally, the last part of the coffee-room was demolished in 1840, and two rows of houses called Spa Cottages were erected in the Gardens. Molloy resided in the proprietor's house in Lloyd's Row *(Plate 17)* and preserved the Well: he advertised the waters and protected the Well in an outbuilding attached to the east side of his dwelling, but the waters ceased to flow around 1860. Daniel said nothing remained of the establishment except the 'original chalybeate spring, which is still preserved in an obscure nook, amidst a poverty-stricken and squallid (*sic*) rookery of misery and vice'[73] *(Plate 18)*.

The remains of the grotto, with stone pilasters and steps down to the Well, survived in 1894[74], and the Wroths (also in 1894) found that the outbuilding housing the Well was used as a 'dwelling-room of a very humble description. Standing in this place, it was impossible to realise we were within a few feet of the famous Well. A door, which we had imagined on entering to be the door of a cupboard, proved to be the entrance to a small cellar two or three steps below the level of the room. Here, indeed, we found the remains of the grotto that had once adorned the Well, but the healing spring no longer flowed'[75].

Eliza Place disappeared when Rosebery Avenue was formed 1887-92, and the last vestiges of *Islington Spa* only remain in the name Spa Green Estate on the eastern side of Rosebery Avenue opposite Sadler's Wells Theatre: two of the blocks of housing, Wells House and Tunbridge House, designed by Tecton, the architectural firm led by Berthold Romanovitch Lubetkin (1901-90), and erected immediately after the 1939-45 War, also serve as a reminder of this lost London Spa[76].

Chapter II References: The Clerkenwell Group I

1 Timothy Bright (*c*.1549-1615), physician and writer on shorthand.

2 These would have been Princess Amelia Sophia Eleanor (1711-86) and Caroline Elizabeth (1713-57), both daughters of King George II (reigned 1727-60) and Queen Caroline (formerly Princess Caroline of Brandenburg-Ansbach [1683-1737]).

3 Edward Ward (1667-1731), satirist.

4 George Colman the Elder (1732-94), playwright and theatre-manager.

5 George Bickham (1683/4-1758), engraver and writing-master.

6 Hugh Smith (d. 1790), physician.

7 Anonymous (*c*.1774) *passim*.

8 Anonymous (1684*a* and *b*). *See* also Cunningham (1850): *Islington*.

9 24 September 1685.

10 Ames (1691); Hembry (1990); Pinks (1880) 398-9; Ward (1699); Ward **ii** (1709) 63 ff; Wroth & Wroth (1896) 16.

11 Gambling-room, usually involving dice. It may have been little more than a temporary shed with an adjoining hovel.

12 Ames (1691). N.B. 'Opera' rhymes with 'play'.

13 Pinks (1880) 400.

14 A woman's loose outer gown, a corruption of *manteau*.

15 From Ames (1691).

16 Ward (1699).

17 At the time this 'low word' as Samuel Johnson called it (1755) suggests one who gets into embarrassing or awkward predicaments through imprudence and thoughtlessness. It could also refer to persons indulging in awkward bows or salutations in which the foot was drawn backwards on the ground. In addition, the word was used to refer to one drawing a bow over a violin (so was a derogatory term for a fiddler); to a money-grubber; to an unscrupulous plunderer or thief; to an appliance for removing dirt from the soles of boots or shoes; to a cocked hat; and to one who hurriedly decamps.

18 Ward (1699).

19 *Ibid*.

20 Ames (1691). The raisins in plum-cakes were sometimes said to resemble flies, and certain ales were conducive to flatulence: the implication is that the fare was of poor quality.

21 *Ibid*. François-Henri de Montmorency-Bouteville, Duc de Luxembourg (1628-95), and Nicolas Catinat (1637-1712) were French military commanders under Louis XIV.

22 10 Will. III *c*.23. The reference to the Royal Oak Lottery is Ward **ii** (1709) 355.

23 Ward (1699).

24 *Ibid*.

25 Ames (1691).

26 Ward (1714).

27 Misson (1719) 161.

28 Stone **ii** (1845) 276. Lady Mary complained of vertigo and somnolence after imbibing.

29 *Gentleman's Magazine* (May 1820) 398.

30 *Fogg's Journal* (2 June 1733).

31 Delany (1862).
32 Quoted in Pinks (1880) 401.
33 The state of being partly undressed, or dressed in a careless or negligent manner.
34 Bickham (1737-9).
35 This term had connotations in 1733 concerned with fine, showy dress, with what was brilliant, attractive, or charming, with light-hearted joyous mirth, with exuberant cheerfulness, but also suggested an addiction to social pleasures and dissipations, and, sometimes, loose or immoral behaviour. It did not have today's meaning.
36 Here the meaning is suggested by its context, and must have been intended to refer to awkward salutations.
37 Hat with a crown rising to a point in the middle.
38 Man's great-coat or overcoat, or a hood with a mantle worn by women.
39 Bickham (1737-9). I owe the alternative *Ridotto al'Fresco* version to Jeremy Smith, to whom I am indebted for much help.
40 A low prostitute, a drab, strumpet, or trollop.
41 Drake (1734). A 'gull' was a credulous person, a dupe.
42 A harlot or strumpet, or a woman who capriciously deceives her lover.
43 A silly fellow, a dupe, one who is deceived by a strumpet.
44 Pertaining to the Pox (Syphilis).
45 Ward (1699) 12, Ames (1691), Colsoni (1951) 6.
46 Saint (*Gen. Ed.*) (2008*b*) 86.
47 Amelia and Caroline went thither almost daily, it would seem: on occasion their sister Anne, Princess Royal (1709-59), who married William (Charles Henry) IV, Prince of Orange, in 1734, accompanied them, but only for a brief period before her nuptials.
48 Lockman (1734), Bickham (1737-9).
49 Abbreviation of 'Citizen', often applied, more or less contemptuously to a townsman or 'Cockney' or to someone not a Gentleman.
50 Anonymous (1733); *Art History* **xxii**/4 (November 1999) 495-513; Drake (1734); F.G., F.R.S. (1733); *Gentleman's Magazine* (May-June 1733) 267, 324,
51 Wroth & Wroth (1896) 18-20.
52 Book 13, Ch. 2.
53 *A Harlot's Progress* consisted of six paintings, all of which were destroyed in a fire at Fonthill, Wiltshire, in 1755, but they enjoyed considerable fame as engravings.
54 *Journal of the Royal Society of Medicine* **xciv** (2001) 143-7. *See* also Munk **ii** (1878) and *Gentleman's Magazine* 1st Ser. **iv** (1734) 218.
55 Pinks (1880) 403.
56 Chlorosis, a form of anaemia, named for the greenish tinge of the skin of a sufferer. Today it is called *hypochromic anaemia*. It was also called *morbus virgineus*, a 'disease of maids' occasioned by celibacy: the cure need not be spelled out.
57 Scrofulous disease, supposedly cured by the touch of the King.
58 Painful retention of, or difficulty in discharging, urine.
59 Something that removes obstructions by opening the pores and natural passages of the body.
60 *London Chronicle* (April 1760), quoted in Pinks (1880) 403-4. Disreputable persons were indeed discouraged: one notorious woman, on being recognised, was ejected from the establishment by a Constable in 1752, and the incident was recorded in *The London Daily Advertiser* (25 June 1752).
61 *Notes and Queries* Series 8 **vi** (1894) 69.
62 Wroth & Wroth (1896) 20.
63 Called both 'John' and 'Henry' in various sources.
64 Quoted in Pinks (1880) 404. *See* Garrick (1775), Wroth & Wroth (1896) 21, and Anonymous (*c.*1776) 47-8.
65 Cromwell (1828) 355-6; Pinks (1880) 404; Anonymous (*c.*1776) 47-8.
66 Wroth & Wroth (1896) 21. *See* also *Public Advertiser* (5 May 1775) for music in Holland's time.
67 Quoted in Pinks (1880) 404.
68 Quoted in Wroth & Wroth (1896) 21.
69 *ODNB* **xxv** (2004) 929.
70 Malcolm **ii** (1802-7) 230-1.
71 Cromwell (1828) 357.
72 Coull (1864).
73 Daniel **i** (1842) 31.
74 *Notes and Queries* Series 8 **vi** (1894) 458.
75 Wroth & Wroth (1896) 22-3.
76 Saint (*Gen. Ed.*) (2008*b*) 96-108. *See* also Addison (1951); Andrews (*Ed.*) (1899); Hembry (1990); Margetson (1963, 1964, 1965); Scott (1948); Wroth & Wroth (1896).

CHAPTER III

SADLER'S WELLS

Introduction; Sadler's Wells: A Place of Entertainment; Epilogue

'If at Sadler's Wells the wine should be thick,
The cheesecakes be sour, or Miss Wilkinson sick,
If the fumes of the pipes should prove powerful in June,
Or the tumblers be lame, or the bells out of tune,
We hope that you'll call at our warehouse at Drury,
We've a good assortment of goods I can assure you'.
SAMUEL FOOTE (1721-77): Prologue: to ARTHUR MURPHY (1727-1805): *All in the Wrong*
(London: John Bell 1792).

'I thought this season to have turned physician,
But now I see small hopes in that condition,
Yet how if I should hire a black flowered jump,
And ply at Islington, doctor to Sadler's pump!'.
NAHUM TATE (*c*.1652-1715): Prologue to *A Duke and No Duke: A Farce*
(London: Henry Bonwicke 1685).

INTRODUCTION

Sadler's Wells is the last survivor of the sundry Spas and Wells that once graced the northern slopes of Clerkenwell. It was founded on the supposed medicinal properties of chalybeate water, but from its very beginnings it was associated with entertainment in the form of music, plays, and the drinking of alcohol. The site was due north of the *Islington Spa*, on the opposite side of the New River, and extended from the Outer Pond at New River Head to the Islington Road (now St John Street) *(see Plates 9 & 10)*. What we know of the site is not a great deal, although the Bohemian artist, Wenceslaus Hollar (1607-77)[1], produced views of the area, including one looking south-east from the Outer Pond of the New River Company *(Plate 19)* which suggests a somewhat bare landscape without much planting: this would have been rather typical of rural or semi-rural scenery before the beautification of the countryside got under way in the eighteenth century.

The story begins when Edward Sadler took a 35-year lease of the site from the Earl and Countess of Clarendon in 1671, although it seems he had connections with the New River Company in the 1660s[2]. He fenced it and erected a 'brick messuage' there, but shortly afterwards he discovered a Spring 'of extraordinary Medicinall Vertue' some time between 1674 and 1684: Sadler appears to have used the water to make beer until he started to market the water for its own 'Vertue'. In a pamphlet of 1684 it was claimed that some 500 persons a day resorted to Sadler's establishment to take the waters there[3]. From that date another pamphlet refers to *Sadlers New Tunbridge Wells near Islington*, which confuses *Islington Spa* with *Sadler's Well*, but Guidott, in *his* pamphlet, refers to 'Sadler's Wells', which suggests that either more Wells were discovered, or that Sadler owned more than one Well. Be as it may, his establishment became known as *Sadler's Wells*, and the water was described as 'ferruginous chalybeate', similar to the water at

Plate 19: Wenceslaus Hollar's illustration of 'by the Waterhouse' (1665) looking south-east over the Outer Pond of the New River Head. The site of *Sadler's Wells* appears to be defined by the fence-posts in the distance. On the right is the wall around the circular New River Head which is visible in Lens's drawing of 1730 *(Plate 12) (LMA SC/GL/PR/F1/NEW/Ce7692/cat.no.p5439605).*

Tunbridge Wells in Kent, though not tasting so strongly of metal, and having more sulphur. The water was taken with a few 'carraway-comfits'[4], some elecampane[5], 'capillaire' (syrup flavoured with orange-flower water), or a little pressed angelica[6] to ease the stomach (and probably make the taste more agreeable). Some Rhine wine might also be drunk with the liquid, and a pipeful of tobacco was also recommended for *medicinal*[7] purposes. There have been claims that the Well was one of those recorded by Stow as having been a source of water in the mediaeval period, but this seems as unlikely as those made that Sadler was some sort of Surveyor: he was actually a Vintner[8], and in 1677 was described in the Clerkenwell 'Census' as a Victualler.

A drawing, by an anonymous artist, supposedly of a Pump-House near the theatre at *Sadler's Wells*, shows a vernacular building, probably timber-framed, typical of the seventeenth century: it suggests that the waters were known earlier than Sadler's involvement *(Plate 20).*

A PLACE OF ENTERTAINMENT

Sadler's 'Musick House' appears to have predated the discovery of the Well, and was really a large public-house with musical entertainment provided as an allurement. By the 1690s both *Sadler's Wells* and *New Tunbridge Wells* were attracting those who wished to drink the waters: Sadler's place also provided dancing, billiards, Royal Oak, and lotteries[9]. Both *New Tunbridge Wells* and *Sadler's Wells* tempted a mixed bag of company[10], but Sadler's concern seems to have offered more in the way of food and drink, and had the added diversion of an organ[11], singers, fiddlers, and even a sword-dancer. Very soon the music seems to have become more important than any curative properties of the waters, with performances lasting for a couple of hours. Sadler certainly advertised his business, laid out the Gardens with flowers and shrubs, and constructed a basin from which the water could be dispensed. Tumblers and others performed there, a band played, and recitals on the dulcimer

Plate 20: View of a Pump-House near the Theatre at *Sadler's Wells* by an anonymous artist (pen/pencil/wash) of *c*.1775 *(LMA SC/GL/PR/F1/NEW-F1/SAD/Ce8610/ cat.no.p544117x).*

were given at the end of the Long Walk. However, the water-supply seems to have slowed to a trickle during the middle of the 1690s, until the Well was advertised again in 1697 as 'opened and currant', so this would probably account for the many other diversions on offer. Once the flow was restored, the waters were claimed to be full of vigour, strength, and virtue, and effective for curing all 'hectick' and 'hypochondriacal heat' as well as 'beginning consumptions', 'melancholy distempers', 'the scurvey', 'diabetes', 'bringing away gravel, stones in the kidneys and bladder, and several other diseases'[12].

Sadler died in *c*.1699 and one James Miles (d.1724), took over. Under his régime *Sadler's Wells* became noted for its rather low entertainment, rowdiness, and even debauchery. One of the more revolting 'entertainments' on offer was the eating of a live cock, feathers and all, by a creature known as the 'Hibernian Cannibal', who washed down this unappetising repast with large quantities of brandy, with 'only a plate of oil and vinegar for sauce'[13]: the Georgians could be decidedly unrefined in their tastes at times. Thus the tone of *Sadler's Wells* appears to have been unelevated, despite Miles's efforts to improve and 'beautify' the music-house which is shown in several illustrations (*see Plate 12* and *Plate 21*). In 1712 an Ingram Thwaits was killed in the gallery of the 'musick-house', and subsequent to this melancholy occurrence the house seems to have been closed for a period. In 1718, however, the *Weekly Journal*[14] announced that *Sadler's Wells* was

Plate 21: 'North View' by an unknown artist of *Sadler's Wells* in 1731, clearly the same building shown in Bernard Lens's drawings of 1730 *(see Plate 12) (ILHC L4.22).*

'lately opened', and was likely to 'be a great resort of strolling damsels, half-pay officers, peripatetic tradesmen, tars, butchers, and others musically inclined'[15]. When Miles died, having 'diverted the town', and been 'the favourite of Beaux, Butchers, Bawds, &c.', *Sadler's Wells* passed to Miles's son-in-law, a barrister, Francis Forcer (d.1743), who enlarged the buildings.

Forcer's improved buildings appear in the finely engraved decorations *(Plate 22)* by Thomas Kitchin (d.1784) in *Universal Harmony; or, the Gentleman and Lady's Social Companion*, published by John Newbery (1713-67) in 1743 with subsequent editions. This image was also shown as 'View of the Theatre in its former State' beneath a *South West View of Sadler's Wells* drawn by R. C. Andrews and published (1814) by Robert Wilkinson of No. 58 Cornhill *(Plate 23)*. Certainly, under Forcer, there was an improvement in tone, for at *Sadler's Wells* could be found a pleasant resort:

> 'There you may sit under the shady trees
> And drink and smoke fann'd by a gentle breeze'[16].

The collection[17] alluded to above contains *A New Song on Sadler's Wells*, 'set by Mr Brett'. The words suggest the *Wells* had improved:

> 'At eve, when Silvan's shady scene
> Is clad with spreading branches green,
> And vary'd sweets all round display'd,
> To grace the pleasant flow'ry mead;
> Then those who are willing joys to taste,
> Where pleasures flow and blessings last,
> And God of Health in transport dwells,
> Must all repair to Sadler's Wells.
>
> There pleasant streams of Middleton[18]
> In gentle murmurs glide along;
> In which the sporting fishes play,
> To close each weary'd Summer's day:
> And Musick's charms in lulling sounds
> Of mirth and harmony abounds;
> While nymphs and swains, with beaus [*sic*] and belles,
> All praise the joys of Sadler's Wells.
>
> The herds around o'er herbage green,
> And bleating flocks are sporting seen;
> While Phœbus, with its brightest rays,
> The fertile soil doth seem to praise:
> And Zephyrs with their gentlest gales,
> Breathing more sweets than flow'ry vales,
> Which give new health, and heat repells;
> Such are the joys of Sadler's Wells'[19].

However, this may have been a rose-tinted

Plate 22: The west front of *Sadler's Wells* in *c*.1743 showing the extension by Forcer, from a collection of sheet-music published as *Universal Harmony: or, The Gentleman and Ladie's Social Companion* by John Newbery (1743) and engraved by Thomas Kitchin *(TILUO: Harding Mus. E.995, p.60 'Sadler's Wells')*.

Plate 23: *View of the Theatre in its former State* published by Robert Wilkinson in 1814, clearly another version of the illustration shown in *Plate 22 (Collection JSC).*

view, for in 1740, when this song was said to have been composed, the 'usual diversions' were advertised at *Sadler's Wells* to begin at five o'clock 'with a variety of rope-dancing, tumbling, singing, and several new grand dances, both serious and comic. With a new entertainment, call'd "The Birth of Venus; or, Harlequin Paris". Concluding with "The Loves of Zephyrus and Flora". The scenes, machines, dresses, and musick, being entirely new'[20]. Two years later, 'rope-dancing' and the 'famous ladder dancer' were trumpeted[21].

However, Dr John Doran (1807-78) leaves us in no doubt[22] that *Sadler's Wells* was a place of low entertainment, and in 1744 it was described by the Grand Jury of the County of Middlesex as a location for 'great extravagance, luxury, idleness, and ill fame': the proprietors of the 'House and Diversions called Sadler's Wells, adjoining the New River Head,.... late one Forcer's, now pretended to be opened and carried on by John Warren' had done little to improve the place, for it was 'frequently a resort of great numbers of loose, disorderly people'[23]. Under Warren's régime *Sadler's Wells* was closed down[24].

From Christmas 1745 a new lease of 21 years was taken by Thomas Rosoman (d. 1782), actor, former manager of the *New Wells* in Bridewell Walk, an 'Interlude House' built by a Dr Joseph Hooke in 1735, a place of vulgar entertainment which had a chequered history, of which more anon. When Rosoman took *Sadler's Wells* he was in partnership with Peter Hough, a tumbler, and various buildings were erected, including a galleried wooden theatre (1748-9) and a two-storey set of 'drinking-rooms' (1748). These 'drinking-rooms' seem to have been open-fronted alcoves set on three sides of a court, rather like a cloister, with a stage facing the court set between rows of alcoves *(Plates 24 & 25)*. The buildings on the site included a brewery, store, stables, granary, and various sheds and outhouses, apart from the theatre, outdoor theatre, and 'drinking-rooms'. There was also a substantial two-storey house with garret.

'Diversions' on offer in 1764 included a ballet concerning the Battle of Culloden (then regarded as a great victory over Pretenders, Papists, and Traitors [not to mention wild Highlanders], so appealed to Popular Patriotism), and an entertainment based on Hogarth's *Harlot's Progress*, with songs by Johann Friedrich (John Frederick) Lampe (1702/3-51). However, by far the greatest attraction in 1747 was the Sadler's Wells Ale:

'Ye cheerful souls who wou'd regale
On honest, home-brew'd British ale,
To Sadler's Wells in troops repair,
And find the wished-for cordial there;
Strength, colour, elegance of taste,
Combine to bless the rich repaste;
And I assure ye to my knowledge
'T has been approv'd by all the Colledge [*sic*],
More efficasious [*sic*] and prevailing
Than all the Recipes of Galen[25].
Words scarce are able to disclose
The various blessings it bestows;
It helps the younger sort to think,
And wit flows faster as they drink;
It puts the ancient a new fleece on
Soon as Mædea did to Eson;
The fair with bloom it does adorn,
Fragrant and fresh as April morn;
Haste thither, then, and take your fill,
Let Parsons say whatever they will,
The ale that every ale excells [*sic*]
Is only found at Sadler's Wells'[26].

Performances included displays by 'Equilibrists' (acrobats or tight-rope walkers such as Anthony Maddox [d.1758 – who entertained with remarkable feats of balance and dexterity]); by the dancer on the high wire, Isabella Wilkinson (who also performed on musical glasses); and by the hand-bell ringer 'Mr

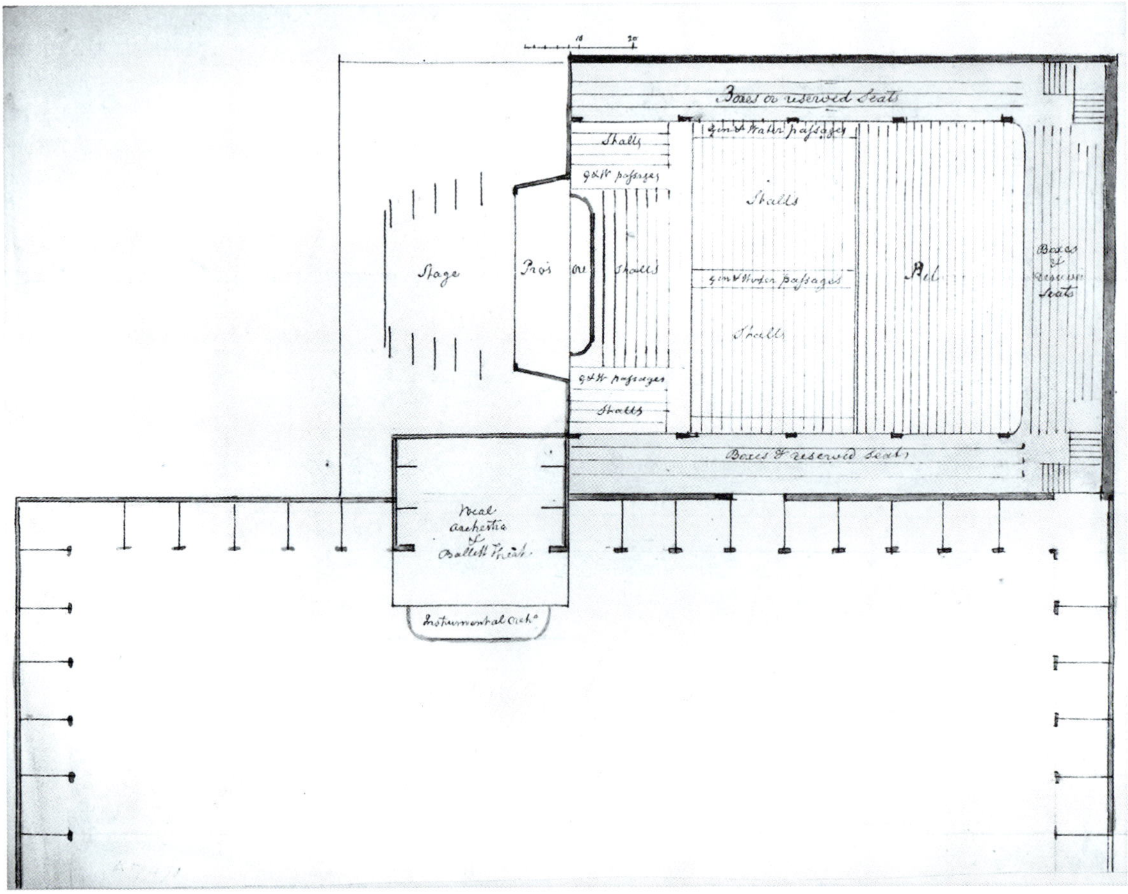

Plate 24: Sketch-plan for a theatre, probably Rosoman's *Sadler's Wells*, of the 1740s, showing the series of 'drinking-rooms' and stage with space for instrumentalists *(MoL).*

Plate 25: Elevation of the court with two storeys of 'drinking-rooms', small stage facing the court (with space for instrumentalists), and theatre behind, probably intended for Rosoman's *Sadler's Wells (MoL).*

Plate 26: West front of *Sadler's Wells* as rebuilt by Thomas Rosoman in 1764, shown in a print of *c.*1791 *(Collection JSC).*

Franklyn'. 'Winifred Jenkins' in *Humphry Clinker* (1771) by Tobias George Smollett (1721-71), described 'tumbling and dancing on ropes and wires' at *Sadler's Wells*, 'rolling of wheel-barrows on a wire', and much else, including a 'fine gentleman' who showed 'his cloven futt' when he 'went for to be rude', causing her much 'flustration'. Clearly the implication was that places like *Sadler's Wells* were famed as places of assignation as much as they were for medicinal, musical, or entertainment purposes.

The theatre was rebuilt in 1764 and the dwelling was also either built from scratch or remodelled: it was of two storeys with garret, was four windows wide, and had a handsome aediculated entrance with pediment over *(Plate 26)*. Theatrical performances include dances by Giuseppe Grimaldi[27] (1709x16-88 – *maître de ballet* during the summer months from 1763 until 1767), Harlequinades, and similar entertainments, some over-obviously and clumsily 'patriotic', some unashamedly vulgar, and others appealing to an audience thoroughly soaked in drink. One of the cleverest 'turns' was that of the trained 'funambulistical'[28] monkey of Signor Spinacuti (*fl.* 1760s) which was all the rage in 1768: the creature performed on a tight-rope, and amazed the spectators with a series of remarkable balancing-acts *(Plate 27)*.

In 1771 the lease was sold to Thomas King (1730-1805), actor-manager, who had had an interest in the *Wells* since 1769: King improved the quality of the music, but although he attempted to raise the tone, vast amounts of alcohol were still consumed (the purchase of a three-shilling admission ticket entitled the holder to a pint of 'Port, Lisbon[29], Mountain[30], or Punch, and further pints of such drinks could be obtained for six pence[31]). Henry Charles William Angelo (1756-1835), fencing-master and memoirist, recalled concoctions sold at *Sadler's Wells* including 'Cream of Tartar Punch', and wine of the 'Sloe Vintage'[32]: with alcohol imbibed in such prodigious quantities the patrons must have been extremely rowdy and certainly drunk. Nevertheless, the performers at the *Wells* included Thomas Lowe (*c.*1719-83), who had enjoyed considerable success as a singer from around 1740; James Byrne (1756-1845), the Harlequin; Marie Theresa Bland (*née* Romanzini

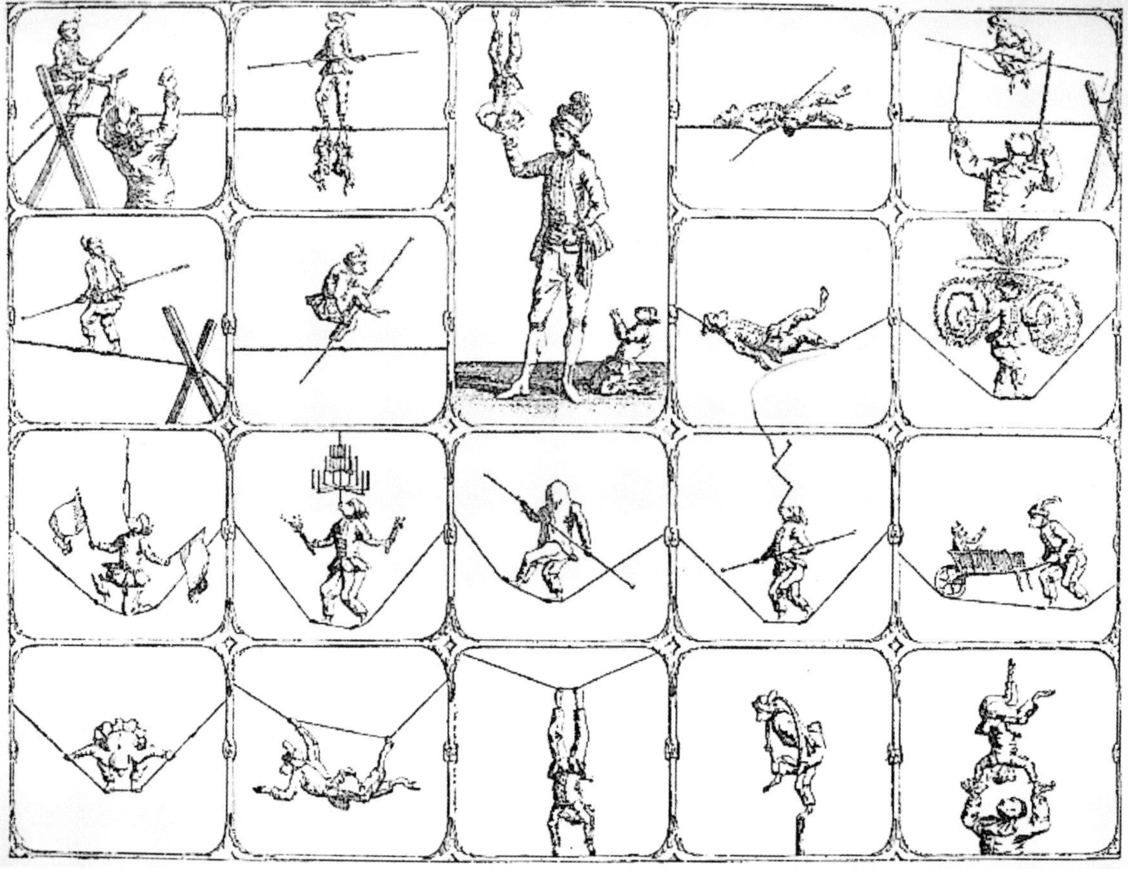

Plate 27: Signor Spinacuti's monkey performing at *Sadler's Wells* in 1768 *(Collection JSC).*

[1769-1838]), the ballad-vocalist; John Braham (*c*.1777-1856)[33], the tenor and lover of the famous soprano, Nancy Storace[34] (1765-1817 – the first Susanna in Mozart's *Le Nozze di Figaro* [1786]); and many other celebrated entertainers.

The 'altered and beautified' theatre was not the only improvement carried out by King: he built a low wall and iron railing along the walk opposite his house and planted a row of poplars that for many years was a landmark. In 1778 further improvements were made to the theatre, and again in 1787. R. C. Andrews produced a drawing of *Sadler's Wells* in 1792 *(Plate 28)* which shows some of the young poplars: William Wise engraved it and it was published by Robert Wilkinson in 1814. The building is obviously that shown in *Plate 26*, and beneath is a vignette of Rosoman's theatre based on the image shown in *Plates 22 & 23*. However, the altered auditorium was quite smart, although there appears to have been little or no separation between stage and the area occupied by musicians, so performers and any apparatus they needed (especially in the cases where acrobats were involved) were not confined to the space behind the proscenium-arch. Seating in the 'pit' consisted of benches, but boxes were provided at the sides with metal balustrades *(Plate 29)*.

In 1781 Joseph Grimaldi (1778-1837)[35] made his first appearance (as a child-dancer) at *Sadler's Wells* in a pantomime written by Charles Isaac Mungo Dibdin (1768-1833)[36], whose brother, Thomas John Dibdin (1771-1841), was also engaged to write for *Sadler's Wells* under the new proprietors (from 1792), Richard Hughes and William Siddons (1744-1808), husband of the celebrated Sarah (*née* Kemble [1755-1831]). The Hughes/Siddons régime not only brought in writers of the Dibdins' stature, but promoted a new respectability, making the *Wells* socially

Plate 28: *South-West View of Sadler's Wells*, from a drawing by R. C. Andrews of 1792, engraved by William Wise (*fl.*1790-1808) and published by Robert Wilkinson (*fl.* 1785-1825) in 1814. The building is clearly that shown in *Plate 26*, and the New River is depicted. Beneath there is a vignette 'View of the Theatre in its Former State', identical to the image shown in *Plate 22 (Collection JSC)*.

acceptable. Raising tone, however, did not improve takings, as King had found out when he replaced the 'meaner sort' of persons with those of higher social standing, and Siddons claimed the establishment had actually run at a loss between 1795 and 1801 despite appearances by the singer Robert Dighton (1751-1814) and the actor Edmund Kean (1787-1833). Dibdin, by 1801, regarded the theatre at *Sadler's Wells* as hopelessly old-fashioned and seedy[37]. Something drastic had to be done, and it was: Dibdin himself took over the management, and, in response to the public taste for spectacle and patriotic sentiment, almost immediately revived the *Wells*'s fortunes. In 1802, Dibdin and his brother, Thomas, became major shareholders in the theatre, and various innovations were made.

The auditorium was given a thorough facelift to designs by Rudolphe Cabanel (*c.*1763-1839)[38], acquiring superior sight-lines, a semi-circular circle, and galleries: supports for the last two were provided by slender cast-iron columns, an early instance in which this material was employed for such a purpose. On either side of the proscenium were boxes, but the Dress Circle no longer had these, and a proper subdivision was provided for the orchestra. An even more radical addition (1804) was the provision of a huge metal tank under the stage which made possible the production of 'aqua-dramas'. Water was provided from the New River by means of an 'Archimedean Wheel'. In 1808 further facilities were added to provide waterfalls. Dibdin advertised *Sadler's Wells* as an aquatic theatre 'with realistic naval battles and Newfoundland dogs rescuing drowning children'[39] and other elevating spectacles. In a view of Cabanel's[40] interior published in *The Microcosm of London*[41] by Rudolph Ackermann (1764-1834)[42] with texts by William Henry Pyne (1769-1843) and William Combe (1742-1823), the audience is seen viewing an aquatic spectacle, a scene from Dibdin's

Plate 29: Typical entertainment at *Sadler's Wells*, showing rope-dancers and the refurbished auditorium of 1787. The metal balustrades in front of each box and the galleries above should be noted, as should the rather crude benches in the 'pit' (what today would be known as the stalls). From a water-colour by C. H. Matthews (*fl.* 1830-40) based on an engraving of 1794 by Benedict Anthony Van Assen (1767-c.1817) *(LMA SC/PZ/FI/O2/038).*

extravaganza, *The Ocean Fiend*[43], of 1807 *(Plate 30)*, with music by William Reeve (1757-1815)[44], a composer of negligible talent, whose opera, *The Caravan* (1803)[45] was successful, not because of the music, but because at the climax a dog jumped into a tank of water and rescued a child: such shows appealed more than fine music to the London public. This gave Dibdin the idea to instal the large tank of (usually fœtid) water at *Sadler's Wells*, and the public seemed to enjoy the novelty, but a foray into the texts of such works as *The Ocean Fiend* has proved unrewarding (at least to one reader), and an exploration of Reeve's scores has revealed them to be models of dullness. However, for a brief period, such empty entertainments worked, and drew the crowds, including ladies of a 'volatile description'[46] and a further innovation was the introduction of pony-racing round a specially constructed track in 1802 *(Plate 31)*: with fireworks, an aquatic theatre, waterfalls, and pony-races, not to mention the popularity of 'Joe' Grimaldi[47], the *Wells* enjoyed a period of prosperity.

Among the additions made to the buildings in the first decade of the nineteenth century (apart from the water-tank) were stables for the ponies and horses, a large scene-room, and a 'piazza' along the south side. A 'piazza' was a covered way, colonnaded walk, or pentice, a term seemingly derived from the roofed arcades as at Covent Garden, designed by Inigo Jones (1573-1652) and built 1631-7: this was a development around a square, perhaps partly suggested by the Piazza at Livorno (Leghorn), and partly by

Plate 30: The auditorium at *Sadler's Wells* in *c.*1807 showing an aquatic scene from Dibdin the Younger's *The Ocean Fiend*, or *The Infant's Peril*, with musical numbers by William Reeve. Illustration derived from a plate in Pyne & Combe (1808-10) by A. C. Pugin and Thomas Rowlandson *(Collection JSC).*

the Palace des Vosges, Paris (1605-12). At *Sadler's Wells* the covered way may be seen in an illustration entitled *Aquatic Theatre, Sadler's Wells*, published in 1813 by James Whittle (d. 1818) and Richard Holmes Laurie (1777-1858) *(Plate 32).*

From around 1818, however, after the departure of Dibdin and the retirement of Grimaldi, the *Wells* lost money, and its fortunes again declined. Attempts were made to smarten up the auditorium, revive and improve the pony-races, and provide a new scene-dock and dressing-rooms. But nothing seemed to work for long, and the establishment sank in reputation and popularity. The house was converted to provide a wine-room, a saloon, a coffee-house, and a box-office, but that, too, was of little avail. The 'piazza' was demolished and a large porch was erected, but views of *Sadler's Wells* in the late 1820s and 1830s do not show much that is attractive. The poplars, it is true, had grown, and the New River still flowed, but the essentially rural surroundings were fast disappearing as land was developed for housing and other purposes. Islington Road became St John Street Road (later St John Street), and it is from that road that we have an impression of *Sadler's Wells* from the east in *c.*1830, with brick piers as gate-posts, SADLERS on one pier and WELLS on the other: both piers had notices stuck to them *(Plate 33).*

Fortunes revived from 1843, when new managers took over: these were Thomas Longdon Greenwood (1808-79) and Samuel Phelps (1804-78), who introduced Seasons of Shakespearian productions, quite a risky venture as the *Wells* was some distance from fashionable London. The new management banished the badly-behaved, and drove vendors away from the vicinity. The result was an amazing reversal of decline: not only did an audience patronise the theatre, but

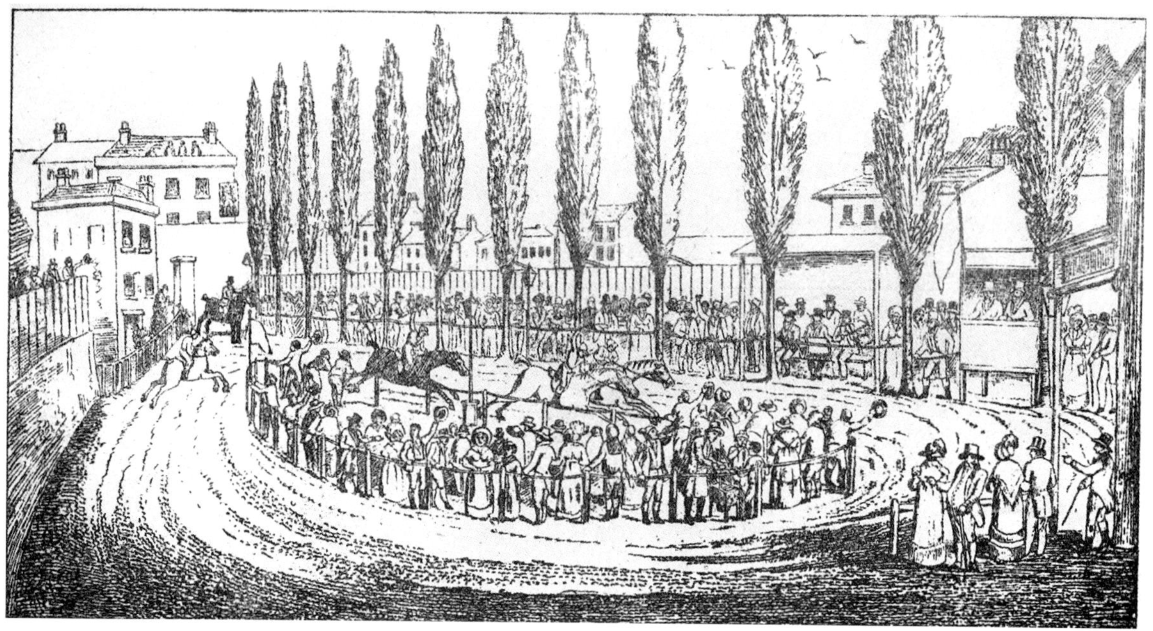

Plate 31: The pony-track at *Sadler's Wells* (1806) *(ILHC L4.22).*

Plate 32: View of *Aquatic Theatre, Sadler's Wells,* looking north-west across the New River, in 1813. The lean-to pentice or 'piazza' can be seen along the south side of the theatre. Compare with *Plate 26.* Published by Whittle and Laurie of Fleet Street, London *(ILHC L4.22).*

the place became a school for training performers who would go on to success in the West End. A large new portico was added, improvements were carried out in the auditorium, and accommodation was added for actors: the architect was Richard Tress (1809/10-75).

As more land was developed for housing, and the last vestiges of a rural setting began to be whittled away, Greenwood retired and Phelps ceased to be much involved at all from 1862. Under several managements a mixed theatrical fare was provided (melodrama, light plays, and some Shakespeare), and the theatre was also used for public meetings (some of a religious-revival nature). In 1876 the buildings were converted to cater for the new craze of roller-skating, and a mixed bag of uses was proposed (concerts, Sunday services, public meetings, lectures, fairs, exhibitions, athletics, wrestling-matches, flower-shows, cat- and dog-shows, and swimming). An obscure architect, John Warrington Morris (*fl.*1864-83), prepared plans (he was also a shareholder in the grandly-named *Sadler's Wells Skating Rink and Winter Gardens Ltd.*), but very soon the roller-skating mania had passed, and it was decided to rebuild the interior as a theatre.

Under Mrs Sidney Frances Bateman (1823-81), widow of Hezekiah Linthicum Bateman (1812-75), business partner of Henry Irving (1838-1905) at the Lyceum Theatre, the *Wells* was substantially rebuilt, not only to satisfy Mrs Bateman but to comply with the 1878 *Metropolis Management and Building Acts Amendment*[48] which compelled owners to remedy defects. Works were carried out to designs by Charles John Phipps (1835-97), and included a new auditorium, a very large stage, and vastly improved facilities, fire-safety, and much else. However, Mrs Bateman died in 1881, further alterations were carried out to designs by Bertie Crewe (d.1937), and the theatre was let to the Music Hall Proprietary Corporation from 1902 to 1911. Used as a part-time cinema (1896-1915), *Sadler's Wells* became shabby and down-at-heel, although there were theatrical performances too, none of the edifying kind. The theatre closed in 1915, was badly vandalised in 1919, and was then taken over by Ernest C. Rolls who carried out minor changes and cosmetic repairs to designs by Crewe and Stanley Harry Burdwood (1878-*after* 1920), but *Sadler's Wells* did not re-open, and once again became derelict.

EPILOGUE

Inspired by Reginald Rowe (d. 1945) and Lilian Mary Baylis (1874-1937), on the lookout for a second home for the *Old Vic*, an appeal for finance was established in 1925 and plans for a reconstruction of Sadler's Wells were drawn up by Francis Graham Moon Chancellor (1869-1940), Senior Partner in the firm of Frank Matcham & Co., but the work of rebuilding was not completed until 1931. The first Ballet production took place in that year, and under the Irish-born Ninette de Valois (*née* Edris Stannus [1898-2001])[49] a Ballet School was founded at the *Wells*. For a few years Ballet and Drama alternated, but from 1935 *Sadler's Wells* became a theatre for Ballet, and the *Old Vic* specialised in Drama. Extensions were planned by Stanley Alexander Hall & Easton & Robertson[50], but the success of the Ballet led to its move to Covent Garden in 1946 to become the Royal Ballet, and de Valois then formed the Sadler's Wells Ballet Touring Company which performed at the *Wells* during its London Seasons.

The *Wells* had also been a venue for Opera, but in 1968 Sadler's Wells Opera was transferred to the vast *London Coliseum* and later became English National Opera. All this threatened the future of *Sadler's Wells* and various proposals were made to demolish the theatre and replace it with other uses. From 1994, however, an ambitious scheme by RHWL Architects, involving the rebuilding of the foyer, stage, and rear-stage areas, all with up-to-date equipment, several rehearsal-rooms, and facilities for educational and community use, was developed. The complex also includes the Lilian Baylis Theatre, a lecture-room, a bar, a Garden Court Café, and much more. It incorporates the 'Georgian House', the back of the 1822 stables, now used as offices. Nicholas Hare Architects were also involved as consultants for the fragmented exterior, where glass plays a dominant rôle (and has not escaped damage from motor-vehicles in Arlington Way). The works were completed in 1996-8, and the first performance took place in October 1998. The

Plate 33: *Sadler's Wells* seen in a water-colour from St John Street Road, looking west, in *c*.1830. The New River can be seen on the left, but gone are the pleasant rural surroundings as London's demand for housing swallowed up available land, and owners of estates cashed in on demand *(NMR/MBC/653/SAD/SW/1824)*.

location of the original Well (long dry) is near the rear corner of the auditorium at the Arlington Way side[51].

So *Sadler's Wells* has had an extraordinarily chequered history, and many activities are reported to have taken place there, including balloon ascents (1826 and 1838); exhibitions by Giovanni Battista Belzoni (1778-1823), not of Egyptology, but to show off his gymnastic skills as the 'Patagonian Sampson', as he was improbably billed, having keen born in Padua; and other displays, performances, and entertainments[52]. Its importance as a medicinal spring was short-lived, and Sunderland[53] categorised it as a 'spurious' Spa, despite claims that a Holy Well once had existed there[54].

Chapter III References: Sadler's Wells

1 For Hollar's Views, *see* Hind (1922) esp. Pls. xliv, xlv, and xliii.

2 Saint (*Gen. Ed.*) (2008*b*) 141.

3 Guidott (1684).

4 Confection containing caraway-seeds.

5 Species of sweetmeat flavoured with a preparation made from the bitter aromatic root of horse-heal, a perennial composite plant (*Inula Helenium*): it was once used as a tonic and stimulant.

6 The aromatic and fragrant root of *Archangelica officinalis* or sometimes the large ribs of its leaves were used to flavour a candied confection, once thought to be an antidote to poison and pestilence.

7 How times have changed!

8 Saint (*Gen. Ed.*) (2008*b*) 141-3.

9 Colsoni (1951) 6, 19.

10 *See* Ames (1691), for example.

11 Ward (1699) 12-15.

12 Wroth & Wroth (1896) 44; Pinks (1880) 412.
13 Pinks (1880) 412. It is hard to credit how *anyone* could be capable of such a dubious feat.
14 15 March 1718.
15 Pinks (1880) 414.
16 Garbott (1728).
17 *Universal Harmony*, etc. (1743).
18 A reference to the man behind the creation of the New River.
19 The song is supposed to date from 1740. It is quoted in Pinks (1880) 417.
20 *London Daily Post* (17 July 1740).
21 *Ibid.* (3 July 1742). Rope-dancing was a tight-rope performance; a ladder-dance was so-called because the performer stood on a ladder which he or she shifted from place to place and ascended or descended without losing the equilibrium or permitting the ladder to fall.
22 Doran **i** (1864) 477.
23 Pinks (1880) 417-8.
24 Noorthouck (1773) 350.
25 Greek physician (*c.*AD 130-*c.*200).
26 *General Advertiser* (14 May 1747). Quoted in Pinks (1880) 418.
27 Known as 'Iron Legs' (*Gamba di Ferro*). He performed in Harlequinades, choreographed and took part in numerous set-pieces, and practiced as a 'surgeon-dentist'. He had contracted Syphilis by 1767, which did not inhibit his voracious sexual appetites. For the Grimaldis *see* Stott (2009).
28 Obsolete term pertaining to rope-walking.
29 A white wine produced in the Province of Estremadura in Portugal and exported from Lisbon.
30 A type of Malaga wine, made from grapes grown on the mountains.
31 Pinks (1880) 419.
32 *See* Angelo (1904) for other information.
33 Son of a German Jew, Johann Abraham (d. after 1779), Braham was the only English male singer of international renown at the time. His celebrated patriotic song, *The Death of Nelson*, was hugely popular, with its ringing climax, *England expects*.
34 Anna Selina Storace, English soprano, was the daughter of an Italian double-bass player. Her brother, Stephen John Seymour Storace (1762-96), was a composer and friend of Mozart: the great German composer wrote for her the beautiful Concert Aria, *Ch'io mi scordi di te* (K.505), with its *obbligato* for piano (which Mozart played at the first performance in 1786).
35 *See* Stott (2009).
36 Known as Charles Dibdin the Younger, or as Charles Isaac Pitt, he was the son of Charles Dibdin (1745-1814) and the actress, Harriett Pitt (*c.*1748-1814).
37 Speaight (*Ed.*) (1956) 17-33.
38 *Ibid.* 47.
39 *ODNB* **xvi** (2004) 31.
40 For Cabanel *see* Colvin (2008) 209-10.
41 Pyne & Combe (1808-10).
42 Plates by Augustus Charles Pugin (1769-1832) and Thomas Rowlandson (1757-1827).
43 Dibdin (1807).
44 *See*, for example, Reeve (1807). *See* Highfill, Burnim, & Langhans **xii** (1973-93).
45 First given at Drury Lane 5 December 1803.
46 Cutting (21 April 1787) Percival Collection **ii** BL.
47 Stott (2009).
48 41 & 42 Vict. *c.*32.
49 *ODNB 2001-2004* (2009) 1126-32.
50 John Murray Easton (1889-1975) and Howard Morley Robertson (1888-1963).
51 For details of the various works on the theatre *see* Saint (*Gen. Ed.*) (2008*b*) Ch. V.
52 Pinks (188) 420-36 is informative on these matters, as is, to a lesser extent, Wroth & Wroth (1896) 48-53. *See* also Foord (1910) 82-89. A useful synopsis of the fortunes of Sadler's Wells can be found in Cosh (2005) 62-3, 66-7, 86, 97-9, 99, 117, 159-7, 176, 271-3, 282, 328, 334.
53 Sunderland (1915) 18, 86-7.
54 *See* Hembry (1990): Margetson (1963, 1964, 1965); Scott (1948); Wroth & Wroth (1896). For opera at Sadler's Wells and afterwards *see* Gilbert (2009).

CHAPTER IV

THE CLERKENWELL GROUP II

Introduction; Spa Fields Pantheon; The London Spaw; New Wells; The English Grotto or Grotto Garden; The Mulberry Garden; Merlin's Cave; Lord Cobham's Head; Sir John Oldcastle Tavern; Coldbath Spring; Peerless Pool; The Clerk's Well; Other Establishments; Afterword

'The Spring is gratefully adorned with rails,
Whose fame will last till the New River fails'.
May-Day: or, The Orginal of Garlands (London: J. Roberts 1720).

'But shou'd I paint
The language, humours, custom of the place,
Together with all curtsy's, lowly bows,
And compliments extern, 'twould swell my page
Beyond its limits due'.
WILLIAM WOTY (*c*.1731-91): *The Shrubs of Parnassus*
(London: J. Newbery for the Author 1760).

INTRODUCTION

This Chapter will mention sundry establishments, none of which was so celebrated as *Islington Spa*, *Sadler's Wells*, or some of the other places mentioned in this book. However, they catered in their way for an eighteenth-century phenomenon: the demand for Pleasure-Gardens and other sites where the social mix was broad, where persons could show themselves and inspect others, and where refreshments could be obtained and entertainments enjoyed. They also offered opportunities for assignations, for upper-class persons who enjoyed the thrill of 'slumming' or at least of mixing with social inferiors, and for the lower classes to view those higher in the social pecking-order with the aim of emulating their dress and deportment. That they might also be convenient places for strumpets, pickpockets, and tricksters to ply their trades cannot be denied, but they sometimes offered medicinal waters, wholesome ales, innocent or semi-innocent amusements, and food, and some even had bathing facilities. In many cases the fare on offer was similar, as one successful enterprise would be copied by the proprietors of other establishments in order to prosper. Thus we have tumblers, musicians, dramatic turns, harlequinades, fireworks, spectacles, and so on. Sometimes remarkable claims were made for the properties of Springs and Wells, and waters would not only be made available for drinking on site but in bottles too for consumption elsewhere. Alcohol was drunk in quantity, and varied food was also provided in several institutions[1].

SPA FIELDS PANTHEON

The area called Spa Fields was to become one where many resorts evolved from the closing decades of the seventeenth century. Various public-houses were not just Taverns, but also had Gardens: bear-baiting, dog-fights, cock-fights, and bowling-greens were among the

Plate 34: The City of London from Spa Fields in 1665 looking south-east, by Wenceslaus Hollar. Old St Paul's Cathedral is in the centre (destroyed from 1666). The two buildings in the foreground are the *Dog and Duck* public-house *(right)* and *The Fountain* public-house *(left)* on a footpath facing Spa Fields: that footpath is now Exmouth Market *(LMA SC/PZ/FI/01/245).*

attractions on offer, and the fields were also blessed with duck-ponds, used for setting dogs among ducks, often involving wagers. A public-house, the *Dog and Duck* (also known as *Ducking-Pond House),* had 'ducking' ponds in its grounds as well as orchards, gardens, and pleasant seating-areas. This establishment may be seen in a view from Spa Fields of 1665 by Wenceslaus Hollar *(Plate 34)*[2].

However, in 1769 the Gardens of the *Dog and Duck* acquired a spectacular addition in the form of the *Spa Fields Pantheon*, the grandest of all the pleasure-pavilions in Clerkenwell. From the 1750s the *Dog and Duck* had been run by the ubiquitous Thomas Rosoman, and the *Pantheon* was opened in 1770 as a 'Tea Drinking House'. It was a large circular drum covered by a high domed roof, and may have been designed by William Newton (1735-90), who, in 1750, had been apprenticed to William Jones (d. 1757), the architect of the Rotunda at *Ranelagh Gardens*, Chelsea (1742-1805), of which Newton published an engraving in 1761. The *Pantheon* had semicircular projections for staircases and entrances, and, inside its drum, three tiers of superimposed columns supported the two galleries and the domed roof *(Plate 35)*. We know that Newton[3] was interested in structural innovation, and so the building was an important and original work.

Although apparently designed as a theatre, the building does not appear to have been used as such, although the persons who frequented it for tea-drinking and so on might be regarded as both actors and spectators (of each other). There was an organ to provide music, and a central stove to heat the space. The building attracted customers in droves to drink tea, coffee, punch, negus, port, and other beverages, and in the adjoining *Dog and Duck* there were several tea-rooms, apartments for gaming, and facilities for dining. The Garden, covering some four acres, had its ducking-pond converted into a canal well-stocked with fish, and alcoves fitted out with seats and tables were grouped around it. Walks were laid out among the fruit-trees and shrubberies, and there was also a summer-house and a statue of Hercules set on a high pedestal.

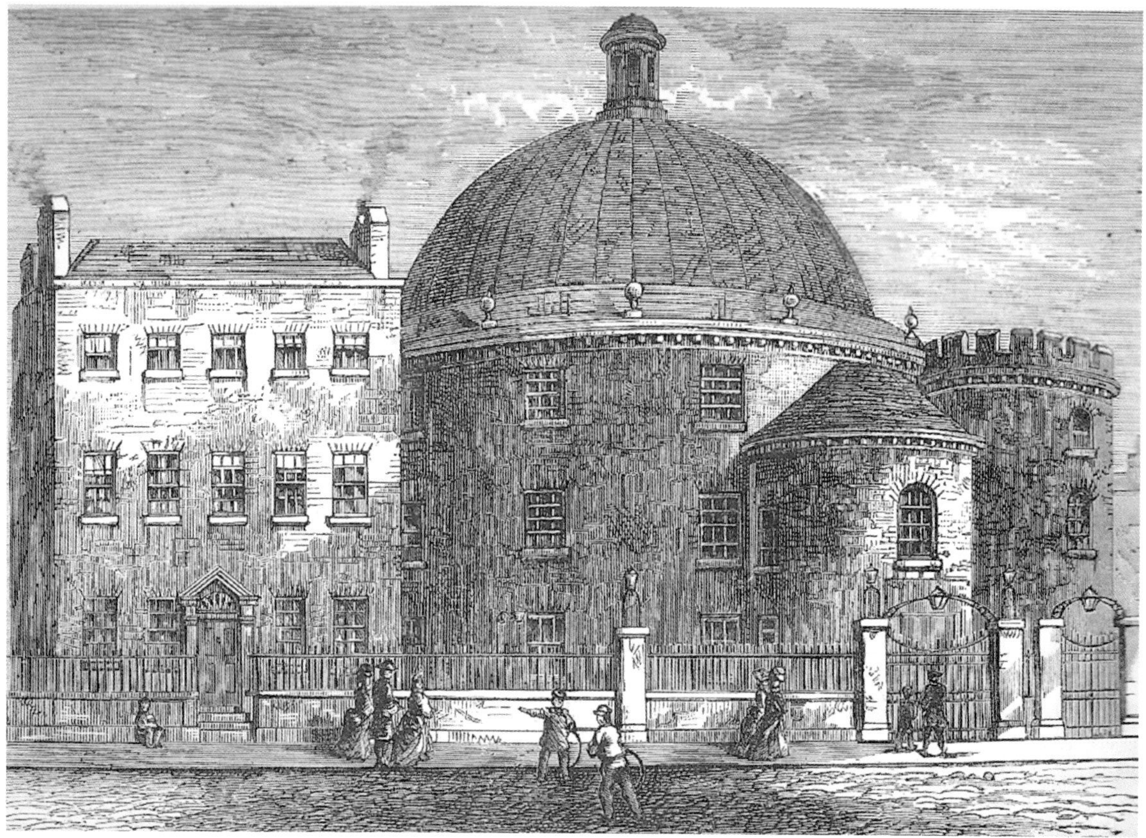

Plate 35: *The Pantheon*, Spa Fields, in the 1780s, after its conversion for use as a chapel for the Countess of Huntingdon's Connexion. The handsome five-window-wide house on the left was the former *Dog and Duck* Tavern (as rebuilt in 1756), by then the Countess's residence *(From Thornbury & Walford* ***ii*** *[1879-85] 300: Collection JSC).*

Although the *Pantheon* brought commercial success, it was principally resorted to 'by apprentices and small tradesmen', and by 'journeyman tailors, hairdressers, milliners, and servant maids'[4]. However, observers professed to be shocked by the behaviour of numerous young women who accosted them with requests for 'dishes of tea' as a means of soliciting. The Middlesex Justices silenced the organ on Sundays in 1772[5], presumably on the grounds that the music inflamed passions that were, however, also aroused by the 'amorous flutterings' of 'duck and drake' on the canal[6]. In any case, in 1774, the building and grounds were put up for sale on account of the bankruptcy of the proprietor (who had leased the establishment from Rosoman), and closed as a place of entertainment in 1776. The *Pantheon* was used as a depôt for the sale of carriages for a short time, and in 1777 became the Northampton Chapel, a place of Anglican worship, in which parsons preached moralising sermons on the profane history of the building, but in 1779 it was opened as the Spa Fields Chapel for the Countess of Huntingdon's Connexion. The activities of Selina Hastings (1707-91), Countess of Huntingdon, at Spa Fields led to her secession from the Established Church (to which she had professed loyalty): she moved into the old *Dog and Duck* which she used as her private residence, and had a door knocked through into the chapel which she claimed was merely an extension to her house. A Consistorial Court forbade Anglicans to preach there, and so what became Spa Fields Chapel became a Dissenting Chapel in 1782[7].

William Shrubsole (1760-1806) became the organist at Spa Fields Chapel[8], and composed the celebrated hymn-tune for 'All hail! the power of

Jesu's name' by Edward Perronet (1721-92)[9], and a wealthy and influential congregation was established in an area where the population was increasing at a rapid rate. Soon after the *Pantheon* became a chapel, the statue of Fame, complete with trumpet, was removed from its position surmounting the cupola, and a new lantern was formed. Various other alterations were made to designs by Thomas William Constantine (*fl.* 1850-68) in the 1850s, and a massive portico was added in 1867, but the building was demolished in 1886-7, and the Church of Our Most Holy Redeemer was erected on the site to designs by John Dando Sedding (1838-91) and Henry Wilson (1864-1934). This remarkably handsome building (1887-1916), in an Italianate style, is a monument to the Anglo-Catholicism and Anglican Ritualism of Warwick Reed Wroth (1825-67), Vicar of St Philip's, Clerkenwell, from 1854 until his death[10].

One of the saddest transformations of any London Pleasure-Ground was the fate that befell the *Dog and Duck* Gardens. Part was built over, and soon the residue was completely surrounded by houses on Exmouth Street, Northampton Row, and Northampton Road, leaving some two acres which became the infamous Spa Fields Burial-Ground. This ghastly place was a purely commercial concern, and was unconnected with the Spa Fields Chapel or its successor. By the early 1840s, when 'Graveyard' Walker was publishing his investigations, some 80,000 corpses had been 'buried' there, many of them 'resurrected' for the anatomy-schools or hideously maltreated to make way for yet more interments[11]. The details involved sawing and chopping up bodies, burning flesh and coffins, and other horrible practices, leading to vile smells, great distress among local residents, and much lurid copy in the Publick Prints. *Laissez-faire* attitudes died hard, however, and it was not until 1853 that Spa Fields Burial-Ground was closed, but attempts to make it into a garden were unsuccessful as many plants died, so poisoned was the ground. After works of drainage, levelling, and gravelling, the area became a children's playground in 1886, a recreation-ground and gardens in 1936, was extended in the 1950s, and newly landscaped in 2006-7[12].

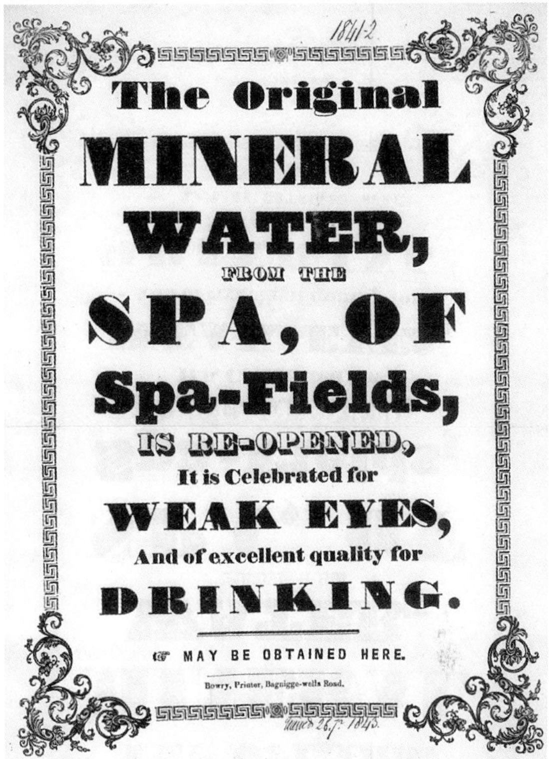

Plate 36: Advertisement printed by Bowry of Bagnigge Wells Road, probably puffing the waters of the *London Spa*. Note the beautiful Greek Key and other decorations as well as the robust lettering *(LMA SC/GL/NOB/C/001/1-12)*.

Given such 'changes of use', it is interesting to consider a handsome advertisement of the 1840s printed by Bowry of Bagnigge Wells Road: it trumpets the 'Original MINERAL WATER, from the SPA, OF Spa-Fields', claiming the place (or the Mineral-Water) was 'RE-OPENED', and that the waters were 'celebrated for WEAK EYES, And of excellent quality for DRINKING' *(Plate 36)*. Now although this document does not specify exactly which Spa is referred to, it cannot be *Bagnigge Wells*, and so must have advertised either the waters of the *London Spaw* or *Islington Spa* as these were both in Spa Fields. It is more likely to refer to the *London Spaw* (by then called *Spa*), in which case the contents of the waters cannot have been wholesome, given the proximity to the hellish ground of the Spa Fields graveyard. Nevertheless, the typography is worthy of admiration.

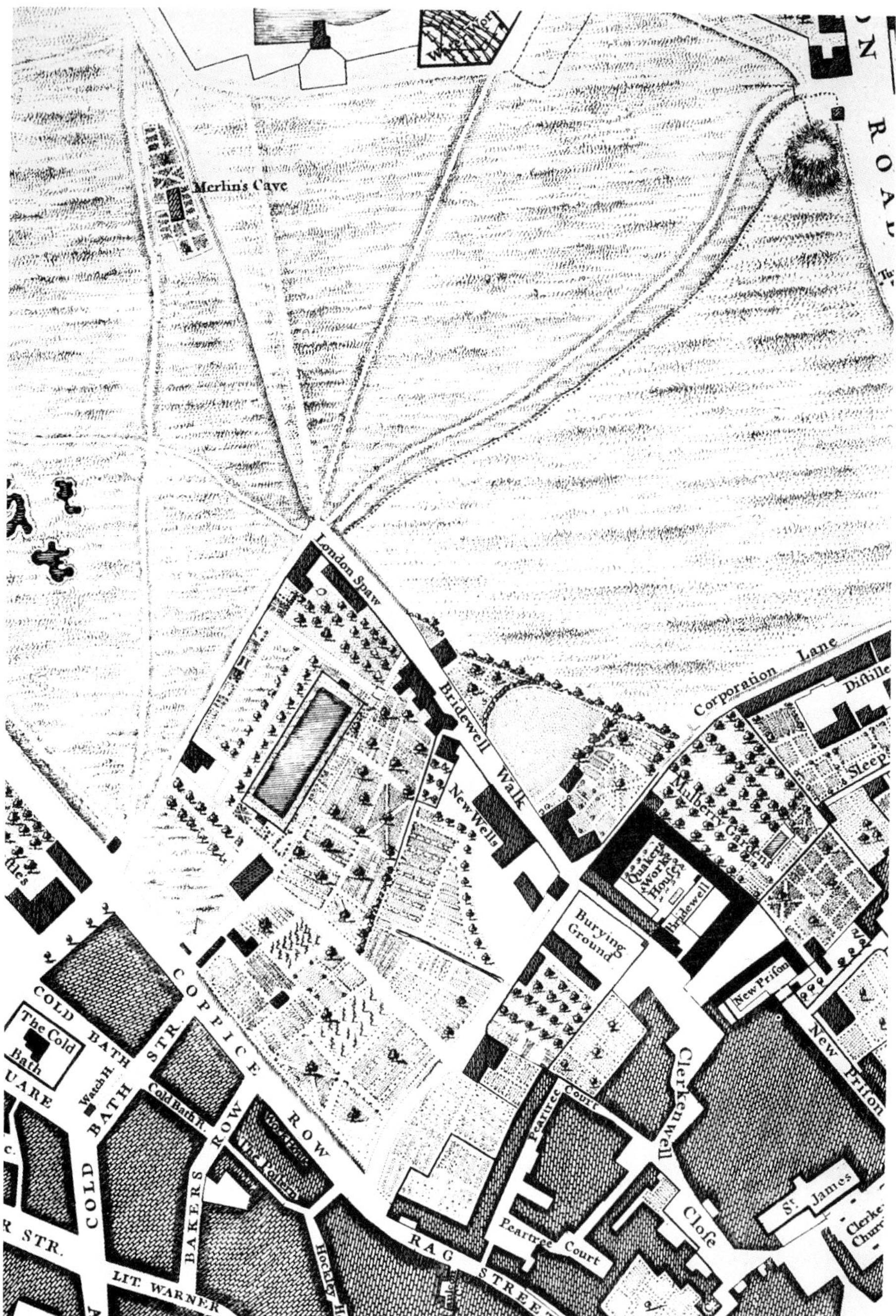

Plate 37: Part of Rocque's map of 1746 showing the expanses of Spa Fields, *Merlin's Cave (top left)*, part of the New River Head *(top)*, Islington Road *(top right)*, the centre of Clerkenwell around the Parish-church of St James *(bottom right)*, the *Cold Bath (bottom left)*, and the area bounded by Bridewell Walk, the path running north-east from Coppice Row (later Farringdon Road) across the Fields, the *London Spaw*, the *Dog and Duck* (on the path by Spa Fields), the *New Wells* in Bridewell Walk (now Northampton Road), and the formal Gardens, orchards, and pleasure-grounds. From Rocque (1746) *(Collection JSC)*.

THE LONDON SPAW

The land-surveyor and cartographer, John Rocque (*c*.1704-62), produced his celebrated survey of London with George Vertue (1684-1756 – engraver and antiquary), the sheets being engraved by John Pine (1690-1756) and published in twenty-four sheets by Pine and John Tinney (*c*.1706-61) in 1746. Part of Rocque's map shows the sites of both the *Dog and Duck* and the *Fountain* (by 1685 re-named *The London Spaw*) *(Plate 37)*. It is to this establishment (visible in *Plate 7*) that we now turn.

Almost due south of the New River Head, an alleged mediaeval Well, dating from 1206, was rediscovered in 1685, but a public-house called *The Fountain* was certainly there in the 1660s, at the junction of what was then Bridewell Walk (now Rosoman Street) and a path which became Exmouth Street and then Market. One John Halhed, vintner and victualler, who was the proprietor, renamed the place *London Spaw* in 1685, supposedly with the support of none other than the Natural Philosopher Robert Boyle (1627-91), whose *Imprimatur* suggested the waters were the strongest and very best 'of these late found out medicinal' variety[13], containing plenty of iron. Halhed laid out a skittle-ground and planted an orchard in the Garden of his establishment. The poor were allowed to drink the waters *gratis*. By the early years of the eighteenth century the *Spaw* became popular, helped, no doubt, by the beer brewed using the waters, a beverage for which medicinal properties were therefore claimed by 'an eminent, knowing, and more than ordinary ingenious apothecary, and other sufficient men'[14]. In competition with other establishments, especially *Islington Spa* and *Sadler's Wells*, the *Spaw* was never fashionable, and its tone always seemed to be rather low and common:

> '... no fabl'd Deities are found
> At London Spaw, to consecrate the ground'[15].

Besides, the area known as Duck or Ducking-Pond Fields, later called Spa Fields in Clerkenwell, was much infested by 'sneaking footpads' who knocked down pedestrians and despoiled them of hats, wigs, silver buckles, watches, and money. Link-boys were in constant attendance at the doors of *Sadler's Wells* to light revellers home as they crossed the lonely fields to the streets of Islington, Clerkenwell, Holborn, The City, or Westminster. Link-boys also plied their trade (and not solely concerned with illumination, it seems) from other Spas or Pleasure-Gardens, but the *London Spaw* was not high on their list for possible customers.

From around 1714 the *Spaw* seems to have run into difficulties, but soon it was observed that

> '... nine-pin alleys, and now skettles grace,
> The late forlorn, sad, desolated place;
> Arbours of jasmine fragrant shades compose
> And numerous blended companies
> enclose'[16].

Ward mentioned that the *Spaw* was popular in 1714[17], and by 1720

> 'The Well neglected, now each from the
> Spring
> Her pail fills up, the news to Town they bring.
> The rabble flock in shoals who hear its fame,
> To try its Virtue – each Childless Dame,
> Holiday fools to see the wonder throngs;
> Now all the trade to London Spaw belongs'[18].

The yearly Welsh Fair[19], which was held in Spa Fields, ensured additional custom, and the Spring, 'adorned with rails', enjoyed 'fame' that would 'last till the New River fails'[20]. Entertainments were provided, and dishes such as 'roast pork with the oft-famed flavoured Spaw ale'[21] were available. It appears that, as with *Sadler's Wells*, the ale soon eclipsed the waters in popularity, although the *Spaw*'s product seems to have induced a 'phrensical fit' in a drunken Custom-House officer, prompting him to attack several persons in the *Spaw* with a dagger, 'in a most frightful manner'[22], so the quality of the beverage may have been suspect, or the 'officer' simply imbibed too much of it.

The facetious 'Almanack', *Poor Robin*, recorded that

> 'Sweethearts with their sweethearts go
> To Islington or London Spaw;
> Some go but just to drink the water,
> Some for the ale which they like better'[23].

Plate 38: Bucolic junketings on May Day at *The London Spaw*, 1720: the patrons do not appear to have emerged from the first echelons of polite society. The formal avenues of trees and the secluded arbours should be noted. From *May-Day* (1720) *(Collection JSC).*

To judge from contemporary descriptions and illustrations *(Plate 38)*, the *London Spaw*, despite claims for its waters and efforts to provide arbours and walks among the trees, was always somewhat rough. The buildings, which appear to have been of timber, clad in boarding *(Plate 39)*, were replaced with brick structures in 1766-8, and the skittle-alley continued in use, but the Spring dried up early in the nineteenth century, although the name endured as that of the public-house, rebuilt in 1835 *(Plate 40)*, and then rebuilt again in 1898 to designs by William Arthur Aickman (1859-1941), possibly working with J. K. Bateman, but the *London Spa* (as it was then known) ceased to function as a pub in 2002: the apartments over the ground floor are still known (2009) as 'London Spa Court'. The builder of the 1835 structure was a Richard Erlam, who may have been related to the architects of that surname who flourished in the 1820s, 1830s, and 1840s. The handsome public-house (which recorded the date 1206 on its frieze) may be seen in a beautiful photograph of Finsbury Town Hall of 1895 *(Plate 41)*.

Immediately to the south of the long strip of *London Spaw* gardens was the *Red Lion*, otherwise *New Red Lion*, which boasted a cock-pit, certainly active in 1730: the 'Royal Sport of Cockfighting' was supposed to be 'something peculiar to the English, there not being such dangerous cocks anywhere else'[24]. Apparently this 'amusement' occurred daily at four p.m., for 6 guineas a battle, although sometimes twenty guineas were wagered. These were enormous sums at the time.

One final note should be added to this brief description of the *Spaw*. The change of name from 'Fountain' to 'London Spaw' suggests, in Sunderland's words, 'an ignorant, quackish impudence which is amusing and staggering'[25]. The pretentious title given to a 'backyard spring' was intended to attract customers who would spend money on the amusements and ale provided. Sunderland put the *London Spaw* into his 'spurious' category, and it would be difficult to dissent from this view[26].

Plate 39: *The London Spaw* from the east in 1731: attributed to Clement Lemprière (1683-1746) in Frederick Crace's (1779-1859) *Catalogue*, edited by his son, John Gregory Crace (1809-89) (*see* Crace [1878] 588 No 41) *(LMA SC/PZ/FI/01/237/Ce23351/p5442731).*

Plate 40: The *London Spa* public-house, as rebuilt in a robust Italianate style in 1835 at the corner of Exmouth *(right)* and Rosoman *(left)* Streets. From a water-colour of 1897 by John Philipps Emslie (1839-1913) made just before the building's demolition *(LMA SC/PZ/FI/01/248)*.

NEW WELLS

Inspired no doubt by the commercial possibilities of *Islington Spa*, Dr Joseph Hooke, as previously noted, opened the *New Wells* in Bridewell Walk on what had formerly been *Red Lion Bowling-Green*, in 1735. There, his 'Interlude House' put on popular comical theatrical pieces or farces, but seems to have run into difficulties as a result of legislation passed in 1736[27]. However, the Gardens included a miniature zoo (with rattlesnakes, a crocodile, 'an African cat between the Tyger and Leopard, perfectly tame', and several 'darting and flying squirrels' among the attractions[28]) and 'Merlin's Cave', in addition to a Spring said to have medicinal value, but Sunderland again considered the place to be a 'spurious' Spa[29]. The price of admission to the theatrical performances was a pint of wine or punch, and there were charges for seeing the zoological exhibits and for other diversions, including firework-displays, tight-rope stunts, tumblers, a dance featuring a Polish male dwarf partnering a seven-feet tall Saxon lady, the Battle of Culloden, and a boy of 16 years already seven feet four inches tall. Among the 'operas' put on there was a curious piece called *The Generous Freemason; or, The Constant Lady; with the Comical Humours of Squire Noodle and his man Doodle* by William Rufus Chetwood (d. 1766), sometimes referred to as the first Masonic opera, published in London by J. Roberts in 1731.

The *New Wells*, then, was hardly an establishment noted for its high-minded entertainments, and in 1744 was described as a 'place where large numbers of disorderly people meet'[30]. Advertisements for it were denounced for 'seducing persons to places kept apart for the encouragement of luxury, extravagance, idleness, and other wicked and illegal purposes, to the destruction of many families, and to the great dishonour of the kingdom in general, and this

Plate 41: Photograph by H. W. Fincham of 1895 showing Finsbury Town Hall, looking south along Rosebery Avenue and left into Garnault Place: the *London Spa* public-house at the corner of Exmouth Street (now Market) and Rosoman Street may be seen. The handsome Town Hall was designed by William Charles Evans-Vaughan (*c*.1857-1900) *(ILHC L3.131)*.

country in particular, especially at a time when we are so much overburdened with taxes, that it is as much as a prudent man may do, without a taste to extravagant and illegal pleasures, to support himself and family'[31].

The *New Wells* closed in 1747, but, in 1750, under the aegis of Thomas Yates (sometimes called Yeates), landlord of the *Red Lion* public-house to the north of the *Wells*, re-opened with performances by the 'Grand Turk' *(Plate 42)* on a slack-rope and by Hannah Snell (1723-92), the sexual impostor, who passed herself off as 'James Gray', in which guise she had taken part in the attack on French-held positions as a Marine, and was wounded several times in 1748. The 1750 Season, however, appears to have been the last, and Nemesis came in the formidable shape of John Wesley (1703-91) who converted the premises into a Methodist tabernacle, opened for worship on 17 May 1752[32].

Charlotte Charke (1713-60), the actress and transvestite, youngest child of the actor and playwright, Colley Cibber (1671-1757), had performed at the *New Wells* as 'Mrs Sacheverell' in 1746, and so knew the place. She was horrified when she visited 'Mr. Yates' New Wells' and was 'persecuted for an hour with words without meaning, and sound without sense... No mortal but Mr Yates would have thought of letting the place for that use, and I believe the first symptoms of his religion will be discovered if there should be a suppression of this mockery of godliness in the loss of his unsanctified tenants, and the sad chance of his tenement standing empty'[33]. It happened. The buildings were demolished in 1756 when Rosoman's Row (later Rosoman Street) was built[34]. What seems clear is that the term 'Wells' had very little to do with water: the establishment was simply a place of vulgar entertainment.

Plate 42: The 'Grand Turk', 'Mahomed Caratha', the 'Equilibrist', performing at the *New Wells*, near the *London Spaw*, shown in an engraving by Robert Sayer (1724/5-94) *(LMA SC/GL/WAK/S3-W1/Ce19231/cat.no.5376307).*

THE ENGLISH GROTTO OR GROTTO GARDEN

This was a timber-mill, timber-clad, which was in existence in 1760, and had a Grotto Garden in its grounds by 1769 complete with 'enchanted fountain', pond, a water-mill which, when working, emulated the effects of fireworks and rainbows in its sprays, and a few other delights. Run by one Jackson, a constructor of rock-work grottoes and contriver of firework-displays, it was situated almost opposite the *London Spaw* at the south-west corner of Cistern or Water House Field, on ground owned by the New River Company at the west end of what is now (2009) Joseph Trotter Close. The entrance-charge was sixpence, and the place gloried in the name of 'Grand Grotto Garden and Gold and Silver Fish Repository', but had a short life, and the pond reverted to the New River Company in 1781. This establishment does not appear to have been a Spa of any kind, but only a resort of mild and innocent diversion, without theatricals or any other distractions[35]. A view of the place published in 1760 was drawn and engraved by Jean-Baptiste Claude Chatelaine (1710-*c*.1758) *(Plate 43).*

THE MULBERRY GARDEN

Due east of *New Wells* was *The Mulberry Garden*, later to disappear beneath the Middlesex House of Detention in 1816-18, the new prison designed by Samuel Ware (1781-1860), itself to be replaced with a bigger structure in 1845-6, designed by William Moseley (*c*.1799-1880), which, in turn, was demolished in 1890. The *Garden* was opened in 1742, and was unusual in that the proprietor, one Body, made no charge for admission, relying for his profits on the sale of refreshments. The grounds were extensive, with a large pond, gravelled walks lined by avenues of trees, a skittle-alley, and seats beneath a venerable

Plate 43: *A View of the English Grotto, near the New River Head,* possibly based on a drawing by Chatelaine, *c.*1760 *(LMA SC/GL/PR/F1/NEW-F1/SAD/Ce7686/cat.no.p5440927).*

mulberry-tree. Attractions included a 'Grand Orchestra' of wind and strings, illuminations, and fireworks, and from the beginning the tone was patriotic, only British musicians being employed and British music played, in preference to the 'effeminate softness' of Italian performers and compositions. Pyrotechnic displays were given from time to time. There was a Long-Room where diversions could be enjoyed during inclement weather, but the *clientèle* was largely drawn from artisans and tradesmen[36].

Provision was made for eating and drinking, with customers 'waited on in the most genteel manner'[37]. Despite the fact that the proprietors attracted custom from the middling strata of society, some illustrations show very well-dressed young men playing ninepins in the shade of the mulberry-tree *(Plate 44)*. Nevertheless, *The Mulberry Garden* derived considerable benefit from the Welsh Fair, as did other establishments in the vicinity. Breakfasts were offered, coffee and tea, bread and butter, and so on, but although the *Garden* undoubtedly had charms, it cannot be regarded as a Spa, and no Spring or Well seems to have provided waters, chalybeate or otherwise, unless the pond was fed by a Spring, which seems likely. Body invited his customers to 'come here' for they would be used 'honestly', unlike other establishments which lost no opportunity to fleece the punters[38]. Nothing is known of the *Garden* after 1752[39], although the grounds were used for a time as the exercise-ground of the Clerkenwell Association of Volunteers, and the House of Detention was erected on them.

MERLIN'S CAVE

In *c.*1700 some cottages were erected on high ground at the eastern edge of Spa Fields, near the New River Head on land now occupied by Merlin Street and Charles Rowan House, lying between Wilmington Square and Amwell Street. One of these houses was a Tavern called *The Hutt*, but re-named *Merlin's Cave* around 1720. It was

Plate 44: Swells at the *Mulberry Garden* *(From Pinks [1880] 128: Collection JSC).*

rebuilt *c.*1737 by the Joseph Hooke who had set up the *New Wells Theatre* further south, and was a two-storey brick building three windows wide with cellars and garrets, and had a Long-Room for entertainment and promenades. In the Garden was a skittle-alley. Now although *Merlin's Cave* could hardly be described as a Spa, its Long-Room, skittle-alley, and Garden were facilities shared with Spas. If waters were available, the evidence is thin. The name, *Merlin's Cave,* has been associated with Queen Caroline's Merlin's Cave, a rustic thatched cottage in Richmond Park, but the name was used in Clerkenwell somewhat earlier.

A fashion for Spas and Pleasure-Gardens led to the creation of numerous resorts attached to existing Taverns (the landlords of which were keen to exploit contemporary tastes). *Merlin's Cave* was clearly one of those. Conspicuously sited on high ground south-west of the New River Head and due north of the *English Grotto, Merlin's Cave* lay in charming open country, and was frequented by Londoners, especially on Sundays[40]. It appears that the Tavern possessed some sort of imitation of the Richmond Cave, adorned with astrological symbols and waxworks, including a statue of Merlin, the Wizard.

Merlin's Cave, however, is remembered today for the three Spa Fields meetings held in the winter of 1816-17, mass-assemblies of considerable importance in the history of English Radicalism, for Henry 'Orator' Hunt (1773-1835) addressed the multitudes from one of the windows of the Tavern on all three occasions. Post-war distress was evident in 1816, and Radicals decided to use well-attended public meetings as a 'springboard for insurrection'[41]: at the first such gathering on 15 November 1816 of 'Distressed Manufacturers, Mariners, Artisans, and Others', demands were made for Parliamentary Reform, the widening of the franchise, and relief of poverty caused by unemployment and a slump after the French Wars. Although there were attempts by extremists to foment riots, and some looting occurred in Smithfield after the second (2 December) meeting, Hunt insisted on constitutional methods, and addressed orderly crowds in Spa Fields. J. Sidebotham published (1 March 1817) a caricature of Hunt speaking from *Merlin's Cave* on 10 February 1817 (the third and last mass-meeting): it was drawn by George Cruikshank and inscribed with some doggerel verses, among which a few examples will suffice:

'Blythe Harry Hunt was an Orator bold!
Talked away bravely and blunt;
And Rome in her glory and Athens of old,
With all their loud talkers of whom we are
told,
Could n't match Orator Hunt!

Blythe Harry Hunt was a slightly man,
Something 'twixt giant and runt;
His paunch was a large one, his visage was
wan,
And to hear his long speeches vast
multitudes ran,
O rare Orator Hunt!

He hated a pension, he hated a place;
Gave them a groan and grunt;
Call'd Ministers *Villains*, and Crowns *a
Disgrace;*
And wish'd to cut short the monarchical race,
O rare Orator Hunt!

Orator Hunt he could both read and write,
Meagre his mind tho' and stunt;
His knowledge of grammar indeed was so
slight,
That a sentence of English he couldn't indite,
O rare Orator Hunt!

How Orator Hunt's many speeches will close,
Tedious, bombastic, and blunt,
In a halter or diadem, God only knows;
The sequel might well an arch-conjurer pose,
O rare Orator Hunt!'[42] *(Plate 45).*

Very soon, however, buildings started to go up opposite *Merlin's Cave*, so further Spa Fields meetings addressed from the 'tribune window'[43] of the Tavern were not possible. Images of *Merlin's Cave* are not plentiful, however, and we have to rely on descriptions[44].

A public-house called *New Merlin's Cave* was subsequently built at nearby 34 Margery Street. It was famed for its jazz entertainments in modern times, but was closed in the 1990s to make way for development.

THE LORD COBHAM'S OR COBHAM'S HEAD

It will be recalled that Hooke's *New Wells* also boasted a 'Merlin's Cave'. It may be mere coincidence that 'Merlin' was a name given to Sir Robert Walpole (1676-1745)[45], and that Walpole's enemy, Richard Temple, 1st Viscount Cobham, might have been suggested to contemporary observers by *Cobham's Head*[46], 1 Cobham Row, Cold-bath Fields. However, *Cobham's Head*, sometimes referred to as *Lord Cobham's Head*, was not in fact Temple, but John Oldcastle, Baron Cobham (d. 1417), soldier, heretic, and rebel, the first Protestant Martyr. This Tavern was opened in 1728 and in its large Garden was a canal well stocked with fish: anglers were invited to board at the Tavern in order to catch carp and tench. By 1742 the *Cobham Head*'s Garden was planted with trees, had gravel-walks, and claimed to sell the strongest and most agreeable beer in London. Music was provided, and the gravelled walks were illuminated at night. In 1744 a fine organ was installed, and the landlord, Robert Leeming, promoted concerts of 'musick by the best Masters'[47], including, of course, Händel. Fireworks, dancing, and dramatic enaction of events such as 'the manner of Prince Charles's distressing the French after he passed the Rhine'[48] were also provided. There seem to have been

Plate 45: *The Spa fields Orator HUNT-ing for Popularity to DO-GOOD!!* drawn by George Cruikshank and published by J. Sidebotham. It shows Orator Hunt addressing the multitude from an upstairs window of *Merlin's Cave*, Spa Fields, in February 1817. His demands include 'Universal Suffrage, Annual Parliaments, No Sinecurists, No Taxes, No Monarchy, No Laws, No Religion', while the crowd cries 'Hunt for ever' and 'Huzza!'. A ranter wishes to reform the Church, abolish Bishops, and take away their Loaves and Fishes & 'D—n them all' *(BM/Satires/12869-PPA145210).*

attempts to offer bottled waters at the *Cobham Head*, but where these came from is unclear. By the last quarter of the eighteenth century the Tavern also laid on billiards, shuffle-board, and several skittle-alleys[49]. By 1811 there was only a large yard behind the pub, all that was left of the Gardens[50].

THE SIR JOHN OLDCASTLE TAVERN

To confuse matters further, another Tavern in Coldbath Fields was called *Sir John Oldcastle* (the same person as Baron Cobham), to the rear of which were extensive Gardens, planted with trees, and for a brief period in the 1740s musical entertainments were given there. The walks were illuminated with lamps, and firework-displays often ended the evenings. Music included *From Scourging Rebellion* by John Lockman set by Händel as a tribute to the Duke of Cumberland's great victory at Culloden, as well as favourites of the time such as *Observe the Fragrant Blushing Rose*: performances seem to have been of a reasonably high standard.'Chinese' Masquerades with fireworks were also announced for 1751, but the regular open-air entertainments seem to have ceased in 1746[51]. However, despite the elevating music, fireworks, and other delights, including refreshments, the *Sir John Oldcastle* was demolished in 1762[52]. Although not strictly a Spa, it is included here because it offered entertainments which Spas and Wells provided, and it does seem that waters were available, probably from the vicinity.

COLDBATH SPRING

Situated in Cold Bath Square, near the *Sir John Oldcastle* and the *Cobham Head*, to the west of what is now Farringdon Road, the *Cold Bath* was an ancient Well rediscovered and exploited from 1697: it was medicinal, was described as an 'antient Conduit and Spring', and the driving force behind its exploitation was a lawyer, Walter Baynes, part-owner of the estate in which the Bath was sited in Coldbath Fields. Baynes called in an advocate of hot-and-cold bathing, Dr Edward Baynard (*c.*1641-1717), who also had a reputation as a poet of disputatious temper. An advocate of Balneology, he also recognised the pernicious effects of heavy drinking, and published much on health and the preservation of the body from the inroads of Excess[53]. Helped by Baynard's puffs, the owners of the estate replaced the ancient conduit with a Bath and Bath-house, but it was inadequately supervised,

Plate 46: The *Cold Bath*, Clerkenwell, from the south, in 1731. It shows the gabled building and walled Garden with corner-pavilions. This looks as though it was a product of the same hand responsible for the view of the *London Spaw* in 1731 *(Plate 39) (ILHC L1.7 Coldbath Square)*.

so a dwelling was erected and a resident manager appointed. Even this did not work, so Baynes moved his family from the Temple to the Bath-house which he greatly extended, adding facilities for bathers including a buttery. In the teeth of a lack of enthusiasm on the part of his associates, Baynes made the place a commercial success, and bought out the non-believers. By 1715 the *Cold Bath* was surrounded by a large walled Garden with pavilions at the southern corners roofed with ogee-shaped caps *(Plate 46)*.

The Clerkenwell *Cold Bath* played a major rôle in the revival of cold bathing for the infirm. Baynes himself claimed the Bath provided remedies for

> 'Dissiness, Drowsiness, and heavyness of the head, Lethargies, Palsies, Convulsions, all Hectical creeping Fevers, heats and flushings, Inflamations and ebullitions of the blood and spirits, all vapours, and disorders of the spleen and womb, also stiffness of the limbs and Rheumatick pains, also shortness of breath, weakness of the joints, as Rickets, &c., sore eyes, redness of the face, and all impurities of the skin, also deafness, ruptures, dropsies, and jaundice. It both prevents and cures colds, creates appetites, and helps digestion, and makes hardy the tenderest constitution'[54].

There were many capable of singing the praises of the *Cold Bath*: Sir Richard Steele (1672-1729 – the Irish politician and writer), for example, composed verses *On the Cold Bath at Oldcastle's*:

> 'Hail sacred Spring! Thou ever living Stream,
> Ears to the Deaf, Supporters to the Lame,
> Where fair Hygienia ev'ry morn attends,
> And with kind Waves her gentle Succour
> lends.
> While in the Cristal Fountain we behold
> The trembling Limbs, Enervate, Pale and
> Cold;
> A Rosy Hue she on the face bestows,
> And Nature in the chilling fluid glows,
> The Eyes shoot Fire, first kindled in the Brain;
> As beds of Lime smoke after showers of
> Rain,
> The fiery Particles concentred there,
> Break ope' their Prison Doors and rage in Air;
> Hail then thou pow'rful Goddess that presides
> O'er these cold Baths as Neptune o'er his
> Tides,
> Receive what Tribute a poor Muse can pay
> For Health that makes the Senses Brisk and
> Gay,
> The fairest Offspring of the heavenly Ray'[55].

Plate 47: *South View of the Cold Baths Cold Bath Fields erected near 120 Years, and supposed to be the Coldest Spring in London*, published 1812 by Alexander Beugo (*fl.* 1799-1817) of 38 Maiden Lane, Covent Garden *(LMA SC/GL/PR/F1/COL-FI/COR/Ce8502/cat.no.p5370693)*.

Baynes's house appears to have survived into the early years of the nineteenth century when it was partially demolished after it was acquired by the London Fever Hospital. A view of the house, published in 1812 *(Plate 47)*, shows a building with three gables, tall chimneys, and composed in a manner similar to (but not the same as) the impression of 1731. William Henry Prior (1812-82) produced a version of this 1812 view for George Walter Thornbury (1828-76) & Edward Walford's (1823-97) *Old and New London*[56] which is probably more accurate than the view in Pinks[57]. However, the Baths themselves survived when redevelopment took place in 1818-19, and indeed seem to have been enlarged and improved. Thomas Kitson Cromwell (1792-1870), writing in the 1820s, mentioned facilities for showers and warm as well as cold baths[58].

There was never any question of the *Cold Bath* at Clerkenwell ever having been a 'Bagnio', with all the connotations of loucheness the name could conjure: it was always associated with curative properties, and provided waters not only for bathing, but drinking-water of the chalybeate type considered efficacious in the cure of 'scorbutic complaints, rheumatism, chronic disorders, &c.' as well as 'the most nerval' of maladies[59]. The Bath itself was a spacious pool lined with marble, and the waters were 'impregnated with Steel and Sea Salt'[60]: it is shown in an illustration of November 1873 with steps descending to the pool and water pouring in from a lion-headed spout *(Plate 48)*. Persons who were too weak to descend into the Bath unaided were lowered into the water by means of a chair suspended from the ceiling.

The Bath flourished until 1878, but in 1887-8 the property was cleared for the construction of Rosebery Avenue, and today nothing remains of this extraordinary Bath that flourished for more than two centuries[61]. Even Sunderland did not list the *Cold Bath* as one of his 'spurious' Spas, and there seems no doubt that, with its prodigious inflow of chalybeate water, it was a genuine medicinal establishment.

PEERLESS POOL

Another bathing concern, just outside the Parish of Clerkenwell, not far from St Luke's Church in Finsbury (now Islington), was on ground behind St Luke's Hospital, Old Street: its existence is

Plate 48: Handbill for the *Cold Bath,* Clerkenwell, showing the pool, a scale of charges, and other information *(ILHC L1.7 Coldbath Square).*

BATHE & PRESERVE YOUR HEALTH.

ESTABLISHED UPWARDS OF 200 YEARS.

The Ancient Chalybeate COLD SPRING BATH

The Daily Influx of This Bath is Computed at 20,000 Gallons.

COLD BATH SQUARE,

CLERKENWELL.

The Finest Medicinal Spring Bath in London, strongly recommended for its invigorating and health restoring properties in all cases of Nervousness and General Debility.

TERMS OF SUBSCRIPTION:	£	s.	d.
Single COLD PLUNGE BATH	0	0	6
One Dozen Tickets ,, ...	0	4	0
Monthly ,, ,, ...	0	6	0
Quarterly ,, ,, ...	0	14	0
Half-yearly ,, ,, ...	1	0	0
Yearly ,, ,, ...	1	10	0
Cold or Warm Shower Bath ...	0	1	0

Open from 6 in the morning till 10 in the Evening.

NOTE,—Dr Hamilton Roe, of the Consumption Hospital, Brompton, and other Eminent Medical Gentlemen, send many of their Patients to this Bath for its bracing and strengthening qualities.

6d. WARM BATHS 6d.

First Class, 1s.

The Celebrated DAPHNE MARINA SALT for Baths, 6d per packet.

Private Baths for Ladies, 6d. and 1s.

With Female Attendance.

COLD BATH SQUARE,

Near Exmouth Street, Clerkenwell.

J. HUTCHINS, PROPRIETOR.

Plate 49: The Pleasure-Bath, *Peerless Pool,* City Road, from an advertisement of *c.*1846. The arcades were the changing-rooms, and the whole ensemble was impressive *(Collection JSC).*

THE PLEASURE BATH,
PEERLESS POOL, CITY ROAD.

TERMS OF SUBSCRIPTION.

PLEASURE BATH	£.	s.	d.
Month	0	9	0
Two Months	0	10	0
Year	1	1	0
Single Bathe with Towels and Box ...	0	1	0
Ditto without	0	0	6

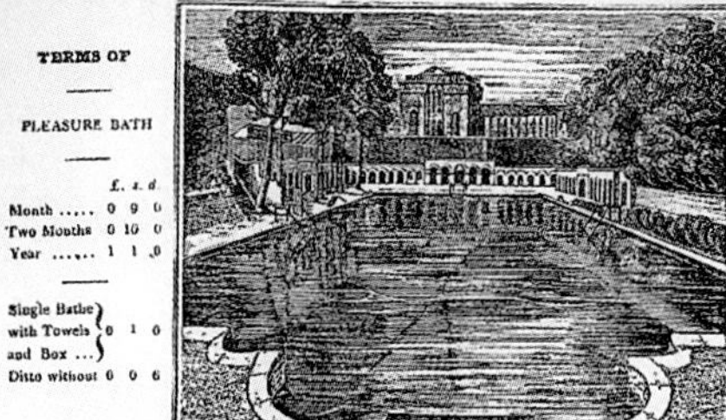

COLD BATH	£.	s.	d.
Month.....	0	10	0
Two Months	0	17	0
Year	1	10	0
Single Bathe	0	1	0

1, Bath Buildings Entrance—2, Baldwyn Street Entrance—3, Cold Bath—4, Pleasure Bath—5, Dressing Boxes—6, Shrubberies.

THE PLEASURE BATH
OF PEERLESS POOL,

THE largest in England, is situated in the immediate neighbourhood of the heart of the City, within Ten minutes' direct walk of the Bank and Exchange. (vide plan.) Surrounded by trees and shrubberies, open to the air, although entirely screened from observation, and most ample in its dimensions—170 FEET in length, by 108 in breadth—it offers to the Bather the very advantages he would least expect to find at so short a distance from the centre of the metropolis. Its depth, which increases gradually from 3 feet 6 inches to 4 feet 8 inches, is such as to afford free scope to the Swimmer, while it precludes all fear of accident to any. and the temperature of the water rises to a height sufficient to ensure all the comfort and luxury of Bathing, without the risk of injury to health, from a too violent contrast with the external air.

THE COLD BATH,

THIRTY-SIX feet by EIGHTEEN, is the largest of its kind in London, and both Baths are entirely supplied by Springs, which are constantly overflowing.

The City Road is the line from all parts of the WEST END *to the City. Omnibuses pass both ways nearly every minute throughout the day.*

Plate 50: *The Peerless Pool in 1811 (HP 11002).*

commemorated by Bath Street, the northern continuation of Bunhill Row, and by Peerless Street. Strictly speaking, it was an agreeable resort for sport and recreation, rather than a place sought by those for medical reasons. Stow tells us that

> 'Somewhat North from *Holywell*, is one other well curbed square with stone, and is called *Dame Annis the cleare*, and not farre from it but somewhat west, is another cleare water called *Perillous pond*, because diverse youthes swimming therein have been drowned, and thus much bee said for Fountaines and Wels'[62].

In the seventeenth century the pond was favoured for the sport of duck-hunting with dogs, but in 1743 one Kemp, a London jeweller, convinced he had derived benefit from his immersions in the 'Parlous Pond', embanked the pool, opened it to subscribers as a pleasure-bath, and changed its name to *Peerless Pool*[63]. Having leased adjacent ground, he also constructed a large fish-pond 320 feet long, 90 broad, and 11 deep, and stocked it with carp, tench, and other fish: its high banks were 'thickly covered with shrubs, and on top were walks shaded by lime trees'[64]. Kemp also formed another pool, the *Cold Bath*, east of the fish-pond and quite distinct from the *Pool* itself, 36 feet long and 18 wide, fed by a Spring: its total depth was 9 feet, but at a depth of 4 feet was 'lettice'[65] work to prevent persons sinking and drowning. As for the *Peerless Pool* proper, it was a swimming-bath 170 feet long, over 100 feet wide, and from 3 to 5 feet deep. Trees were planted around it, and the descent to the *Pool* was by means of marble steps. At the bottom of the *Pool* was fine gravel through which water

Plate 51: Impression of the fish-pond at *Peerless Pool* by John Cleghorn *(From Hone **i** [1835] 975: Collection JSC).*

from the Springs was filtered. Entry to the *Pool* was from a bowling-green on the south side, and through a saloon adjoining which was an arcade containing the changing-rooms. A small library was provided in the saloon. From around 1750 the *Pool* was much patronised by subscribers, and occasional non-subscribers paid two shillings per visit. There were facilities for anglers *(Plate 51)*, and in cold weather skating was permitted.

In the early years of the nineteenth century, Joseph Watts (*c*.1770-*c*.1835), a bricklayer, originally from Northamptonshire, leased the property from St Bartholemew's Hospital for £600 per annum, and built over part of the grounds, laying out Baldwin Street, off the City Road, where the fish-pond (which he drained and filled) had been. Kemp's house, which stood in a garden set among an orchard of apple- and pear-trees, Watts pulled down, and in its stead he built Bath Buildings (completed 1811)[66]. Watts continued to manage the *Cold Bath* and *Pool*, charging a shilling per person per visit. William Hone (1780-1842) claimed the *Peerless Pool* was, 'both in magnitude and convenience, the greatest bathing-place in the metropolis. Here, the lover of cleanliness, or of a "cool dip" in a hot day, may at all times... enjoy the refreshment he desires, without the offensive publicity, and without the risk of life, attendant on river-bathing'[67]. Every Thursday and Saturday afternoon in Summertime, the Blue-Coat Boys from Christ's Hospital bathed there, under the watchful eyes of the Beadles: their 'hilarity' testified to their 'enjoyment of the tepid fluid'[68].

Peerless Pool was still frequented in 1850[69], and after Watts's death the concern was managed by his widow, Sarah (*née* Phillips [1773-1857]), and his sons, Thomas (1811-69 – the famous Librarian of the British Museum) and Joshua (1808-75)[70]: it continued in use until the site was built over in the late 1850s or early 1860s[71].

Obviously the waters available were of at least two kinds, for that supplied to the *Pool* was 'tepid' and that which flowed to the *Cold Bath* was not, so the establishment had some claims to be of importance in the context of the present work[72]. Those who frequented the *Pool* and *Bath* could take refreshments at *The Shepherd and Shepherdess* ale-house, which supplied cream, cakes, and 'furmity' (a dish made of wheat boiled in milk and seasoned with cinnamon, sugar, etc.) as well as tea, coffee, and alcoholic beverages. This public-house is listed among the many Tea-Gardens frequented by Londoners until around 1825, when part of its site was redeveloped for the *Eagle Tavern*[73]. Some versifier recorded that

'To the Shepherd and Shepherdess then they go
To tea with their wives, for a constant rule;
And next cross the road to the Fountain[74] also,
And there they all sit, so pleasant and cool,
And see, in and out,
The folks walk about,
And gentlemen angling in 'Peerless Pool'[75].

THE CLERK'S WELL

To return to Clerkenwell, it is worth remembering a few more establishments. Clerkenwell, of course, gets its name from the *Clerk's Well*. Stow tells us that '*Clarkes well*, or *Clarken well*' was 'curbed about square with hard stone, not farre from the west ende of *Clarken well* Church, but close without the wall that incloseth it:... Other smaller welles were many neare unto *Clarkes well*, namely *Skinners well*, so called for that the Skinners of London held there certaine playes yearely playd of holy Scripture, &c... Then was there *Fagges well*, neare unto *Smithfield* by the *Charterhouse*, now lately dammed up, *Todwell*, *Loders well*, and *Radwell*, all decayed, and so filled

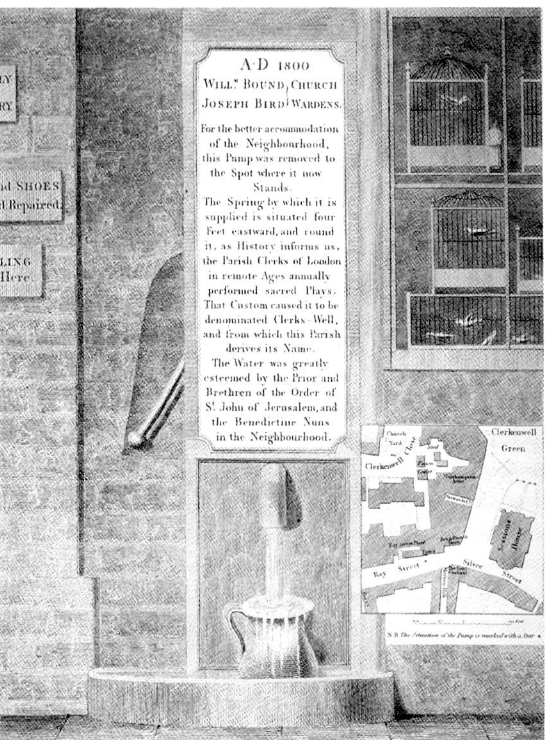

A·D 1800
WILL.M BOUND, JOSEPH BIRD CHURCH WARDENS.
For the better accommodation of the Neighbourhood, this Pump was removed to the Spot where it now Stands.
The Spring by which it is supplied is situated four Feet eastward, and round it, as History informs us, the Parish Clerks of London in remote Ages annually performed sacred Plays. That Custom caused it to be denominated Clerks-Well, and from which this Parish derives its Name.
The Water was greatly esteemed by the Prior and Brethren of the Order of St. John of Jerusalem, and the Benedictine Nuns in the Neighbourhood.
Clerkenwell Green

Plate 52: The *Clerk's Well* in 1822, published by Robert Wilkinson (*fl.*1785-1825), 125 Fenchurch Street, drawn by H. Gardner and engraved by Bartholomew Howlett (1767-1827). The inset plan shows the location of the pump in relation to the Middlesex Sessions House and the churchyard of St James's Church *(LMA SC/GL/PR/FI/NEW-F1/SAD/Ce8603/cat.no. p5439976).*

up, that there places are hardly now discerned'[76].The *Skinners Well* was traditionally said to be on the west side of the Church of St James, Clerkenwell, and the *Clerk's Well* was situated near the south-west corner of the grounds of St Mary's Nunnery. Good water, of course, was essential for the brewing of beer and the making of Gin, and there were plenty of Wells in the area at one time. The *Clerk's Well* still exists, under 14-16 Farringdon Lane: it was only rediscovered in 1924[77] *(Plate 52).*

OTHER ESTABLISHMENTS

There were many places in the vicinity that provided Pleasure-Gardens and refreshments in the eighteenth and early nineteenth centuries. The site now occupied by Nos. 16-17 Bowling Green Lane, Clerkenwell, for example, was the *Hockley-in-the-Hole* bear-garden, where edifying spectacles such as bull-baiting, 'mastiffs throttling bears', and even armed fights between men and between women could be enjoyed by a wide spectrum of society. The place was called 'His Majesty's Bear Garden', and the 'diversions' that went on there need not detain us here: they are described and illustrated by William Biggs Boulton (1869-*after* 1901)[78], and there are many references to *Hockley-in-the-Hole*:

> 'When through the streets, with slow and solemn air,
> Led by the nostril, walks the muzzled bear;
> Behind him moves, majestically dull,
> The pride of Hockley Hole, the surly bull;
> Learn hence the periods of the week to name,
> Mondays and Thursdays are the days of game'[79].

But *Hockley* was not the only place where dog-fights, bear- and bull-baiting, and so on took place. Ferocious dogs (backed by hefty bets) were praised by their proud owners:

> 'Both Hockley Hole and Marybone
> The combats of my dog have known'[80].

Occasionally, the bears got their revenge, for in 1709 Christopher Preston, the then proprietor of the Bear Garden, was attacked and partly eaten, but the usual fate of a chained bear was to be attacked by dogs (some of which would be killed) *(Plate 53)*[81]. *Hockley-in-the-Hole* seems to have been a magnet for bloodthirsty types, but several public-houses also promoted cock-fights and the occasional display of fisticuffs. Bowling-greens, however, offered more sedate and seemly recreation (there seem to have been three of these in what became Bowling Green Lane and Corporation Row [formerly Lane]), and there were several others north of what is now Pentonville Road.

The *White Conduit House*, however, provided a wide range of entertainment, including fireworks and music. This large establishment was situated on the north side of what is now Tolpuddle Street, at the corner of Barnsbury Road, and is supposed to have opened as early as 1649[82],

Plate 53: Bear-baiting, from a drawing by Henry Thomas Alken (1785-1851) *(Collection JSC)*.

sited near a mediaeval conduit-house from which fresh water was piped to the Charterhouse. At the beginning, the *White Conduit House* was a small ale-house out in the country *(Plate 54)*, but around the middle of the eighteenth century it was impressively extended and improved *(Plates 55 & 56)* by its proprietor, Robert Bartholomew (d. 1766). Among the innovations was a Long Walk with a 'handsome circular fish-pond, a number of shady pleasant arbours inclosed with a fence seven feet high'[83], to prevent 'gentlemen and ladies... being the least incommoded from people in the fields' (the House was still then in rural surroundings)[84]. Hot loaves and butter, milk directly from the proprietor's own cows, 'coffee, tea, and all manner of liquors in the greatest perfection' were available, and Bartholomew assured his customers that his cows ate no grains, nor was there any adulteration of the milk and cream he served. He also built a handsome Long-Room: from it 'copious prospects and airy situation' could be enjoyed, better than any others then in vogue, with views north towards Hampstead and Highgate. In addition, cricket was played in the meadows adjoining the House: bats and balls were provided, and matches were played by many, including members of the nobility[85].

By the 1770s the Gardens were laid out with pleasing walks, avenues of trees, and 'genteel boxes' decorated with paintings let into the hedges. Respectable Londoners regularly longed for Sunday to come when mirth brightened every face and painted 'the rose upon the housemaid's cheek'[86]. The apprentice, his 'meal meridian' over, 'to White Conduit House' hied, and human beings 'in couples multitudinous' formed 'the drollest groups that ever trod fair Islingtonian plains': in short, while tea and cream and buttered rolls were able to please, and while rival beaux and belles existed, *White Conduit House*, it was claimed, would enjoy success[87].

Christopher Bartholomew (d. 1809) did much to improve the House and grounds, but his taste

Plate 54: *White Conduit House* from the south, *c.*1731: it was a small ale-house near the Conduit-House itself *(left)* from which water was supplied to the Charterhouse *(From Pinks [1880] 535: Collection JSC).*

for gambling ruined him, and he died in poverty. Under later proprietors a new tea- and dancing-saloon was erected, the 'boxes' were enlarged, a miniature steeple was built, and a maze was formed. A band-stand, small stage, fountains, and statuary further beautified the grounds. Additional entertainments included bowls, archery, and Dutch-pins (a form of ninepins or skittles), and there were also balloon-ascents, firework-displays, and concerts, so that in 1825 the place was advertised as 'The New Vauxhall'. Despite musical performances, masquerades, juggling, and the presentation of various dioramas, the establishment lost its rural setting as London expanded, and its tone deteriorated by the end of the 1820s and beginning of the 1830s. Its reputation became tarnished, behaviour of patrons was often rowdy, and custom came almost exclusively from the artisan class. In 1849 the House was demolished and the area developed. It was extensive: its southern boundary was approximately the line of the present Tolpuddle (formerly Culpeper and before that Albert) Street; its western extremity was at Penton Street; its eastern boundary was White Conduit Street (later Cloudesley Road); and its northern limit was Denmark Grove.

So why is it included here? It was neither a Spa nor a Well, but it shared with establishments such as *Islington Spa* and *Bagnigge Wells* (*see* below) many aspects such as Gardens, arbours, a Long-Room, and similar kinds of entertainment. Thus quite humble public-houses aped places that laid

Plate 55: *White Conduit House (Collection JSC).*

Plate 56: William Henry Prior's impression of *White Conduit House* as it was *c.* 1820 *(From Thornbury & Walford **ii** [1879-85] 283: Collection JSC).*

claim to higher things or even medical cures, however spurious those might have been[88].

Dobney's Bowling Green[89], previously *Prospect House*[90], stood on the site of what is now Claremont United Reformed Church, White Lion Street, and had carriage access from Islington High Street. It was a large property, and had bowling-greens in the seventeenth century. One very attractive illustration shows the western bowling-green at *Dobney's c.*1730, looking south towards the City *(Plate 57)*: it demonstrates how agreeable the heights of Pentonville once were, and that the bowling-greens of *Dobney's* were extensive. The buildings associated with *Dobney's* are elusive, however, and accounts are unclear. An illustration *(Plate 58)* in Pinks's *Clerkenwell*[91], labelled 'Busby's Folly' is probably *Prospect House*, but the precise location of 'Busby's Folly' is uncertain: some writers seem to have confused it with other establishments[92]. The success of Bartholomew's *White Conduit House* prompted Dobney's proprietor, William Johnson, to try to attract custom by constructing an amphitheatre for equestrian displays (*Plate 60*): one amazing show in 1772 involved a rider standing upright on a horse, one foot on the horse's neck and the other on the saddle, with a mask of bees on his face. At the sound of a pistol-shot half the swarm marched over a table, while the other took off into the air. The skeleton of a whale was exhibited, but success, such as it was, of *Dobney's Prospect House*, despite the showmanship, was short-lived, and, in 1772 it became the *Jubilee Tea-Gardens*: booths decorated with scenes from Shakespeare served as 'tea-boxes' for the enjoyment of that beverage.

A horse also featured as an attraction at the

Plate 57: Western Bowling-green at *Dobney's*, *c.*1730, looking south towards the City and St Paul's Cathedral. The figures walking on the footpath on the left are following the line of Penton Street. Drawing by Bernard Lens *(BM/1853/0409.50-P&DB706).*

Plate 58: Eighteenth-century view, probably of the north front of *Prospect House,* later called *Dobney's Bowling-Green* *(From Pinks [1880] 530: Collection JSC).*

Plate 60: *A Representation of the Surprising Performances of Mr. Price at Dobney's Bowling Green,* c.1767 (Collection JSC).

Belvidere[93], Pentonville Road. This Tavern also boasted a Tea-Garden and bowling-green. It was established as *Penny's Folly*, and in 1769 a German named Zucker took a lease on the establishment, where he exhibited his 'Learned Little Horse' while his wife played 'favourite airs' on musical glasses. The *Belvidere* was also known for its racket-court, Saturday-night discussion-meetings, and its large Garden with trees and accommodation for tea-drinkers. Skittles and quoits, billiards, and, of course, food and drink, were also available[94] *(Plates 59 & 61).*

Plate 59: Gardens and Rackets-court at *The Belvidere* in the 1820s. On the left are 'tea-boxes' or booths similar to those found in Spas and Wells *(From Pinks [1880] 530: Collection JSC).*

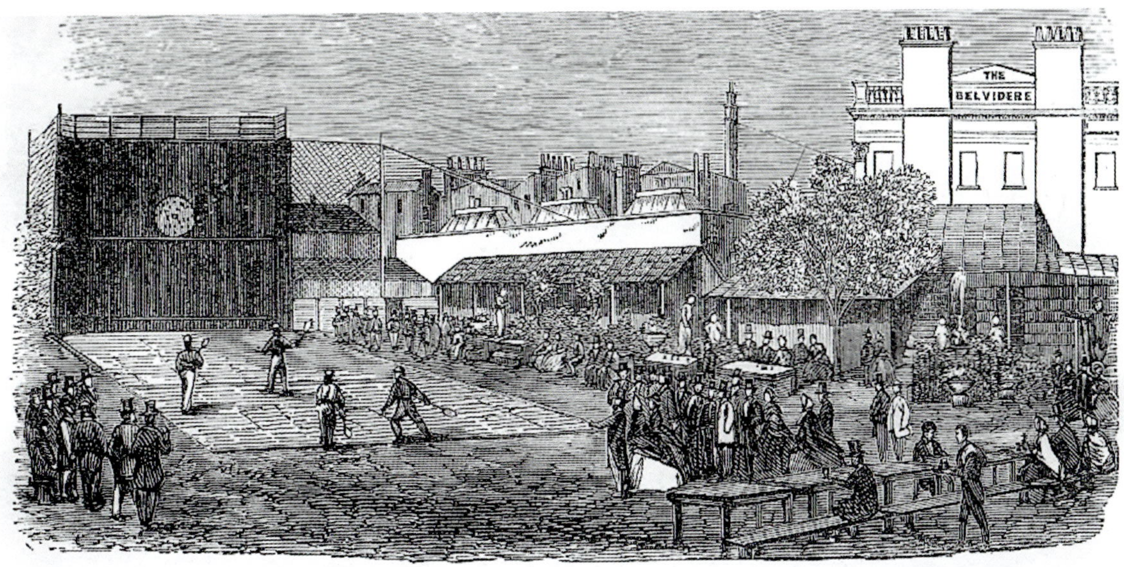

Plate 61: Rackets-court and remaining Gardens at *The Belvidere*: the Tavern itself can be seen on the right. The building was replaced by another designed by William Edward Williams (1810/11-94) and built 1875-6. The handsome Italianate building shown here probably dates from a major face-lift and extension of the mid-nineteenth century. This view, of *c.*1874, shows how omnivorous London was devouring the countryside *(From Pinks [1880] 532: Collection JSC).*

Plate 62: *Summer Amusement*, drawn by Robert Dighton (*c.*1752-1814), published by Bowles & Carver, 69 St Paul's Churchyard, London, *c.*1784, but showing a mid-eighteenth-century scene, possibly the Gardens of *Lord Cobham's Head*, or perhaps those of the *White Conduit House* *(LMA SC/GL/SAT/1784/Ce18818/cat.no.p5448745).*

Plate 63: Johnson, the 'Irish Tartar', showing off his skills at the *Three Hats* in 1758, engraved for the *Grand Magazine of Universal Intelligence, and Monthly Chronicle of our Own Times*, published 1758-60 by Ralph Griffiths (*c.*1720-1803) *(Collection JSC).*

There were many such London establishments which had Gardens, amusements, and other attractions to which patrons were drawn. *The Three Hats*, Upper Street, Islington, for example, featured equestrian prowess, notably by Thomas Johnson (*fl.* 1758-67), 'The Irish Tartar', who was one of the earliest performers, galloping round the grounds standing first on one horse, then on a pair, and then on three horses: on at least one occasion he rode on one horse standing on his head *(Plate 63)*. He was succeeded in 1767 by one Sampson (who appeared with his wife, and subsequently went on to perform his equestrian feats at the Circus, St George's Fields [*see* Chapter X]). There were other diversions more appropriate to the Circus, perhaps, advertised in various suburban Tavern-Gardens, and these deserve a volume on their own[95]. Just as public-houses find it difficult to survive in the twenty-first century unless they provide food and other attractions, eighteenth-century Taverns had to cater for what ever was the fashion of the moment, and, prompted by the success of certain Spas and Wells, attempted to emulate such places. Pressure to develop land for housing, however, soon destroyed the pleasant rural surroundings that were such a feature of Middlesex and Surrey in the immediate vicinity of London, and the grounds of most Taverns soon vanished under buildings.

AFTERWORD

We are left with tantalising glimpses of such places in illustrations and descriptions. One typical view entitled *Summer Amusement (Plate 62)*, was published by Henry Carington Bowles (1763-1830), who, with Samuel Carver (born *c.*1755), traded as Bowles & Carver from 1793 until his death, although the firm did not vanish from the scene until 1832 (presumably the year of Carver's demise): it shows a waiter moving across the Garden, tray and kettle in his hands, with 'tea-boxes' in the background set against foliage, and a summer-house or gazebo reached by steps on the right. Many prints and drawings of the second half of the eighteenth century depict tea-drinking (often in secluded three-sided alcoves set behind arcades or colonnades), waiters hurrying across Gardens, gambolling dogs, and persons conversing in pairs or groups. From public-house Gardens to the most celebrated Spa such scenes were usual. The next Chapter, however, will concentrate on one famous Spa, which had a great many attractions, and lay just to the west of the Parish boundary of Clerkenwell.

Chapter IV References: Clerkenwell Group II

1 For eighteenth-century outdoor culture *see*, for example, Bermingham & Brewer (*Eds.*) (1995), esp. 341-61; Benedict (1995) 203-19; and Gay (1716). *See* also Borsay (1989, 2006) *passim*. For Georgian Vice *see* Cruickshank (2009).

2 For Hollar *see* Hind (1922), in which several views are reproduced.

3 Colvin (2008) 745-7.

4 Wroth & Wroth (1896) 25.

5 *The Gazetteer and New Daily Advertiser* (20 June 1772).

6 *Town and Country Magazine* (April 1770) 195.

7 *ODNB* **xxv** (2004) 775-8.

8 *ODNB* **l** (2004) 455.

9 *ODNB* **xliii** (2004) 806.

10 He was the father of Warwick William (1858-1911) and Arthur Edgar Wroth (*fl.*1870-96), authors of Wroth & Wroth (1896). For the Chapel *see* Saint (*Gen. Ed.*) (2008*b*) 55-7.

11 Curl (2004) 113. 115, 117, 129-31, 133, 136, 178. *See* also Walker (1839, 1843).
12 Saint (*Gen. Ed.*) (2008*b*) 57-8. For the conversion of burial-grounds *see* Holmes (1896).
13 Wroth & Wroth (1896) 29. *See* also Esser & Fuchs (*Eds.*) (2003) 161-83. For Boyle *see* Hunter (2009).
14 Curl (1979) 60.
15 *May-Day: or, The Original of Garlands* (1720).
16 *Ibid.*
17 Ward (1714), Rogers (1896) 46.
18 *May-Day* (1720).
19 *Daily Advertiser* (2 August 1744).
20 *May-Day* (1720).
21 Wroth & Wroth (1896) 30.
22 *Daily Post* (17 March 1741).
23 *Poor Robin* (1733).
24 *Daily Post* (9 March 1730).
25 Sunderland (1915) 89.
26 *Ibid.* 88.
27 10 Geo. II *c.* 191 and 28.
28 *Daily Post* (July 1739).
29 Sunderland (1915) 91.
30 Pinks (188) 169.
31 *Ibid.* For Georgian vice *see* Cruickshank (2009).
32 Pinks (1880) 170.
33 Charke (1755), quoted also in Pinks (1880) 170.
34 Cromwell (1828) 254-5; Pinks (1880) 169-171.
35 Wroth & Wroth (1896) 37-9.
36 *Ibid.* 40-42.
37 Pinks (1880) 127.
38 *Daily Advertiser* (21 June 1742).
39 Wroth & Wroth (1896) 40-42.
40 *Ibid.* 54-5.
41 *ODNB* **xxviii** (2004) 841.
42 Printed under the Cruikshank caricature (London: J. Sidebotham 1 March 1817).
43 *The Observer* (4 May 1817).
44 *See*, however, Crace (1878) 592, nos. 70 and 71.
45 *Eighteenth-Century Studies* **x** (1976) 1-20.
46 Sometimes given as *Lord Cobham's Head*, it would also have had resonances from 1733, when Lord Cobham was robbed at *Islington Spa.*
47 *Daily Advertiser* (20 July 1744). *See* Wroth & Wroth (1896) 68-9.
48 *Ibid.* This was a reference to Prince Karl Alexander of Lorraine (1712-80) who in 1743 led a successful Austrian campaign against the French and Bavarians.
49 Saint (*Gen. Ed.*) (2008*b*) 30.
50 Wroth & Wroth (1896) 69; Pinks (1880) 120.
51 Wroth & Wroth (1896) 70; Pinks (1880) 738.
52 Anonymous (1764) 81; Ashton (1889) 117; Pinks (1880) 65, 121-3, 495, 503; Larwood & Hotten (1868) 97; Tomlins (1858) 172; Ward (1714).
53 *ODNB*, **iv** (2004) 469-10.
54 *Post Boy* (28 March 1700): *see* Pinks (1880) 112.
55 Quoted in Pinks (1880) 112.
56 Thornbury & Walford **ii** (1879-85) 113.
57 Pinks (1880) 113.
58 Cromwell (1828) 308.
59 Sunderland (1915) 42; Pinks (1880) 112. Sunderland also reproduced Prior's illustration of the house (opposite p. 42).
60 Cromwell (1828) 308; Saint (*Gen. Ed.*) (2008*b*) 458 notes 18 and 19.
61 Saint (*Gen. Ed.*) (2008*b*) 27.
62 Stow **i** (1908) 16 and **ii** 273.
63 Wroth & Wroth (1896) 81.
64 *Ibid.* 82.
65 That is, a lattice-work or net-like structure, more usually spelled *lettise.*
66 Hughson **iv** (1806-13) 414.
67 Hone **i** (1835) 970-1.
68 *Ibid.* 972.
69 Cunningham (1850).
70 *ODNB* **lvii** (2004) 741-2.
71 *Notes and Queries* Series 7 (14 September 1889) **viii** 214-5.
72 *See* Foord (1910) 112-14; Crace (1878) 608 Nos 8 & 9; Dodsley (1761) on the Pool; Noorthouck (1773) 756 ff.; Trusler (1786) 124; and Wheatley (1891) **iii**.
73 Wroth & Wroth (1896) 86-7. *See* also Larwood & Hotten (1868) 352-3.
74 Another Tavern near by.
75 Hone **i** (1835) 975.
76 Stow **i** (1908 edn.) 15-16, **ii** 272
77 *Transactions of the London and Middlesex Archaeological Society* N.S. **v**. (1923-8) 57, 67-84.
78 Boulton **i** (1901) 1-6, 10, 11-12, 16 ff., 29ff.
79 Gay (1716) bk **ii**.
80 *Ibid.*
81 *See* Pinks (1880) 157-61.
82 *Ibid.* 533.
83 *Ibid.*
84 *Ibid.*
85 *Ibid.* 542.
86 *London Chronicle* (1760) **vii** 531.
87 Pinks (1880) 534.
88 For the *White Conduit House see* Noakes (1970).
89 Wroth & Wroth (1896) 141-4.
90 Saint (*Gen. Ed.*) (2008*b*) 327-8, 349, 373, 375, 385-6.
91 Pinks (1880) 530.
92 Cromwell (1828) 530. *See* Saint (*Gen. Ed.*) (2008*b*) 327-8. 'Busby's Folly' may have become the *Belvidere.*
93 Wroth & Wroth (1896) 145-6.
94 Saint (*Gen. Ed.*) (2008*b*) 352.
95 *See* Boulton (1901) and Wroth & Wroth (1896).

CHAPTER V

BAGNIGGE WELLS

Introduction; The Background; A Place of Resort, Pleasure, and Dissipation; Nemesis

'I abhor, too, the roaming lover, nor do I drink from every well;
I loathe all things held in common'.
(μισῶ καὶ περίφοιτον ἐρώμενον οὐδ᾽ ἀπὸ κρήνης
πίνω· σικχαίνω πάντα τὰ δημόσια)

CALLIMACHUS (*c*.305-*c*.240 BC): RUDOLF CARL FRANZ OTTO PFEIFFER (1889-1979) (*Ed*.): *Callimachus* (Oxford: Clarendon Press 1949-53) Epigram 28.

'Will you go to Bagnigge Wells, Bonnet builder, O!
Where the Fleet-ditch fragrant smells, Bonnet builder, O!
Where the fishes used to swim, So nice and sleek and trim,
But the pond's now covered in, Bonnet builder, O!'

ANONYMOUS: *The Little Melodist, or Vocal Pocket Companion* (London: J. Bysh *c*.1817-39).

INTRODUCTION

Bagnigge Wells was a large establishment situated on the west side of what is now King's Cross Road, opposite Wharton Street and Gwynne Place (which leads up 'Riceyman Steps'[1] to Granville Square). It occupied a long strip of land: its northern perimeter coincided with what is now Acton Street, and its southern boundary was defined by a lane (now Calthorpe Street). The western edge of the Gardens lay slightly to the west of the present Cubitt Street, and the eastern boundary (along which most of the buildings stood) coincided with the narrow lane which became King's Cross Road. Wells and Fleet Squares commemorate the Spa and the river that once ran through the Gardens. This Chapter will be devoted to *Bagnigge Wells* alone, a place that once was many things to many men.

THE BACKGROUND

Bagnigge House, the building which formed the centrepiece of the place of entertainment called *Bagnigge Wells*, was said to have been a summer residence of Eleanor (Nell) Gwyn (*c*.1651-87), actress and Royal mistress. The house was situated in a hollow called Bagnigge Wash (noted in 18th-century Cantelowes manor court rolls as Bagnall's Marsh or Wash), so was sheltered and protected from winds: it is alleged to be shown in an attractive water-colour of 1865 by Waldo Sargeant (*fl*. 1865-90) as a three-gabled structure of some size, set in grounds behind a brick wall. Above a doorway in the wall was fixed a stone carved with the inscription

S+T
THIS IS BAGNIGGE
HOUSE NEARE
THE PINDER A
WAKEFEILDE[2]
1680

beneath a carved head of a bearded male *(Plate 64)*. Apparently the stone was once set over a gateway in a wall to the north of the Long-Room

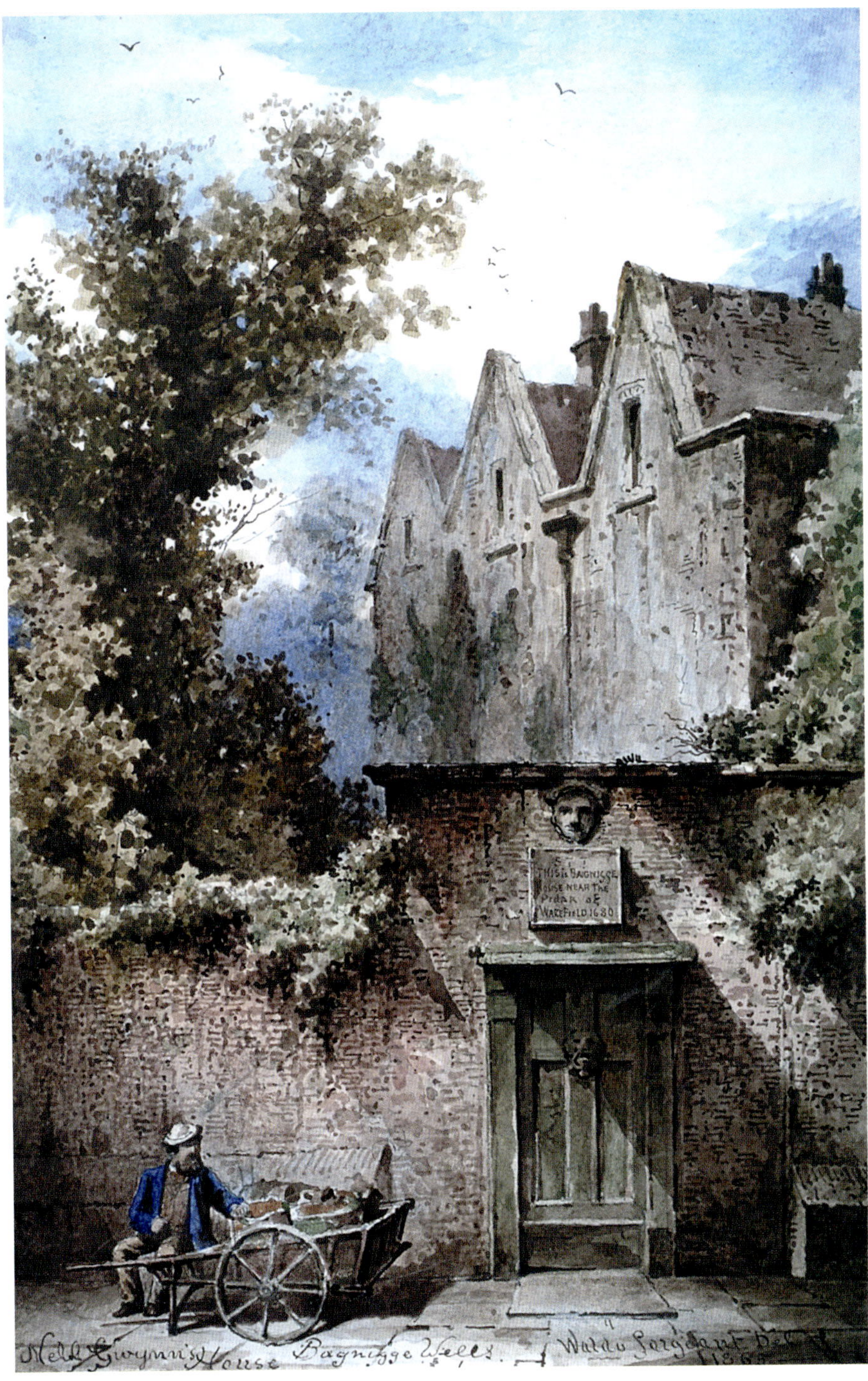

Plate 64: View of 'Nell Gwyn's house', Bagnigge Wash (or Vale), from a water-colour by Waldo Sergeant of 1865. The three gables suggest a seventeenth-century date for the building. Over the doorway to the garden is a stone slab with inscription relating to 1680 and 'Pinder a Wakefeilde', but the head over was probably associated with the Tavern known by that name, and seems to have been part of a figure once set in the north wall of the Long-Room: the view is apparently taken from the east *(LMA SC/GL/PR/ P3/BAG/Ce17031/cat.no.p5379470).*

(*see* below) of *Bagnigge Wells*[3], and remained there until the 1840s when it was moved to Coppice Row (later Farringdon Road) and then affixed to the front of Nos. 61-63 King's Cross Road[4]. The *Pindar of Wakefeilde* was a Tavern, and the head probably shows the 'Merrie Pinner', otherwise known as George-a'-Green, the pound-keeper of Wakefield who defeated all comers with his quarterstaff, including 'Robin Hood' (the story was told by William Carew Hazlitt [1834-1913][5] in his *Tales and Legends* [1892]). A public-house called *The Pindar of Wakefield* in Gray's Inn Road

Plate 65: View of 'Nell Gwynne's house, Bagnigge Wells Road' in 1852. Anonymous sketch showing the 'Pinder a Wakefeilde' stone over the doorway to the Garden. As this is an earlier impression than that of Waldo Sergeant, the conclusion must be that one of them must be romantic wishful thinking. The 1852 drawing shows only one complete gable, one truncated gable, and a brewery. However, the building labelled 'Bagnigge Wells Brewery' has very unusual features, including rudimentary crenellations and most peculiar treatments of what were obviously once windows. The tall tapered chimney should be noted (compare *Plates 67* and *83*). The fact that there is no head over the tablet suggests that it was placed there after the Long-Room was demolished *(LMA SC/GL/PR/P3/BAG/Ce17032/cat.no.p5379464).*

appears in the earliest extant Licensing Records for 1721. The name survived several rebuildings until *c.* 1990, when it was bought by the Grand Order of Water Rats, the entertainers' charity, and renamed *The Water Rats*.

Some have assumed that Bagnigge House was a place of public entertainment in 1680, but there is no evidence for this: nevertheless it was a place of entertainment for the King in another sense. It would appear that the carved head was a representation of 'George-a'-Green', in the guise of a Green Man: this character was the subject of a play, possibly by Robert Greene (*c.*1560-92), though some doubt this. The head appears to have been part of a figure in relief, once set into the end-gable of the Long-Room at *Bagnigge Wells*.

A rather rudimentary drawing entitled 'Nell Gwynne's House Bagnigge Wells Road' shows the tablet set over the doorway leading to the Garden with buildings described as 'Bagnigge Wells Brewery', but there is no sign of the head. Admittedly the gate is in the same relation to the gabled house as is that in Sergeant's water-colour, but it looks as though one gable has been cut down and another has vanished *(Plate 65)*. Of course at one time Bagnigge House stood in rural surroundings, and an idyllic view of the 'Original Garden-Entrance' shows how it must have appeared at the end of the eighteenth century *(Plate 66)*.

In 1757, one Hughes, seemingly the tenant of Bagnigge House, noticed that the plants in his Garden, when watered from the Well near by, appeared not to thrive. Concerned, he called in Dr John Bevis (1695-1771), physician and astronomer, who undertook lengthy chemical investigations of the water, and declared it a very good chalybeate. Another Well was sunk in the grounds adjoining Bagnigge House, and Bevis's analysis showed the water from that possessed cathartic[6] properties. Bevis[7] published a booklet on these two Wells in 1760 which was reprinted several times to 1819 and proved to be an admirable aid to attracting custom[8].

Hughes quickly grasped the commercial possibilities that two Wells (each with water having differing properties) offered, and opened the house and Gardens to the public. Water from the two Wells was brought to one point and then drawn by means of a double pump housed within

Plate 66: 'Original entrance (1698) Baggnigge Wells Gardens' (*c.*1800). The lane that passes over the bridge is the line of the present Calthorpe Street. In the foreground a child squats on the bank of the river Bagnigge (Fleet – which flowed through the Gardens, dividing them in two), retrieving with a stick a stray hat. Note the washing hanging on the line in the garden to the right. The monopitched roof over the boarded hut is probably a privy. Engraved from a drawing by John Thomas Smith (1766-1833) by Alexander Carse (1770-1843), probably dating from *c.*1820 when Carse left London for Edinburgh *(LMA SC/GL/PR/P3/BAG/Ce17035/cat.no.p537956x).*

a small circular structure consisting of columns supporting a domical roof: unsurprisingly this was called The Temple, and was situated behind the House. Hughes' chalybeate water had a 'ferruginous character, with an agreeable sub-acid tartness, apt to produce a kind of giddiness with an amazing flow of spirits and afterwards a propensity to sleep if exercise be not interposed'[9]: it was very clear, but had a sulphurous smell, and discharged 'great quantities of air bubbles', with a highly 'ferrugineous' (*sic*) taste, and was effective in curing 'violent, scorbutic disorder', breathing difficulties, weak and inflamed eyes, swellings, 'fierce hot humours', cutaneous disorders, stone, 'obstinate gleet from virulent gonorrhoea', breast cancer, vomiting, loss of appetite, and gout, among almost every ailment that affects Mankind[10]. The odour of Commerce and Quackery pervades much of eighteenth-century London Spa and Wells literature, and Bevis's effort was no exception. The 'purging' or 'cathartic' water from the other Well left a 'distinguishable brackish bitterness on the palate', and we are informed that three half-pints of the waters were 'sufficient' for most purposes without the addition of other 'salts to quicken their virtue'. One wonders if the purging qualities might not be due to pollution, but we cannot analyse the waters now.

There does not appear to have been any claim that these Wells had any medicinal properties before the Hughes/Bevis promotions of 1760: some authorities have suggested, however, that the Wells at one time belonged to one of the religious houses of Clerkenwell, and that one of the Wells was associated with the Blessed Virgin Mary, but, the 'name of the Holy Virgin having in some measure fallen into disrepute after the Reformation, the title was altered to Black Mary's Well,... and then to Black Mary's Hole'[11]. Others claimed that the appellation was nothing to do with the Virgin Mary, but was connected to a 'black moor woman' called Mary Woolaston who used to dispense waters in the vicinity in the seventeenth century. Yet another variation relates of a woman named Mary who kept a black cow, the milk from which was mixed with waters from the Well for curative purposes[12], which sounds very doubtful. The most likely explanation relates to the Holebourne (*see* Chapter I).

Be that as it may, Hughes charged three pence for anyone drinking at the pump. Half a guinea was levied for use throughout the Season. Later, when *Bagnigge Wells* was developed with Tea-Gardens, a charge of sixpence was made for admission[13].

A rather amateurish pen-and-wash drawing survives from *c*.1762 which shows *Bagnigge Wells* in its earliest form as a Spa. The circular building is depicted as a drum rather than as an open Temple with circular colonnade, and the ranges of booths for parties of drinkers of whatever beverages they choose are also delineated. The bridge over the river carries a road, and to the left is the brewery: the crenellations and tall chimney (though badly drawn) suggest that the brewery was at one end of the Garden and the Long-Room, etc., at the other *(Plate 67)*.

A PLACE OF RESORT, PLEASURE, AND DISSIPATION

From the day of its opening, *Bagnigge Wells* enjoyed favour with those aspiring to be fashionable. Gardens were hastily planted in a formal style, with arbours and gazebos, and broadsheets and doggerel were produced to spread the fame of this Spa. Many persons went there in the mornings to drink the waters, and the establishment cashed in further by providing early breakfasts. A versifier of the period, William Woty (*c*.1731-91), in *The Shrubs of Parnassus*, tells us that

> 'where each by turns
> His venal Doxy[14] woo'd, and stil'd the place
> Black Mary's Hole – there stands a Dome superb,
> Hight Bagnigge; where from our Forefathers hid,
> Long have two Springs in dull stagnation slept;
> But taught at length by subtle art to flow,
> They rise, forth from Oblivion's bed they rise,
> And manifest their Virtues to Mankind[15].'

Plate 67: A somewhat crudely-drawn view of *Bagnigge Wells* in 1762 by an unknown artist. The bridge over the river (which flowed through the Gardens) is shown, as is the circular structure within which were the pumps dispensing the waters. The ranges of booths were developing within which compartments drinks and meals could be consumed. To the left the crenellated building with the chimney is the brewery shown in *Plate 65*, so the view is taken from the west, looking north-east *(LMA SC/GL/PR/P3/BAG/Ce17040/ cat.no.p5381923)*.

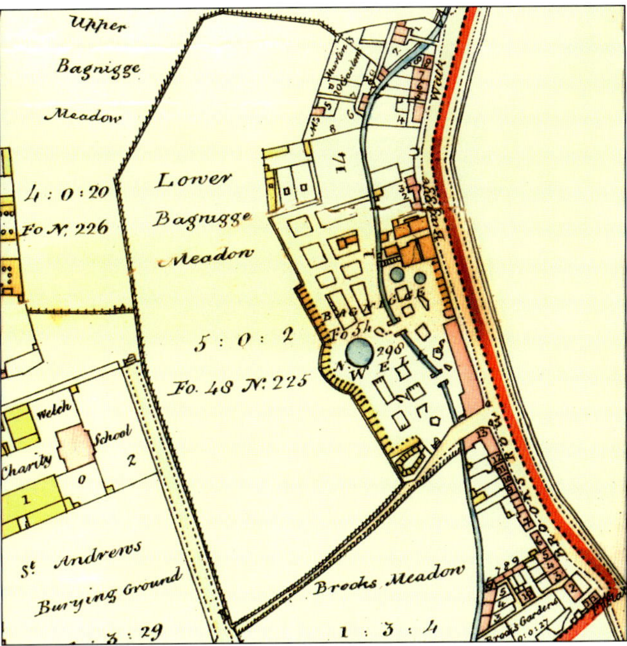

Plate 68: St Pancras Parish Map *c.*1800 drawn by John Tompson, showing *Bagnigge Wells* along today's King's Cross Road, with the Tavern fronting the lane that is now Calthorpe Street to the south. The Spa's main buildings are coloured yellow (note the booths) and pink (the Tavern and Long-Room). The River Fleet meanders through the grounds *(HP).*

Those 'virtues' included the dilution and dissolving of 'vicious humours'[16], the ability to 'obtund[17]' and 'correct... acrimonious and bilious ones', as well as having powers to 'temperate... acidities and inordinate fermentations', to 'restraine... effervescences of the blood', and to 'recreate... the spirits beyond other medicines'[18]. Woty did not shrink from describing the effects of the purgative waters:

'Of these the one will purge the human frame
... and thro' posterior channel
Precipitate its way, or meeting there
With violent repulse, come tumbling up
In horrible cascade'[19].

Bagnigge Wells acquired a Long-Room which, like the Gardens, was thronged with tea-drinkers, especially on Sundays. Waters and tea were popular, but so were stronger beverages, a speciality of the house being bowls of negus[20] to attract topers. So those in search of cures, hypochondriacs, drunks, and all seeking entertainment could find something to their tastes at *Bagnigge Wells*:

'Ye gouty old souls and rheumaticks crawl on,
Here taste these blest springs, and your
tortures are gone;
Ye wretches asthmatick, who pant for your
breath,
Come drink your relief, and think not of
death.
Obey the glad summons, to Bagnigge repair,
Drink deep of its streams, and forget all your
care.

The distemper'd shall drink and forget all his
pain,
When his blood flows more briskly through
every vein;
The headache shall vanish, the heartache
shall cease,
And your lives be enjoyed in more pleasure
and peace.
Obey then the summons, to Bagnigge repair,
And drink an oblivion to pain and to care'[21].

In the *Daily Advertisement* of July 1775 *Bagnigge Wells* had become 'Royal', and readers were informed that the establishment 'between the Foundling Hospital and Islington', provided 'chalybeate and purging waters' of 'the greatest perfection as ever known'[22]. There were occasions when the Long-Room became a venue for parading Beaux and Belles, known collectively as an Exquisite Mob, much given to ogling and quizzing, as is made clear in a view of the Long-Room entitled *The Bread and Butter Manufactory, or the Humors of Bagnigge Wells* published as a mezzotint by John Raphael Smith (1751-1812) and based on a drawing by John Sanders (*or* Saunders – 1750-1825): it shows the Long-Room 'filled with a gay and numerous company attired in the fashion of the period' *(Plate 69)*. 'Some are promenading, others are seated at tables partaking of tea; the room is lighted' by chandeliers with wax lights, 'hanging from the ceiling, and the organ is visible at the distant end. The artist has, after the manner of Hogarth, well depicted the humours of the motley company,

Plate 69: The Long-Room at *Bagnigge Wells* in 1772 showing men and women, dressed in the height of fashion, ogling and quizzing each other. The chandeliers should be noted, as should the organ at the far end of the room on the right. The artist was John Sanders and the published mezzotint, printed by Henry Parker of Cornhill, was by John Raphael Smith. Several versions of this picture appeared in publications at the end of the nineteenth and beginning of the twentieth centuries *(LMA SC/GL/PR/P3/BAG/Ce17026/cat.no.p5379085).*

who are quizzing one another, and being ogled in turn; the prominent feature of the sketch is a richly bedizened madam on the arm of a gallant, who is receiving a polite salute from an officer, by whom she is recognised, at which her companion seems to be somewhat chagrined'[23]. At one end of the Long-Room was a distorting mirror and at the other an organ. Over one of the chimney-pieces was a bust in alto-relievo of a woman as a Roman matron, supposed to represent Nell Gwyn: it was set in a roundel surrounded by festoons of fruit and flowers, coloured to represent Nature[24]. There appears to have been a water-organ in the grounds as well, and recitals were given regularly on both instruments[25]. The Long-Room organ was presided over by one Charley Griffith, 'The Bagnigge Organfist', shown in an illustration *(Plate 70)* accompanied by a verse based on *A Song for St Cecilia's Day* of 1687 by John Dryden (1631-1700):

> 'What passion cannot Music raise & quell
> When G....[26] struck his corded shell
> The listning Drunkards[27] stood around
> And wond'ring on their faces fell'[28].

This picture of Griffith was inscribed 'vide Dry[s] Ode to S Cecilias Night Pub'd for the Benifit [*sic*] of decayed Musicians'.

It is said that the distorting mirrors were used to terrify visitors, some of whom were 'hyp'd to death' (i.e. affected with hypochondria, depressed, or low-spirited): one punter was so appalled by his reflections in the concave and convex mirrors that he consulted a quack who advised imbibing huge draughts of the Spa Waters and charged a whacking fee for the

Plate 70: Charley Griffith, the Long-Room 'Bagnigge Organfist', at work in *c.*1765 in an anonymous etching. The book inscribed 'Davis' refers to John Davis who seems to have been the lessee after Hughes, and ran the place until his death in 1793. Under Davis the establishment acquired a *louche* reputation: is the name on the book a warning of what was to come? *(LMA SC/GL/PR/P3/BAG/Ce17038/cat.no.p5381900).*

counsel. Having Taken the Cure, the patient was led to a straight mirror which reflected a healthy, well-proportioned, well-nourished man, who repaired to his lodgings convinced of the virtues of the Wells. Such shameless trickery was not at all unusual at the time[29].

Pavilions, Gardens, secluded arbours, and seats laid out by the banks of the Fleet River made *Bagnigge Wells* popular among all classes of society, a position it enjoyed for half a century. The grounds were planted with hedges of box and holly, and there were numerous fine trees, some 'curiously trimmed', and a pretty flower-garden. There were ponds, too, containing gold and silver fish, and the main pond in the centre had a fountain in the form of a Cupid astride a swan from the beak of which rose streams of water. Along the river-banks were willows, large docks, and coarse plants, elder-bushes, and other shrubs in luxurious profusion. It appears that the artist, Luke Clennell (1781-1840), repaired to *Bagnigge Wells* on many occasions to make studies of the foliage. Three bridges spanned the stream to link the two parts of the Gardens, and there were two lead statues set among the trees: one represented a rustic figure with a scythe, and the other a Phyllis[30] of the hay-fields, a rake in her hand. It seems that by the banks of the river were several seats for such as 'chuse to smoak or drink cyder, ale, &c.', which were not permitted in other parts of the Garden. The river was then relatively unpolluted, and 'Copywell' mentioned that

'Close by the Garden Wall meand'ring stream
Its jetty Wave devolves, degraded oft
With term of Ditch. Insinuation vile!
Dishonourable name! and rough to ear
Of Water-drinking Mortal. Silence! thou,
Do thou the lips of bitter Malice close,
If once she dare the gliding Lymph prophane,
Or with unhallowed tongue proclaim it foul'[31].

Nevertheless, some pollution did occur, some of it occasioned by the customers of the *Wells*:

'A *holey* Temple there invites the view
To *Cloacina* sacred. Here repair
In order due her Votaries well-pleas'd,
And offer up their Morning Sacrifice
With lowly reverence, performing rites
With modest face, averted from the Fane'[32].

Arbours were covered with honeysuckle and sweet briar, and were frequented for dalliance and tea-drinking. There were also structures like

Plate 71: *Old Bagnigge Wells Tavern and Tea Gardens* (*c*.1825). In the foreground a game of skittles lies abandoned. The ranges of 'boxes' in which groups of persons could sit are shown as is the circular 'Temple' from which the waters were dispensed. The two-storey Gothick castellated 'grotto' is shown, beyond which is the Long-Room attached to the Tavern *(LMA SC/GL/PR/P3/BAG/Ce17033/cat.no.p5379234)*.

three-sided rooms, open on one side to the Gardens (visible in *Plate 68*), which gave privacy to persons who wished to take the waters, dishes of tea, or stronger liquors. At the end of one such series of rooms was a pretty two-storey castellated building in Rococo Gothick style, brightly decorated with shells, fossils, and fragments of broken glass[33]. The Gardens also boasted a bowling-green and skittle-alley, and the waters were dispensed within the circular Temple covered by a dome, the 'Dome superb' of Woty's poem, crowned by a weather-vane. A drawing entitled 'Old Bagnigge Wells Tavern and Tea Gardens' *(Plate 71)* shows the two-storey Gothick pavilion behind which is the Long-Room, and behind that the Tavern (so we are looking south), with the circular Classical Temple-like structure sheltering the water-pumps: around the open space are sequences of 'boxes' in which persons could take refreshments. Tables and chairs were also set out, and there is a skittle-alley in the foreground.

One can imagine, when looking at the selections of views of *Bagnigge Wells*, a veritable shrine of Æsculapius, its fountains ministering to various ailments (Consumptions, Fevers Quartan and Tertian, Gouts, Quinsies, Vapours, and Winds, among others), where Phyllida sought, and was sought by, her Amor, and the Exquisite Mob enjoyed Dishes of Tea in many an alcove or sheltered bower, glared at, no doubt, through many a rheumy and watery eye. The swank of post-Church promenades was followed by a glass or two of chalybeate to aid the digestion of a long sermon, and perchance hints of carmine might brighten the pallor of many a cheek, patched or not. Perhaps a *Magot*[34] or two lurked among the hedges, coloured green, vermilion, yellow, and blue, as part of the furniture of Rococo *Chinoiserie*, and porcelain Mandarins looked on sagely as the Rout progressed, and exotic Cathay was conjured by lanterns and gongs, as scarlet heels sparkled among the dark hollies and box, and Columbine, Pierrot, Pantaloon, and Harlequin entertained the Mob. Fluttering fans and handkerchiefs, yellow masks, and pretty flying lace added to the pulse of movement. The hilarious account of an eighteenth-century Spa provided by Compton Mackenzie (1883-1972) in his *The Passionate Elopement* of 1911 gives a marvellously vivid impression of what ephemeral places such as *Bagnigge Wells* were actually like, with their stilted conversations, their absurd affectations, and their etiquette presided over by self-appointed Arbiters of Taste. Even disasters, as when 'my lady Bunbutter tore her gown on a monkey's tail' during the Grand Minuet of Cathay[35], have a period feel, and one can imagine some elaborate and fanciful concoction of *Chinoiserie* doing the inevitable damage.

Bagnigge Wells had its ups and downs, and was often lampooned as a place of low fashion:

'Ah, I loves life and all the joy it yields,
Says Madam Fussock[36], warm from Spittlefields [*sic*],
Bon Ton's the space 'twixt Saturday and Monday,
And riding in a one-horse chair o' Sunday!
'Tis drinking tea on summer's afternoons
At Bagnigge Wells, with chayney and gilt spoons'[37].

In the opening lines of a satirical poem said to have been by Charles Churchill (1732-64), but, as it was published in 1779, several years after his death, it was probably not by him:

'Thy arbours, Bagnigge, and the gay alcove,
Where the frail Nymphs in am'rous dalliance rove;
Where 'prenticed Youths enjoy the Sunday feast,
And City Matrons boast their Sabbath's rest;
Where unfledg'd Templars[38] first as fops parade,
And new-made Ensigns *sport* their first cockade'[39].

This suggests that the tone of *Bagnigge Wells* seems to have dipped at times:

'Come, come, Miss Prissy, make it up, And we will lovers be,
And we will go to Bagnigge Wells, And there we'll have some tea;
It's there you'll see the lady-birds upon the stinging-nettles,
And there you'll see the waiters, ma'am, with all their shining kettles.
Oh la! Oh dear! Oh dash my vig, how funny!

It's there you'll see the waiters, ma'am, will serve you in a trice,
With rolls all hot and butter-pats serv'd up so neat and nice;
And there you'll see the fishes, Ma'am, more *curioser* than Whales.
Oh! they're made of gold and silver, ma'am, and they wag their little tails.
Oh la! Oh dear! Oh dash my vig, how funny!

And there you'll hear the organ, ma'am, and see the water-spout,
Oh, we'll have some rum and water, ma'am, before that we go out.
We'll coach it into town, ma'am, and won't return to shop,
But we'll go to Thingimy hall, ma'am, and there we'll have a drop.
Oh la! Oh dear! Oh dash my vig, how funny!'[40]

Certainly *Bagnigge Wells* was

'... frequented oft, when male and female meet,
And strive to drink a long adieu to pain,
In the refreshing Vale with fragrance fill'd...'[41]

Woty (or 'Copywell') went on to describe the *clientèle*:

'Here ambulates th'Attorney looking grave,
And Rake from Bacchanalian rout uprose,
And mad festivity. Here, too, the Cit[42]
With belly turtle-stuffed, and Man of Gout
With leg of size enormous. Hobbling on,
The pump-room he salutes, and in the chair
He squats himself unwieldy. Much he drinks
And much he laughs to see the females quaff,
The friendly beverage. He, nor jest obscene,
Of meretrician wench, nor quibble quaint
Of prentic'd punster heeds, himself a wit
And dealer in conundrums...'[43]

William Clarke (1800-38) seems to have observed *Bagnigge Wells* in decline, for he explained that

'...Cits[44] to Bagnigge Wells repair,
To swallow dust and call it air'[45],

a remark attributed to 'Miss Edgeworth[46], in one of her tales', by Pinks[47] and others. Clarke attributes the couplet to 'an author,... describing a summer Sunday in London', alluding 'to this old place of plebeian entertainment', and goes on to tell us that the

> 'proprietor administers large doses of music gratis to his customers... the music is vocal as well as instrumental, and professional persons are engaged to conduct the concerts. You go in free, call for what you think proper, and are ever and anon indulged, while sipping your grog, or tippling your burton, with a piece from the works of Handel, Arne, or Mozart, on the organ, – a song, – a catch, – or a recitation. We do not much admire these tap-tub concerts, and therefore do not very earnestly recommend our reader to explore his way to Bagnigge Wells. If, however, he happen to be in the neighbourhood, which is not probable, for it lies in the very Van Diemen's land of the metropolis, that is to say, behind Battle-bridge and Gray's Inn Lane Road, he may do worse than take his tumbler of toddy, and snatch a glance at one of the amusements of the apprentice order of cockneys at Bagnigge Wells'[48].

Plate 72: *A Bagnigge Wells Scene, or No Resisting Temptation* (1780). The suggestive Swan/Cupid fountain can be seen between the two young women, as can the roof of the 'Temple' from which the waters were dispensed, and some of the tall, clipped hedges: the picking of the roses alludes to deflowering. Mezzotint published by Carington Bowles *(LMA SC/GL/PR/P3/BAG/Ce17028/ cat.no.p5379116).*

Carington Bowles (1724-93) produced numerous droll prints that pass commentaries on the social preoccupations of his time, often with rumbustious humour[49]. One of his publications, entitled *A Bagnigge Wells Scene, or No Resisting Temptation* (1780) shows two young women dressed in the height of fashion: they are near the Cupid/Swan fountain in full spate, and one is picking the roses *(Plate 72)* while the other looks at her askance. The so-called 'Temptation' which keeps the woman waiting is an assignation with a lover: the plucking of the roses suggests deflowering of virginity, and the allusion in the fountain's flood is suggestive, so these apparently droll illustrations have layers of meaning that deserve to be understood. Bowles also published *Mr Deputy Dumpling and Family enjoying a Summer Afternoon* (1780) in which Mr and Mrs Dumpling are depicted as very fat, he bewigged and perspiring, and she with monstrous hat and opened fan. A boy (presumably Dumpling Junior) pulls a carriage-like pram in which sits his sister holding a doll dressed like a fashionable young woman. Mr Dumpling carries another daughter. The print *(Plate 73)* also shows the western side-entrance to *Bagnigge Wells* with Chinese frets over which is a Gothick element in the form of an ogee (the road is now Calthorpe Street).

Two other Carington Bowles mezzotints are worth including here. One is *The Young Wanton (Plate 74)*, with a quotation from *Proverbs* (**vi** 25-6 – 'Lust not after her beauty in thine heart; neither let her take thee with her eyelids. For by means of a whorish woman *a man is brought* to a piece of bread; and the adulteress will hunt for the precious life'): it shows a presentable, but clearly very worldly, young woman in a suitably low-cut dress, seated on a handsome chair; in the next

Plate 73: *Mr Deputy Dumpling and Family enjoying a Summer Afternoon* (1780). Note the entrance to the Gardens under the Gothick element and the Chinese fret on the door. The shuttered canted bay-window of the Tavern should also be noted. Mezzotint published by Carington Bowles *(LMA SC/GL/PR/P3/BAG/Ce17027/cat.no.p5379180).*

Plate 74: *The Young Wanton*, printed for and sold by Carington Bowles. Mezzotint with moralising quotation from *Proverbs*, in Anonymous (1779): *Bagnigge Wells: A Poem: in which are pourtrayed the characters of the most eminent filles-de-joye.* With notes and illustrations (London: Henry Hawkins [or Haukins]) *(GLCL A.5.2 no.13).*

room, visible through the open door, is a large bed, one of the curtains of which is enticingly drawn back. The other, entitled *The Blooming Peach and Shrivell'd Apple... or Amorous Notions at Fourscore (Plate 75)*, depicts an elderly gentleman propositioning a younger woman (who is obviously not from the Top Drawer) in the Gardens of *Bagnigge Wells.*

To return to the main building, one of the canted, shuttered bay-windows is shown, with the Garden-gate and superimposed Gothick ornament, in *Plate 73*. These aspects are confirmed in the illustration entitled *Bagnigge Wells, near Battle Bridge, Islington (Plate 76)*, another version *(Plate 77)* of which (*c*.1800) has differences of detail, but the tall windows of the Long-Room are clearly delineated in both pictures. The polygonal structure to the right of the Long-Room is presumably the back of the two-storey Gothick structure before it was crenellated (or perhaps after the crenellations were removed). Thus both *Plates 76* and *77* depict the appearance of *Bagnigge Wells* when approached from the south-east, that is, travelling northwards: the Gardens were to the west of the buildings, and the brewery lay to the north. Yet another version of this view *(Plate 78)* shows the Gothick gate to the Gardens, the general disposition of the elements, including the windows of the Long-Room, and the polygonal structure, but this time the seven windows of the Long-Room are not disposed equidistant from each other, for there is a larger expanse of blank wall between the group of five and the group of two, and the polygonal structure has windows and appears to partly oversail the wall. The ground-floor windows in the symmetrical front of the Tavern are set to either side of a projecting porch, and the projecting windows on the side of the Tavern are not the same.

Plate 75: *The Blooming Peach and Shrivell'd Apple, or Amorous Notions at Fourscore*, printed and sold for Carington Bowles. Mezzotint of 1773 in the same 1779 volume as Plate 74 *(GLCL A.5.2. no.13).*

A similar view to that shown in *Plate 71* was published in Pinks's *Clerkenwell*[50] *(Plate 79)*: this deserves to be studied, as although it has similarities to the drawing, it is of especial interest because a sculpted figure with head-dress can be discerned on the north wall of the Long-Room, the head of which is shown in its new position, above the inscribed tablet referring to the 'Pinder a Wakefeilde' illustrated in Sargeant's water-colour *(see Plate 64)*. Yet another impression of the Gardens (1780) shows the pond with Cupid/Swan fountain, the two-storey Gothick pavilion behind it, and a temporary booth set up for diners and drinkers *(Plate 80)*: it is by J. Mérigot (*fl.* 1772-1814).

The frontispiece of the *Sunday Ramble*, engraved by Page, 'Being a View in Bagnigge Wells Garden' *(Plate 81)*, published in *c.*1774, shows the fountain, formally cut and planted trees and hedges, a young woman making free with a gentleman, and a dog chasing another over which a waiter trips and drops his tray. The caption records:

'Salubrious Waters, Tea, and Wine,
Here you may have, and also dine;
But, as ye through the Garden rove,
Beware, fond Youths, the Darts of Love'[51].

Plate 76: *Bagnigge Wells*, near *Battle Bridge, Islington, c.*1800. Note the Gothick structure over the Garden-gate, the canted bay-windows of the Tavern, and the polygonal structure beyond the Long-Room. In the foreground is what would become King's Cross Road, and on the left Calthorpe Street *(LMA SC/GL/PR/P3/BAG/Ce17039/cat.no.p5379228).*

Plate 77: Water-colour (*c.*1800) of the exterior of the Tavern and Long-Room at *Bagnigge Wells*, showing the Gothick Garden-gate in what is now Calthorpe Street *(left)* and the tall windows of the Long-Room. Note that the windows of the Tavern appear to be shown flush, not as canted bays, and the two tall projecting windows differ from those shown in *Plate 76 (LMA SC/GL/PR/P3/BAG/Ce17029/cat.no.p5380881).*

Plate 78: *Exterior of Bagnigge Wells in 1780*: note the Gothick gate on the left, the different fenestration when compared with Plates 76 & 77, and the polygonal projecting element on the right *(north)*. Engraving by William Henry Prior (1812-82) *(From Thornbury & Walford **ii** [1879-85] 294: Collection JSC).*

This may all look very innocent, but there is a much more suggestive comment in the illustration, not least in one dog pursuing another and the broken crockery (promiscuity). Indeed, *A Sunday Ramble* suggested that *Bagnigge Wells* was a place of assignation, where sexual transgression occurred. This publication drew on a literary genre which described all sorts of scenes of high and low life in London, in this instance on a Sunday, aimed at a visitor from the country. The texts seem to deplore the 'Follies' of contemporary mores, yet refer to 'genteel seats' provided and the presence of 'genteel females', as the author (the Guide) takes the newcomer to London through the Gardens, pointing out various personages. One young man takes the waters as a cure for his 'melancholy'; an effeminate male mixes with the company; and a brazen young woman cuckolds an old 'Cit'. Indeed, this young woman, an 'exquisite' beauty, the best-looking of all the 'genteel' females, had

Plate 79: *Bagnigge Wells Gardens, c.*1800. Note the circular Temple within which were the pumps dispensing the two types of water. Surrounding the Gardens are boxes *(see Plate 68)* within which parties could take the waters, tea, alcohol or other refreshments. The two-storey Gothick building on the left was encrusted with shells, broken pottery, and glass, and in the foreground is a skittle-alley. Between the two-storey Gothick pavilion and the tall buildings of the Tavern proper is a Long-Room: on the end-wall facing the Gothick pavilion is a figure the head of which is clearly that subsequently placed over the inscribed tablet relating of 'Pinder a Wakefeilde' *(see Plate 64)* *(Collection JSC).*

actually been a lowly servant of the old 'Cit', but had inveigled him into marriage by falsely claiming to be with child, and suggesting her father's rage might vent itself against the old fool. On the way out of the Gardens the Guide and his companion are accosted by two ladies of 'easy virtue', but decline their favours[52].

As well as supposed 'genteel females' there mingled others of less elevated reputations, including pickpockets, prostitutes, and others[53]. The highwayman, John Rann (*c.*1750-74), nicknamed 'Sixteen-String Jack', whose self-esteem was legendary, appeared at *Bagnigge Wells* clad in scarlet coat, tambour[54] waistcoat, silk stockings, laced hat, and other finery, including eight silk strings attached to each knee of his breeches (hence his nickname)[55]. Dissolute, self-indulgent, and an unrepentant thief, Rann, like many flamboyant cads, was a favourite among the ladies. On one occasion his behaviour at *Bagnigge Wells* gave such offence to the company that he was thrown out of the Long-Room windows[56]. Nemesis came when he robbed Dr William Bell (1731-1816), Chaplain to Princess Amelia, and was duly arrested, tried, and sentenced. On his way to be hanged at Tyburn he wore a bright pea-green coat, and a huge nosegay was fixed to the button-hole of that garment[57].

A perusal of the considerable literature leads the reader to conclude that places such as *Bagnigge Wells* were responses to the demands of a growing middle class which had money to spend and desired to be seen to spend it in 'genteel' pastimes. What, therefore, did that word mean? It suggested aspirations to be included among the gentry, or at least of a rank above that of the common herd, which would involve stylishness (or attempts to be stylish) appropriate to Persons of Quality. 'Genteel' was characteristic of the station of a gentleman or gentlewoman, and involved copying the habits of persons of a superior station in life in dress, manners, refinement, speech, and so on. However, the word, while synonymous with what was polite and elegant, became associated with the aspirations of the 'Cit' whose new-found wealth often outstripped the acquisition of manners and behaviour, and threatened the established social order. The upwardly mobile or aspirational 'Cit' and his family were frequently the butt of verses, essays, songs, and texts for attempting to join in fashionable activities, entertainments, modes of dress, and conspicuous consumption, for they were often embarrassingly clumsy and unsuccessful in such attempts. And *Bagnigge Wells* was described as an establishment where the overweight, expensively but inelegantly dressed, and affected Cit and his family could be seen taking part in 'genteel' forms of entertainment. The Reverend Doctor John Trusler (1735-1820 – who wrote numerous works, some on self-help, some on farming, some on medicine, some on politeness, and some on gardening [among other topics], and who was a 'fearless compiler' of others' literary efforts)[58] mentioned *Bagnigge Wells* in the context of 'tea gardens' on the outskirts of London where the 'common people' resorted in numbers, and that the *Wells* was 'much resorted to' by what he referred to as 'women of the town'[59]. But in this respect *Bagnigge Wells* was by no means unusual: public or semi-public spaces in the eighteenth century became increasingly frequented by those who could afford to put themselves on display. The work of Peter Borsay may be read with profit on these matters[60].

Cultural sites in the eighteenth century were also places of performance for those visiting them: theatres and exhibitions drew audiences and visitors who were both spectators and actors, actively participating in the swank of self-promotion and public display[61]. In the Pleasure-Grounds, Promenades, Gardens, and Long-Rooms of London's 'Spaus' and Wells, to see and be seen were among the most sought-after entertainments, and this was especially true in establishments where a wide, broad, social mix could be found. Notions about so-called 'polite' behaviour were widely disseminated by means of cheap publications, and Pleasure-Gardens attached to Spas and Wells were the arenas in which the middle classes (or those aspiring to the middle class) could practice behaviour and deportment, and note the latest fashions. The blurring of class-boundaries presented writers and artists with vast ranges of opportunities to poke fun at polite Taste and those who attempted to follow the habits of their social superiors[62].

Bagnigge Wells, with its range of activities, offered splendid opportunities for satire. The alleged medicinal properties of the waters attracted hypochondriacs as well as genuine invalids who flocked thither in the mornings to take the waters and breakfast, and later in the day males and females patronised the establishment to take tea, hear music, promenade, flirt, steal, make assignations, and to eat, drink, and play. *Bagnigge*, like other London Spas and Wells, could provide several forms of entertainment in a relatively small space: it was partly a Spa, partly a Pleasure-Garden, part a Tea-Garden, and part a place for promenades, and, because of its proximity to London, attracted a *clientèle* from a broad spectrum of society, unlike the much more exclusive upper-class and aristocratic Spas of Bath and Tunbridge Wells[63], where accommodation had to be purchased and a great deal of time was necessary, neither of which would be possible for middling to lower-class Londoners. *Bagnigge Wells* offered 'scaled-down' types of entertainment found at more expensive, fashionable resorts[64].

Apart from social climbers, highwaymen, Cits, whores, and so on, *Bagnigge Wells* could boast others suggested in the verses that comprise the Anonymous work entitled *A Poem: In which are pourtrayed the characters of the most eminent filles-de-joye. With notes and illustrations*[65]. The 'gay alcove'[66] where the 'frail Nymphs[67] in am'rous dalliance rove' sets the tone, and the mixed character of the customers is suggested by the lines

> 'Sing, Muse, conversant in the various Styles,
> Which deck St James's, or adorn St Giles:
> Now here, now there, who'st view'd the
>   various face
> Shine forth at Haddock's[68], decorate King's
>   Place[69];
> Now toping burnt Champagne[70] 'mongst
>   G - - dby's whores,
> Or Flannel now with Pickpockets at
>   Moore's'[71].

'St James's' alludes to the Court, and to the upper echelons of society, but 'St Giles' refers to the filthy, overcrowded rookery in Holborn, where the dregs of society roomed. These extremes were both found at the *Wells*, together with the 'Nymphs', 'Cits' and their wives, apprentices, student lawyers, and many other types all in search of entertainment and pleasure. Only a minority sought health from the waters. The poem emphasises the social mix, the ranges of *dramatis personæ*, and the curious contrasts: there were an author, a milliner, a moralist or two, a pickpocket, and sundry harlots: indeed a fair proportion of the publication deals with strumpetry in its many forms, the aim being to warn against the dangers of a 'modish' life if followed by any woman from 'city maid' to an 'o'er gay wife' ('gay' meaning addicted to social pleasures and dissipations, leading a loose or immoral life, impertinent, over-familiar, living by prostitution, flashy, or brilliantly showy – a gay man was one who delighted in public entertainments, was perhaps dissipated, and enjoyed rakish pleasures: the word did not have the homosexual meanings it has today). The author of the piece[72] contrasted reality with illusions (or appearances), describing the alleged beneficial properties of the medicinal waters and the moral depravity and promiscuity that went

Plate 80: View of the Gardens (1780) at *Bagnigge Wells* showing the Cupid/Swan fountain in its pond, one of the tall clipped hedges, poplar-trees, the two-storey Gothick pavilion (which is shown with an ogee-shaped roof), and a temporary booth set up for dinners and drinks. By J. Mérigot, engraved by 'H.F.' *(LMA SC/GL/PR/P3/BAG/Ce17036/cat.no.p5379205).*

on at the Wells as opposites: he drew especial notice to the dangers not only of being robbed, but of contracting appalling (and then incurable) sexually transmitted diseases.

So *Bagnigge Wells* seems to have attracted much attention. From around 1810, however, its tone seems to have dipped, and it became almost exclusively a resort of the 'lower orders': even those who might still enjoy 'slumming' appear to have deserted it. The then lessee was bankrupted in 1813[73], and the establishment was offered for sale: everything was auctioned, including the organ, the Long-Room chandeliers, the water-organ, the dinner- and tea-services (all apparently Worcester china), the furniture, and vast quantities of ale and stout. Even shrubs were sold.

In 1814 a W. Stock took over, and although the Gardens were reduced to the parts east of the Fleet (by that time an increasingly malodorous stream), some efforts were made to revive the business. Nevertheless, the *Wells* changed hands again in 1818, and in 1831 a Mr Monkhouse advertised a Concert-Room open every evening for musical entertainments, and these appear to have been the main attractions of *Bagnigge Wells*, even though the place changed hands in 1833 and 1834. From 1838 the new lessees, called Foster, announced performances which do not appear to have been very edifying: songs included such numbers as *Pat was a Darling Boy*; a Highland Fling was performed by 'Mr McDougal'; and there were 'delineations' of Greek statues as well. Scenes from Shakespeare were given, though apparently without scenery or period costumes. A lithograph of *c.*1840 showing the Gardens

Frontiſpiece for the Sunday Ramble;
Being a View in Bagnigge Wells Garden; drawn on ye Spot.
Page sculp.
Salubrious Waters, Tea, and Wine;
Here you may have, and also dine;
But, as ye through the Garden rove,
Beware, fond Youths, the Darts of Love.

Plate 81: Frontispiece for the *Sunday Ramble; Being a View in Bagnigge Wells Garden, drawn on ye Spot.* The Long-Room is in the background, with the Tavern partly visible behind the tall clipped hedge. The domed roof of the Temple sheltering the two pumps is visible, complete with weather-vane. On the left, a 'fond Youth' is being embraced by a somewhat forward young woman, dressed to the nines. In the foreground a youthful waiter drops his tray, breaking the teapot and crockery as he trips over a dog being chased by another: the overturned and fractured vessels allude to sexual promiscuity, while the uninhibited lust of dogs also suggests a certain wantonness *(Collection JSC).*

Plate 82: Figures in the Tea-Garden at *Bagnigge Wells*: a raffish young man offers a drink to a young woman seated at a table set for tea, but she refuses it, perceiving, no doubt that, as he is spilling a jug, he is probably tipsy. Lithograph by F. Alvey of *c.*1840 *(LMA SC/GL/PR/P3-P3/BAG/Ce24497/cat.no.p5379547).*

would not suggest High Culture *(Plate 82)*. 1841 was the last year in which entertainments were given there: they consisted of comic songs, farces, and glees, but they did nothing to revive fortunes. The dilapidated Gothick grotto was wrecked by a passing mob early in April 1841, and by 1843 all that still survived was the north end of the Long-Room. The Wells were filled up with rubbish, and a new public-house (*The New Bagnigge Wells Tavern*) was erected: in 1850 the tenant was the appropriately-named Mr Negus, but he, too, was bankrupted shortly afterwards[74].

Plate 83: View of the remains of *Bagnigge House* in 1844 from the ruined Gardens of the *Wells*. In the background is King's Terrace, King's Cross Road (erected 1831-2), part of which survives in 2009. Note that the drawing shows the crenellated parapet of the Brewery and the chimney (visible in *Plate 65*) *(LMA SC/GL/PR/P3/BAG/Ce17030/cat.no.p5379458).*

NEMESIS

An etching by an unknown artist of 1844 shows the remains of the 'Residence of Nell Gwyn' at *Bagnigge Wells*, presumably drawn from the ruins of the Garden. It is a melancholy view *(Plate 83)*. That is not quite the end of the story, however, for the inscribed stone and part of the sculptured figure that once adorned the north wall of the Long-Room survived for a time, having been re-set, and even the name of *Bagnigge Wells* was transferred to the *Bayswater Tea-Gardens*, 'situated in a region once noted for its springs and salubrious air'[75], and also called *The New Bagnigge Wells* and the *Flora Tea Gardens* (*see* Chapter VIII), but of the original these were a mere shadow[76].

Chapter V References: Bagnigge Wells

1 Title of novel (1923) by Enoch Arnold Bennett (1867-1931). *See* Bennett (1923).
2 Given incorrectly in most sources as WAKEFIELDE.
3 Wroth & Wroth (1896) 56.
4 Cosh (2005) 56.
5 Hazlitt (1892).
6 That is cleansing, purifying, and purgative water.
7 *ODNB* **v** (2004) 614.
8 Bevis (1760).
9 Bevis (1760); Boulton **i** (1901) 51; Wroth & Wroth (1896) 57.
10 Bevis (1760) *passim*.
11 Pinks (1880) 560.
12 Dodsley **i** (1760) 324; *Gentleman's Magazine* **lxxxiii**/2 (1813) 557.
13 Wroth & Wroth (1896) 57.
14 A mistress; a woman of loose character.
15 Woty (1760).
16 A 'humour' was a fluid held to determine temperament or dispositions of mind.
17 Blunt, dull, or deaden.
18 Bevis (1760) *passim*.
19 Woty (1760) 107-11 especially.

20 Port or Sherry with hot water, spiced and sweetened. Sometimes claret was used as the main ingredient.

21 *London Magazine* (June 1759) quoted in Wroth & Wroth (1896) 60.

22 Quoted in Pinks (1880) 564.

23 *Ibid*. 566.

24 Said by Pinks *et al* . to have been made by Sir Peter Lely (1618-80).

25 Feltham (1802).

26 In Dryden's original, this is Jubal: G, of course, stands for Griffith.

27 Given as 'brethren' in Dryden's original.

28 Image 17038 at LMA.

29 Pinks (1880) 567-8.

30 Mythological female associated with almond-trees.

31 Woty (1760) and Pinks (1880) 565. By 'Lymph' is meant pure water.

32 Woty (1760): a *Fane* in this sense refers to a temple, but it also can allude to a place where Fashion prevails. For Cloacina *see* Gay (1716).

33 Wroth & Wroth (1896) 62.

34 Small grotesque Chinese figure.

35 Mackenzie (1911) Ch. XVIII.

36 Given as Fupock in some sources, but 'Fussock' seems to be correct: it means a fat, unwieldy woman. Also *Fuzzock*.

37 Garrick (1775): Colman's *Prologue*.

38 A student lawyer living in The Temple, London.

39 Anonymous (1779) 1-2.

40 *The Prentice and his Mistress*, an old song that is found in many versions, some fruitier than others. It is given in different forms in Pinks (1880) 568; Thornbury & Walford **ii** (1879-85), 207; and Wroth & Wroth (1896) 62-4. This version appears to be more nineteenth- than eighteenth-century in tone.

41 Woty (1760).

42 Samuel Johnson (1709-84) defined a Cit as 'A pert low townsman; a pragmatical trader', and bracketed the Cits of London with the Boors of Middlesex.

43 Woty (1760).

44 Given as 'City' in some sources, e.g. Thornbury & Walford **ii** (1879-85) 297.

45 Clarke (1827) 36.

46 Maria Edgeworh (1768-1849), Anglo-Irish writer.

47 Pinks (1880) 565; Wroth & Wroth (1896) 62.

48 Clarke (1827) 36.

49 *ODNB* **vi** (2004) 958.

50 Pinks (1880) 567.

51 Anonymous (*c*.1774).

52 *Ibid*. 23-31.

53 *See* Anonymous (*c*.1774 & 1779).

54 Rich gold and silver embroidery.

55 *ODNB* **xlvi** (2004) 43.

56 Wroth & Wroth (1896) 61.

57 *ODNB* **xlvi** (2004) 43.

58 *ODNB* **lv** (2004) 470-1.

59 Trusler (1786) 164 and *passim*.

60 Borsay (1989, 2006).

61 Bermingham & Brewer (*Eds*.) (1995) 341-61.

62 O'Byrne (2003-4) 25.

63 Benedict (1995).

64 O'Byrne (2003-4) 25.

65 Anonymous (1779).

66 That is, an alcove where naughtiness might occur.

67 Euphemism for harlots.

68 Bagnio or hotel.

69 Chosen by the 'chaste and pious Prince Ch...s the Second as a place for the further education of young ladies'.

70 Burnt Champagne was *Branntwein*, corrupted to *Brandy*, meaning spirit distilled from wine: 'burnt Champagne' was therefore Cognac.

71 Anonymous (1779) 1-2. 'Flannel' in this sense meant 'drink' or talk nonsense, or indulge in ostentatious behaviour.

72 *Ibid*. *passim*.

73 Wroth & Wroth (1896) 64.

74 Pinks (1880) 569-70; Wroth & Wroth (1896) 64-7.

75 Wroth & Wroth (1896) 117.

76 For Rococo *see* Symes (2005).

CHAPTER VI

ST PANCRAS, ISLINGTON, AND HACKNEY

Introduction; St Pancras Wells; The Adam and Eve Tavern; Copenhagen House; Assembly-House, Kentish Town; Canonbury House Tea-Gardens; Highbury Barn; The Devil's House; Hornsey Wood-House Tavern; Other Establishments

'Pancras and Kentish-town repose
Among her golden pillars high
Among her golden arches which
Shine upon the starry sky.'
WILLIAM BLAKE (1757-1827): *Jerusalem. The Emanation of the Giant Albion* 'To the Jews' Pl. 27.L.9 (London: W. Blake 1815) .

INTRODUCTION

From previous Chapters it should be clear that many eighteenth-century places of entertainment offered similar attractions such as alcohol, teas, coffee, food, musical performances, acrobats, rope-walkers, and so on: some had pretensions to provide waters of supposedly beneficial kinds, and these establishments often bottled the waters for sale on the premises or elsewhere. As has been pointed out, distinctions between 'Spas', 'Wells', and 'Taverns' were often blurred: it should also be remembered that many places of resort had their own Wells, and if beers were brewed on the premises (as was not infrequently the case) the water came from a supply on site before the general availability of piped water. This Chapter will deal with establishments north of the eastern end of the New Road (today's Pentonville/ Euston/Marylebone Roads), the first London bypass, created 1756. It will commence with *St Pancras Wells*, which had many attributes associated with Spas, but will also include several other places of resort that also provided similar facilities, yet were not necessarily 'marketed' as Spas or Wells.

ST PANCRAS WELLS

St Pancras, Pancridge, or *Pankrege Wells* flourished for about a century from 1697, south of Old St Pancras Church, off today's Pancras Road (the Church was substantially 'remodelled' in 1848 by the architects A. D. Gough [1804-71] and R. L. Roumieu [1814-77]). The extensive Gardens eventually disappeared beneath the sundry tracks and yards of the Midland Railway's St. Pancras Station[1]. Just to the west the River Fleet ran on its way to Blackfriars.

The proprietor (one Edward Martin) of a Tavern called *The Horns* issued a handbill in which he spelled out the virtues of the waters, which he claimed through 'long experience' were powerful antidotes to such problems as 'rising of the Vapours', 'Stone', and 'Gravel': in addition, the waters were efficacious agents in the cleansing of the body and sweetening of the blood, as well as being 'sovereign' helps to Nature. Martin did not rely on the waters alone to attract custom: in 1697 his Tavern also held dances and other diversions for a moderate charge of three pence.

At the time open fields stretched north-west from *Bagnigge* and *St Chad's Wells*, and there was unspoiled countryside lying to the north of St Pancras too. Indeed, the *Wells* and its various buildings are shown in rural surroundings in a view based on what Martin's establishment was like in the eighteenth century. There were extensive Gardens with straight avenues shaded by trees, two Pump-Rooms, a House of Entertainment, and a Long-Room.

However, very soon 'Pancredge Wells' was beset by problems, doubtless because 'pretty nymphs' frequented the place thereby attracting further 'scandalous company', and the Long-Room had become not a place for promenades and other diversions, but a common dance-hall[2]. In 1722 the then proprietor was attempting to raise the tone by excluding *louche* company, and the waters were promoted, not only on the premises, but in bottled form, sold elsewhere[3]. In 1729, the *Wells*, 'being in new Hands', were 'refitted, the House and Walks alter'd much to Advantage, so as to render them very Pleasant, and the most Commodious of any within many Miles of London'. The 'Ladies Hall and Apartments' were 'made agreeable and convenient', all entertainments were 'suitable', and the 'Waters... were much resorted' to 'by Persons of all Ranks and Distinctions, many years before any other about the Town were taken Notice of'. This Notice (July 1729) observed that as 'the Credit of these Wells hath much suffered for some late Years, by encouraging scandalous Company, and making the Long Room a common Dancing-Room, originally built and designed only for the Use of Gentlemen and Ladies, that drink the Waters; due care will be taken for the future, that nothing of that kind shall be allowed, or any disorderly Person permitted to be in the Walks'[4]. Thus 'Pancridge Wells', which had been advertised to be let earlier that year, complete with Garden, stable, and other 'conveniences', began to regain something of its besmirched reputation, and Pancras, Bristol, Bath, Pyrmont, and 'Spau' waters were advertised for sale 'at the lowest Prices', a dozen bottles of Pancras water costing six shillings[5].

By *c*.1730 the establishment seems to have recovered somewhat, and various views of the Gardens, with the buildings, were prepared *(Plate 84)* which extolled the properties of the purgative and chalybeate waters *(Plate 85)*.

> 'These *Wells* are Situate about a Mile Northward from *London* the *Mineral Waters* of which are Surprisingly Successfull in Curing the most Obstinate *Scurvy, King's-Evil, Leprosy* & all other breakings out & defilements of the *Skin*: *Running Sores, Cancers, Eating Ulcers,* the *Piles* (herein far Excelling the Waters of *Holt*[6]) *Surfeits* or any Corruption of the *Blood* and *Juices* the *Rheumatism* and all *Inflamatory Distempers*'.

Furthermore, the waters were useful in the treatment of 'most *Disorders* of the *Eyes*', 'Pains' of the '*Stomach* and *Bowels*', 'loss of *Appetite*', and even 'sinking of the *Spirits*' and that most fashionable of maladies, the '*Vapours*'. They were also capable of curing

> 'The most violent *Colds, Worms* of all kinds in either young or old, the *Stone* and *Gravel*, the *Stranguary* or total suppression of *Urine*, most decays of *Nature* & *Weaknesses* in either Sex'[7].

Clearly there were few 'distempers' which could resist attack from these efficacious waters. 'Eruptions', 'Scorbutick and even Leprous Cases, Surfeits,... Asthmas, Beginning Consumptions, Inward Ulcers', and many other unpleasant conditions, it was claimed, could be cured, and the waters could also 'powerfully provoke Urine, purge pleasantly, and answer any Ends where these Discharges are necessary'[8].

In 1732, 'Bristol, Pancras, and Bath Water' was advertised for sale at Richard Bristowe's establishment, *The Three Bells*, Fleet Street: Bath water, however, was expensive, at 7 shillings and 6 pence per dozen large bottles. At Bristowe's emporium the five stones voided by Daniel Harrod could be viewed (they are illustrated in several advertisements), and 'Pancras Mineral Waters' were warmly recommended: in addition to the remarkably long list of 'distempers' they

Plate 84: Bill of *St Pancras Wells*, showing it as it was from the south in *c*.1700 or *c*.1730. In the foreground are the straight rows of the 'New Plantation', and north of the fence is the 'Old Walk' beyond which is the Long-Room, six windows wide and two storeys high, to the left of which are the Pump-Houses. The tall blank wall with three chimney-stacks is the House of Entertainment, and the lower building to its left with two chimneys is the 'Ladies Walk & Hall'. The cultivated Garden to the left of the Old Walk is the Kitchen-Garden, and the road on the left is the 'Coach Road to Hampstead & Highgate', off which are two roads giving access for coaches to the *Wells*. To the left of the New Plantation is a field for the grazing of cows, and on the right of the New Plantation is the footpath from Gray's Inn Road and the City of London. North of the buildings is St Pancras Old Church and its extensive burial-grounds, and to the left of the church-tower is the *Adam and Eve Tavern*. The hill immediately above the Church is Hampstead, and the hill in the distance on the right is Highgate. Just above the row of trees on the northern side of the burial-ground where they join the row on the eastern side is Kentish Town, and the hill on the top left is Primrose Hill. The meadow on the right had a footpath from Islington *(LMA SC/GL/PR/P3/WEL/Ce20074/cat.no.p5382704).*

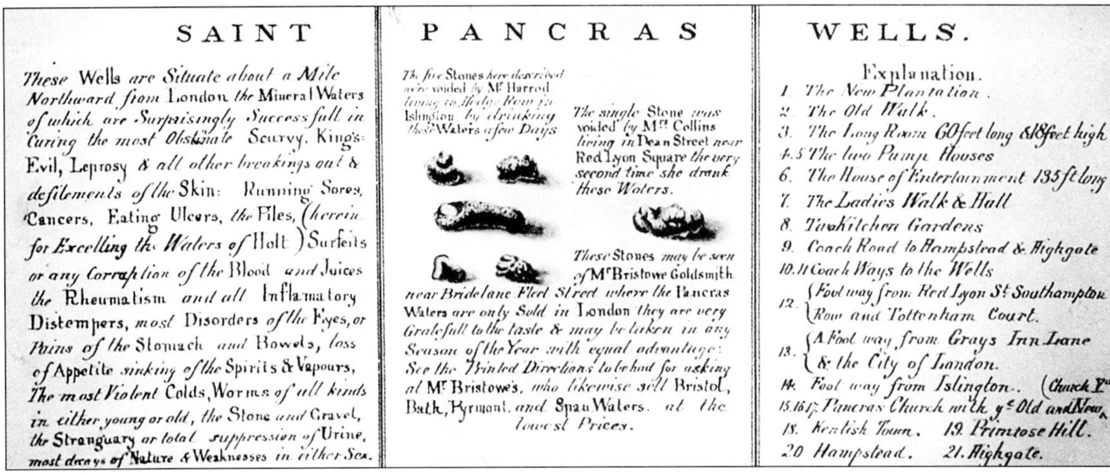

SAINT PANCRAS WELLS.

These Wells are Situate about a Mile Northward from London the Mineral Waters of which are Surprisingly Successfull in Curing the most Obstinate Scurvy, Kings-Evil, Leprosy & all other breakings out & defilements of the Skin: Running Sores, Cancers, Eating Ulcers, the Piles, (herein for Excelling the Waters of Holt) Surfeits or any Corruption of the Blood and Juices the Rheumatism and all Inflamatory Distempers, most Disorders of the Eyes, or Pains of the Stomach and Bowels, loss of Appetite sinking of the Spirits & Vapours, The most Violent Colds, Worms of all kinds in either young or old, the Stone and Gravel, the Stranguary or total suppression of Urine, most decays of Nature & Weaknesses in either Sex.

The five Stones here described were voided by Mr Harrod living in Hedge Row in Islington by drinking these Waters a few Days

The single Stone was voided by Mrs Collins living in Dean Street near Red Lyon Square the very second time she drank these Waters.

These Stones may be seen at Mr Bristowe Goldsmith near Bridelane Fleet Street where the Pancras Waters are only Sold in London they are very Gratefull to the taste & may be taken in any Season of the Year with equal advantage: See the Printed Directions to be had for asking at Mr Bristowe's, who likewise sell Bristol, Bath, Pyrmont, and Spau Waters. at the lowest Prices.

Explanation.

1. The New Plantation.
2. The Old Walk.
3. The Long Room 60 feet long & 18 feet high
4.5 The two Pump Houses
6. The House of Entertainment 135 ft long
7. The Ladies Walk & Hall
8. Two Kitchen Gardens
9. Coach Road to Hampstead & Highgate
10.11 Coach Ways to the Wells
12. Foot way from Red Lyon St Southampton Row and Tottenham Court.
13. A Foot way from Grays Inn Lane & the City of London.
14. Foot way from Islington.
15.16.17. Pancras Church with ye Old and New Church Yards
18. Kentish Town. 19. Primrose Hill.
20 Hampstead. 21. Highgate.

Plate 85: Key or 'Explanation' of the Prospect of *Pancras Wells* shown in *Plate 84*, with a text on the supposed healing properties of the 'Pancredge Waters' *(left-hand panel)*. In the *centre* panel five stones are depicted, 'voided by Mr Harrod', as well as a large stone 'voided by Mrs Collins': these stones could be viewed by the curious in the establishment of 'Mr Bristowe, Goldsmith', near Bride Lane, Fleet Street, where the *Pancras Waters* could be purchased. Bristowe also did a good line in *'Bristol, Bath, Pyrmont,* and *Spau Waters at the lowest Prices' (LMA SC/GL/PR/P3/WEL/Ce20074/cat.no.p5382704).*

could cure were added 'Glandular Diseases', ability to 'promote... due Secretions', and to cause 'a free and brisk Circulation'. They were capable of removing 'all vapourish and melancholy Disorders', were excellent 'in all Inflammatory Distempers' and were an effective 'Cure' for 'the Piles'.

A trawl through ephemera, especially notices, reveals that among the attractions at *St Pancras Wells* was 'that diverting and manly Exercise commonly call'd Hurling, by twenty-four Men, twelve of a side, in the Long Field adjoining to Pancras-Wells'[9]. This 'Diversion' was also subject to wagers[10], and other enticements were lectures on heads[11], an 'Entertainment' by 'Mr Clench of Barnet'[12], and other curious activities. However, the main draw was the water, which in 1741 was claimed to be helpful in curing 'violent Colds, breakings out in the Flesh, carrying off old Gleets, and especially... most of those Diseases that are contracted by the Intemperance so common in this great City'. In 1748 'Musick' for 'Country Dancing' was advertised to appeal to 'all Gentlemen and Ladies who are disposed to go a Maying[13] in the Morning': this was no idle claim, for festivities began between four and five *in the morning*. The Georgians were enthusiastic revellers.

In 1769 the then proprietor, John Armstrong, claimed that the waters were 'in the greatest perfection and highly recommended by the most eminent Physicians', and 'genteel and rural' Tea-Gardens catered to fashionable demand, providing hot loaves, syllabubs, and fresh milk from the resident cows[14]. More substantial meals could also be obtained, washed down with 'neat'[15] wines, 'curious'[16] punch, and 'Dorchester, Marlborough, and Ringwood[17] beers'[18]. Armstrong, 'to prevent mistakes' was careful to locate *St Pancras Wells* 'on that side of the churchyard towards London', presumably to distinguish his property from the *Adam and Eve Tavern* near by. His tea, coffee, and other beverages, including 'Burton, Yorkshire, and other fine ales', could be depended upon, as could the 'cyder'. His cows were 'kept to accommodate ladies and gentlemen with new milk and cream, and syllabubs in the greatest perfection'. His two Long-Rooms could hold two hundred diners 'compleatly'[19].

Tantalisingly, *St Pancras Wells,* apart from its Tea-Gardens, Kitchen-Gardens, Mineral-Springs, and cows, seems at one time to have possessed a building, or part of a building, devoted to the Muses, where James Robinson Planché (1796-1880)[20] made some of his earliest appearances on

Plate 86: The *Adam and Eve Tavern* and St Pancras Old Church in today's Pancras Road. This drawing is part of the so-called *Kentish Town Panorama* drawn by James Frederick King (1781-1855). It was reproduced by the London Topographical Society in 1986 in conjunction with the owners, the London Borough of Camden, with an editorial commentary by John Richardson. The original *Panorama* consists of three rolls, totalling 39 feet, and features each building from Swains Lane in the north to St Pancras Old Church, and the *Mother Red Cap* public-house at Camden Town in the south. It was thought that Mr King's drawings depicted each building *c.* 1800, but the rolls were found to have been drawn on paper watermarked 1850. It is likely that some of King's sketches were made in his early years, but some were obviously done from a keen memory later in his life. Mr King's comments beneath this part of the roll relate that: 'No 39 is a building belonging to the Parish of St Giles, the back of which, a portion of the Tea Gardens, is converted into a Burial Ground usually filled by Catholics. On the other side of "Tea Gardens" four houses are built which leaves but a very small portion of the ground belonging to the Adam and Eve Tavern, but is all sufficient for its present purposes' *(Kentish Town Panorama publ. by London Topographical Society and CLSA, 1986).*

the stage. It would appear that 'Pancridge Wells' possessed (probably as early as 1735) some kind of facility for putting on theatrical or 'variety' entertainments (perhaps not unlike those given at *Sadler's Wells* and other establishments), but these were, strictly speaking, illegal, for theatres were controlled by law to attempt to prevent the spread of seditious ideas[21]. Regrettably, little is known about any theatrical performances that may have been given at the *Wells*, but it is highly unlikely, given the competition at *Sadler's Wells* and elsewhere, that they did not occur.

Water from *St Pancras Wells* continued to be esteemed towards the end of the eighteenth century, but when Daniel Lysons (1762-1834) was recording his impressions, the *Wells* had been enclosed in the garden of a private house[22]. The catastrophic arrival of the railways did immense damage to the environs of this once-pleasant spot, and by 1870 the *Wells* was 'neglected and passed out of mind'[23]. John Timbs (1801-75) stated, somewhat laconically, that St Pancras 'had formerly its mineral springs, which were resorted to. Near the old churchyard, in the yard of a house, is the once celebrated St Pancras' Well, slightly cathartic'[24].

THE ADAM AND EVE TAVERN

'Stand amongst the railway arches and shunting grounds at the back of St Pancras Station and realise, if you can, the pleasant gardens of Pancras Wells in the middle of hayfields, with a view of the northern heights of Primrose Hill and Hampstead, reckoned fine, the old church of St Pancras on its borders, and footpaths from Gray's Inn in full view of the gardens, whence the proprietor could count his customers approaching and form his estimate of their wants'. *Pancras Wells*, too, had a 'competitor at its gates' in the *Adam and Eve Tea Garden*, where cows were kept for the 'making of syllabubs', 'men played trapball[25] of a summer's evening, and the children watched a little squadron of toy frigates on the pond'[26].

Quite so: but to imagine such a pleasing scene requires a major effort these days. The *Adam and Eve Tavern* stood near the west end of Old St Pancras Church, and was in existence at least as early as 1729-30. It is shown in the bird's-eye view of *St Pancras Wells (see Plate 84)*, but at first it seems to have had a slightly sinister reputation. In 1731 James Dalton (*c*.1700-30), a notorious robber, was drinking with a linen-pedlar at the *Adam and Eve*, and, under the pretext of lighting himself and the pedlar home knocked the unfortunate man down and robbed him in the fields between Tottenham Court and Bloomsbury. Dalton was hanged at Tyburn on 12 May 1731[27].

The site of the Tea-Gardens of the Tavern is now part of the disused burial-ground of St-Giles-in-the-Fields, adjacent to the churchyard of Old St Pancras Church *(see Plate 86)*. These Gardens 'were the common resort of holiday-folk and pleasure-seekers'[28]. By the mid-eighteenth century the *Adam and Eve* had become a resort of the 'Cit'[29], and by 1778 it could boast a Long-Room fitted out with gilt-framed pier-glasses, five of which were stolen, as we know from a report in the *London Evening Post*[30]: theft of such substantial objects would have required some ingenuity, so one wonders about the tone and *clientèle*. However, the *Adam and Eve* was advertised in 1741 as a rival to *St Pancras Wells*, as the following makes clear:

> 'PANCRAS-WATERS have been noted for many Years past, even Time out of Mind: But a new Spring has been discover'd at the Adam and Eve in the year 1736, not inferior to the old, but much of the same Quality, tho' if anything pleasanter to the Taste, and finer to the Eye: It has been approv'd by several Physicians, and gives Satisfaction to all those who have made a use of it, and in several Hospitals and Workhouses in London. It is daily sent for to all Parts of the Town, and other Places, by the Order of different Physicians. It will keep for many Years bottled, and continue the Taste and Spirit as if just out of the Well. It will purge of itself, without Salts, or any other Ingredients, both by Urine and Stool; and likewise has occasion'd the voiding several Stones of a considerable Size'[31].

The puff continued to claim the waters were a 'certain Remedy for the Piles', as well as the usual cure for 'all Gleets' and disagreeable 'Distempers' brought on by 'Intemperance'. The mind boggles. Bottled water was labelled *Spencer's Pancras-Wells Waters*, sold as 'thirteen Bottles to the Dozen' at 'Six Pence a Gallon'[32].

In 1786 the attractions of the Gardens were advertised by the landlord, Charles Eaton, who had fitted them out with the usual flowers, shrubs, and arbours[33], and at the end of the eighteenth century the place was puffed as having 'enchanting prospects' by G. Swinnerton, Jun., & Co., Proprietors, who claimed to have 'greatly improved' the Gardens by laying them out 'in an elegant manner' with walks, and kitting out the Long-Room 'with paintings, &c.'. This establishment, it was said, was 'justly... esteemed' as 'the most agreeable retreat in the metropolis'. The Long-Room was 'capable of dining any company', and the proprietors had, 'at great expense, fitted out a squadron of frigates, which, from a love to their country', they wished they could 'render capable of acting against the natural enemies[34] of Great Britain', in order to give 'additional pleasure to every well-wisher to his country'. The proprietors hoped 'for the company of all those' who had the 'welfare of their country at heart, and those in particular' who were 'of a mechanical turn'. The gardens of the *Adam and Eve* were 'genteel and rural'. Coffee, tea, and hot loaves were available every day, and the 'neat wines' and all sorts of fine ales on offer (as well as syllabubs made from the milk of the resident cows) suggest that the establishment deliberately attempted to ape *St Pancras Wells*. The landlord (who presumably rented from Swinnerton & Co.), one George Lambert, hoped that the 'gentlemen... who favoured him with their bean-feasts[35] last season' would grant him their 'future favours'[36].

The Long-Room would accommodate one hundred persons, and bowls and trap-ball were diversions on offer, as a couplet announced:

> 'All those who love trap-ball to Lambert's repair
> Leave the smoke of the town, and enjoy the fresh air'[37].

Doubtless the players would appear in their shirt-sleeves and shaven heads, their wigs and long-skirted coats being picturesquely distributed on the adjacent hedges, under the guard of their three-cornered hats and Malacca canes. Hollands[38], punch, and claret, drawn from the wood at three-and-sixpence a quart, would lubricate proceedings.

In 1803 over three acres of the Gardens were taken to form the St-Giles-in-the-Field burial-ground adjacent to Old St Pancras Churchyard. The Tavern survived for a few years, but by the 1860s it was just an ordinary public-house, and later in the nineteenth century it was demolished[39]. During the eighteenth century, however, the facilities were very similar to those provided at numerous other Spas and Wells[40]. A view of St Pancras Old Church shows the Tavern as it was early in the 19th century.

Plate 87: *Copenhagen House* in *c.*1830. On the left is the extension containing the tea-rooms, billiard-room, and large parlour: the building with the shaped gables is probably of the late seventeenth century, and to the right are the Gardens *(From Hone **i** [1835] 857-8: Collection JSC).*

COPENHAGEN HOUSE

Due north of *St Pancras Wells* was *Copenhagen House,* which stood alone off Maiden Lane, the thoroughfare leading from Battle Bridge to Highgate, now called York Way. It was certainly known as a place of public entertainment in 1725[41], and in 1695 the site was marked as 'Coopen-hagen' on maps[42]: it was clearly an inn at least as early as the beginning of the eighteenth century. Hone stated that it was 'certain that Copenhagen-house' was 'licensed for the sale of beer, and wine, and spirits, upwards of a century: and for such refreshments, and as a tea-house, with a garden and grounds for skittles and Dutch pins[43], it was 'greatly resorted to by Londoners'[44]. 'No house of the kind' commanded 'so exclusive and uninterrupted a view of the metropolis and the immense western suburbs, with the heights of Hampstead and Highgate, and the rich intervening meadows'[45].

The name is supposed to have derived from a house built to house a party of Danes on a visit to King James I and VI in the early seventeenth century[46]. The original building does not appear to have existed before 1624, and had shaped gables (this would appear to be of eighteenth-century vintage): to its west end an extension was added containing a large parlour in which customers could drink and smoke, and it also contained a billiard-room. Upstairs was a large Tea-Room. The image of *c.*1830 shows it with that extension *(Plate 87)* which seems to have been built after the establishment was brutally robbed in 1780. The robbers did so much damage that a subscription was invited to relieve the unfortunate landlady, and more money was received than the value of what had been stolen, enabling the place to be greatly improved and beautified. The notoriety of the robbery (the perpetrators were hanged) led to a great increase in custom, and *Copenhagen House* became known for the quality of its entertainments, including Fives[47], in which the skills of John Cavanagh (d. 1819), the Irish house-painter and Fives-player, were legendary. The wall against which the combatants played was, on the inside, the kitchen, and when that wall resounded louder than usual with the impact of play, the Cook came out with the immortal line:

> 'Those are the *Irishman's* balls'[48],

and indeed, according to William Hazlitt (1778-1830), Cavanagh's 'eye was certain, his hand fatal, his presence of mind complete'[49]. From around 1780, then, Fives was a 'chief diversion' at *Copenhagen House*, and the landlady (a Mrs Harrington) was 'careless of all customers, except that they came in shoals to drink tea in the gardens and long room upstairs, or to play at fives,

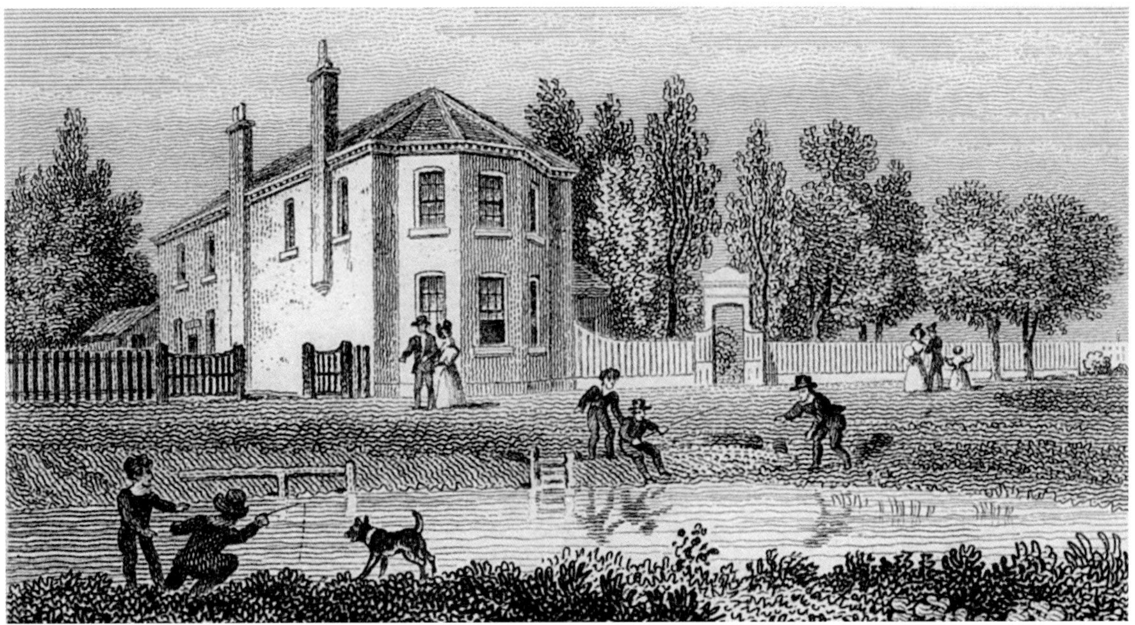

Plate 88: *Copenhagen House*, drawn and engraved by J & H S Storer, published in Thomas Cromwell's *Walks Through Islington* (1835). It shows the post-1780 block containing the new accommodation, with the entrance to the Gardens: the new building completely masks the earlier Tavern *(Collection HP).*

skittles, and Dutch pins, and swill and smoke'[50].

The next landlord, called Orchard, had connections with the London Corresponding Society which held 'tumultuous meetings' in the adjoining Copenhagen Fields'[51] and advocated Parliamentary reform with suffrage for the working classes. During the French Wars it was proposed to bring sea-water through pipes to Copenhagen Fields and to construct Baths, a project which, it was estimated, would bring a tidy profit, but although this was supported by 'several eminent physicians'[52] interested in Balneology, there were insufficient funds raised to make it possible. Clearly *Copenhagen House* would have benefited from this had it been realised.

Orchard was succeeded by one Tooth, under whose régime tone deteriorated. Where Fives had been played, the ground was

> 'filled by bull-dogs and ruffians, who lounged and drank to intoxication; as many as fifty or sixty bull-dogs have been seen tied up to the benches at once, while their masters boozed and made match after match, and went out and fought their dogs before the house, amid the uproar of idlers attracted to the "bad eminence" by its infamy. This scene lasted throughout every Sunday forenoon, and then the mob dispersed, and the vicinity was annoyed by the yells of the dogs and their drunken masters on their return home. There was also a common field, east of the house, wherein bulls were baited; this was called the bull-field. These excesses, though committed at a distance from other habitations, occasioned so much disturbance, that the magistrates, after repeated warnings to Tooth, refused him a license in 1816, and granted it to Mr Bath, the present landlord, who abated the nuisance by refusing to draw beer or afford refreshment to any one who had a bull-dog at his heels. The bull-field has since been possessed and occupied by a great cow-keeping landlord in the neighbourhood...'[53].

From the post-war period until around 1830 *Copenhagen House* was a favourite resort of the respectable middle classes who flocked there, especially during the Summer[54]. In 1841 the Tavern and Gardens were still in existence, and attached to them was a cricket-pitch[55], but the buildings were demolished in 1853[56] to make way for the Corporation of London's huge Metropolitan Cattle Market (1850-5), designed by James Bunstone Bunning (1802-63): the great Clock-Tower, the centrepiece of Bunning's superb creation, stands on the approximate site of *Copenhagen House*[57]. Most of Bunning's fine composition, in turn, has been demolished, apart from the Clock-Tower and the Italianate public-houses that stood at the corners of the splendid ensemble[58].

Copenhagen House was an interesting place *(Plate 88)*, and it is rather sad that it was completely obliterated by a development that, in turn, has virtually disappeared as well. The proposal to bring sea-water to it was interesting, and it would have been fascinating to know if it ever had a chance of success: clearly the potential subscribers thought it would not. Hone wrote of the 'drinking-benches' in the Gardens and the 'boisterous company' within. Tomlins claimed that the House was occupied by a currier[59] in 1753, and suggested that it was not a hostelry then, but other evidence seems to prove it was a Tavern well before that[60]. Like many such establishments it also had a Well, but there does not seem to be any evidence that the water was ever claimed to have special properties.

ASSEMBLY-HOUSE, KENTISH TOWN

To the west of *Copenhagen House* was the *Assembly-House* or *-Rooms*, Kentish Town, a large inn (probably in existence in the early eighteenth century), partly built of timber, with a Long-Room, entrance to which was gained by an exterior covered stair *(Plate 89)*. Cheerfully illuminated at night, it provided, for 1788, 'a choice assortment of wines, spirits, and liquors, together with mild ales and cyder of the best quality', all of which the landlord was '*determined* to sell on the most *valuable* terms'[61]. Dinners were available for 'public societies or private parties', and tea, coffee, and other refreshments were provided. The extensive Gardens boasted 'a good trap-ball ground and skittle ground', a pleasant Summer-house, 'and every other accommodation for the convenience of those' who made an 'excursion' to the place during the Summer months[62].

The Gardens were built over and the Rooms demolished in 1853: the old resort is commemorated by the *Assembly House*, a lavish pub of 1898 designed by Thorpe & Furniss. Astonishingly, the name survives in these days of 'catchy' pub names. A *Well* existed, but again it does not appear to have been exploited for commercial gain or for medicinal purposes[63].

Plate 89: *The Assembly-House*, Kentish Town, depicted in the *Kentish Town Panorama* by James Frederick King (*see* caption to *Plate 86*). It shows the stair leading up to the Long-Room. In 1725 a gentleman called Robert Wright donated an oval, marble-topped table inscribed in Latin to record his belief that his health had recovered by his walking to the *Assembly-House* for breakfast each morning. The table, still there in 1986, was stolen a few years later
(Kentish Town Panorama publ. by the London Topographical Society and CLSA 1986).

Plate 90: Canonbury Tower, with *(right)* the inn-sign of *Canonbury House Tea-Gardens, c.*1830 *(From Hone **i** [1835] 633-4: Collection JSC).*

Plate 91: Canonbury Tower, by F J Pasquier, published in 1846, with part of the old ponds in the foreground *(Collection HP/121).*

CANONBURY HOUSE TEA-GARDENS

To the east of *Copenhagen House*, near the site of the mansion built for the Priors of St Bartholomew, Smithfield, stood a small ale-house from *c.*1754, which was extended and acquired a Tea-Garden under the name of *Canonbury House*. In the 1780s improvements were made to the Gardens (which consisted of about five acres) and Tavern, and a bowling-green was laid out. By the 1790s *Canonbury House* had become a place of 'decent retreat' for tea and 'sober treatment'. An Assembly-Room was built around 1810, and the grounds were further embellished to cater for devotees of Dutch-pin, trap-ball, and other diversions. Outhouses of the old Tavern were used as a bakery, and the *Tea-Gardens* continued in use until around the mid-1840s. Around the middle of the nineteenth century the *Canonbury Tavern* was rebuilt as a handsome Italianate edifice with a substantial garden (though this was only a small remnant of the Gardens that had once been such an attraction). A view of around 1830 shows Canonbury Tower, with the inn-sign and gardens of *Canonbury House Tea-Gardens* on the right *(Plate 90).*

Although *Canonbury House Tea-Gardens* would seem hardly to qualify for inclusion in the present work, their extent (within the old park wall of the Priors' House) included the remains of the extensive fish-ponds of the mediaeval house, and these were fed by a Spring: their remnants may be seen in an image of the Tower *(Plate 91)*. Several brick arches were excavated in the vicinity which appear to have been connected with water-supplies, and there is no doubt that there were plentiful Springs in the vicinity. However, they do not appear to have been exploited as drinking-water by the proprietors of the *Tea-Gardens*[64].

HIGHBURY BARN

This establishment was once connected with the Priory of St John of Jerusalem in Clerkenwell, and seems to have been a small ale-house which also dispensed cakes in the 1740s. It was sited almost due north of *Canonbury House*, and it was at *Highbury Barn* that The Highbury Society (a Protestant Dissenting Society formed to commemorate the abandonment [1714] of the *Schism Bill* [which would have required all Dissenters who were teachers to obtain a licence to teach from the Anglican Bishop of their Diocese]) met from 1740: it had previously gathered at *Copenhagen House*.

The *Barn* was the occasional venue for meals

Plate 92: *Highbury Assembly-House, near Islington, kept by Mr Willoughby*, published by Robert Sayer (1724/5-94) & Co, subtitled *Highbury Barn in 1792*. The extensive Gardens are shown, with the substantial buildings *(Collection JSC)*.

by Oliver Goldsmith (*c*.1728-74) and his friends[65], after which they would walk to the *White Conduit House* and then on to other hostelries. From 1785 to 1818 the Gardens were laid out with Bowling-green, trap-ball ground, and other facilities, and a large barn was incorporated within the establishment (it had been part of an adjacent farm) and fitted up as a Long- or Great-Room: there dinner-parties and convivial meetings could be accommodated. In 1800 some 800 persons dined, and 3,000 were accommodated at the Dinner of the Licensed Victuallers in 1841[66]. In the 1790s the property was also called the *Highbury Assembly-House (Plate 92).*

In 1811, the landlord, one Willoughby, grew hops in part of the garden, and established a brewery, using water from the site (there was a large pond in front of the premises). During his time *Highbury Barn* was sometimes called *Willoughby's Tea Gardens*[67]. After the French Wars the establishment became a popular resort as a Sunday Tea-Garden, and enjoyed a respectable reputation for many years. By mid-century the 'monster' dinner-parties and 'bean-feasts' ceased to be common, and in 1854 the then landlord introduced musical entertainments. A huge dancing-platform with an Orchestra at one end was erected in 1858, the whole place illuminated

Plate 93: *Highbury Barn Tea Gardens c*. 1825. *(Collection HP/3823)*

by gas. There was an avenue lined with trees between which were statues of females, each supporting a gas-lamp. Alcoves were formed, and the five acres of grounds became a favoured place for enjoyment. In the 1860s a large hall was erected as a supper-room-cum-ball-room: musical entertainments included Rebecca Isaacs (1828-77) and George Vernon Rigby (1840-*after* 1869), both of whom had illustrious careers as singers, and 'splendid Illuminations' were provided. Other attractions were 'Blondin' (Jean-François Émile Gravelet [1824-97]), the tight-rope walker; 'Natator', the 'man-frog', whose aquatic displays were legendary; and a pair of Siamese Twins, but gradually tone declined, and riotous behaviour led to sundry complaints so that licences were refused, and in 1871 *Highbury Barn* closed. By 1883 the site was developed for other purposes[68], but a public-house of the same name today stands on part of it.

THE DEVIL'S HOUSE

This Chapter will end with mention of a few resorts in the vicinity of *Highbury Barn* and *Canonbury House*. First was *The Devil's House*, Holloway, to the north-west of *Highbury Barn* and south-east of the junction of the present Seven Sisters and Hornsey Roads. It was an unusual building, timber-framed and moated, and appears to have been the old Manor House of Tolentone or Highbury. In 1767 the then landlord tried to change the name to the *Summer House*, and offered to anglers and walkers the usual refreshments of hot loaves and tea, with 'new milk' from the cows that grazed in the adjoining meadows. At that time the wide moat was still in existence, and there was a substantial orchard with a canal well stocked with carp and tench. The building was approached via a bridge over the moat, and there were attractive Gardens. During the French Wars *The Devil's House* was refurbished as an inn, and the moat was partially filled in[69]. It was still in existence in 1850, but succumbed to development shortly afterwards[70].

The Devil's House was associated, perhaps spuriously, with the highwayman, card-sharper, drinker, and ladies' man, Claude Duval (*c*.1643-70)[71], otherwise Du Vall or Devol, which probably explains the confusion with the inn, a corruption of the name. Duval was hanged at Tyburn, and is supposed to have been interred in St Paul's, Covent Garden, the slab over his grave inscribed

Plate 94: *The Devil's House*, Holloway, in 1825, from a drawing by William Henry Prior, in a wood-engraving by Joseph Swain (1820-1909). There is water to the right, and what appears to be some sort of flimsy bridge over it *(From Thornbury & Walford v [1879-85] 378: Collection JSC)*.

> 'Here lies Du Vall. Reader, if Male thou art
> Look to thy Purse: if Female, to thy Heart'[72].

However there is no mention of his name in the burial-registers of the church, nor does Strype, in his edition of Stow's *Survey of London* of 1720, mention either epitaph or slab. It is also highly unlikely that a felon would have been buried in a church at all, as robbers usually ended up on the anatomist's table.

Despite the moat, Gardens, canal, and other attractions, *The Devil's House* does not appear to have been architecturally impressive *(Plate 94)*.

HORNSEY WOOD-HOUSE TAVERN

Almost due north was *Hornsey Wood-House Tavern* on high ground east of Hornsey village, at the entrance to Hornsey Wood (the remains of which lie within Finsbury Park, in today's London Borough of Haringey, just outside of Islington). It seems to have been a 'genteel tea-house' with a

Plate 95: *Hornsey Wood-House Tavern* drawn and engraved by J & H.S Storer, published in Thomas Cromwell's *Walks through Islington* (1835) 139 *(Collection HP).*

Long-Room and Gardens from around the middle of the eighteenth-century[73]. The pleasures on offer would hardly have appealed to the Top Drawer, and consisted of 'eating rolls and butter and drinking of tea at an extravagant price'[74], walking in the Wood, and enjoying the view of the surrounding countryside. Apparently the establishment was once called *The Horns*:

> 'A house of entertainment – in a place
> So rural, that it almost doth deface
> The lovely scene: for like a beauty-spot,
> Upon a charming cheek that needs it not,
> So Hornsey Tavern seems to me'[75].

Around 1800 the House was demolished and a substantial building of brick was erected for the enormous sum of £10,000: it was from that time it was known as *Hornsey Wood-House Tavern (Plate 95)*. The Tea-Gardens were enlarged and beautified, and a lake was formed for boating and fishing *(Plate 96)*: this involved the destruction of several venerable oak-trees, but the remaining part of the Wood continued as an attraction for Londoners, especially when they went 'palming'. A word of explanation is needed.

> 'Palm Sunday remains in the English calendars. It is still customary with men and boys to go a palming in London early on Palm Sunday morning; that is, by gathering branches of the willow or sallow with their grey shining velvet-looking buds, from those trees in the vicinity of the metropolis: they come home with slips in their hats, and sticking in the breast button holes of their coats, and a sprig in the mouth, bearing the "palm" branches in their hands'[76].

This custom was already dying out in the 1830s, although a few hawkers still sold branches to those willing to buy (though they did not know why, nor did they know that the branches did not come from palms)[77].

Accommodation in the *Tavern* was spacious, although a painted-leather folding-screen in the main room was 'in ruins'[78], and the *Tavern* soon became a 'well-frequented' house, the 'pleasantness of its situation' being 'a great

Plate 96: The lake at *Hornsey Wood-House Tavern*, *c*.1835. The shelters were for fishermen *(From Hone **i** [1835] 761-2: Collection JSC).*

attraction in fine weather'[79]. Everything was demolished in 1866 to make way for Finsbury Park, which opened for public recreation in 1869[80].

OTHER ESTABLISHMENTS

To the south-east of *Highbury Barn* were two other establishments: *The Spring Garden*, Stoke Newington, and *The Black Queen Coffee-House and Tea Gardens*, Shacklewell. The former was situated south of Newington Green, and the latter to the east of what is now Stoke Newington Road, to the north of Dalston Lane. The *Spring Garden* is mentioned in Henry Warner's *Survey and Admeasurement* of 1735[81], and in 1753 the Tavern associated with the *Spring Garden* was advertised as providing afternoon teas as well as, curiously, 'beans in perfection'[82]. It never seems to have been fashionable, and had no associations with other entertainments[83], although ale and cakes were once 'plenty' in Newington.

Rather more salubrious was *The Black Queen* on Shacklewell Green, which had its Tea-Gardens planted with fruit-trees, limes, poplars, and yews, and was also endowed with a bowling-green. Other than a statement that it was the resort of 'genteel company', not much is known of it[84]. However, tantalisingly, Shacklewell is said to have been named after some Springs or Wells which stood in high regard in former times[85], so the possibility exists that *The Black Queen* had a water-supply that was once esteemed.

We will finish with brief mentions of two other hostelries to the south of *Canonbury House Tea-Gardens*. The first, *The Barley Mow Tea-House and Gardens*, Islington, was situated to the east of the Essex Road and to the west of Frog Lane, now Popham Road. *The Barley Mow* was a public-house much frequented by George Morland (1763-1804)[86], the landscape- and genre-painter, who succumbed to the Demon Drink and mountains of debt, and the place had a Garden where tea and cakes could be consumed, but this was built over, probably early in the nineteenth century. There does not appear to have been any attempt to sell or advertise waters there[87].

Plate 97: Vignette showing an early-nineteenth-century man enjoying a pipe and a tankard in a pub Garden (From *Hone **i** [1835] 769-70: Collection JSC).*

Finally, there was *The Castle Inn and Tea-Gardens*, Colebrooke Row, Islington, which was, for a short period (*c*.1754-*c*.1800), popular with the London 'Cit' where he could consume cider and heart-cakes[88] and smoke a pipe or two *(Plate 97)*. When Nelson wrote his volume on Islington[89], published in 1811, the place was no longer putting on public entertainments. Until *c*.1822 there was a six-acre nursery-garden to the rear of Colebrooke Row, but both pub and Tea-Garden have proved ephemeral, leaving hardly any residue behind.

The next group to be discussed will be that to the north-west, comprising the important watering-places of Hampstead and Kilburn Wells.

Chapter VI References: St Pancras, Islington, and Hackney

1 Roffe **iii** (1865) 10.

2 Brown *et al.* (1702) ii.

3 Foorde (1910) 79-81; Sunderland (1915) 77-9; Wroth & Wroth (1896) 123-6.

4 Notices of July and 27 September 1729.

5 Anvers (1729-30) 7 March.

6 Not Holt, Norfolk, but Nevill Holt, near Rockingham, Leicestershire, where a Spring was discovered in 1728: the waters were bottled and made available in many locations, including London. In an advertisement of July 1729 Holt in Wiltshire is mentioned, and indeed there was a Spa there from 1720.

7 From a Bill of St Pancras Wells, *c.* 1730.

8 Notice of July 1729. Thanks are due to Jeremy Smith for this item.

9 18 September 1738.

10 As advertised in 1737.

11 16 September 1765.

12 20 July 1731.

13 Celebration of or participation in May-Day.

14 Foorde (1910) 81.

15 A commonly used word at the time, it signified free from impurities, clear, unadulterated, undiluted, when applied to food or drink.

16 Subtle, made with care, exquisitely prepared, delicate, choice, excellent, and fine.

17 Ringwood, Hampshire, where the 'most orthodox ale in the Kingdom' was brewed.

18 Wroth & Wroth (1896) 124.

19 10 June 1769, advertisement, quoted in Thornbury & Walford **v** (1879-85) 339.

20 *ODNB* **xliv** (2004) 515-17.

21 *See* Cooper (1735), who referred to 'Defiance of the Royal Licence'.

22 Lysons **iii** (1795) 381, and Lysons (1811) 283.

23 Palmer (1870). *See* also Britton **x**/iv (1816) 175; Brown **ii** (1702); Clinch (1890); Dodsley (1761); *Gentleman's Magazine* **ii** (1813) 556; Lewis (1854) 37; Lysons **iii** (1795) 381; Lysons (1811) 283; Miller (1874); Palmer (1870); Roffe (1865) 10; Thornbury & Walford **v** (1879-85) 339.

24 Timbs (1867) 641.

25 Game in which a ball, placed upon one slightly hollowed end of a pivoted wooden *trap* or *cat*, by which it is thrown upwards by the batsman striking the other end with his bat, with which he then hits the ball away.

26 Boulton **i** (1901) 66.

27 *ODNB* **xiv** (2004) 1013; Pinks (1880) 549; Wroth & Wroth (1896) 127.

28 Thornbury & Walford **v** (1879-85) 338.

29 *The Connoisseur* (1754) **xxvi**.

30 11-14 July 1778.

31 Advertisement for the *Adam and Eve Tavern*, 1741, kindly provided by Jeremy Smith, LMA.

32 *Ibid.*

33 Clinch (1890) 157.

34 The French, of course.

35 Meal given by an employer to his work-people. The term seems to have been applied especially to a dinner served up at a country tavern.

36 Advertisement reproduced in Thornbury & Watford **v** (1879-85) 338.

37 *Ibid.*

38 Grain spirit, called *Hollands Gin*, or *Hollands Geneva*, or *Jenever*.

39 Feltham (1802) 370. *See* also Miller (1874) 45 & 49; Palmer (1870) 244-5; Roffe (1865) 3; Wheatley **iii** (1891) 20-23.

40 Wroth & Wroth (1896) 127-8.

41 Nelson (1823) 20.

42 Tomlins (1858) 204-5. *See* also Hone **i** (1835) 858-62.

43 A form of Ninepins or Skittles.

44 Hone **i** (1835) 860.

45 *Ibid.*

46 The Queen-Consort, Anne or Anna (1574-1619), was a Dane, the daughter of King Frederick II (reigned 1559-88).

47 Game in which a ball is struck by the hand against the front wall of a three-sided court. Variations included the use of a bat or racquet. It originated in Ireland.

48 Hone **i** (1835) 868.

49 *The Examiner* (7 February 1818) 94-5. *See* also *ODNB* **x** (2004) 592.

50 Hone **i** (1835) 869.

51 Wroth & Wroth (1896) 158.

52 Hone **i** (1835) 869.

53 *Ibid.* 870.

54 Cruchley (1829); Hone **i** (1835) 859, 870.

55 *See* Lewis (1842 and 1854).

56 Tomlins (1858) 205.

57 Curl (2007) 170, 179.

58 The Cattle Market closed in 1939, and the Meat Market in 1963. *See* Miller (1874) 269.

59 One whose trade was the dressing and colouring of leather after it was tanned. *See* Tomlins (1858) 204-5.

60 Hone **i** (1835) 860, for example.

61 Thornbury & Walford **v** (1879-85) 320.

62 *Ibid.*

63 *See* Wroth & Wroth (1896) 129-30. *See* also Elliott (1821) 65; Millar (1874) 294 etc.; Palmer (1870) 62 ff.; and Roffe (1865) 10-11.

64 For Canonbury *see* Anonymous (1774*b*); Brayley **iii** (1829) 269ff.; Feltham (1802, 1829); Kearsley (1791); Lewis (1854) 310; Nelson (1823) 252; Nichols (1788) 33.

65 Forster **iv** (1848) Ch. II.

66 Wroth & Wroth (1896) 162.

67 Feltham (1802).

68 For *Highbury Barn see* Cromwell (1835); *Era*

Almanack (1871) 3-4; Feltham (1802, 1829); Kearsley (1791); Lewis (1842, 1854); Ritchie (1858); Thornbury & Walford **ii** (1879-85) 273 ff.; Tomlins (1858); and Williams (1883) 33 ff.

69 *See* Nelson (1823) but *see* edn. of 1980 133, 173.

70 Larwood & Hotten (1868) 294-5; Lewis (1842) 67, 279-80; Lysons (1792-6) on Islington 127; Thornbury & Walford **ii** (1879-85) 275; Tomlins (1858).

71 *ODNB* **xvii** (2004) 445-7.

72 *Ibid*. 446, quoting WALTER POPE (1670): *The Memoires of Monsieur Du Vall: containing the History of his Life and Death* (London: Henry Brome) 16.

73 *The Connoisseur* **lxviii** (15 May 1755); *The Idler* **xv** (July 1758).

74 Anonymous (1764) 46.

75 Hone **i** (1835) 759.

76 *Ibid*. 397.

77 *Ibid*. 398. *See* also Cromwell (1835) 138.

78 Hone **i** (1835) 759.

79 *Ibid*.

80 *See* Anonymous (1764) 46; Anonymous (1776, 1797); Dodsley (1761); Feltham (1802, 1829); Kearsley (1791); Lambert **iv** (1806) 274; Hone **i** (1835) 759 ff.; Lewis (1842, 1854); Lloyd (1888) *passim*; Murray **ii** (1845) 82 ff.; Thornbury & Walford **v** (1879-85) 430 ff.; Wroth & Wroth (1896) 169-71.

81 *See* Warner (1810).

82 Quoted in Wroth & Wroth (1896) 172.

83 Cromwell (1835) 199. *See* also Anonymous (1764) where it is referred to as a resort of the lower orders.

84 *The Daily Advertiser* (3 September 1793) and Wroth & Wroth (1896) 173.

85 Thornbury & Walford **v** (1879-85) 530.

86 *ODNB* **xxxix** (2004) 199-202.

87 Cromwell (1835) 194 ff.; *The Morning Herald* (22 April 1786); Nelson (1823) 128, 197; Thornbury & Walford **ii** (1879-85) 262; Wroth & Wroth (1896) 153.

88 Heart-shaped cakes, popular in the eighteenth century.

89 Lewis (1842) 351-2; Nelson (1980) 385; Wroth & Wroth (1896) 147.

CHAPTER VII

HAMPSTEAD AND KILBURN

Introduction; Hampstead Spa; Belsize House: An Alternative Attraction; A New Lease of Life; The Spaniards Inn; Kilburn Spa or Wells

'With the early part of the eighteenth century England – as well as other countries – entered upon a period of Wells and Spas. They sprang up all over the country, sometimes supported by a fair excuse, but more often by only the pretence of one. If there really happened to be a chalybeate or saline spring at the chosen spot, so much the better; if not, there was water of some sort, and, encouraged by an imaginative physician as sponsor, the public would readily rise to the lure, especially if the place was easily accessible and the neighbourhood picturesque'.

THOMAS JAMES BARRATT (1841-1914)[1] : *The Annals of Hampstead in Three Volumes* **i** (London: Adam & Charles Black Ltd. 1912) 175.

INTRODUCTION

Barratt's perspicacious remarks which are quoted above sum up much of what has been related in previous Chapters. The problem, when it was decided to exploit water, was how to get the public to patronise a 'Spaw' and make it profitable. Long before the Spa was developed, Hampstead had been a popular resort in Summer, and many Persons of Quality actually resided there, finding the air, elevated position, and proximity to the countryside agreeable. However, a much wider patronage was needed so that it could rank with places such as Bath, Boston Spa, Buxton, Cheltenham, Epsom, Harrogate, Malvern, Scarborough, or Tunbridge Wells, and so, in addition to claims for the waters themselves, numerous amusements had to be provided to draw in the punters[2].

The main problem with which Hampstead had to contend was the fact that it was too near London to be as fashionable as the more celebrated Spas (e.g. Bath, Scarborough, or Tunbridge Wells), all of which called for longish periods of residence, and required, therefore, fair sums to finance such stays with all the attendant attractions. Nearer London were places such as the *Marylebone Gardens*, *Spring* (later *Vauxhall*) *Gardens*, and *New Tunbridge Wells* at Islington, all of which provided music, dancing, raffling-shops, and sequestered walks for daily visitors, so Hampstead had to provide at least these facilities otherwise nobody would bother to travel up the hill at all. 'So it came about that both the water-drinkers and the mere pleasure-seekers were after a time duly catered for, and during a decade or two Hampstead enjoyed a considerable reputation as a popular resort'[3].

HAMPSTEAD SPA

Unquestionably, one of the most important of the eighteenth-century Spas of London was Hampstead. A medicinal Spring was known from the earliest of times, and in 1698 this Spring and some six acres of land, later known as the Wells Charity Estate, were given to the Hampstead poor by Susannah Noel (*née* Fanshaw) and her son, Baptist (1684-1714), 3rd Earl of Gainsborough from 1690.

Apparently one Dorothy Rippin sold water from this Well, and a token issued by her, dated 1670, survived[4]. However, thanks to William Gibbons (1649-1728), physician, the medicinal properties of the water received notice, and in 1700 the chalybeate waters of *Hampstead Wells* were compared to those of *Tunbridge Wells*, were bottled, and sold at several establishments in the City, Westminster, and elsewhere, at threepence a flask (which had to be returned promptly)[5]. Gibbons considered the Hampstead waters to be 'not inferior to any of our Chalybeate Springs, and coming very near to Pyrmont in quality'[6]. He also declared the Hampstead product was 'full as efficacious in all cases where ferruginous waters are advised as any chalybeate waters in England, unless Scarborough Spa, which is purgative'[7], but such encomia, even when augmented by further endorsements by quacks resident elsewhere, were not enough to ensure success. Other diversions had to be provided, and when both the waters and the entertainments were well-advertised, a certain amount of custom was assured, but the proprietors had to be certain of keeping up with, or even being slightly ahead of, fashion, provided they did not back losing horses, so to speak. It was not long before Hampstead acquired its share of buildings and amusements, augmenting the lure of the waters, which some London medical men were soon prescribing to alleviate or cure 'several distempers'[8]. The medicinal water was bottled at the original Tavern, called *The Lower Flask*, and a carrier's wagon called there every day to take supplies into London. These waters were not from the Spring in Well Walk, however, but from the Head Spring or Pond (called the Bath Pond) higher up the hill in Well Road[9]. Gibbons, incidentally, was ridiculed as 'Mirmillo' by Sir Samuel Garth (1661-1719), physician, because of Gibbons's siding with the Apothecaries against the Royal College of Physicians in opposition to the establishment of Dispensaries for the poor in the 1690s. Garth supported the Dispensaries project, and made 'Mirmillo' say

> 'While others meanly asked whole months to slay,
> I oft despatched the patient in a day'[10].

Garth was a member of the Kit-Cat Club (so-called because meetings were held at the house of Christopher Katt [*or* Cat], pastry-cook, whose mutton-pies were called *Kit-cats*[11]). William King (1663-1712) observed of Cat that

> 'His Glory far, like Sir *Loyn's* Knighthood flies,
> Immortal made, as *Kit-cat*, by his Pyes'[12].

The Club was formed by some forty-eight (or perhaps thirty-nine) prominent Whigs (including Joseph Addison [1672-1719], William Congreve [1670-1729], John Somers [1651-1716], Richard Steele [1672-1729], Jacob Tonson [1656-1736], and Sir John Vanbrugh [1664-1726]). Sir Richard Blackmore (1654-1729) described the first meetings of the 'Poetic Tribe' at *The Fountain* in The Strand:

> 'Hence did th' Assembly's Title first arise,
> And *Kit-Cat* Wits spring first from *Kit-Cat's* Pyes'[13]

in his poem, published by Egbert Sanger (*c.*1684-1713) and the irrepressible Edmund Curll (1683-1747)[14]. Thus it would appear that the Club, for a time the most prestigious in London, originally met in public-houses, but in 1703 it moved to a purpose-built room at Tonson's house in Barn Elms, Surrey, although there are also occasional references to Summer meetings in the *Upper Flask Tavern*, Hampstead[15].

Sunderland considered that 'Hampstead Wells had more claim to the title' of Spa

> 'with its full significance than many of the other Old London spas. The beautiful scenery, the bracing and invigorating climate, a pure *chalybeate* water, and the attractions provided in the way of amusement, including good music, made it very popular with Londoners'[16].

He went on to note that

> 'It was resorted to in Queen Anne's reign by all kinds of people, distinguished, fashionable, notorious, and uninteresting, some of whom were drawn thither in search of health, others to find amusement and distraction'[17].

However, Hampstead's residents drew most of their water from the *Shepherd's Well*, which was located where Fitzjohn's Avenue is joined by Akenside and Lyndhurst Roads, an area formerly

Plate 98: *The Shepherd's Well*, Hampstead, in 1827, showing water-carriers
*(From Hone **iii** [1835] 381-2: Collection JSC).*

known as Conduit Fields. Water-carriers collected the water at *Shepherd's Well (Plate 98)* and carried it to households at a charge of a penny or more for a bucket. There were other sources of water, but the *Shepherd's Well* seems to have been of considerable importance. Hone stated that most Hampstead Springs were 'impregnated with mineral substances', but that the *Shepherd's Well* provided water that was exceptionally pure, and thus in great demand, although the 'poor things' who made a 'scanty living by carrying it to houses' had 'much hard work for a very little money'[18]. Hone mentioned that the *Shepherd's Well* water was 'remarkable for not being subject to freeze'[19], and that there was another very pure Spring at Kilburn that, with the ponds in the Vale of Health, were 'the ordinary sources of public supply to Hampstead. The chief inconvenience of habitation in this delightful village', however, was 'the inadequate distribution of good water. Occasional visitants, for the sake of health, frequently' sustained 'considerable injury by the insalubrity of private springs, and charge upon' the air they breathe the 'mischiefs they derive from the fluid they drink'[20]. Concerning the *Shepherd's Well*, however, Hone waxed lyrical:

'The verdant lawns which rise above the rill,
Are not unworthy Virgil's past'ral song'[21].

Buildings associated with the *Hampstead Spa* were erected on the south side of what is now Well Walk, and Gardens were laid out and planted. The largest room of the complex was known as the Great-, Long-, or Assembly-Room: it was illuminated by tall windows, and within it there were musical performances and dances for the diversion of visitors until *c.*1733. The first recorded entertainment there was in 1701, when there was a 'Consort' of 'vocal and instrumental musick' composed by the 'best masters'[22]. It appears that performances began in the mornings at ten o'clock (cost one shilling), and dances took place in the afternoons (sixpence per person). In the Autumn of that year a concert was given one morning by James ('Jemmy') Bowen (*fl.* 1695-1701)[23], a celebrated boy soprano, who is known to have performed in works by Jeremiah Clarke (1673x5-1707), Johann Wolfgang Franck (*c.*1641-*after* 1696), and Daniel (*c.*1670-1717) and Henry (1659-95) Purcell at Drury Lane and elsewhere[24]. Bowen was accompanied at Hampstead by two violinists, and there were the usual dances in the afternoons, though in 1708 'good music' was provided for 'dancing all day long'. Child singers seem to have been fashionable, for in 1710 a nine-year-old girl was advertised in a programme of operatic songs beginning at five in the afternoon, for the 'convenience' of 'gentlemen's returning', but the princely sum of half-a-crown was charged for the privilege.

However, to return to 1701, one of the 'very special concerts' was given 'at the request of several people of Quality living at Hamstead [*sic*] and round about' for which tickets cost five shillings, an astronomical sum then. The attraction was John Abell (1653-*after* 1716), the celebrated Scots alto singer and lutenist, who had been dismissed from the Chapel Royal as a 'Papist' in 1688, and later sang in Warsaw before the King of Poland, before returning to England in *c.*1699[25]. Other performers at Hampstead included the tenor Francis Hughes (1666/7-1744), and music by diverse composers, including John Eccles (*c.*1668-1735 – whose 'Instrumental Musick' for the Coronation of Queen Anne [1702] was given) and John Weldon (1676/7-1736).

Hampstead was developed as a Spa when John Duffield took a lease of the land and Springs (except the Upper, or Flask Spring) from 2 June 1701 at a yearly rent of £50 for 21 years[26]. The lease provided that inhabitants of Hampstead and their children and servants should be permitted to drink or carry away *gratis*, every day, as much of the 'purging waters' as they needed, but these could only be collected between five and twelve in the 'forenoon' so as not to disturb the afternoons and evenings[27].

Duffield's Great- or Assembly-Room *(Plate 99)* was also called the Pump-Room, about two-thirds of which was used for assemblies and balls, the rest set aside to contain a large basin filled directly from the chalybeate Spring for the convenience of those who wished to take the waters. The Gardens were laid out, as elsewhere, with lawns, winding paths, arbours, flower-beds, and a bowling-green. A new Tavern was erected, lodging-houses for visitors were built, and shops were opened. *Hampstead Wells* also provided bun-houses, tea-shops, emporia for fine clothes, and 'raffling'-shops. Initial success encouraged other businesses to be set up: in 1709 the 'Thatch'd House and Flask' and 'Bowling Green and New Wells' were opened, with 'Musick every Saturday' and an 'Ordinary' every day at 2 o'clock.

In 1705 a Cold Bath was erected, connected to one of the best Springs of the Heath, lying between the Old and New Greens, adjoining 'the Spaw-Water': there was 'all conveniency' for hot and cold bathing[28]. This was the time when *Hampstead Heath*, a comedy by Thomas Baker (1680/1-*after* 1709), given at Drury Lane in 1705, capitalised on the fame of *Hampstead Spa*, where could be found 'Court Ladies that are all Air and no Dress' with 'City Ladies... over-dress'd' with no Air, and 'Country Dames' with 'broad brown faces like a *Stepney* bun; besides an endless number of *Fleetstreet* Semptresses, that dance Minuets in their Furbeloe[29] scarfs', and their 'Cloaths hang as loose about 'em as their Reputations'[30]. Baker's play, despite the fact that it only ran for a few nights, was published, and went into several editions, but it describes something of the raffish nature of Hampstead, a 'charming place', where a lady could 'dance all Night at the Wells', be 'treated at *Mother Huff's*[31], have Presents made one at the Raffling-Shops, and then take a Walk in *Cane Wood*[32] with a Man of Wit that's not over rude'.

Besides places like *Mother Huff's* and the raffling-shops, a chapel was erected at Belsize, with a clergyman ready to perform short marriage-services for a fee of five shillings (provided the wedding-feast was held 'in the gardens'). Sion Chapel (as this dubious House of God was known) seems to have operated as a sort of southern Gretna Green for some twenty years, closing around 1719, and some of the ceremonies held there were of dodgy legality. The exact site of this Chapel is not known, though Wroth & Wroth claimed it was 'in the vicinity of the Great Room'[33]. Barratt, however, stated it was at Belsize, near Old Belsize House[34].

Public morals, it seems, were not only endangered by bogus marriages, *Mother Huff's*[35], and the various temptations to gamble, but by the erection of a play-house in 1709 to which the Vicar and various parishioners vociferously objected. However, it seems that some sort of assurances were given, for the new play-house was advertised as 'to be conducted with greater decorum than before'[36], so it would appear the worst excesses were avoided. Nevertheless, Hampstead attracted a rakish and disreputable element as well as more innocent pleasure-seekers, and the proprietors of the Spa did not mind who patronised the place so long as the money kept rolling in. The concerts attracted a more cultured *clientèle* which required facilities for coaches from London: this also meant the horses (and coachmen) had to be fed and watered, so stables and public-houses were provided[37].

There were also persons who actually did go to Hampstead to drink the waters and bathe, and they also consulted the local medical-man in attendance. From descriptions[38] it is clear the water was quite heavily impregnated with iron, for Professor Charles Heisch (1820-92), in 1889, inspected the Spring, and found evidence of considerable deposits of oxides of iron. Despite these doubtless efficacious cures, the attractions of the Promenade in Well Walk, the music, and all the other diversions on offer, by around 1724 tone had declined[39]. Loose women arrived from Town 'vampt up in old Cloaths to catch the

Plate 99: The first *Assembly-Rooms* in Well Walk. Watercolour by John Philipps Emslie, 1879. The entrance is flanked by two rooms on either side (this elevation looks as though it was revamped in the early-nineteenth century), with other accommodation above, and the Long- or Assembly-Room behind *(CLSA).*

Apprentices', and my Lord Lovemore might hotly pursue his 'mimic charmer'[40], but more reticent persons tended to eschew the Walks. Gambling continued, but losers lost with ill-grace, and the Great-Room became a Chapel in 1725, continuing in that use until 1849. The walls that had been raised and to the Devil assigned (within which gamesters and dicers blasphemed) eventually were found to be fit for nothing but to serve the Lord: it was a 'surprising change of purpose and of sound', but Consecration, we are told, 'made it holy ground'[41].

The Room was then used as a drill-hall for the Hampstead Volunteers, and was demolished in 1882.

BELSIZE HOUSE: AN ALTERNATIVE ATTRACTION

When things become really bad, they often mend, and Hampstead was no exception to this. The gambling, dissipations, irregular marrying, and general loucheness that had taken hold were perhaps partly because *Belsize House*, a rather grand, symmetrical pile of somewhat Dutch appearance *(Plate 100)*, had been sublet in 1700 to one Charles Povey (*c*.1651-1743), writer, inventor, and coal-merchant, who, failing to find a suitable tenant, did his best to vulgarise it, and his was the genius behind the early marriages of 'Sion Chappel neare Hamstead' as well as attempts to establish a deer-hunt at *Belsize House*. Povey made much of his protestations of patriotism, and ranted long and loudly against 'Popish uses'. By 1720 *Belsize House* and Gardens were opened to the public, 'fitted up for the entertainment of gentlemen and ladies during the whole summer season; the same will be opened with an uncommon solemnity of music and dancing'. This undertaking, the public was assured,

Plate 100: *Belsize House*, a seventeenth-century symmetrical building, demolished before 1798 *(Collection HP/4828).*

'will exceed all of the kind that has hitherto been known near London, commencing every day at six in the morning, and continuing till eight at night, all persons being privileged to admittance without necessity of expense, etc.'[42].

The Park, Wilderness, and Garden were 'wonderfully improved' and 'filled with a variety of birds, which compose a most melodious and delightful harmony'. Persons 'inclined' to walk and 'divert' themselves might breakfast on tea or coffee 'as cheap as at their own chambers'. In addition, twelve 'stout fellows', well armed, patrolled the footpaths between Belsize and London in order to protect potential and satisfied customers from footpads[43]. Georgian London was not exactly a safe place, and later the number of 'heavies' became thirty.

In the 1720s Belsize became a Pleasure-Resort, and was, for a short time, fashionable, thanks to a visit by the Prince and Princess of Wales[44], who dined there 'attended by several Persons of Quality, where they were entertained with the diversions of hunting, and such others

Plate 101: *Belsize House* as rebuilt in 1810 to designs by James Thompson Parkinson (*fl.*1795-1840). It was demolished in 1853 *(LMA SC/GL/LYS/002/003/Ce23790/cat.no.p5377956).*

as the place afforded'[45]. This degree of honour was never to be bestowed on the *Wells*, and soon horse-racing was introduced to attract even more custom, including the nobility and gentry[46]. However, the horse-racing caught on, and another course was opened on the west side of the Heath, which was certainly not a high-class rendezvous, and really attracted a concourse of rabble, so that it was prohibited by the Justices[47].

Belsize was lampooned in 1722 in print. The author claimed that

> '*Sodom* of old was a more righteous Place;
> For Angels hence four righteous Souls could call;
> But at Bellsize, by Heav'n! there's none at all'[48].

Povey's tenant, one William Howell (referred to as 'The Welsh Ambassador', a character who had once 'Done Time' [or Bird] in Newgate Gaol), had many ways to raise money,

> 'For 'tis not only Chocolate and Tea,
> With Ratifia[49], bring him Company;
> Nor is it Claret, *Rhenish* Wine or Sack[50],
> The fond and rampant Lords and Ladies lack,
> Or Ven'son Pasty, for a certain Dish,
> With several Varieties of Fish;
> But hither they and other Chubs[51] resort,
> To see the *Welsh Ambassador* make Sport,
> Who mounting an a Horse, rides o'er the Park,
> While Cuckolds wind the Horn, and Beagles bark,
> And in the Art of Hunting has the luck
> To kill in fatal Corner tired Buck,
> The which he roasts, and Stews, and sometimes bakes,
> Whereby *His Excellency* Profit makes...'[52].

Patrons of *Belsize House* could consume drinks in a coffee-room, and mix with

> 'Coquets, Prudes, and self-conceited Beaux,
> Who are not known for Merit but their Cloaths'[53].

Thus all sorts of types could be found in this establishment. Courtesans, gamblers and such like, with sufficient money and suitably dressed, could frequent the place, doubtless to take advantage of the gullible. As for Howell's armed men, the poet had his own views:

> 'But whether one half of this Rabble-Guard
> Whilst t'other half's Asleep on Watch and Ward
> Don't Rob the People they pretend to Save
> I to th'Opinion of the Readers leave'[54].

Daniel Defoe (*c*.1660-1731), in his celebrated *Tour*[55], noted that the 'old seat of the Earls of *Chesterfield* called *Belsize*', which 'for many years had been neglected', but, 'being tenanted by a certain *projector*, who knew by what Handle to take the gay part of the world, he made it into a house of Pleasure and Entertainment', where great 'Concourses' of persons were 'effectually gratified in all Sorts of Diversion'. However, 'there being too great a License used, it alarmed the Magistrates', and the House hastened 'apace to Ruin'[56]. *Belsize House*, indeed, reverted to residential use, but, regrettably, the fine pile had been badly treated, and was demolished before 1798. It was rebuilt in a plain Georgian style *(Plate 101)*, and was tenanted, among others, by Spencer Perceval (1762-1812 – Prime Minister from 1809 until his assassination): that house, in turn, was demolished in 1853, and the site and park developed as the Belsize Park Estate[57]. So, as Barratt noted, after its 'brief spell of prosperity, Belsize was beyond revival as a pleasure resort. It was over-boisterous; it had lost its manners; polite society declined to be drawn by its coarse attractions'. Indeed,

> 'The Megs and Molls of Georgian times, and the demi-reps, gamblers, thieves, and rowdies, who ran riot over the once beautiful grounds towards the end of "the Welsh Ambassador's" time, were a blot on Hampstead's fair name, not to be tolerated. The authorities... ultimately restrained the more boisterous elements, and the gates of Belsize had to be closed upon the pleasure-seekers. The painted grenadiers which had stood in mimic guard on each side of the entrance during the years of revelry were taken down'[58].

A NEW LEASE OF LIFE

The Hampstead waters had never quite fallen from the favour of that part of the populace to which such treatments appealed, and, cleansed of the more disreputable activities that Duffield and his colleagues had encouraged, *Hampstead Wells* once more became a fashionable resort and 'haunt of literary men'[59]. More importantly, the benefits of the waters were extolled by medical practitioners. Among the literary figures who took the waters to alleviate the effects of 'colic' was John Gay (1685-1732), an enthusiastic consumer of alcohol, whose *Beggar's Opera* (1728) contained various characters which would not have been unfamiliar to the habitués of *Belsize House, Hampstead Wells* in its decline, and the dangerous footpaths between the Heath and London. John Arbuthnot (1667-1735), author of *An Essay concerning the Effect of Air on Human Bodies* (1733), spent time drinking the water to attempt to cure himself of troublesome kidney-stones and the effects of too many years of gluttony. Alexander Pope (1688-1744) often resorted to Hampstead not only to see Arbuthnot, but to spend time (from 1736) with his great friend, William Murray (1705-93 – 1st Earl [from 1776] of Mansfield): the two men often walked in the grounds of Caen Wood, long before Murray purchased it as Kenwood for his residence in 1754[60]. This is referred to in the lines:

> 'And late, when MURRAY deign'd to rove
> Beneath Caen-Wood's sequester'd grove,
> They[61] wander'd oft, when all was still,
> With him and POPE on Hampstead-Hill'[62].

Pope could be witty and amusing, but he had a keen eye (and ear) for the absurd, and was often acidic in his comments. When a woman of his acquaintance went to 'some such soft retreat as Hampstead' he penned the epigram *On Certain Ladies*:

> 'When other fair ones to the shades go down,
> Still Chloe, Flavia, Delia, stay in town:
> Those ghosts of beauty wand'ring here
> reside
> And haunt the places where their honour
> died'[63].

Dr Gibbons was dead by then, but a new champion had appeared in 1734: he claimed not only all the virtues sung by 'Mirmillo', but many others as well. His name was Dr John Soame (d. 1738), and his book on the *Wells* was dedicated to John Mitchel, 'Proprietor of the *Hampstead-Wells*'[64]. Soame held that the Hampstead waters were 'as good, if not better, than any in these Parts of *Great Britain*', and that their virtues would justify calling the Spring 'The Inexhaustible Fountain of Health'. He held that most of the evils from which the British suffered were due to the deplorable habit of tea-drinking, which would stunt the growth of future generations. Soame recommended Hampstead waters as *the* sovereign remedy for many ills, although the only strictures he issued regarding tobacco were confined to a consideration of 'the Ladies, who cannot relish well' smoke with 'their Waters'. He cautioned against violent exercise after the 'treatment', and recommended resting for an hour, then partaking of the 'Diversions' on offer. Cheerfulness was encouraged, and after breakfast a ride of four or five miles was advised, because, by the 'Motion of the Horse, the Stomach and Viscera are thereby borne up and contracted, by which means the Waters will be better digested'[65].

Soame recommended Hampstead for its 'pure and balmy Air, with the Heavens clear and serene above'. Compared with the 'great and populous City of *London*' it was a healthy place, for London was 'cover'd with Fogs, Smoaks, and other thick Darkness', forcing the populace to be 'frequently oblig'd to burn Candles in the middle of the Day'[66]. Hampstead was 'bless'd with the benign and comfortable Rays of a glorious Sun, breathing a free and wholesome Air without the noisome Smell of stinking Fogs, or other malignant Furies and Vapours, too, too common in large Cities'[67].

Many associate polluted air, pea-soup fogs, and vile conditions in cities with the Victorian era[68], but if they would study the literature of the Georgian period they would understand that conditions could be extremely grim in the London of the 1730s. Hampstead must have seemed a sylvan retreat indeed. John James Park (1795-1833) considered Soame's 'hyperbolic praise' somewhat deserving of derision[69], but by the time Park was active the Spa had been in decline for some years. Soame praised the neglected Spring, recommending the waters for cutaneous 'affections'[70] and nervous disorders. Various songs and verses of the period extolled the 'Chrystal bub'ling Well' of Hampstead: one, called *The Beautys of Hampstead*, appeared in *The Musical Entertainer*[71], a series of engraved song-sheets by the ubiquitous George Bickham:

'Summer's heat the Town invades,
All repair to cooling Shades;
How inviting, How delighting,
Are the Hills and flow'ry Meads.

Here, were[72] lovely Hampstead stands,
And the Neighb'ring Vale commands;
What surprising Prospects rising,
All around adorn the Lands.

Here, ever woody Mounts arise;
There, verdant Lawns delight our Eyes;
Where Thames wanders, In Meanders,
Lofty Domes approach the Skies.

Here are Grottos, purling Streams,
Shades defying Titans beams,
Rosy Bowers, Fragrant Flowers,
Lovers Wishes Poets Themes!

Of the Chrystal bub'ling Well,
Life & Strength the Current Swell,
Health & Pleasure, (Heavenly Treasure)
Smiling here united dwell.

Here Nymphs & Swains indulge their Hearts,
Share the Joys our Scenes imparts;
Here be strangers, To all dangers;
All – but those of Cupid's darts'[73].

The music provided for this lyric was by Abiell Wichello (*or* Whichello – d. *c*.1745), who was popular as a composer of songs in the early part of the eighteenth century. In 1710 he published *Lessons for the Harpsichord, or Spinett*, so seems to have flourished from *c*.1700, but the tunes for the songs are vapid in the extreme, and of no interest.

Following the publication of Soame's book and his *Imprimatur* for the 'sulphuric chalybeate' waters, another Assembly-Room, called the Long-Room, was built in the 1730s to replace the old Great-Room. It was situated on the opposite, north-western, side of Well Walk, just south of today's Burgh House. This is the building visible in some of the mid-eighteenth-century views of Hampstead, notably *A Prospect of the Long Room at Hampstead from the Heath* by Jean-Baptiste Claude Chatelain (1710-58), engraved by William Henry Toms (*c*.1700-*c*.1758) of Union Court, Hatton Garden, published 1745 *(Plate 102)*. This was obviously the source for *A View of ye Long Room at Hampsted from the Heath* by Chatelain, published by Cluer Dicey (1714/15-75) in 1752: Chatelain was English (despite his name), the son of French Huguenot parents, and could probably have benefited from Spa treatment, for he was a glutton, and if he earned anything immediately resorted to a Tavern where he indulged himself freely to excess. He is supposed to have died after a real bender at the *White Bear*, Piccadilly, and was buried at the Parish's expense in the Pest-fields, Carnaby Market[74]. William Henry Prior produced another version more or less from the same viewpoint in the 1870s *(Plate 103)*. This new structure was a substantial building shown in its final years in *Plate 105*, developed in the 1730s[75]. It was here, in the new Long-Room, that the Balls took place as described by that remarkable observer of the social scene, Fanny Burney (1752-1840): there, 'Evelina' was obliged to refuse offers by 'inelegant and low-bred' types who 'begged the favour of hopping a dance' with her[76]. Miss Burney described the Long-Room as 'very well named' but without 'ornament, elegance, or any sort of singularity': indeed, it was merely 'marked by its length'. From what one can glean concerning other fashionable or upstart Assembly- or Long-Rooms of the period, this description could fit most of them (*Plate 104*). Nevertheless, many frequented the place, including Henry Fielding (1707-54), Samuel Richardson (1689-1761), and Tobias George Smollett (1721-71). Samuel Rogers (1763-1855) recalled that in his youth (around 1783) much excellent company could be found at the 'Hampstead Assemblies', and that he himself danced several minuets there one evening[77]. These Rooms continued in use until the end of the eighteenth century. One can also detect references to Hampstead in Richardson's *Clarissa Harlowe* (1747-8): 'Robert Lovelace' lures 'Clarissa'

Plate 102: *A Prospect of the Long Room at Hampstead from the Heath* by J.-B.C. Chatelain, engraved (1745) by W. H. Toms *(LMA SC/GL/LYS/002/003/Ce23773/cat.no.p5376371).*

to Hampstead where the pair 'alight' at *The Upper Flask* to take refreshment, and *The Lower Flask* was a place where 'second-rate characters were to be found occasionally in a swinish condition'. Other visitors included Edward Young (1683-1765 — author of the celebrated *Night Thoughts* [1742-6]), Thomas Gray (1716-71 – of *Elegy* [1750] fame), Mark Akenside (1721-70 – author of *The Pleasures of the Imagination* [1757]). The invalid wife of Samuel Johnson (1709-84), Elizabeth Porter, *née* Jervis (1689-1752), who 'indulged herself in country air and nice living, at an unsuitable expense', lived at Hampstead for her health, while poor Samuel was labouring as a 'harmless drudge' on his *Dictionary*. Indeed, Mrs Johnson 'by no means treated him with that complacency which is the most engaging quality as a wife', as the ever-observant James Boswell (1740-95) remarked [78]. Johnson himself wrote *The Vanity of Human Wishes, being the Tenth Satire by Juvenal Imitated* (1749) in Hampstead[79], probably because of the necessity to raise money to meet the charges of his wife's retreat[80]. Another Hampstead resident was George Steevens (1736-1800), who bought the former *Upper Flask* Tavern as his own residence, and walked daily to London, and is mostly remembered today as editor of the edition of Shakespeare's works which first appeared in 1765.

Plate 103: *The Old Well Walk, Hampstead, about 1750* by William Henry Prior *(From Thornbury & Walford v (1879-85) 463: Collection JSC).*

The Long-Room was often used for private parties, and under the reign of R. Simmonds[81] during the third quarter of the eighteenth century the Wells was run at a profit and with decorum. Simmonds was not only Master of Ceremonies

Plate 104: Madam Duval dancing a Minuet in the Long-Room, Hampstead *(From a drawing by William Heath [1794/5-1840], otherwise known as 'Paul Pry', published by Jones & Co., 16 February 1822. See* Burney's *Evelina [1822] opposite 277: Collection JSC).*

at Assemblies, but ran a Tavern near by which had Gardens for tea-drinkers. He also appears to have been the proprietor of the Hampstead Brewery, which was supplied with water from the Springs. Joseph Brasbridge (1744-1832) left us descriptions of events at *Hampstead Wells*. Simmonds was so dignified and courteous, he was called 'Baron Hampstead, Viscount Negus, or Earl of Bread and Butter'[82].

During the later Georgian period the *Wells* gradually declined in favour. It was a place, Charles Corbett (1710-52) observed, where a 'Conflux' of all sorts of company was to be seen during the Summer months: some were there 'for the benefit of the Waters, but the chief part' resorted thither 'more for gallantry than any Thing else'[83]. Early in the nineteenth century, however, there were more attempts to revive Hampstead as a fashionable Spa by two medical men, both of whom resided there. They were John Bliss and Thomas Goodwin (both *fl.* early 1800s), and they published works extolling the benefits of Mineral-Waters. Bliss analysed the Hampstead waters and issued a treatise entitled *Experiments and Observations on the Medicinal Waters of Hampstead and Kilburn*[84], and Goodwin's more substantial tome was *An Account of the Natural Saline Waters Recently discovered at Hampstead*[85]. Goodwin was convinced that 'Purgative' Springs might exist as well as the known chalybeate waters, and claimed to have discovered them at the 'south-east extremity of the Heath near Pond-street'. These waters, he assured his readers, had an 'affinity' to the Saline Spa at Cheltenham that had been patronised by the King (George III) in 1788: thus Goodwin made a shrewd connection to ensure support from the public. The 'contiguity' of Hampstead to 'so populous a city' was emphasised, and the 'peculiar advantage' of having the Springs so near 'to relieve complaints arising from too copious or too stimulant ingesta' that were the 'usual companions of wealth and indulgence' was trumpeted. In addition, Goodwin claimed the waters were excellent for 'weakly women... desirous of being mothers' among other groups needing help[86]. However, these eulogies were of little avail, and the waters, at the end, failed to draw the crowds[87].

The second Hampstead Long-Room and Ballroom were badly damaged in the Second World War and despite vigorous protest was later demolished by Hamptead Borough Council and replaced by flats of little architectural distinction.

Plate 105: The Second *Long-Room* in Well Walk, on the north-western side of the road on a site now taken by flats called Wells House *(CLSA)*.

THE SPANIARDS INN

The Spaniards still exists on the north side of the road between the upper and lower Heath at Hampstead *(Plate 106)*. It is of interest in the context of this study because the Gardens attached to the Inn were laid out by William Staples, who appears to have been the landlord[88]. There was a proper bowling-green, and there were pretty arbours, bowers, winding walks, small 'summer-houses', and some forty designs set into the pathways in coloured pebbles: these included representations of the Tower of London, the Signs of the Zodiac, the Colossus of Rhodes, the Pyramids, the Sphinx, Adam and Eve, the Sun in its Glory, the Spire of Salisbury Cathedral, the Shield of David, the 'Pathway of All the Planets', and a curious assortment of various earthly and celestial themes[89]. An artificial mound enabled visitors to see for many miles on a clear day: it was claimed that Banstead Downs in Surrey and that (more improbably) even a steeple in Northamptonshire were visible from its summit *(Plate 107)*.

During the latter part of the eighteenth century the *Spaniards* was much favoured, especially on Sundays[90], by parties enjoying 'dishes of tea' in these Gardens (which, like the Gardens of *New Georgia*[91] in Hampstead had concealed mechanical surprises): Charles Dickens (1812-70), in *The Posthumous Papers of the Pickwick Club* (1837), describes a party of tea-drinkers in the Gardens of *The Spaniards*[92] *(Plate 108)*. There have been various explanations as to why the establishment was so-named: one is that the house was once occupied by a family connected with the Spanish Embassy; another is that the Spanish Ambassador stayed there during the reign of King James I and VI (and complained about the English weather while in residence); another is that, during the reign of Philip and Mary I, some Englishwomen were rescued by some gallant Spanish cavaliers from Fates Worse than Death at the hands of drunken English louts (in gratitude, the ladies caused a belt of trees to be planted there); and yet another is that a Spanish merchant, in the seventeenth century, found the climate of Hampstead to his taste, and spent his leisure moments and eventually his

Plate 106: The *Spaniards Inn* in 1838, where today's Hampstead Lane and Spaniards Road meet. The tollhouse to the left survives and inhibits fast-moving traffic *(Collection HP/4535)*.

Plate 107: *The South View of the Spaniards near Hampstead* by Chatelain, engraved (1750) by J. Roberts *(LMA SC/GL/LYS/002/003/Ce23765/cat.no.p5377821)*.

Plate 108: Decoration by Thomas Onwhyn (1814-86) for Dickens's *The Pickwick Papers* (1837) showing Mrs Bardell's Tea-Party at the *Spaniards* (*Collection JSC*).

retirement at the spot[93]. More mundanely, the name probably derives from a Spanish licensee in 1721. Oliver Goldsmith, too, found *The Spaniards* a pleasant inn where he could drink with like-minded friends.

KILBURN SPA OR WELLS

This Chapter ends with a brief description of *Kilburn Wells* at Abbey Field to the rear of *The Bell* Inn, near the top of Belsize Road *(Plate 110)*. In its day, *Kilburn Wells* was almost as famous as was *Hampstead Wells*. The Spring was known before 1600, and *The Bell* seems to have been established around then. There was a mediaeval Priory at Kilburn, some remains of which still survived in the eighteenth century *(Plate 111)*, and the Spring may have been associated with that foundation. The waters were certainly collected in a brick reservoir (surmounted by a cupola) by 1714, but the landlord of *The Bell* does not seem to have

Plate 109: *View of Kilbourn Wells Spa, Belsize Road.* Anonymous water-colour drawing of *c.*1850 *(LMA SC/GL/PR/H3-H3/CHU/ROW/Ce7822/ cat.no.p5377373).*

Plate 110: *The Bell Inn* in 1789 *(Collection HP).*

attempted to exploit the waters until around the middle of the century: in 1752, however, the *Wells* was mentioned as a place of resort by Richard Owen Cambridge (1717-1802):

> 'Shall you prolong the Midnight Ball
> With costly Supper at Vaux Hall,
> And yet prohibit earlier Suppers
> At *Kilburn*, Sadler's Wells, or Kuper's?'[94].

In 1773 the establishment was advertised as a 'happy spot... delightfully situated on the *scite* of the once famous Abbey of Kilburn on the Edgeware Road, at easy distance, being but a morning's walk from the Metropolis, two miles from Oxford Street; the footway from Mary-bone across the fields still nearer... is now opened for the reception of the public, the Great Room being particularly adapted to the use and amusement of the politest companies'[95]. The waters were claimed to be in the 'utmost perfection', and the Gardens were 'repaired and beautified in the most elegant manner'. The 'rural situation', 'extensive prospects, and the acknowledged efficacy of the waters' were extolled: breakfasts and the popular 'hot loaves' were advertised, and the 'plentiful larder', 'best of wines and other liquors', and other delights were mentioned[96]. Our old friend, Dr Bliss, gave his *Imprimatur*[97] to the waters, but ten years earlier Johann Gottfried Schmeisser (1767-1837) had also analysed them. Schmeisser was a friend of the influential Joseph

Plate 111: William Henry Prior's drawing of the remains of Kilburn Priory, 1750 *(From Thornbury & Walford v [1879-85] 247: Collection JSC).*

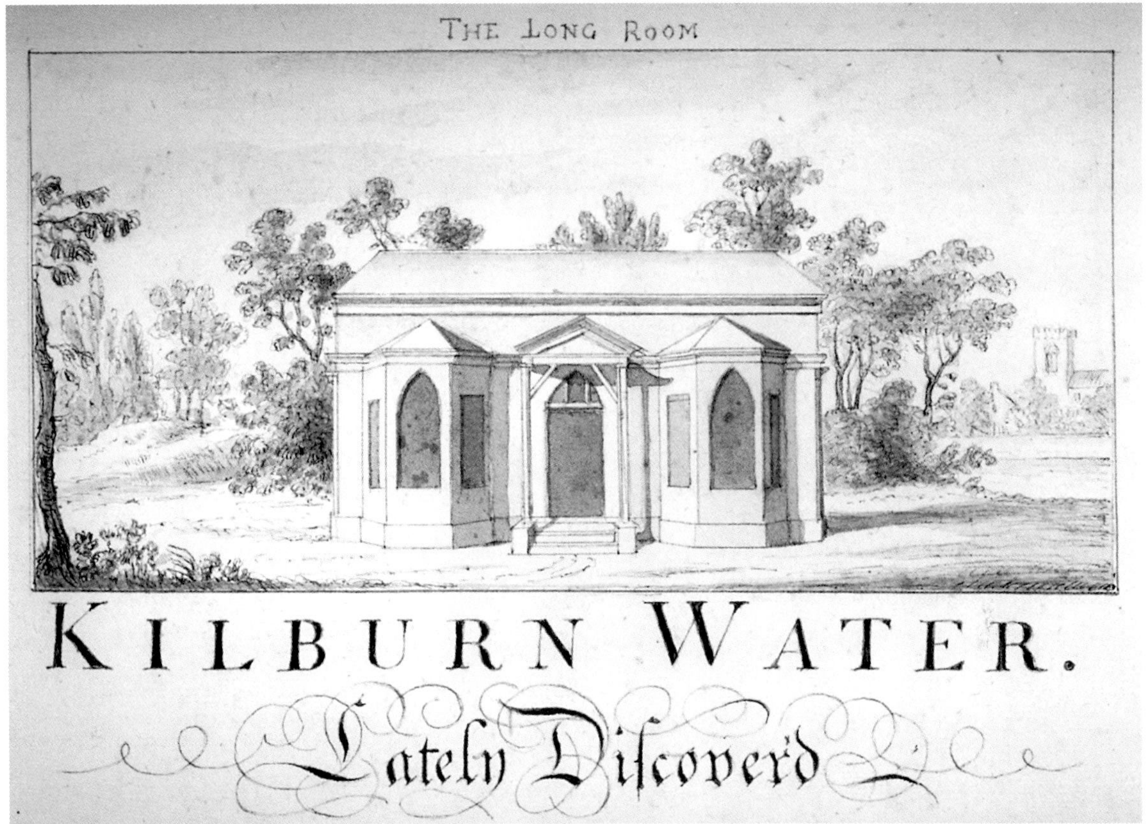

Plate 112: *Kilburn Water Lately Discover'd*, a view of the Great- or Long-Room at *Kilburn Wells* by an anonymous artist. Pen-and-wash drawing, *c*.1820 *(LMA SC/GL/WAK/H2-H4 /Ce19190/cat.no.p5378677)*.

Banks (1743-1820), and during his sojourn in London he was sponsored by the Linnean Society to give a series of public lectures on mineralogy and chemistry. He found that the water was a mild purgative, milky in appearance, and had a bitter saline taste: it contained magnesium and sodium sulphates, and was considered to be efficacious in 'affections' of the liver that had been 'provoked' by over-indulgence at the Groaning Board. It was also more strongly impregnated with carbon dioxide than any other Spring in England, so was naturally effervescent, and especially prized, therefore, by 'those who indulged in convivial potations'[98]. The water was sold at *Kilburn Wells* at three pence a glass, and was advertised as late as 1841[99]. The Gardens remained popular as a 'tea-garden' until around 1830[100].

En passant, it is perhaps of interest that *Kilburn Wells* was not entirely noted for innocuousness, for in the Gardens several duels were fought, including one between James Maitland (1759-1839 – 8th Earl of Lauderdale from 1789) and Benedict Arnold (1741-1801) in 1792. Only shortly before, Lauderdale had challenged Charles Lennox (1735-1806 – 3rd Duke of Richmond and 3rd Duke of Lennox from 1750)[101], but this confrontation was averted. One feels there was a certain robustness among the denizens of Parliament then, before the advent of a wetter professional class of politicians the interests of whom are clearly directed towards themselves.

Some idea of the charming rural situation of 'Kilbourn' Wells may be gained from a water-colour of *c*.1850, by an unknown artist, held by the Corporation of London *(Plate 109)*. The Great- or Long-Room was illustrated in a View of *Kilburn Wells* by another anonymous artist in pen and wash, dated *c*. 1820, entitled 'KILBURN WATER Lately Discover'd' *(Plate 112)*.

Around 1863 *The Bell* (by then *The Old Bell*)

was demolished, and the Gardens were built over. However, it would seem likely that the *Wells* owed something to the religious foundation, and both Sunderland[102] and Macpherson[103] clearly felt *Kilburn Wells* qualified as a Spa, although by the time John Macpherson (1817-90) was writing his tome on the Mineral-Waters of the British archipelago (1871), he was of the opinion that the water had 'lost most of its salts'[104].

Regrettably, the verdict that the south end 'of the down-at-heel shopping street' (Kilburn High Road) 'retains no reminiscences of the spa that existed' in the eighteenth century is true, yet another instance of a delightful spot having been utterly ruined within only a few generations[105].

Chapter VII References: Hampstead and Kilburn

1 Barratt was a remarkable man. His was the genius behind the astonishing success of the advertising campaigns of Pears' Soap, the celebrated *Bubbles* (1886) of Sir John Everett Millais (1829-96). As a wealthy man, he was a passionate collector of British art and of memorabilia of Lord Nelson, a conservationist who bought up open lands to preserve them from development, a distinguished Microscopist, and an historian whose monumental *Annals of Hampstead*, published by Adam & Charles Black Ltd. in 1912, is a superb achievement by any standards. Barratt dedicated it to the Right Honourable George John Shaw-Lefevre (1831-1928), 1st Baron Eversley of Old Ford from 1906, Founder (1865) and Chairman of the Commons Preservation Society, a leader of the national campaign for securing open spaces for the people, and one of the leading lights in the historic struggles to save, protect, and extend Hampstead Heath. Shaw-Lefevre made significant contributions to Conservation, public access to land, the advancement of women, and peasant proprietorship of land in Ireland (*see ODNB* **xxxiii** [2004] 163-6): like many of advanced liberal opinions at the time, he had no known religious beliefs. Barratt himself was unconventional: in 1865 he had married Mary Frances Pears (d. 1916), eldest daughter of Francis Pears and sister of Andrew Pears (1846-1909), but at some time he formed a relationship with Florence Bell, a doctor's daughter, who lived with him and called herself 'Mrs Barratt'. By her he had two sons, the principal beneficiaries of his estate of £405,564 16*s.* 6*d.* (*see ODNB* **iv** [2004] 32-3).

2 Barratt **i** (1912) 176.

3 *Ibid.* 176-7.

4 Boyne **ii** (1889-91) 818.

5 *The Postman* (18-20 April 1700). The Hampstead water-flask was an innovation, and is commemorated by *The Flask* public-house and by Flask Walk.

6 Quoted in Sunderland (1915) 93-4.

7 Quoted in Barratt **i** (1912) 176.

8 *Ibid.* 177

9 Foord (1910) 141.

10 Garth (1699).

11 *See The Spectator* **ix**. *See ODNB* **x** (2004) 524.

12 King (1708).

13 Blackmore (1708).

14 For Curll *see* Baines & Rogers (2007) and Straus (1927).

15 Foord (1910) 146; Sunderland (1915) 94.

16 Sunderland (1915) 94.

17 *Ibid.*

18 Hone **iii** (1835) 382.

19 *Ibid.* 383.

20 *Ibid.*

21 *Ibid.*

22 Wroth & Wroth (1896) 178. *See Postman* (14-16 August 1701).

23 Barratt **i** (1912) 187.

24 *ODNB* **vi** (2004) 910-11.

25 *ODNB* **i** (2004) 68-9.

26 Barratt **i** (1972) 179.

27 *Ibid.*

28 *Ibid.* 188.

29 Showy trimmings, pleated or puckered.

30 Baker (1706).

31 A low Tavern (euphemistically called a 'Tea-House') on the Heath where patrons got 'staggeringly drunk' and sang and ranted 'like the *Jacobite* Party at a piece of ill News'. Cakes, cheesecakes, and the 'Best of Entertainment' were to be had there.

32 Kenwood.

33 Wroth & Wroth (1896) 178).

34 Barratt **i** (1912) 220.

35 *See* Potter (1904, 1907).

36 *Daily Courant* (17 September 1709).

37 *See* Potter (1904, 1907).

38 Baines (*Ed.*) (1890) 218-20.

39 Cox (1724) 'Middlesex'.

40 Welsted (1732).

41 Barratt **i** (1912) 218; Wroth & Wroth (1896) 181. The quotes are from a piece entitled *On Transforming the GAMING-ROOM at HAMPSTEAD WELLS into a CHAPEL.*

42 *Mist's Journal* (16 April 1720).

43 Barratt **i** (1912) 222.

44 George Augustus (1683-1760 – Prince of Wales from 1714, reigned as King George II [1727-60]) and Princess Wilhelmina Charlotte Caroline (1683-1737), formerly of Brandenburg-Ansbach.

45 *Read's Journal* (15 July 1721).
46 *St James's Journal* (7 June 1722).
47 Barratt **i** (1912) 224.
48 Serious Person of Quality (1722).
49 Cordial flavoured with fruits or their nuts, usually peach-, apricot-, and cherry-kernels, with almonds.
50 White wine imported from Spain or the Canaries, or Sherry.
51 Lazy dolt, simpleton, or fool.
52 Serious Person of Quality (1722).
53 *Ibid.*
54 *Ibid.*
55 Defoe (1742).
56 *Ibid.* on Middlesex.
57 *The Illustrated London News* (9 September 1854) 239.
58 Barratt **i** (1912) 231. For Belsize House *see* also Baines (*Ed.*) (1890); Howitt (1869); Lambert **iv** (1806) 256; Palmer (1870) 227 ff.; Park (1814); Thorne (1876) on Hampstead; Thornbury & Walford **v** (1879-85) 494 ff.; Wroth & Wroth (1896) 189-193.
59 Barratt **i** (1912) 239.
60 *ODNB* **xxxix** (2004) 992-1000.
61 That is, The Muses.
62 Coxe (1805): *To Commemorate the Preservation of the Nine Elms, on Hampstead Heath.*
63 Pope (1876) 420.
64 Soame (1734).
65 *Ibid. passim.*
66 *Ibid.*
67 *Ibid.*
68 *See* Curl (2007).
69 Park (1814) *passim.*
70 Soame (1734).
71 Bickham (1737-9).
72 *Sic.*
73 Bickham (1737-9).
74 *ODNB* **xi** (2004) 226-7 and **xvi** (204) 43.
75 *Victoria County History, Middlesex* **ix** 83.
76 Burney (1778) Letter **li**.
77 Rogers (1856) *passim.*
78 Boswell **i** (1924) 151.
79 *Ibid.* 119.
80 Barratt **i** (1912) 260.
81 *Morning Post* (20 November 1779).
82 *See* Brasbridge (1824) *passim.*
83 Corbett (1755) 249.
84 Bliss (1802).
85 Goodwin (1804).
86 *Ibid.*
87 *See* Anonymous (1774); Baines (*Ed.*) (1890); Barratt (1912); Dodsley (1761); Kearsley (1793); Park (1814); Potter (1904); Scott (1879); Thornbury & Walford **v** (1879-85) 467ff.; and Thorne (1876) 281.
88 Park (1814) mentions Staples.
89 Barratt **i** (1912) 234-5.
90 Woodward (1796) 13; Anonymous (1797) 53.
91 Laid out by Robert Caston, *New Georgia* also had a cottage, tea-houses, arbours, and amusing allusions of all sorts, including a pillory into which gentlemen would thrust their heads in order to receive the kisses of the ladies (*see The Connoisseur* **xxvi** [15 July 1754]; *Gentlemen's Magazine* **xviii** [1748] 109; *The Idler* **xv** [22 July 1758]; Lambert **iv** [1806] 255; Lysons **ii** [1792-6] 255; Park [1814]; Prickett [1842] 71ff.; and Thornbury & Walford **v** [1879-85] 446).
92 Chapter **xlvi**.
93 *See* Baines (*Ed.*) (1890); Barratt **i** (1912) 234-7; Park (1814); Potter (1907); Prickett (1841) 71 ff.; Thornbury & Walford **v** (1879-85) 445 ff.; Thorne (1876); and Woodward (1796) 14.
94 Cambridge (1752): 'Kuper's' referred to Cuper's Gardens at Lambeth.
95 *Public Advertiser* (3 July 1773).
96 Barratt **iii** (1912) 115.
97 Bliss (1802).
98 Foord (1910) 161. *See* also Schmeisser & Banks (1792).
99 Barratt **iii** (1912) 116.
100 Feltham (1802, 1829).
101 He was also Duke of Aubigny in the French Nobility.
102 Sunderland (1915) 98-100.
103 Macpherson (1871).
104 *See* also Park (1814) 65-6. For Kilburn *see* Baines (*Ed.*) (1890); Barratt **iii** (1912) 114-16; Howitt (1869); Lambert **iv** (1806) 288; Park (1814); Thorne (1876); Thornbury & Walford **v** (1879-85) 245 ff.; and Wroth & Wroth (1896) 194-6.
105 Cherry & Pevsner (1991) 133.

CHAPTER VIII

MARYLEBONE, BAYSWATER, AND CHELSEA

Introduction; Marylebone Gardens; Marylebone Spa; The Bayswater Tea-Gardens; Other Places in the Vicinity of Marylebone Gardens; Afterword

'The fleshpots of Euston and the hanging garments of Marylebone'.
JAMES JOYCE (1882-1941): *Finnegan's Wake*
Part I (London: Faber 1939) 192 .

INTRODUCTION

Although the density of Pleasure-Gardens was not as great as that in the Clerkenwell area, there were several important resorts north and south of Marylebone Road, some where Regent's Park is now. This Chapter will include these, as well as the few isolated examples that once existed, and another group we might refer to, loosely, as the Chelsea Group.

Many of these were really variations on the popular 'Tea-Garden' theme favoured by the eighteenth-century middle classes (or by those who aspired to be middle-class). Such Gardens were, in a sense, offspring of the older 'promenades' found in places where the waters were taken. Some Tea-Gardens, it is true, possessed Mineral-Springs or Wells, and if they did not, their owners attempted to ensure they acquired them by digging for them. Even if they had Wells or Springs, this did not mean the waters were always exploited for drinking or 'medicinal purposes': just to have a Spring was often enough to attract the public. Gardens, be they for tea-drinking or the consumption of alcohol and food, were sometimes attached to Taverns, and landlords, keen to make the most of their businesses, laid on concerts, built Long-Rooms and Assembly-Rooms, and provided trellis-work alcoves hung with plants, grottoes, fountains, pools, bowling-greens, skittle-grounds, and other attractions.

Where *real* medicinal Springs or Wells existed or were found, it was also important to provide like facilities, and one is struck by the similarities of provision in places of entertainment whether waters were available or not. If they were not, belated attempts were made to provide them, sometimes by selling water bottled elsewhere or trying to ensure water could be found by sinking Wells to obtain them. So spurious Spas copied real ones; places of entertainment that were really only Gardens with a few buildings emulated Spas and spurious Spas; humble public-houses with Gardens attempted to follow fashion, even adding Long-Rooms and laying out arbours and trellis-work outside; and establishments with only the vaguest connections with health and pleasure latched on to the fashion of the day, no matter how mean and primitive were the facilities on offer.

MARYLEBONE GARDENS

These eventually extended to some eight acres lying to the south of what is now Marylebone Road (formerly the New Road), bounded to the south by Weymouth Street (formerly Bowling

Green Lane), to the east by what is now Harley Street, and to the west by the backs of buildings on Marylebone High Street. The main entrance was through the grounds of a Tavern called *The Rose* (sometimes referred to as *Rose of Normandy*), on the eastern side of the High Street opposite the old Marylebone Church (demolished and rebuilt 1741-2, then replaced by St Mary's, Marylebone Road [1813-17], by Thomas Hardwick [1752-1829]), the site of which has been a garden since 1949. What is now Beaumont Street, part of Devonshire Street, part of Devonshire Place, and Upper Wimpole Street were built on what was once Marylebone Gardens to which there was also a northern entrance connected with the High Street and the fields beyond[1].

These once-celebrated Gardens were the remnants of the last stages in the life of Marylebone Palace, the old Manor House (demolished 1791) that stood opposite the church on the High Street. The Gardens were opened as Pleasure-Grounds with many facilities in 1737 and provided the usual eighteenth-century diversions of bowling-greens, fireworks, and musical performances, but long before then there were bowling-greens much frequented by all: John Sheffield (1647-1721), 1st Duke of Buckingham and Normanby from 1703, often went to 'Marybone' which he described as a 'place of air and exercise' a 'small distance' from London, ideal for 'recovering' his weariness and 'recruiting' his spirits[2]. Lady Mary Wortley Montagu (1689-1762), in her *Town Eclogues*, referred to Buckingham:

> 'At the *Groom-Porter's*[3], batter'd bullies play,
> Some *dukes* at Marybone bowl time away',[4]

and that was in 1715: the Gardens of the Manor House were actually detached from it as early as 1650, and soon boasted several bowling-greens, the main one being that attached to the *Rose* Tavern. Indeed, the extensive Gardens of the *Rose* had a circular walk, and several gravel walks flanked by quick-set hedges, with the bowling-green in the centre. This Garden was walled, and surrounded by fruit-trees: it is described in *Grove's Dictionary of Music and Musicians*, quoting a memoir in the *Gentleman's Magazine*, and if this is accurate, the bowling-green, tall hedges 'full grown and kept in excellent order, and indented like town walls' were in existence in 1659, so Pleasure-Gardens at Marylebone seem to have been at least of mid-seventeenth-century date[5].

Samuel Pepys (1633-1703), in 1668, ventured 'abroad' to Marylebone, 'and there walked in the garden'. It was the first time he had ever been there, and found it a 'pretty place'[6]. For many years[7] 'Long's Bowling Green at the Rose' (as it was called) was patronised by the Quality, and the public-house acquired a reputation as a Gaming-House and as a place for convivial sessions: Buckingham himself used to give dinners at *The Rose*, and John Gay's *Beggar's Opera* makes reference to the 'deep play' with consequently money to be 'pick'd up' on the road by thieves. Nevertheless, no less a personage than Camille d'Hostun, Comte de Tallard (1652-1728), French Ambassador Extraordinary and soldier, gave a grand dinner there for Buckingham just before the end of his stay in London in 1701[8]. The 'Bowling-green', then, had its many attractions. In 1718 there were fireworks and other illuminations, and a 'Consort of Musick' in celebration of the King's birthday[9]: this was a year of general rejoicing, for the King obtained from the Holy Roman Emperor a guarantee of the Hanoverian Succession and a scheme of collective security for Western Europe.

In 1737, Daniel Gough, proprietor of *The Rose* and its Gardens, decided to beautify them and make a charge for admission issuing metal tickets for the purpose[10]. 'Marybone Gardens' was advertised as a place of entertainment in 1738 where airs, overtures, and concerts were given by a band from the Opera: a covered concert-platform was built, called a 'garden-orchestra', and in it in 1740 an organ was erected by Richard Bridge (d. 1758)[11]. A Great-Room was designed and put up for balls and suppers in 1739-40, and when John Trusler[12] took over as proprietor of the establishment in the 1750s the place achieved considerable success, not least because Trusler was a cook and his daughter produced succulent almond cheese-cakes, delicious plum-and-seed-cakes, and other delicacies. Trusler was the uncle of John Sherratt (1718-88), entrepreneur and social reformer, and the two men went into partnership to run the *Marylebone Gardens*[13]: this

Plate 113: *Marylebone* or *Marybone Gardens*, 1755-61, showing the orchestra on the balcony *(right)* and a fashionably dressed Mob sitting among the trees. Note the trellis-work *(Collection JSC).*

probably occurred in the early 1750s but Sherratt had been bankrupted in 1746, and in 1754 he and Trusler filed jointly for bankruptcy as a result of financial difficulties with the Gardens. A 'Mr Beard' took over as proprietor in 1755, and Trusler was appointed manager in 1756, a position he held until 1763 (minus Sherratt, who had gone on to invest in a privateer [captured by the Spaniards in 1757], to reform mad-houses, and to create mayhem as Consul for Cartagena, Spain). Trusler appears to have died in *c.*1766, but his reign at Marylebone (though spoiled by the unfortunate association with his disputatious, belligerent, and reckless nephew) brought the praise of many, including Sir John Fielding (1721-80)[14], magistrate and reformer, who was a devotee of *Marylebone Garden*'s music, plum-cakes, and wine. From around 1740 the Gardens were open for public breakfasts in the Great-Room, and concerts began at noon. The musicians were no hacks, and included men of the stature of Thomas Augustine Arne (1710-78), the composer, his son, Michael (*c.*1741-86), and John Frederick Lampe (1702/3-51)[15], composer and bassoonist, 'Mr Ferrand' performed on the 'Pariton, an instrument never played in publick before' (this was actually the *Baryton*, or *Viola di Bordone*, or *Viola Paradon*, a bowed instrument with a body similar to that of a bass *Viola da Gamba* with six gut strings and sixteen or more wire strings close to the belly[16]). In 1747 Mary Ann Falkner (d. 1796/7)[17] made her *début* as principal female singer at the Gardens. She had sung Eurydice in Lampe's *Orpheus and Eurydice* at Covent Garden in 1745[18], and she established a firm reputation at *Marylebone Gardens* (where she sang until 1752), aided, no doubt, by her striking good looks. She performed many works by Arne[19], Willem De Fesch (1687-1761 – who directed the orchestra in the gardens 1748-9), and, of course, 'Mr. Handel'. She also sang Polly in Gay's *Beggar's Opera*, and seems to have enjoyed considerable success. She became the mistress of George Montagu Dunk (1716-71), 2nd Earl of Halifax from 1739, who established her at Hampton Court House adjoining Bushy Park, Middlesex[20].

There is a further Mozartian connection with the Gardens. Stefano Storace (d.1783), double-bass player, had married Elizabeth (*c*.1739-1821), daughter of John Trusler and sister of Dr John Trusler, the author[21]: the Storaces were the parents, therefore, of Stephen John Seymour Storace and his sister, Ann Selina (Nancy) Storace, friends of Mozart. The elder Storace, with the younger Trusler, made an adaptation of *La Serva Padrona* (The Servant Mistress) by the Neapolitan composer, Giovanni Battista Pergolesi (1710-36), first given in 1733: the Storace-Trusler *Burletta* was first performed at Marylebone in 1758 to considerable acclaim, and was often repeated there for years afterwards[22].

Hone relates a story of 'while Mary-le-bone gardens were flourishing, the enchanting music of Handel, and probably of Arne, was often heard from the orchestra there'. His correspondent, Norrisson Cavendish Scatcherd (1779-1853)[23], noted that when his grandfather and Händel were walking together in the Gardens, a new piece was 'struck up by the band'. Händel suggested they should sit and listen to the music and after some time the old parson said

> 'It is not worth listening to – It's very poor stuff'.
>
> Händel agreed, saying he thought so himself when he had written it[24].

This was probably 'Mr Fountaine'[25], who ran the fashionable Marylebone Manor House School.

Marylebone Gardens, then, seems to have enjoyed a fashionable reputation, and put on entertainments a cut above the sort of thing usual in certain other establishments mentioned earlier. To judge from the published views of the place, it seems to have been rather splendid, with buildings lit by tall arched windows, an orchestra playing on a balcony, and an Exquisite Mob strolling in the grounds (where there were plenty of trellised alcoves) *(Plate 113)*. Gentlemen were asked not to 'smoak' on the walks, ladies were assured they would not be 'incommoded' by firework-displays, and the latticed alcoves (a common feature of most public Gardens of the period) provided pleasant, private, secluded places for parties to take refreshments, chat, and laugh together. The Great-Room was occasionally used for masquerades and balls as well as concerts, and on the whole *Marylebone Gardens* was a place where decorum was observed, and could claim to host some of the largest and politest assemblies of the time, although Prince William Augustus (1721-65), Duke of Cumberland from 1726, is supposed to have behaved in a scandalous manner, if Trusler[26] is to be believed: this may reflect the Duke's unpopularity in certain quarters, even though he had been acclaimed as a national hero after Culloden in 1746, received the accolade of Händel's composition *See the Conquering Hero Comes* from *Judas Maccabaeus* (composed 1746) played at the Thanksgiving Service in St Paul's Cathedral for the victory over the Jacobites, and his admirers adopted the flower 'Sweet William' as his emblem. In the last years of his short life, however, his stock again rose, and he was once more held in high esteem[27].

Even *Marylebone Gardens* was not free from danger: the neighbourhood was by no means safe in the middle of the eighteenth century, for the ways to and from there lay through fields infested with footpads[28] and highwaymen. In the 1760s the proprietor of the Gardens offered rewards for the 'apprehension' of any highwayman found on the road to the Gardens, and a horse-guard had to be provided to patrol the way to and from the City. The audacious and famous Richard (Dick) Turpin (1705-39) once publicly kissed a lady related to old Dr Fountaine in the Gardens, advising her not to be alarmed, for she could boast that she had been kissed by the great Turpin, or so it has been claimed[29]. This story, however, is probably only an example of how a criminal metamorphoses into a mythical hero, thus achieving immortality in juvenile drama, and it is probably apocryphal.

Marylebone Gardens and adjoining premises, in 1763, were taken at an annual rent of £170 by Thomas Lowe (*c*.1719-83), the singer and author, who had made a name for himself as a tenor in the 1740s, singing works by Arne, Händel, and others. In 1750 he made his first appearance at *Marylebone Gardens*, with which establishment he was to remain loosely associated for the next quarter of a century. Lowe engaged numerous fine vocalists, including the young and beautiful Ann Catley (1745-89)[30], but, in spite of her mellifluous warbling, Miss Trusler's plum-cakes, the support of the elder Storace, and audience participation in glees and choruses, exceptionally wet Summer weather (and perhaps lax management) found Lowe ruined in 1767, and by a Deed early in 1768 he assigned all his receipts and profits arising from the *Gardens* to his creditors, who carried on the enterprise until Dr Samuel Arnold (1740-1802), the composer, took over in 1769, offering ambitious and substantial musical entertainments alongside refreshments and a variety of spectacles, including firework-displays. Arnold seems to have made something of a speciality of arranging and composing short *Burlettas* (miniature comic operas), of which his own *Don Quixote* was the last he gave at Marylebone in 1774. Under Arnold the drainage was improved so that the Gardens were less likely to become waterlogged, and in 1769 he organised a Benefit for his entire staff: in addition, the variety of musical entertainment was astonishing, and he managed to secure the services of many 'names', including François-Hippolyte Barthélémon (1741-1808 – violinist and composer, who had met the Mozarts in London in 1765), James Hook (1746-1827 – organist and composer, who also performed at the *White Conduit House*, Clerkenwell), Charles Bannister (1741-1804 – the bass singer, who specialised in sentimental songs), and many others. Thomas Chatterton (1752-70) wrote a *Burletta*, *The Revenge*, which he sold to the management of *Marylebone Gardens*: although not published until 1795, it may have been given at the *Gardens* in 1770, the year of Chatterton's death from overdoses of arsenic and laudanum[31], probably attempts to cure himself of the diseases he had contracted in the bawdy-house where he lodged (he claimed to have slept with his landlady[32] and her girls). Unfortunately, no *Burletta* called *The Revenge* appears in advertisements for the Gardens from 1770, even though the published version claimed Bannister sang Bacchus. However, the published *Burletta* clearly states it was 'acted at Marybone Gardens, MDCCLXX', and we know that Bannister, Frederick Charles Reinhold (1741-1815 – who sang Jupiter), and Mrs Thompson (1736-74 – known also as Jane Poitier – who sang Juno) were all active at Marylebone in 1770-3. Mrs Thompson, incidentally, was Bannister's mistress, and was referred to as 'the liveliest baggage on the modern stage'[33]. She created the parts of Dorcas in Arne's *Thomas and Sally* (1760) and Fanny in *The Maid of the Mill* (1765): her Lucy in *The Beggar's Opera* was celebrated.

For a couple of years, from 1772 to 1774, spectacular displays of fireworks by the pyrotechnician Giovanni Battista Torré (*fl.*1753-76) drew the crowds. Torré's exhibitions were more than mere firework-shows: they were performances around a narrative (often taken from Classical Mythology), so his entertainments drew on stage-effects as well as on conventional firework-shows[34]. Local residents found Torré's displays a nuisance, and Arnold was summoned before the magistrates: having equipped himself with a licence from the Board of Ordnance, however, he was permitted to continue with these shows. Arnold was certainly no slouch when it came to obtaining performers for the *Gardens*, and Bannister (who seems to have been of a humorous disposition) gave imitations not only of celebrated singers, but of the French, German, and Italian modes of singing. Compositions by Hook, Storace, Arne, and others were performed, and even the boys from the choir of St Paul's Cathedral were roped in to sing choruses. During one of Torré's Classical firework-displays an orchestra played martial music under Hook's baton, and in 1773 Händel's charming masque or serenata, *Acis and Galatea*[35], was given.

Nevertheless, by 1774 the *Marylebone Gardens* star seemed to be growing more dim, and attempts were made to revive fortunes by means of the *Fête Champêtre*[36], but the Publick Prints were unimpressed, castigating the management for charging extra for entertainments enlivened only by a few extra lamps and some sad festoons. The public were not amused either, and vented its displeasure. Dr Johnson was no exception, his curiosity having been excited by the praises bestowed

> 'on the celebrated Torré's fireworks at Marybone Gardens, he desired Mr Steevens[37] to accompany him thither. The evening had proved showery: and soon after the few people present were assembled, public notice was given, that the conductors to the wheels, sun, stars, etc., were so thoroughly water-soaked,

> that it was impossible any part of the exhibition should be made. "This is mere excuse", says the Doctor, "to save their crackers for a more profitable company. Let us but hold up our sticks, and threaten to break those coloured lamps that surround the orchestra, and we shall soon have our wishes gratified. The core of the fireworks cannot be injured; let the different pieces be touched in their respective centres, and they will do their offices as well as ever." Some young men who overheard him, immediately began the violence he had recommended, and an attempt was speedily made to fire some of the wheels which appeared to have received the smallest damage; but to little purpose were they lighted, for most of them completely failed. The author of *The Rambler*, however, may be considered on this occasion as the ringleader of a successful riot, though not as a skilful pyrotechnist'[38].

The spectacle of the Sage of Lichfield inciting uproar must have been extraordinary, a reminder, perhaps, that life in Georgian England was not all genteel behaviour and elegance. Nevertheless, musical performances continued every week-day evening in 1774, the artists including Reinhold, 'Miss Wewitzer'[39], Charles Clementine Dubellamy (d. 1793 – the tenor), and John Abraham Fisher (1744-1806 – violinist and composer). The last married (1784) Nancy Storace, then *prima buffa* at the *Burgtheater*, Vienna, but was ordered to leave the city by Kaiser Joseph II[40] because of his scandalous ill-treatment of his wife.

The *Gardens* were going through a bad patch, however, and it appears that in the 1770s the place had become seedy. Hardly anybody went there any more; table-cloths were dirty; the detritus from Signor Torré's fireworks lay uncollected, and the few shapeless trees and two or three grubby gravel paths were unenticing. Tea-drinkers had deserted the *Gardens*, and all in all things were in steep decline[41]. Clearly something had to be done to revive fortunes[42].

MARYLEBONE SPA

It appears that in 1773 a Mineral Spring was discovered in the Gardens, and the proprietors decided to call their establishment *Marybone Spa* in 1774 in order to try to recoup losses. Sunderland suggested the water was of the chalybeate type, said to be useful for 'indigestion, and for nervous, scorbutic or other disorders'[43]. The Spa was opened from six in the morning for the drinking of the waters, and tea, coffee, and other refreshments were available[44]. Claims for the water included the strengthening of the stomach and the promotion of good appetite and digestion[45].

Thus the 'medicinal waters' ploy, unusually, was introduced *very* late in the life of *Marylebone Gardens*, unlike the cases of places like *Islington Spa* or *Sadler's Wells*. Lectures of an improving and educational nature (on Shakespeare) were introduced, delivered by William Kenrick (1729/30-79), and firework-displays were again given. In 1775 was presented *The Modern Magic Lanthorn* in three parts, 'being an attempt at a sketch of the Times in a variety of Caricatures, accompanied with a whimsical and satirical Dissertation on each Character'[46] by Robert Baddeley (1733-94), and George Saville Carey (1743-1807) gave his *Lecture on Mimicry* which was subsequently published[47]. Carey is of some interest in the Spas context, as he was the author of a volume on the watering-places of England[48].

There was a conjurer, and various other 'turns' were introduced to try to bring in custom. Torré's *Forge of Vulcan* was revived, a pyrotechnical display (by Caillot) at the end of which a curtain rose to reveal Vulcan and the Cyclops at the Forge behind Mount Etna: Venus and Cupid entered, the Mount erupted, and 'lava' poured down. In contrast, a Parisian scene was contrived, with the boxes in front of the ballroom converted into shops[49], a curious idea, but one that can be better understood when it is realised that most Londoners stayed put, and that places like Paris were almost mythical to them.

The whole business of the Spa does not seem to have improved the fortunes of *Marylebone Gardens*, which, in any case, in the words of Henry Charles William Angelo (1756-1835)[50], was a place more 'adapted to the gentry than to the *haut ton*'[51]: in other words, the establishment was too genteel, and fashion had passed it by. 'After existing for upwards of a century, and undergoing many vicissitudes, the gardens were closed about the year 1778[52], and the site was soon afterwards turned to building purposes'[53]. This was the reason why the Gardens closed: as London expanded, land became far too valuable to remain a Pleasure-Garden, with Well or no Well, especially as the history of the place shows it was by no means always a successful business, and several individuals lost a great deal of money trying to run it. The Spa was really an afterthought, an attempt to give new life to something that was moribund, and could not withstand the demands for development. In any case, *Marybone Gardens* was always quite small, and even by 1773 it was clear that it was becoming a part of London as new buildings were going up in great numbers in the vicinity[54]. Sunderland was of the opinion that *Marybone Spa* was one of the 'spurious' variety, and it does seem he was correct in that diagnosis. The actual site of the Well was supposed to be in the centre of a stable at the back of what in 1915 was No. 28 Weymouth Street[55].

From 1778, then, new streets were formed, and houses began to rise. A few trees that once graced the Gardens still stood at the beginning of the nineteenth century: these were at the north end of Harley Street[56]. The Orchestra disappeared beneath Devonshire Place: Smith identified No. 17 in that street as being precisely over the site[57]. In 1794 a small part of the Gardens survived, and an attempt was made to court public favour as a place of recreation, without a successful financial outcome[58]. The *Rose of Normandy* (complete with its skittle-alley) was still going until 1848-50, when it was rebuilt: this Tavern was taken by Samuel Vagg (1825-65), who had made a reputation as an 'Irish' singer, using the name of 'Sam Collins', performing such immortal works as *The Limerick Races, The Rocky Road to Dublin,* and other songs, dressed in his 'Oirish' costume complete with *shillelagh*. It is doubtful if he ever set foot in Ireland. Vagg converted the concert-room in the Tavern to a Music-Hall, and ran it until 1861, when he moved to *Collins's Music Hall*, Islington. The *Marylebone Music-Hall,* with public-bar, was the Victorian successor to the once-celebrated *Marylebone Gardens*.

The Wroths[59] noted that in 1887 the architect Thomas Harris (1829/30-1900) prepared an

Plate 114: Etching (*c.*1780) of *The Tea Gardens North side of Bayswater Road* by Paul Sandby, who lived near by at the time *(LMA SC/GL/NOR/TEA & MUSIC Vol. 9. p.15).*

'ingenious reproduction... of the latticed alcoves, lamp-hung trees, &c., of the old Marylebone Gardens', and mention a pamphlet entitled *A Booke of ye olde Marybone Gardens*. Harris's book[60] cited in the Select Bibliography, and Mollie Sands's[61] excellent study will satisfy the student of these lost Gardens, however, although *A Booke...* has eluded the present writer. There is much about *Marylebone Gardens*, however, to keep one entranced for many a day: there are at least 400 volumes of music that can be specifically identified with the Gardens, and there are probably many more publications in which a connection is not spelled out. What is clear, however, is that the *Marybone Gardens* attracted many eighteenth-century Persons of Quality, so must have had something rather special[62].

THE BAYSWATER TEA-GARDENS

The success (for a time) of *Bagnigge Wells* (see Chapter V) prompted the transfer of the name to another establishment, the *Bayswater Tea-Garden* (or *-Gardens*), situated, as previously observed, 'in a region once noted for its springs and salubrious air'[63], also called (in deference to, or perhaps, more likely, opportunistically) *The New Bagnigge Wells*. It was also, confusingly, named the *Flora Tea-Gardens*, and it was by this name that it was known when shown in a watercolour of *c*.1840 *(Plate 115)*. The place was situated in rural surroundings, captured in a drawing by Paul Sandby (1731-1809) entitled *The Tea Gardens North side Bayswater Road*: it shows the Gardens to the rear of the unpretentious building depicted in *Plate 115*, and is really like the garden of many an English country pub used to be before the advent of horrors such as 'Bouncy Castles' and other pollutants. Folding tables, benches, and sparse planting in a Garden by a little stream conjure up simple pleasures *(Plate 114)*. It was much frequented by the inhabitants of the Oxford Road (as it then was), but its tone does not appear to have been elevated. It appears to have had ranges of alcoves, like those of *Bagnigge Wells*, and views published in 1796 give some flavour of what it was like *(Plate 116)*[64].

The *New Bagnigge Wells* was a spurious[65] Spa, laid out in the Physic Garden of the physician, natural philosopher, actor, and playwright Sir John Hill (1714-75): however, the Garden contained several Springs of water lying close to the surface, and the place remained open until 1854 when housing developments at Lancaster Gate encroached. At that time it was known as the *Victoria Tea-Gardens*. During the 1830s it was associated with experiments using balloons, but the waters do not appear to have been used to attract custom, although Hill used them in the preparation of some of his nostrums, including 'Water Dock Essence' and 'Balm of Honey'[66]. Charles Churchill (1731-60) satirised Hill as a *Proteus* in *The Rosciad*:

> 'For who, like him, his various pow'rs could call
> Into so many shapes, and shine in all?
> Who could so nobly grace the motley list,
> Actor, Inspector, Doctor, Botanist?'[67]

He was far more interesting than many of his contemporaries thought, and was knighted by Gustavus III of Sweden (reigned 1771-92) in 1774 for his pioneering works on botany[68]. David Garrick (1717-79) remarked of him that

> 'For Physick and Farces, his Equal there scarce is,
> His Farces are Physick, and his Physick a Farce is'[69].

Posterity, however, suggests that Hill was rather better than that.

The presence of so many Springs was a characteristic of Bayswater, and indeed the Westbourne river was named Bayswater Brook. Sunderland observed that Bayswater had 'plenty of springs', and there existed for some time a celebrated conduit called the 'Bayswater' or 'Roundhead' (from its circular shape with conical roof) situated about half-way between the Parish Church at Paddington and the gardens of Sir John Hill *(Plate 117)*.

The *New Bagnigge Wells* was more celebrated for its tea and cakes than for any 'medicinal' qualities in its waters. Hill's reputation as a herbalist probably helped to ensure that the place remained, in essence, a Tea-Garden, perhaps slightly more elevated than was the *London Spaw*, but probably a lot less fun. Vice, then and now, has its undoubted attractions.

Plate 115: View of the *Flora Tea-Gardens*, also known as *The Bayswater Tea-Gardens*, of *c*.1840, by an anonymous artist *(LMA SC/GL/WAK/P1-S2/Ce19089/cat.no.p5434683).*

IN THE VICINITY OF MARYLEBONE GARDENS

To the east of *Marylebone Gardens*, north of the New (now Euston) Road[70], at the junction with Hampstead Road (immediately north of the end of Tottenham Court Road) was the *Adam and Eve Tea-Gardens*, not to be confused with the establishment of the same name at St Pancras. There had been a Tavern on the site for some time, and even in the seventeenth century, Londoners in festive mood would flock to the 'City out-leaps' for cakes, cream, and ale[71]. The *Adam and Eve* is identified as at 'Tottenham Court', and there are references to female servants being fined for drinking on the Sabbath Day[72]. William Wycherley (1641-1716) referred to visits to certain Gardens, including the *Mulberry Garden* and 'Totnam Court', in his *Gentleman Dancing-Master* (1671).

Early in the eighteenth century the *Adam and Eve* had a Long-Room furnished with an organ, and its spacious Gardens possessed the usual arbours set among fruit-trees. Facilities for skittles and Dutch-pins were provided, and in the forecourt, sheltered by mature trees, were tables with benches for those who wished to take refreshments out-of-doors. There was a pond stocked with goldfish, and in the Gardens could be seen a heron, a monkey, some parrots, and sundry wild fowl[73]. In addition, there was a 'strange and wonderful fruit growing' there 'called a Calabath, which is five feet and a half round, where any person may see the same gratis'[74].

A famous, if unexpected, visitor to the Tavern Gardens was the balloonist, Vincenzo Lunardi (1759-1806), whose large balloon landed unintentionally there in 1785[75]. However, the establishment became hemmed in with buildings, even though the Gardens remained spacious, and were patronised by many holiday-makers, although some sources hint at a less than respectable *clientèle*, including highwaymen, footpads, and 'low women'[76]. Others, however, paint an agreeable picture of the Tea-Gardens with middle-class customers, and organ-recitals in the upstairs room where punch, tea, and wine

Plate 116: The *New Bagnigge Wells,* otherwise known as *The Bayswater Tea-Gardens,* shown in illustrations entitled *View of the Tea Gardens at Bayswater*. At the bottom is a decidedly middling group of persons enjoying a meal, and above is a waiter jesting with another while scalding the leg of a customer with a hot drink: a range of alcoves may be seen behind. Drawings by George Moutard Woodward (*c*.1760-1809) engraved by Isaac Cruikshank (1764-1811 – the father of the more famous George Cruikshank [1792-1878] and published [1796] Allen & West of 15 Paternoster Row) *(LMA SC/GL/NOR/TEA & MUSIC Vol.9 p.15).*

were served[77]. Some time shortly before 1811 the organ was removed, the Gardens partly sold off for building, and the skittle-grounds were destroyed.

What makes the *Adam and Eve* more interesting in the context of the present study is that near by, in the New Road, was a Cold Bath, in existence certainly by 1785, for the use of ladies and gentlemen. It was supplied with plentiful water from a Spring, and was set in a pleasant Garden. The waters were supposed to benefit those suffering from nervous disorders and 'dejected' spirits, sometimes referred to as 'the Vapours'.

Hone described the *Adam and Eve* as

> 'now denominated a coffee-house, and that part which has been built of late years, and fronts the Paddington New road, with the sign-board at the top corner, is used for tavern purposes, and connects with the older part of the building; the entrance to which is through the gateway with the lamp over it, in the Hampstead road[78].'

He also could recollect when it was a 'house standing alone, with spacious gardens in the rear and at the sides'[79]. The illustration Hone provided shows quite a humble establishment, and from it it is obvious that the Gardens no longer existed, and the days when 'sullibubs' might be taken, with 'cakes and creame' among the milkmaids,

Plate 117: *View of the Conduit at Bayswater* (1796), by Edward Dayes (1763-1804), engraved by Sparrow, and published by John Stockdale (*c*.1749-1814) in Hunter (1811) *(LMA SC/GL/PR/P1-P1/EDG/Ce16957/ cat.no.p544499x).*

Plate 118: The *Adam and Eve* by William Henry Prior *(From Thornbury & Walford iv [1879-85] 475: Collection JSC).*

were well and truly over[80]. William Henry Prior produced another version of this illustration for Thornbury & Walford *(Plate 118)* which was captioned '1750', which must be incorrect, for we are looking at a building near the end of its life.

Due north of *Marylebone Gardens* were two humbler places of entertainment, long gone, but standing in grounds that are now part of Regent's Park: these were the *Queen's Head and Artichoke* and the *Jew's Harp*. The former was in Marylebone Park, some hundred yards north of the New (now Marylebone) Road. Its strange name probably derives from the image of Queen Elizabeth I and the possibility that the house was once the dwelling of one of her gardeners. The familiar shady bowers, where cakes, cream, and tea could be enjoyed, were provided in the Gardens, and there were facilities for skittles and bumble-puppy (an ancient game resembling bagatelle but played out-of-doors with marbles or 'dumps'[81] of lead, also called 'nine-holes'). No exploitation of the Well on the site appears to have taken place[82].

The latter lay to the north-west of the former, with fields between them. It was frequented by Arthur Onslow (1691-1768), Speaker of the House of Commons (and a 'man of rare integrity in an age of corruption'[83]) who used to go there for a quiet pipe and glass (as one used to do before such combined pleasures were forbidden). By the 1770s it had acquired the obligatory 'bowery tea-gardens'[84], skittle-grounds, a trap-ball ground, and even a tennis-court. There was a room on the first floor, approached by an external stair, where large groups could dine or dances could be held. A semicircular enclosure filled with alcoves or 'boxes' provided a secluded space where tea and ale could be consumed. An innovation was the 'guard' provided by painted figures of soldiers[85].

Such establishments were no doubt very pleasant, but the walk home from them was often fraught with danger, as in 1808, when someone who had been in the *Jew's Harp* to enjoy the skittles (and no doubt a drink or two) was robbed and murdered in the Marylebone Fields[86].

Then, due west of the *Marylebone Gardens*, on the south side of the Marylebone Road, not far from Edgware Road, was the famous public-house, the *Yorkshire Stingo*[87], which had extensive Tea-Gardens and a bowling-green. For the first four decades of the nineteenth century the Gardens were patronised by the middle classes, notably on Sundays when admission was by means of a sixpenny ticket which entitled the holder to refreshments, a system which excluded the roughs and lower orders, who otherwise would walk about and not spend any money 'because they had no money to spend'[88]. This establishment also had its Apollo, also called Royal Apollo, Saloon in which concerts and *Burlettas* were performed. Fireworks, balloon ascents, and other diversions were provided in the grounds. The Tea-Gardens and bowling-green were closed around 1848 and the site built over.

The *Yorkshire Stingo*'s bowling-green was on the site chosen for the exhibition of the iron bridge designed by Thomas Paine (1737-1809) and cast by Walker Brothers of Rotherham: in 1790 it was erected and seen by many, but it did not receive backing from those who attended, so the Walkers repossessed it and took it back to Rotherham where it was broken up in 1791[89].

AFTERWORD

All the groups of Spas, Wells, Pleasure-Gardens, Taverns, and so on previously mentioned seem to have been influenced by each other to a greater or lesser degree. Each group had connections with water, however tenuous, but some groups, like

Plate 119: View of Chelsea Bridge in 1761 drawn by Zachariah Boreman (1738-1810), engraved by J. Lodge, and published by Robert Sayer and John Bennett. On the left is *Jenny's Whim* in its rural setting *(Collection JSC).*

the Clerkenwell and Hampstead groups, were especially the result of the fashion for taking the waters. At Marylebone, the Spa element was almost an afterthought, a last throw to try to lift a failing concern from the doldrums.

There is another group, loosely termed 'Chelsea', which included the spectacular Rotunda at Ranelagh (by William Jones (d. 1757), a truly remarkable building by any standards, but none of the establishments (*Ranelagh House and Gardens*, the *Star and Garter*, *Strombolo House*, *Jenny's Whim*[90] *(Plate 119)*, and *Cromwell's Gardens* [the last sited some distance to the west, south of what is now the Cromwell Road]) in that group had any connection with pretensions to be Spas or Wells. And although Ranelagh had an amazing building, kitted out with an organ, orchestra, and central element containing the chimney *(Plate 120)*, was patronised by the Great and Good, and held masquerades, routs, balls, and all manner of entertainments (including the inevitable fireworks), the indifferent tea, bread, and butter had limited charms, and visitors found the place terribly dull. Terms such as *insipid*, *ennui*, and *mauvaise musique* were bandied about: the splendid walks, Temple, canal with Chinese House *(Plate 121)*, and illuminations did little to alleviate the tedium, but there is no denying the innovative architectural importance of the huge Rotunda, the grandest of all *fabriques* in the Pleasure-Gardens of eighteenth-century London[91].

Later still, the *Cremorne Gardens*[92] enjoyed a brief vogue. In existence *c.*1843-77, these Gardens were laid out on the site of the suburban residence and estate of Thomas Dawson (1725-1813 – 1st Viscount [from 1785] Cremorne), to the west of old Battersea Bridge on the north side of the river, west of Cheyne Walk and south of King's Road. The usual illuminations, ornamental buildings, grottoes, theatre, concert-room, dining-hall, and other facilities were provided, and there occurred dancing, balloon ascents (with one fatality), and fireworks. In 1859 the paintings in the 'supper-boxes' at Vauxhall were purchased and set up in the dining-hall at *Cremorne Gardens*. A large Tavern provided drink, food, and other delights. The dancing-platform in *Cremorne Gardens* was a late and exotic example of *Chinoiserie*, and an elegant one at that: it was the subject of a pretty painting (1864) by the

Plate 120: Interior of the Rotunda at *Ranelagh Gardens*, 1754. Note the organ on the right, the central fire and chimney, and the stupendous size of the place. Oil on canvas by Giovanni Antonio Canal (Canaletto) (1697-1768). From a reproduction in the *Burlington Magazine*, January 1922 *(Collection HP)*.

Plate 121: The Chinese House, Canal, Rotunda, avenues of trees, and the 'Company in Masquerade' at *Ranelagh Gardens*, produced by Bowles *(Collection JSC)*.

Plate 122: The Dancing-Platform at *Cremorne Gardens*. Painting by Phoebus Levin, signed and dated 1864, showing the late flowering of *Chinoiserie (MoL/001658)*.

German-born artist, Phoebus Levin, who worked in London 1855-78[93] *(Plate 122)*.

Johann Wilhelm von Archenholz (1743-1812), Prussian historian and soldier, who lived in England 1769-1779, remarked that the English, especially Londoners, took great delight in Public Gardens near the metropolis where they assembled to drink tea together in the open air. He noted that the number of such Gardens in the neighbourhood of the capital was amazing, and the order, regularity, neatness, and even elegance of them was truly admirable. He also perceived that they were rarely visited by people of fashion, but that the middle and lower classes went there often, and seemed delighted with the music of an organ which usually graced an adjoining building. Such a description could have been applied to numerous establishments mentioned above[94], all of which have vanished, remembered only in descriptions, images, and fading ephemera.

Chapter VIII References: Marylebone, Bayswater, and Chelsea

1 Smith (1861) 39. *See* also Sands (1987).

2 Buckingham **ii** (1726) 214.

3 Officer of the English Royal Household (abolished under George III): his duties involved regulating all matters connected with gaming within the precincts of the Court, to provide cards, dice, etc., and to settle disputes arising from play. In the plural it meant loaded dice.

4 Montagu (1861) *The Town Eclogues: Friday: The Bassette-Table:* 'Cardelia'. This was first published in 1716 as *Court Poems* 'for J. Roberts'. But for Edmund Curll's involvement *see* Baines & Rogers (2007) and Straus (1927). *The Bassette-Table* has been attributed (erroneously) to Pope.

5 The entry on 'Marylebone Gardens' in *Grove* is a useful summary (*see* Grove **v** [1966] 605-6). The

entry in the *Gentleman's Magazine* is given in Grove and in Wroth & Wroth (1896) 110 as Volume **lxxxiii** 524, and is entitled *The Garden at Marylebone Park* (from *Memorandums* by Samuel Sainthill, 1659). I am indebted to Lucas Elkin of the University Library, Cambridge, for this.

6 Pepys **iii** (1953) 223 (7 May 1668).

7 It is mentioned in *The London Gazette* (11 January 1692), and the Tavern seems to have been favoured by the well-to-do-at that time.

8 He was created Marshal of France in 1703. His hurried departure from England in 1701 was because, on the death of the exiled James II & VII in that year, Louis XIV recognised his son as King of England (as James III & VIII), thereby provoking anti-Jacobite opinion.

9 George I (reigned 1714-27).

10 For details see Wilkinson **ii** (1819-25) *passim*, but *see* Pl. No. 19.

11 Grove **v** (1966) 605.

12 The father of the clergyman, John Trusler (1735-1820), author of *The London Advertiser and Guide* (*see* Trusler [1786]).

13 *ODNB* **l** (2004) 332-3.

14 Half-brother of the novelists Henry (1707-54) and Sarah (1710-68) Fielding.

15 Original names Johann Friedrich, a native probably of Braunschweig.

16 Franz Josef Haydn (1732-1809) wrote well over 170 Sonatas for this instrument.

17 Niece of the Dublin publisher, George Faulkner (*c*.1703-75), she was also called Anna Maria Falkner.

18 *General Advertiser* (23 November 1745).

19 *See* Arne (1751). *See* also Grove (1966) *passim*.

20 *ODNB* **xviii** (2004) 984-5.

21 *See* Trusler (1786).

22 Grove **v** (1966) 606.

23 Scatcherd, the Yorkshire antiquary, was the son of Frances Fountaine, one of the schoolmaster's daughters. He was a regular contributor to Hone's publications.

24 Hone (23 April 1832) 501.

25 Sometimes given as 'Fountayne'.

26 Trusler (1806) 57.

27 Trusler apparently regretted publication of his rambling 1806 *Memoir* and attempted to destroy all the copies he could find: it is doubtful, therefore, if his work, although entertaining, is reliable as history. For the Duke *see* *ODNB* **lix** (2004) 105-113.

28 Two footpads who had robbed the waiters of *Marylebone Gardens* were hanged at Tyburn on 15 June 1763.

29 Wroth & Wroth (1896) 100-101.

30 Mistress of Sir Francis Blake Delaval (1727-71), the famously dissolute Baronet, owner of Vanbrugh's masterpiece, Seaton Delaval Hall, Northumberland. *See* also Grove **v** (1966) 606.

31 It has been suggested (*ODNB* **xi** [2004] 240) that his death was caused by unwisely mixing the medicines he was taking to cure himself of venereal disease with 'recreational' drugs (opium in the form of laudanum).

32 Inappropriately called 'Mrs Angell'.

33 Sadie (*Ed.*) **iii** (2002) 1042.

34 *ODNB* **lv** (2004) 50-51. For fireworks *see* Brock (1922, 1949), and Dixon (1987).

35 First performed at Cannons, Summer 1718.

36 A rustic entertainment or garden-party.

37 George Steevens (1736-1800).

38 Memoir by Steevens in Boswell **iii** (1924) 386-7. For pyrotechnics *see* Brock (1922, 1949); Dixon (1987).

39 Probably Sarah Wewitzer (1756-1820) or perhaps her elder sister.

40 Reigned as Holy Roman Emperor from 1765 with his mother, Maria Theresia, and as sole Emperor 1780-90.

41 Anonymous (*c*.1776).

42 *See* Smith (1861) for much information about the Gardens.

43 Sunderland (1915) 101-2.

44 Foorde (1910) 167.

45 Wroth & Wroth (1896) 108.

46 *Morning Chronicle* and *London Advertiser* (29 May 1775).

47 London: J. Bew 1776. Carey was the grandfather of the celebrated actor Edmund Kean (1787-1833), whose mother, Ann Carey (d. 1833), divided her time between acting and prostitution.

48 Carey (1799).

49 *See* Rogers (1896) 30 for an impression of this.

50 *See* Angelo (1904) for fascinating glimpses into a world long gone.

51 High fashion.

52 They actually closed on 23 September 1776.

53 Thornbury & Walford **iv** (1879-85) 436.

54 *See* Noorthouck (1773) for interesting observations.

55 Sunderland (1915) 100-3 and 161.

56 Malcolm (1802-7) is informative on changes.

57 Smith **i** (1828) Ch. II.

58 Sunderland (1915) 102.

59 Wroth & Wroth (1896) 109-10 note 2.

60 Harris (1887).

61 Sands (1987).

62 For further information *see* Andrews (*Ed.*) (1899); Angelo (1904); Boulton **i** (1901) 56, 58-60, 78; Grove **v** (1966) 605-6; Harris (1887); Ledger (*Ed.*) (1869) 32 ff.; Margetson (1963, 1964, 1965); Sands (1987); Scott (1948); Smith (1828, 1861); Thornbury & Walford **iv** (1879-85) 431 ff.; Timbs (1865); Timbs (1867) 563-4;Wroth & Wroth (1896) 93-110.

63 Wroth & Wroth (1896) 117. *See* also Pasmore (1988) *passim*.

64 Woodward (1796) 18. *See* also Pasmore (1988).

65 Sunderland (1915) 103-4.

66 *See* Ledger (*Ed.*) (1871); Thornbury & Walford **v** (1879-85) 183, 185, 188; Wheatley (1891) *passim*; and Wroth & Wroth (1896) 117-9 on Bayswater and Lancaster Gate.

67 Churchill (1769) *The Rosciad* 69.

68 *ODNB* **xxvii** (2004) 144-7. Gustavus III's assassination in 1792 inspired *Un Ballo in Maschera* (1859), the Opera by Giuseppe Verdi (1813-1901).

69 Wilson & Kahrl (*Eds.*) **i** (1963) 299.

70 Properly 'The New Road to Paddington'.

71 *See*, for example, Brome (1658) in *The New Acad-*

emy, and Wither (1628).

72 *See* Miller (1874) 161, for example, and the detailed records in Parton (1822) for 1644. *See* also Cunningham (1850) under *Tottenham Court Road*.

73 Wroth & Wroth (1896) 78.

74 Thornbury & Walford **v** (1879-85) 304: 'Calabath' is probably *Calabash*.

75 *Morning Herald and Daily Advertiser* (14 May 1785).

76 *See* Wilkinson (1819-25) *passim*.

77 Feltham (1802) 370.

78 Hone (1832) 47.

79 *Ibid*.

80 *See* also Brayley **ii** (1829) 165; Hone **i** (1832) 317; Larwood & Hotten (1868) 257-8; Miller (1874) 161; Thornbury & Walford **iv** (1879-85) 477 and **v** 303 ff.

81 Roughly-cast leaden counter.

82 *See* Clinch (1890) 40, 45; *Gentleman's Magazine* **lxxxix**/2 (1819) 401 (article by John Bowyer Nichols); Hone (1832) 318; Larwood & Hotten **v** (1868) 311-12; Smith (1861); Thornbury & Walford v (1879-85) 255; Wheatley (1891).

83 *ODNB* **xli** (2004) 874.

84 Hone (1832) 318.

85 Wroth & Wroth (1896) 113.

86 Chambers **ii** (1862-4) 236; Clinch (1890) 48: Feltham (1802) 370; Miller (1874) 238; Thornbury & Walford **v** (1879-85) 255.

87 'Stingo' was strong ale or beer, often associated with Yorkshire and, sometimes, with Shropshire. 'Tea-gardens and stingo-houses' were referred to in Benjamin Disraeli's *Lothair* (1870) xxvii.

88 Thornbury & Walford **iv** (1879-85) 410.

89 *ODNB* **xlii** (2004) 404. *See* also Wheatley (1891) on the *Yorkshire Stingo* and *Newcomen Society Transactions* **lix** (1987-8).

90 *Jenny's Whim*, however, at Pimlico, near Ebury Bridge, was a Tavern and Pleasure-Garden popular in the eighteenth-century. It was possessed of the usual alcoves, bowers, bowling-greens, flower-beds, and so on, but also had a ducking-pond, a cock-pit, a large fish-pond, and a grotto. The Gardens had jokey mechanical devices triggered when a hidden spring was trodden upon, and mermaids and various monstrous fish rose from the ponds at intervals. The place remained as a Tea-Garden for a time but by the French Wars had become a mere public-house. It is shown in a view of Chelsea Bridge of 1761 printed for Sayer & Bennett *(Plate 119)*.

91 De Bellaigue (1984); Chancellor (1931): Jeffery (1906); Sands (1946); Worsley (1986).

92 Croft-Murray (1974); Wroth (1907).

93 Maas (1988) 188. The painting is now in the London Museum.

94 Archenholz (1789) *passim*. This work is fascinating, providing many insights.

CHAPTER IX

OTHER SPAS AND WELLS NORTH OF THE THAMES

Introduction; Acton Wells; Powis Wells; Kensington Wells and other Springs in the Vicinity; Hoxton Wells; Hackney Wells; Tottenham Wells; Muswell; Highgate; Country Wells North, North-East, and East of London; Spring Gardens North of the Thames; Afterword

'You must not pump spring-water unawares
Upon a gracious public full of nerves'.
ELIZABETH BARRETT BROWNING (1806-61):
Aurora Leigh (London: Chapman & Hall 1857) **iii** l.72.

INTRODUCTION

This Chapter will mention the Spas and Wells north of the Thames which cannot be treated as part of a group. They are mostly scattered and isolated, and have at least some claim to be treated as falling into the balneary category. Some were tiny, almost insignificant; some had the familiar appendages of Gardens, Long-Rooms, and so on; and others were really quite impressive establishments. We will begin in the west.

ACTON WELLS

Five miles west of Marble Arch and half a mile north of the Uxbridge Road, was *Acton Wells*, East Acton, a Spa which became fashionable in the reign of Queen Anne. It was a real Spa, attracting those in search of 'cures': the waters were *cathartic* (i.e. cleansing, purifying, purging) in action and said to contain *Glauber Salts* (or sodium sulphate), first artificially made in 1656 by Johann Rudolph Glauber (1604-68), a German chemist, although the term was qualified by 'calcareous', meaning with the nature of carbonate of lime containing calcium. The waters were supposed to be almost as strong as those of *Cheltenham Spa* (again producing water containing sodium sulphate)[1]. *Acton Wells* was situated in the Garden of Acton House, and there were three Springs producing plentiful supplies of waters. From just after 1706 these waters attracted considerable numbers of visitors, and some took rooms in the vicinity during the Season[2]. There do not appear to have been many other amusements associated with the establishment, which, in the words of Sunderland[3], was a 'steady, respectable spa', although 'in the days' when it was fashionable there were race-meetings at Acton (which inevitably meant wagers, the arrival of pickpockets and others with an eye to the main chance, and probably the usual collection of thieves keen to relieve punters of any winnings). The *Acton Wells* waters remained high in reputation until the end of the century. Apparently subscriptions were half a guinea per season, or a guinea for a family for the Season's 'potations', and water was sold in cases at three pence a quart at the Spring as well as by agents in London itself.

Sunderland's claims for respectability were not entirely borne out by James Norris Brewer (*fl.* 1799-1830) in the volume[4] for which he was responsible in the collaboration with Edward Wedlake Brayley (1773-1854) and Joseph Nightingale (1775-1824). 'Acton', he informs us, 'had its share in the day of fashion. An assembly-room was built, and for a few years East Acton and Friar's Place, a small adjacent hamlet, were thronged with valetudinarian and idle inmates, allured by the hope of remedy or tempted by the love of dissipation'[5]. Brewer, writing in 1815, claimed that both these classes had long 'abandoned the spot; and the assembly-room' *(Plate 123)* had for many years 'been converted into a private dwelling' (actually a boarding-school). The military surgeon and writer on medical matters, John Macpherson (1817-90) claimed that Acton waters were popular from around 1730 until 1790, and that horse-races (as noted above) were run for the amusement of the company[6].

The attractions of the *Wells* caused many houses to be erected around Friar's (or Prior's) Place, complete with pleasant gardens[7]. The Spa was actually at Old Oak Common: few travelling by train on what was the old Great Western, can be aware they are passing over one of the fashionable Georgian resorts[8]. Unlike many other Spas, Wells, and Pleasure-Gardens of the period, however, *Acton Wells* seems to have escaped censure in the many satires, squibs, and comedies of the time. On the other hand, serious writers on Mineral-Waters, such as Benjamin Allen (1663-1738)[9], Robert Boyle (1627-91)[10], and August Wilhelm von Hofmann (1818-92)[11], examined the whole chemical analyses of Mineral-Waters, and certainly knew of the reputations of places such as *Acton Wells*, which is shown on the celebrated map of London (1746) by John Rocque (*c*.1704-62). John Bowack (*fl*.1705-37) mentions the famous Mineral-Springs at East Acton[12].

Those (usually ephemeral) pieces of information, advertisements, occasionally reveal

Plate 123: The Assembly-Room at *Acton Wells* in 1795 *(LMA SC/GL/LYS/002/001/Ce33519/cat.no.k1271959).*

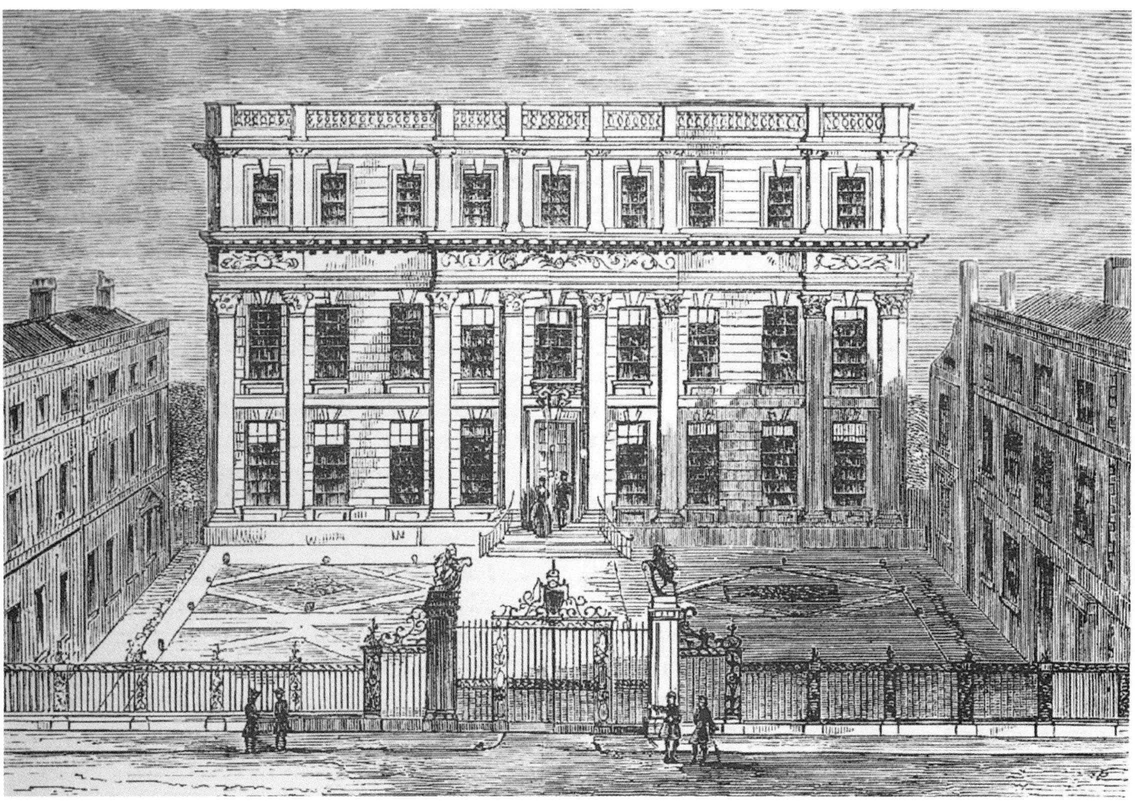

Plate 124: *Powis House*, as rebuilt after the fire *(From Thornbury & Walford* ***iv*** *(1879-85) 553: Collection JSC).*

elusive flavours. We learn from one[13] that by the 'Recommendation of Physicians and the Encouragement of the Nobility and Gentry Acton Wells' were 'newly opened for the benefit of the public. Every Monday, Wednesday, and Friday from Lady Day[14] to Michaelmas[15], are public days for drinking the water and breakfasting'. Subscribers could drink the water in the New Room (presumably part of the Assembly-House, or perhaps that House itself as newly refurbished in *c*.1770) or take it away for consumption elsewhere. Non-subscribers paid a shilling for *water and salts*, which suggests that the mineral contents were sometimes abstracted from the waters and the salt sold as a separate item. However, towards the end of the 1770s, demand for the waters seems to have declined, and sales to subscribers were suspended[16]. By the mid-1790s the Assembly-House was reported as being 'nearly in ruins' and was to be 'converted into two tenements'[17], but, as we have seen, it was for a period a boarding-school[18].

POWIS WELLS

Back in North London, in Lamb's Conduit Fields, not far from the Foundling Hospital, near the north-west end of Great Ormond Street, was a Mineral-Spring producing water of a 'sweetening, diuritic [*sic*], and gently purging quality', reckoned by 'eminent Physicians and Surgeons' to be useful for curing 'breakings out, sore legs, inflammation of the eyes, and other scorbutic and leprous disorders, &c.' as well as 'giddiness and obstinate headaches', and for alleviating symptoms in 'rheumatic and paralytic cases'[19].

Powis Wells water was bottled and sold, and was used for bathing as well as for drinking. The *Wells* were mentioned as situated behind 'a stately Stone House, belonging to Squire Herbert, called Lord Powiss'[20] in 'Ormond Street, by Queen's Square'[21], 'reckon'd Medicinal for sore Eyes'[22]. The year before William Stow (*fl*.1722) published his *Remarks on London*, it was recorded that a man 'going to a little spring on the back of

Lord Powis's house, in Lamb's Conduit Fields, to which there is a good resort on account of its being reported good in several impurities', stooped 'to wash his eyes... fell headlong in and was suffocated'[23].

Powis Place, on the north side of Great Ormond Street, stands on the site of Powis House (demolished soon after 1784): this stood back from the street, was fronted in stone, was nine windows wide, and featured a Giant Order of eight Corinthian pilasters supporting an entablature over which was an Attic storey surmounted by a balustrade *(Plate 124)*.

The waters enjoyed a reputation for their beneficial properties from the 1720s until the 1770s, and a Pump-House and the inevitable Long-Room (for music, promenades, dancing, and refreshments) were built, but, as Sunderland observed[24], despite availability of the water in bottled form, the Spa itself never achieved 'great fame or popularity'. Country dancing and other diversions took place in the Long-Room, with 'good Musick' and 'accommodations'[25].

It is perhaps worth mentioning that in the early 1740s a guard of soldiers accompanied an Exquisite Mob from 'Marybone Gardens' across the fields to the 'Foundlings' Hospital'[26]: perhaps this was in order to take the waters at *Powis Wells*, for at that time no such facilities were provided at Marylebone, or perchance to visit the Hospital itself (where concerts were also given).

KENSINGTON WELLS AND OTHER SPRINGS IN THE VICINITY

To the west, Kensington, it appears, had several medicinal Springs, including one attached to Aubrey House, a building completed by 1698 under a fifty-year lease granted to John Wright, 'Doctor in Physick', John Stone, Apothecary, and others[27]. Dr Benjamin Allen, in 1699, published his considerable work on the chalybeate and purging waters of England[28] in which is an analysis of the product of the Spring on account of its 'being made Illustrious by the Town, in which his Majesty hath been pleased to fix his Mansion Palace'[29]. John Bowack, another name we have previously encountered, wrote that *Kensington Wells* was 'much esteem'd and resorted to for its Medicinal Virtues'[30].

The property passed to a Mr Town by 1720, then, in 1721, to a Mr Reid, and by the 1730s it was in the possession of Jeffrey Gillingham, pinmaker, of Hammersmith, and had acquired a Long-Room and a Brew-House. Two Wells are marked on Rocque's Map of 1746, but in 1744 the lease had been assigned to Edward Lloyd (d. 1795)[31], who later purchased the freehold from Frederick Halsey (d. 1762) together with the rest of Halsey's holdings in the area[32]. It was Lloyd who built the rather grand Aubrey House at the junction of Aubrey Walk and Aubrey Road, Notting Hill, incorporating as its nucleus part of the earlier property of 1698. Aubrey House eventually passed to Sir Edward Pryce Lloyd (1768-1854 – 1st Baron Mostyn from 1831), and was taken by William Cleverly Alexander (1840-1916 – one of the influential patrons of the painter James Abbott McNeill Whistler [1834-1903]) in *c*.1874. Alexander found a Well under the west wing of the house, and another at the east end of the building: both were polluted by then, and he had them filled up[33]. The waters of *Kensington Wells* were similar to those of Epsom[34], so were 'like other aperient waters with which London was so amply supplied'[35].

Thomas Faulkner (1777-1855)[36] and William John Loftie (1839-1911)[37] both mentioned Aubrey House and the *Wells* in their books, but further information about the *Wells* is sparse. Faulkner also referred to a 'medicinal Spring at Earl's Court' which still functioned in the 1820s: it was called *Billing's Well*, after a former proprietor[38], but not much is known about it except that in mediaeval times Counter's Creek in Southern Kensington had been known (among numerous variants) as Billingwell Dycke, probably meaning Billing's Spring or Stream[39]. Counter's Creek, a tidal tributary of the Thames, was one of the principal water-courses for the drainage of west London, and formed the boundary between the Parishes of Kensington and Fulham. Three fields beside the Creek (which now form part of The West London and Westminster Cemetery at Brompton) were known in the seventeenth century as 'The Three Billins Wells', and one (or possibly more) of these was probably the 'medicinal Spring in Earl's Court' mentioned by Faulkner. In the 1820s part of Counter's Creek became the Kensington Canal, but in 1859-63 the Creek was banished underground and the course of it became the West London Extension Railway[40].

Further west, however, there was a Well sunk in 1794 near Norland Square: it was named after Benjamin Vulliamy (1747-1811), the celebrated clockmaker, who, in 1792, had purchased the whole of the Norland Estate (some forty acres). This Well, sunk at great expense beside Vulliamy's residence, Norland House, was very deep, and is said to have been the first of the Artesian variety in Britain, an achievement which Vulliamy reported to the Royal Society in 1797[41]. Sunderland only mentioned this Well without comment[42], even though it provided an ample water-supply for the new developments carried out on the Norland Estate. The Well's existence was commemorated by an inscribed stone set at the rear of No. 130 Holland Park Avenue[43]: this house was the Norland Estate Office, and was occupied by a solicitor, Charles Richardson (*fl.* 1830-69), who had purchased the Estate from Benjamin Lewis Vulliamy (1780-1854) in 1839. The ground at the back of the house had a steam-engine to pump water up from the Well, and there was a large tank on top of the house itself[44].

Three other Wells existed not far from Kensington. These included *St Agnes's Well*, Hyde Park, apparently at one time a Holy Well, which was sited near the head of the Serpentine on the east bank, in part of the Park called Buckden Hill. Sir Richard Phillips (1767-1840)[45] described the Springs, 'greatly resorted to', in the north-west corner of Hyde Park, 'beneath a row of trees, running parallel with the keeper's garden: one was 'a mineral and is drunk' and the other was used for bathing 'weak eyes' and for immersing children. Persons of Fashion used to 'go in their carriages' to the entrance to the enclosure around the former Spring: there, in fine weather, sat 'a woman, with a table and chair and glasses for the accommodation of visitors'. Servants were sent with jugs for the water, and children were encouraged to drink at the Spring. The 'Eye' Spring was 'frequently surrounded with persons, chiefly of the lower order, bathing their eyes'. The water was 'constantly clear, from the vast quantity' the Spring cast up, and 'its continually running off by an outlet from a small square reservoir'[46]. A third Well, in Kensington Gardens,

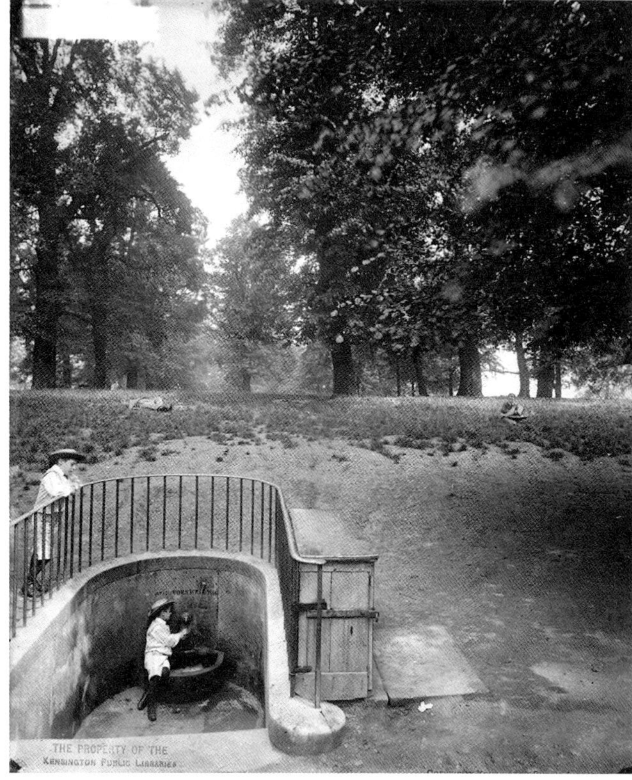

Plate 125: A young boy using *St Gover's Well*, probably end of 19th century *(RBKC)*.

called *St Govor's Well (Plate 125)*, has been mentioned above, but by 1888, Loftie observed that it was polluted and was 'loaded with organic matter'[47]. Dr Samuel Dodd Clippingdale (1836-1925) mentioned the *St Agnes Wells* in his work on West London Rivers: he called the 'Eye' Well the 'Dipping Well'[48]. Sunderland referred to the other Well as 'medicinally potent' and as 'mildly chalybeate'[49].

However, the Springs and Wells mentioned above were only a few of the many that once flowed there: Hyde Park, for example, contained numerous Springs, as did also Regent's Park, St James's Park, and Green Park[50].

HOXTON WELL

Hoxton, due east of Islington, was once a place of conviviality: in Beaumont and Fletcher's *The Knight of the Burning Pestle* reference is made to

> '*Hogsdon* or to Newington, where ale and
> cakes are plenty'[51],

and there is also the couplet

> 'Nutmegs and Ginger, Cinnamon and Cloves,
> And they gave me this jolly red nose'[52].

A medicinal Spring was discovered (or rediscovered) in Hoxton late in the seventeenth century when an excavation was being made for a cellar for a house in Charles Square (just north of Old Street east of City Road). The Hoxton waters were said to contain both sulphur and iron, and were claimed to be able to combat an impressive array of 'distempers'. Dr Timothy Byfield, in his slim volume entitled *A Short and Plain Account of the late found Balsamic Wells at Hoxdon*[53], dedicated to the 'Proprietors of the Wells at the Golden Heart in Hoxdon Square', recommended from one to two quarts (or, at the most, five pints), over a period of two to three weeks, in order to

> 'set up such a pretty bustle or ferment
> In Nature that maketh Gay
> a well-temper'd Healthy Body':

the mind boggles. Byfield claimed there was 'no unwholesome glebe[54] or any dangerous mineral or metal' in the waters to cast 'one unhappy ray into this healing fountain'. Sunderland considered the Hoxton Water probably contained magnesium sulphate and iron, but Macpherson declared that of 'sulphur wells there are none in or near London'[55], and went on to opine that the Hoxton water had 'bituminous' scum on the surface, but had a pleasant aromatic flavour'[56]: it sounds dubious.

HACKNEY WELLS

North-east of Hoxton is Hackney, where there were several Wells. William Robinson (1777-1848), in his two-volume *History and Antiquities of Hackney*[57], mentioned *Churchfield Well* (after which Well Street, Hackney, is named), *Pig's Well* (presumably *Pyke Well*, a prodigious Spring on the Hackney Downs which supposedly never froze), a chalybeate Well to the west, towards Dalston, and another at Shacklewell. Benjamin Clarke (1821-1906), in his *Glimpses of ancient Hackney and Stoke Newington*[58], claimed there was indeed a Well in Well Street, and Robinson mentioned another of very pure water near the old churchyard off Morning Lane[59]. Sunderland observed that *Churchfield Well* had claims to be considered one of the old Holy Wells 'on account of its contiguity to the old Palace of the Priors of St John of Jerusalem, which formerly existed quite near'[60].

TOTTENHAM WELLS

North of Hackney is Tottenham, which once possessed several Holy Wells, including *St Eloy's* or *St Loy's Well*, named after St Eligius or Eloi (*c*.588-660), Bishop of Noyon from 641 and Patron of goldsmiths, blacksmiths, and farriers[61], whose Feast Day is 1 December. The seventeenth-century chronicler of Tottenham was William Bedwell (1563-1632)[62], Vicar of the Parish of All Hallows, Tottenham High Cross, 1607-32, who mentioned the Wells there. *St Eloy's Well* in Bedwell's day, however, was a 'deep pitte in the highway' within memory cleaned out: at the bottom was found a 'faire great stone' which had 'certain characters or letters engrav'n upon it, but being broken and defaced by the negligence of the workmen, and nobody near that regarded such things, it was not known what they were or what they might signify'[63]. Stories about Wells often mention large dressed stones at the bottoms of the shafts. Robinson considered the waters of *St Eloy's Well* to have properties similar to those of Cheltenham[64]. He mentioned that in his time (early nineteenth century) the Well was surrounded by willows, bricked up on all four sides, and about four feet deep[65].

Tottenham also possessed *The Bishop's Well* in a field near the Vicarage once occupied by Bedwell: this Well was reputed to have waters beneficial for eyes, and (a common property among numerous Wells) never froze[66]. It issued out of the side of a hill and fell into the River 'Mose' or 'Mosell' 'afore it hath run many paces'[67]. *Bishop's Well* waters were also supposed to be efficacious in the cure of an impressive list of infirmities, but their purity was held in great esteem, so much so that 'the ladies of the vicinity were in the habit of sending their servants in the morning and evening for water'[68] for their dishes of tea, from which circumstance the Well was rather unfortunately known as 'My Lady's Hole', but the Georgians, like ourselves, were no strangers to ribaldry. The Mosel, or Mosell River gave its name to Muswell Hill, but the *Bishop's Well* dried up when the land for the cemetery at Tottenham was drained prior to its opening in 1858[69].

St Dunstan's Well, Tottenham Wood, in the outskirts of the Parish, was celebrated for its waters, but it appears to have fallen into disuse in the seventeenth century: the site of the Well lies in the grounds of Alexandra Palace[70]. St Dunstan (909-88), Benedictine monk and Archbishop of Canterbury from 960, had many miracles attributed to him, and he enjoyed a nationwide cult: goldsmiths, jewellers, and locksmiths claimed him as their especial Patron, and his Feast Day is 19 May. The Saint was much given to travel to Bath every year for the sake of the hot Springs there[71]: this may account for his association with so many Wells.

At Spotton's Grove, just to the north of what is now Lordship Lane, was another Well, but it seems to have passed from mind at least two-and-a-half centuries ago.

MUSWELL

Due west of Tottenham is Muswell Hill, some five-and-a-half miles north of London, part of a low sequence of hills extending along the northern limit of what was the once-beautiful County of Middlesex. Today its summit is occupied by Alexandra Palace, designed by Alfred Meeson (1808-95) and John Johnson (*c*.1807-78), completed 1873 but burned down almost immediately, then re-opened 1875.

There was a Holy Well there on the southern side of the Hill (called, at various times, *Mouse-Well*, *Mos-Well*, *Moss-Well*, *Mus-Well*, *Mussel*, and, in Rocque's Map of 1741-5, *Muscle*, and even *Pinse-Hall Hill*), and it was associated with a chapel, the Patroness of which was Our Lady of Muswell: John Norden (*c*.1547-1625) tells us that the Well was much resorted to by pilgrims, attracted by the story of a certain King of Scots (chronicles are infuriatingly vague about his identity) who had been cured of some vile condition by the waters[72]. The land on which the Well was situated was, during the Middle Ages, in the hands of the Fraternity of St John of Jerusalem, the London House of which was in Clerkenwell, but after the reign of Queen Elizabeth I the land passed to private ownership. The *Mouse-well* was situated in the area now covered by such streets as Muswell Avenue, Coniston Road, and Methuen Park, all built on land which until 1900 was a detached part of Clerkenwell Parish.

In fact there was another Well in addition to the Holy Well, and both were 'in good preservation' early in the nineteenth century[73]: one Well produced water that was hard, sweet, and pellucid, and liquid from the other resembled rainwater. Both Wells supplied water to local inhabitants, but in the middle of the nineteenth century the landowners sealed one Well to the great inconvenience of the public, so an Action was begun to establish public rights to use the Well, which the plaintiffs won in 1862[74]. In due course the Alexandra Park Company provided a pump, but by the 1880s the Wells ceased to function, and the water by that time seems to have been only polluted surface-drainage[75]. The 'overflowings'[76] of the two Wells formed a rivulet, named *Mosel*, which entered the River Lea. Sunderland stated that there was 'no evidence' that the waters 'had any medicinal virtues'[77], but that does not seem to have deterred King John from visiting the Wells and partaking of them. The water from *Our Lady's Well* was deemed a cure for 'scrofulous and cutaneous disorders', so many were attracted to the Shrine (managed, it seems, by nuns), bringing offerings and their hopes for cures[78].

HIGHGATE

Almost due south of Muswell Hill lies the pretty village of Highgate which possessed a Spring of 'very mild' chalybeate water, situated in Southwood Lane. The waters from this Spring were bottled and sold in London as *Highgate Eye Water*[79] because they were held to be beneficial for bathing eyes. The *Flask* public-house at 77 Highgate West Hill is near what used to be the village green, a remnant of which is Pond Square. This now has no pond and is covered with unattractive asphalt. It appears that, like the *Flask*, the Flask Walk, Hampstead, the inn (part of which dates from the eighteenth century) sold bottled water, hence the name[80]. It would appear that virtually all the waters which appeared as Springs or Wells in the Hampstead-Highgate area were of the chalybeate character, supposedly efficacious in 'cases of nervous debility'[81].

COUNTRY WELLS NORTH, NORTH-EAST, AND EAST OF LONDON

For many centuries London was intimately connected with its surrounding counties, especially Essex, Hertfordshire, Kent, Middlesex, and Surrey. Middlesex, of course, has been swallowed up by London, and the same process is happening to Essex, northern Surrey, and the other counties. Even from the Middle Ages Londoners would often venture out to the country, and with the growing fashion for rural experiences, fresh air, and taking refreshment outside Town, many were attracted to places that offered food, drink, and waters.

Samuel Pepys travelled out to visit the Wells at East Barnet, Hertfordshire, in 1664, where he drank five glasses of the water, but that evening felt very unwell[82]. This did not deter him from venturing there again, in 1667, where he 'found many people a-drinking', after which he went to the *Red Lion* in Barnet and ate 'some of the best cheese-cakes' he had ever consumed in his life[83]. *Barnet Well* water was purgative, with a brackish flavour, and was impregnated with magnesium sulphate: it was said to be 'of great efficacy in cholics'[84].

The *Well* lay south of High Barnet, in a field beside the road from Barnet to Elstree, and was known locally as the *Physick Well*. It seems to have been first promoted in the middle of the seventeenth century, and its medicinal qualities were lauded[85]: it quickly rose to some prominence in the 1660s, being mentioned by Joshua Childrey (1623-70) as 'very famous'[86], and Thomas Fuller (1608-61) wrote of the 'catalogue of the cures done by this Spring' amounting to a 'great Number, inasmuch as there is Hope, in process of Time, the water rising here will repair the blood shed hard by, and save as many lives as were lost in the Fatal Battle[87] at Barnet'[88].

The Yorkshire physician, Robert Witty (*or* Wittie – 1613-84), established Scarborough's reputation as a Spa, and his many patients testified to the success of his treatment[89]. The publication in 1660 of his celebrated *Scarborough Spaw*[90] coincided with the Restoration of the Monarchy and made his reputation: he had experimented with the waters by taking them himself (*c*.1637-8), and prescribed them for an impressive list of conditions ranging from Gout to Convulsions. He claimed the waters contained vitriol, nitre, alum, salt, and iron, findings which were disputed by 'Chymists' in York and Newcastle, so vituperative disputes followed in which no holds were barred: 'viperous Brat' and 'base Bachelor of Arts' were only two examples of the invective that flowed as generously as the waters. Witty included Barnet in his poetic gem, rivalling William McGonagall (*c*.1825-1902)[91] in its bathos:

> 'Let Epsom, Tunbridge, Barnet,
> Knaresborough be
> In what request they will, Scarborough for
> me'[92].

Sir Henry Chauncy (1632-1719) adopted a more elevated tone for his monumental work on the *Antiquities of Hertfordshire*[93]: he claimed the Barnet waters were impregnated with 'allom' (a double sulphate of aluminium and potassium, or other compounds including iron, magnesium, etc), or some other 'mixt salt' hard to analyse, but useful in the treatment of 'cholics'. A century later, William Martin Trinder (*c*.1747-1818) carried out 'Chymical Experiments' on the *Barnet Well* water, and found it somewhat 'brackish' to the taste, though not unpleasant, containing a large percentage of sulphate of magnesia: taken in moderation, it was a useful purgative. The Well-House was demolished around 1840, and the Well covered, but a pump was installed, and the water was 'occasionally resorted to by invalids'.[94] Foord reported being able to see the pump in 1906, and Sunderland[95] said it was visible at the back of Well House Farm, Well House Lane, in 1914, but no water could be drawn from it[96].

At Lower Cuffley, Hertfordshire, between Northaw and Cheshunt, was a saline-chalybeate Spring, once used by the denizens of Theobalds, the great house (virtually all demolished) erected for William Cecil (1520/1-98), 1st Baron Burghley from 1571, Elizabeth I's leading statesman. Dr Donald Monro (1727-1802), in his *Treatise*[97], mentioned the analyses carried out on the *Northaw Spring* waters by Dr John Rutty (1698-1775)[98] and published: it would appear from these works that the Barnet and Northaw waters were very similar, but the Northaw water seems to have contained a greater proportion of iron.

Foord said it was colourless, but when it was boiled and poured on tea, the iron in the water combined with the tannin in the tea to form an inky liquid that astonished the tea-makers as much as it delighted practical jokers[99].

East of Northaw and due south of Epping is *Chigwell*, Essex, and there, at least since Saxon times, was an ancient Spring from which *Chigwell* was supposed to get its name. This was, literally, the *King's Well* (from the Old English *Cyng* and *Wielle*, *Wella*, and other variations). Philip Morant (1700-70)[100] described *Chigwell* as lying between the forests of Epping and Hainault, and the ancient Spring seems to have been distinct from the medicinal Spring at Chigwell Row, east of *Chigwell*, discovered near the end of the seventeenth century. A charming view from Chigwell Row by Philippe Jacques de Loutherbourg (1740-1812) was published by Robert Bowyer (1758-1834) in 1805: it shows an idyllic countryside before London's suburbia engulfed it *(Plate 126)*.

Anthony Walker (d. 1692) mentioned *Chigwell* in a rather curious volume entitled *Fax fonte accensa*[101], listing it with other sources such as Bath, Epsom, Scarborough, and Tunbridge Wells, so it would appear that the Spring at *Chigwell Row* was esteemed at the end of the seventeenth century: its waters[102] had purgative properties, so they probably contained sulphate of magnesia. Walford tells us that the Spring was 'written up by Dr. Frewen, a native of *Chigwell*, but it never attained any great celebrity or popularity'[103]. Elizabeth Ogbourne (1763/4-1853) mentioned the Spring of Mineral-Water near Chigwell Row, 'formerly so celebrated, but now considered of little account, and entirely neglected': this was in 1814[104].

There was another Mineral-Spring at *Woodford Wells*, west of *Chigwell* and south of

Plate 126: View from Chigwell Row, Essex, aquatint after Philippe Jacques de Loutherbourg, published by Robert Bowyer (1758-1834) in 1805 *(LMA SC/GL/LYS/004/001/Ce32004/cat.no.p539298x)*.

Plate 127: *The Horse and Well*, Woodford Wells, then in Essex, showing the drinking-fountain with tall roof *(left)* to perpetuate the memory of the Wells *(From Walford **i** (1884) 463: Collection JSC).*

Buckhurst Hill, at the southern edge of Epping Forest, now in the London Borough of Redbridge. Sunderland[105] was of the opinion that the water was of the chalybeate kind: the source was visited by numerous people during the eighteenth century, but, according to *Twenty-five Miles Round London* in *Ambulator: or, A pocket Companion in a Tour round London*[106], the waters had lost their reputation by the 1790s. The Spring was only a short distance away from a Tavern called *The Horse and Groom*, afterwards called *The Horse and Well*: this large and handsome public-house had a Garden attached to it, and was illustrated in Walford's *Greater London*[107] *(Plate 127).*

There were several other Wells in Essex near Romford, Brentwood, Upminster, and Tilbury, that were claimed to have medicinal qualities, but none achieved great fame, though waters were bottled and sold in London. Trinder described the water from ten of these in 1783[108], with analyses and recommendations for their use. These included *Tilbury Hall* water, containing 'calcareous earth, true nitre, sea salt, and mineral alkali' used for diseases 'arising from acidity in the first passages' and for gout[109]. The water rose near the River Thames at Tilbury Hall, and was sold in both Pall Mall and Whitechapel[110]. Water from *The Rector's Well*, Tilbury, contained some iron, and was sold, bottled, at Temple Bar and Savile Row. Chalybeate water impregnated with sulphur, magnesia, and so on, came from the *Gidea Hall Spring*, Romford, and was claimed as a cure for dropsy, obstructions of the 'liver, spleen, mesentery[111], and uterus', being 'a corroborant[112], a deobstruent[113], and also a purging water'[114]. Romford, of course, is no longer in Essex, but within the London Borough of Havering, and Gidea Park became Romford Garden Suburb from 1910, where there is still much work inspired by the Domestic Revival of the Arts-and-Crafts Movement that is of interest. About a mile out of Romford, towards Hornchurch, was the *Hornchurch Lane Spring*, producing supposedly almost pure water, impregnated with an alkaline salt, which was advised for the inhibition of 'early gout' and to be used to ease 'acetous fermentation' in the stomach: the water was also recommended for 'fat tenacious humours, as in jaundice, rheumatism, and scurvy', which sounds like powerful stuff. Then, about five miles north of Romford, was the *Forest Spring*, Stapleford Abbotts (which is still in Essex): water from this source contained 'bitter purging salt' of the Epsom kind, iron, and sea-salt, reckoned to be useful for 'colics... bilious, flatulent, or nephritic' as well as to ease cutaneous diseases, sore eyes, and painful legs. Three to four pints of the water taken twice a year were sufficient to thoroughly

Plate 128: Street-scene in Witham, Essex, *c.*1830, drawn by George Bryant Campion (1796-1870), engraved by W. Watkins (*fl.* late 1820s) *(LMA SC/GL/PR/II/TER-II/WRI/Ce30759/cat.no.p7491691).*

cleanse the system[115], or so it was claimed.

North-east of Romford is the Parish of South Weald in Essex, and in a field was the *Weald Hall Spring*: its waters were 'selenitic' (i.e. related to selenious acid and its salts, e.g. sulphate of lime), said to have a 'drying and astringent quality', and were recommended in cases of internal haemorrhages[116]. There were more. The *Upminster Spring*, for example, near Tyler's Hall, Upminster, now in the London Borough of Havering, was one example, The water had a slight greenish tint, tasted like a weak solution of Epsom Salts, and was supposed to help in cases of damaged livers[117].

To the north-east, almost in the centre of Essex, lies Witham, where Dr James Taverner (1709-48) established a Spa at Powers Hall End[118], half-a-mile west of the Parish Church of St Nicolas, where a chalybeate Spring had been discovered in the seventeenth century. The waters were described as 'brisk..., impregnated with a little sulphur and Magnesia Glauber's Salt'[119]. As Witham was the half-way house on the road from London to Harwich *(Plate 128)*, the Spa did very well for a short time, extolled by Taverner[120], who caused an Assembly-Room to be erected: this was originally the Great Hall at New Hall, Boreham, Essex, about four miles south-west of Witham, 'translated', to Taverner's Spa in *c.*1738, according to the historian and clergyman, Philip Morant (1700-70)[121], in his monumental *History and Antiquities of the County of Essex*, a work in which sound common sense, scholarship, and consistency are mercifully more in evidence than in many other similar works of the period. As New Hall was connected with the Earl of Ormond, Thomas Boleyn (father of Anne), the 3rd Earl of Sussex, the Duke of Buckingham, the Duke of Albemarle, the Duke of Wharton, and Lord Waltham, it was a house not without distinction in architectural *or* historical terms, so the Great Hall, rebuilt as the Assembly-Room, must have provided Taverner with one of the grandest of all such Spa buildings in or around London. It is a pity the Spa did not long survive Taverner's own premature demise. A perambulation of Witham[122] also reveals that the Spa (as well as the geographical location of the town) must have brought sufficient prosperity to enable this to be expressed in architecture: Newland Street, largely refaced in the eighteenth century, tells the story with some eloquence. The only visible evidence of Dr Taverner's Spa today is Spa House, incorporating a seventeenth-century timber-framed house.

Then there was the *Springfield Water*, which rose on the 'sedgy' banks of the River Chelmer, about a mile east of Chelmsford. The waters were 'selenitic', impregnated with iron and sulphur, and also contained 'a little of the nitrum calcarium or purging salt of Dr Rutty'[123]. A light and pure chalybeate water similar to 'Tunbridge Water' issued from *Felsted* or *Little Dunmow Spring* (the two villages are quite close together), and the waters of *Markshall Spring*, Coggeshall (where there were several large ponds), were similar in content. Strangely, Trinder did not mention *Markshall Spring* in his survey[124].

North-west of Southend-on-Sea, Hockley in Essex acquired a salubrious Spa complete with Pump-Room. The waters were quite heavily impregnated with sulphate of magnesium, and the Spa attracted custom from the time of the discovery of the Spring in 1838. James Lockyer (1796-1875) designed the Pump-Room (1842-3), which had tall arched windows, Tuscan pilasters, and a heavy, somewhat busy parapet. Lockyer also designed the *Spa Hotel*, but the Spa did not prosper, and the Pump-Room became a Baptist Chapel. Something of the ambience of a Spa still seems to pervade Hockley, however, and it is certainly worth a visit for that reason.

Finally, there were Chadwell St Mary (now part of Thurrock), and Chadwell Heath (now in Barking and Dagenham) near Romford (both of which were historically in Essex): as their names suggest, their connection with St Chad leads to a link with water, and so it turns out to be.

SPRING GARDENS NORTH OF THE THAMES

There were several *Spring Gardens*, some of which will be listed here. One of the most famous was at Charing Cross *(Plate 129)*[125], taking its name from a Spring and Fountain set in a Garden connected to the Royal Palace of Whitehall. Known at least since the time of Elizabeth I, it contained pleasant arbours, and there was a pool for bathing. A bowling-green was laid out in the reign of Charles I, and in the middle of the seventeenth century it appears to have had its devotees. Another was at Knightsbridge, frequented by Pepys, possibly identical with *The World's End*[126]: it seems to have occupied a site approximately where William Street joins Lowndes Square, and ceased to be a place of entertainment in the 1770s. There was definitely a stream which ran along the western side of these Gardens[127].

Yet another Spring Garden, called the *New Spring Garden*, at Chelsea, was a place of public entertainment, and was advertised as providing suppers and dinners in 1792[128]. It was situated near Ebury Street, and seems to have flourished for only a short time. This appears to have been identifiable with a public-house called *The Dwarf's Tavern* in Chelsea Fields, so called after its landlord, the 'unparalleled Norfolk Dwarf, John Coan (d.1764)[129]. The site was later taken for a factory[130]. Sunderland, though admitting the existence of water on the site, could find no evidence that it was exploited, other than to make tea and coffee (and perhaps dilute the alcoholic drinks)[131]. However, a drawing in the Crace Collection is entitled 'The Spring Garden, Belgrave Road, Pimlico, 1774' *(Plate 130)*, and this is clearly the source for the illustration in Thornbury & Walford **v** (1879-85) labelled 'The Spring Garden "World's End"' *(Plate 131)*.

Not far from *The Dwarf's Tavern* was the somewhat forbiddingly-named *Monster Tavern*, which stood at the corner of St George's Row and Buckingham Palace Road, Pimlico. St George's Row is now Ebury Bridge and the beginning of Warwick Way, just as it swings north-east at the top of Sutherland Street. 'Monster' is probably a corruption of 'Monastery', and may be connected with the Monastery of Westminster which, through its Abbot, took a lease on the property in the fourteenth century[132]. This Tavern had behind it a *Monster Tea-Garden* well planted with trees and shrubs. It was an attractive building, and the Garden had a painted sign over the entrance *(Plate 132)*: it was a place 'of popular resort', and it was from the Tavern that the 'Monster' line of omnibuses plied its trade[133]. The Garden had benches, tables, and pleasant alcoves

Plate 129: The pretty *Spring Gardens*, St James's Park, in 1830, showing a Fair held for the Benefit of Charing Cross Hospital. The character of the Gardens, with its trellises and walks, would have been similar to that of other such Gardens of the time. Drawn and lithographed by George Scharf (1788-1860) and printed by Charles Joseph Hullmandel (1789-1850) *(LMA SC/GL/WAK/W2/PAU-YOR/Ce29827/cat.no.p7521630).*

where the usual refreshments could be consumed: although the place never acquired any reputation for the medicinal qualities of its water, nevertheless its teas, coffees, and so on were enjoyed. As far as is known, the *Monster* Gardens were never called 'Spring', however, and it would appear that water played but little part in the fortunes of this establishment, but it is included here because the Gardens were used until the major upheavals caused by the construction of the railway completely changed the character of the area.

The *Spring Garden*, Stepney, was situated north of the Mile End Road, its eastern side coinciding with what is now Globe Road, running north. In the early eighteenth century it was known as *The Jews' Spring Garden*[134], and had a Tavern attached to it: it appears to have been a popular resort on Sundays[135], and Sunderland observes of it that many 'resorted there to eat Stepney buns

Plate 130: *The Spring Garden, Belgrave Road, Pimlico,* 1774 showing the fountain *(LMA SC/GL/NOR/TEA & MUSIC/vol.9 p.36).*

Plate 131: Engraving purporting to be of *The Spring Garden*, 'World's End' at Knightsbridge, but clearly the same building as that shown in *The Spring Garden, Belgrave Road, Pimlico* (Plate 130) *(From Thornbury & Walford v (1879-85) 18: Collection JSC).*

Plate 132: *The Monster Tavern and Tea-Garden* in *c.*1820 drawn by W. H. Prior and engraved by Greenaway *(From Thornbury & Walford v [1879-85] 42: Collection JSC).*

and drink ale and cider'[136]. Nevertheless, Sunderland included this establishment in his list of old London Wells used for drinking purposes, and, as the presence of so many Victorian and earlier breweries in the vicinity shows, there was a good supply of pure water in that district.

Stepney's *Spring Garden* should not be confused with the Well at Sun Tavern Fields[137], Shadwell, ludicrously puffed by Diederick Wessel Linden[138] as a cure for just about any ailment known to Man. There was another Spring in the Parish known as the *Postern Waters* on Tower Hill, near the Postern Gate of the Tower, but of this, like so many, nothing visible remains. Sunderland claimed the waters of the *Postern Spring* was probably of the chalybeate kind[139].

AFTERWORD

Delving through the considerable literature of the 'History and Antiquities' genre, one is conscious of an enormous number of Wells that were once prized for various reasons (sometimes just because they provided pure water) in and within reach of London. Some were associated with Saints, such as *St Chad's Well*, Wapping, and the *Holy Well* at Shoreditch, commemorated today by Holywell Lane EC2, supposed to be somewhere under Bateman's Row in the Parish of St Leonard, Shoreditch. In Stow's time, however, this *Holy Well* was 'much decayed and marred with filthinesse purposely laide there, for the heightening of the ground for garden plots'[140]. This *Fons Sacer* was mentioned by Fitzstephen in the twelfth century[141].

St Chad's Well, Battle Bridge, was, perhaps, one of the most important of the ancient Holy Wells in London, but the Well of *St Agnes-le-Clair* (situated, it seems, at the junction of City Road and Old Street and described as a 'celebrated spring' at the entrance to the small village of Hoxton[142]), was reckoned to be important in the treatment of eye and skin complaints. The Well was probably known in Roman times, but its waters fed the *St-Agnes-le-Clair Bath*, sited where Paul Street joins Old Street at what is now called Bath Place. This Bath was 'greatly extolled by the most eminent professor of this age'[143], and although it seems to have existed from the beginning of the sixteenth century, it was improved and advertised around 1731, when it was called the *Pool of Bethesda* and then the *New Cold Bath*, larger and more commodious than any in or about London. The water flowed constantly at the rate of 10,000 gallons every day, and remained at a constant temperature at all times of the year. Ladies and gentlemen could 'depend upon suitable accommodation and attendance'[144]. These waters were lauded for their properties in the cure of rheumatic and nervous cases and headaches[145], and the usual claims regarding easing of 'cutaneous eruptions' and reducing inflammation and weaknesses of the eyes were made.

There was a Garden attached to the Bath, for in 1748 we learn of the thefts of shells from the rock-work of artificial fruit-trees (why artificial? one wonders), and of two swans made of glass that had adorned the basin of the fountain. In 1778 the Baths were renovated and were puffed as the 'completest' in London. By the 1830s the establishment was called the *St Agnes Le Clair Mineral Baths*, and seems to have had buildings containing between twelve and fourteen rooms. Subscriptions were £1 5*s*. per annum; a single bath was one shilling; and there were facilities for warm and vapour baths at two shillings and sixpence and five shillings each.

In 1845 there was a disastrous fire which destroyed the dwelling-house of the proprietor as well as buildings associated with the Bath, and thereafter the Baths ceased to function, although the waters appear to have been used for industrial purposes well into the second half of the nineteenth century[146]. It is likely that the sources that fed *St Agnes-le-Clair Well* and *Bath* were similar to those supplying the *Peerless Pool* and, presumably, *Hoxton Well*.

Mention should be made of some of the ancient Wells that were considered to have medicinal properties, although they did not evolve into Spas, Pleasure-Gardens, or other places of entertainment. *Crowder's Well* produced water, supposed to taste like new milk, that was recommended for sore eyes: it was situated behind the Church of St Giles, Cripplegate[147]. In addition to the *Clerk's Well* discussed earlier, there was the *Skinner's Well*, west of the Parish Church of St James, Clerkenwell, where, allegedly, festivities were held during the Middle Ages by The Skinners' Company, a supposition that appears to be based on very little[148] other than Stow's statement that 'a great play was played at the Skinners Wel, which lasted eight daies'[149]. Stow's use of the words *Parish Clarks* to describe participants in plays has caused problems, for Parish Clerks as such did not exist before the Reformation: what such references actually meant were clergy, based on Fitzstephen's use of *clerici*, which means not 'clerks' in the modern sense, but clerks in Holy Orders, that is clergymen[150].

There is another problem too, and that is viewing the Middle Ages through romantic rose-tinted spectacles: it was not so much Holy Plays but readings from Scriptures over several days that took place. Stow also mentions wrestling and other diversions, including 'dauncing' by 'Maidens' for 'garlandes', which, having been discouraged, he feared 'worser practises within doores' might occur: clearly he had fornication in mind. He also mentioned 'bayting of Bulles and Bears'[151] and various other edifying spectacles: in short, there is little evidence that a mediaeval crowd was given to piety, or over-zealous in its devotions and religious observances, and the notion of miracle-plays having taken place may stem from a misunderstanding or misreading of mediaeval French words alluding to boisterous games and wrestling. Had the mob been at its quiet devotions by the Clerks' and Skinners' Wells, it is highly unlikely that a Prioress of St Mary, Clerkenwell, would have complained to the King in the strongest possible way about damage to her crops, fields, and hedges[152].

Other Wells in the vicinity included *Loder's Well*, *Fagges Well*, and *Godwell* or *Godeswell* (called to mind by Goswell Road), but there must have been other sources of water, given the important religious houses that existed in the area[153]. Stow also referred to 'Redwell', which appears to have been Radwell in Hertfordshire[154]. The waters of Clerkenwell have been fully discussed above, in Stow, and by Saint[155], and Hassall also made an important series of contributions concerning the conventual buildings of St Mary, Clerkenwell[156], and although future building-works and excavations may reveal more about them, the subject may be left at this point.

Only a few more central Wells may be listed. These are *St Clement's Well*, The Strand, which was north of the Church of St Clement Dane; a *Holy Well* (which may have been the same as *St Clement's Well* or perhaps a separate well submerged beneath the Royal Courts of Justice); and *St Bride's* or *St Bridget's Well*, probably at the east end of the churchyard of St Bride, Fleet Street, in Bride Lane[157]. The last Well is supposed to have given its name to the Palace, and later Hospital and Prison called Bridewell which stood on the site. Hone tells us that the 'last public use of the water of St Bride's well drained it so much, that the inhabitants of St Bride's parish could not get their usual supply. This exhaustion was effected by a sudden demand. Several men were engaged in filling thousands of bottles, a day or two before the 19th of July 1821, on which day his majesty, King George IV. was crowned at Westminster; and Mr Walker of the hotel, No. 10, Bridge-street, Blackfriars, purveyor of water to the coronation, obtained it, by the only means through which the sainted fluid is now obtainable, from the cast-iron pump over St Bride's well, in Bride-lane'[158].

Then there was *Monk Well* in the defunct Monkwell Street (now Monkwell Square between London Wall and the Barbican): the Well was tended by a monk in a hermitage near Cripplegate[159], among whose duties were to pray for the soul of Aymer de Valence (d. 1324), 11th Earl of Pembroke, whose widow, Mary de St Pol (*c*.1304-77), by grants to the Abbot and Convent of the Cistercian establishment (founded 1134) at Garendon, Leicestershire, had arranged for this to be done in Aymer de Valence's memory and for the ease of his soul.

Near *Monk Well* was *St Giles's Well* in the defunct Well Street, which fed a pool. Between Old Jewry[160] and Ironmonger Lane stood (until 1892) the Church of St Olave Jewry, formerly St Olave Upwell, so-called from a well with a pump attached to it. St Mary Woolnoth had a Spring, as we know from the Returns regarding supplies of water made by the parishes to the Board of Trade in 1872. The gist of this list, giving the name, location, and depth (where known) of every public surface-Well in the Metropolis, is published in Foord's useful book[161]. A few of the more important will be given here:

St George-in-the-East: 2 pumps (one in Wellclose Square and other within the churchyard gates); *Whitechapel*: 4 public Wells, all of which, being polluted, were about to be filled; *St Michael's Well, Aldgate* (supposed to have medicinal properties, and much resorted to by the populace), by 1876 found to be so polluted it had to be connected to the New River supply; Well in the churchyard of *St Dunstan-in-the-East*, the pump of which was set against the south wall of the Church; *St Martin Outwich Well* closed 1862 and now lost among later buildings; Well in the churchyard of *St Mary-le-Bow*, Cheapside (commemorated by Well Court between Bow Lane and Queen Street); another in Chancery Lane on the north side of Breams Buildings; and many more.

It is interesting, when delving through old records and maps, to note how many Pumps and Wells associated with them were sited in or near churchyards. It is extraordinary that the connection between disease, polluted water, and decaying matter was not understood until well into the nineteenth century. Many of the pumps were obviously Dispensers of Death, not only through decaying bodies in churchyards, but because infected faeces from the living drained into drinking-water. It was not until after the 1854 outbreak of cholera in Broad (now Broadwick) Street, Soho, Westminster, that Dr John Snow (1813-58) was able to compile his statistical evidence that the disease was carried in water provided by the pump there[162]. As official awareness of the problem became accepted (often in the teeth of popular ignorance and long-established custom [some with an inevitable religious connection]), many of the old Wells were sealed, filled, or closed, and purified water at last became widely available thanks to the mass-production of pipes. It is a sobering thought that not until the Victorians, with their massive programmes of construction involving the removal of sewage and the supply of uncontaminated water, managed to potty-train Urban Man, were towns and cities made safer places and largely protected from the hitherto perennial rampages of water-borne diseases.

Chapter IX References: Other Spas and Wells North of the Thames

1 Lysons (1792-6): *see* especially **iii** (*County of Middlesex*).

2 Sunderland (1915) 105.

3 *Ibid.*

4 Brayley, Brewer, & Nightingale (1810-16): volume **iv** was entirely the work of Brewer.

5 *Ibid.*, quoted in Walford **i** (1884) 16.

6 Macpherson (1871).

7 Walford **i** (1884) 16.

8 *Ibid.*

9 Allen (1711).

10 Boyle (1690).

11 Hofmann (1854).

12 Bowack (1705-6).

13 Dated 3 July 1771.

14 25 March: The Feast of the Annunciation.

15 The Feast of St Michael (29 September).

16 Advertisement of 13 April 1776.

17 Anonymous (1796): *The Ambulator...* published by Scatcherd. *See* Anonymous (1774).

18 *See* Foord (1910) 156-8; Sunderland (1915) 104-5.

19 Advertisement of 1754.

20 William Herbert (1657x61-1745), 2nd Marquess of Powis and Jacobite sympathiser: Powis House was leased to the French Ambassador in 1712, but burned down in 1713. Louis XIV paid for the rather grand rebuilding. Powis was imprisoned during the Jacobite Rising of 1715. For the House *see* Cunningham (1850), Noorthouck (1773), Thornbury & Walford **iv** (1879-85) 556.

21 Now Queen Square.

22 Stow (1722) on Powis Wells.

23 *Weekly Journal* (17 January 1721).

24 Sunderland (1915) 81.

25 Advertisement (4 August 1748).

26 Wroth & Wroth (1896) 100.

27 Sheppard (*Gen. Ed.*) (1973) 87. The present writer had the pleasure of contributing to this volume.

28 Allen (1699) 129-32.

29 *Ibid.*

30 Bowack **i** (1705-6) 20.

31 Created 1st Baronet in 1778.

32 Sheppard (*Gen.Ed.*) (1973) 87.

33 Foord (1910) 171.

34 So contained Glauber Salts.

35 Foord (1910) 171.

36 Faulkner (1820).

37 Loftie (1888).

38 Faulkner (1820) 26; Foord (1910) 172; Sunderland (1915) 54.

39 Gover, Mawer, & Stenton (1942) 2.

40 Sheppard (*Gen. Ed.*) (1983) 241.

41 *ODNB* **lvi** (2004) 613.

42 Sunderland (1915) 28.

43 Sheppard (*Gen. Ed.*) (1973) 278.

44 *Ibid.* 295.

45 Not to be confused with Richard Phillips FRS (1778-1851).

46 *See* Phillips (1805).

47 *See* Loftie (1888).

48 Clippingdale (1914).

49 Sunderland (1915) 54.

50 *Ibid.* 28.

51 Beaumont & Fletcher (1613).

52 *Ibid.* Act **i** Sc. 4.

53 Byfield (1687) *passim.*

54 Chemical substance or solids, lumps, nodules.

55 *See* Macpherson (1871).

56 Foord (1910) 120.

57 Robinson (1842-3).

58 Clarke (1894).

59 Robinson (1842-3). *See* also Foord (1910) 124.

60 Sunderland (1915) 21-2.

61 When shoeing a restive horse, he took the leg off, shod it, and stuck it back on the horse again, which animal suffered no ill-effects. *See* Baring-Gould **xv** (1914) 2-9 for many volumes of grotesquely improbable stuff.

62 He was also an Arabist and Mathematician.

63 Bedwell (1718).

64 Robinson (1840). *See* also Sunderland (1915) 22.

65 Thornbury & Walford **v** (1879-85) 561.

66 Anonymous (1774) for details.

67 Bedwell (1718).

68 Foord (1910) 128.

69 Buried there is William Butterfield (1814-1900), the great Victorian Gothic architect. *See* Curl (2007).

70 Sunderland (1915) 23.

71 Baring-Gould **v** (1914) 276-88.

72 Norden (1723) 36-7. *See* also Foord (1910) 133; Sunderland (1915) 23.

73 Cromwell (1828).

74 Foord (1910) 136.

75 Lloyd (1888). For the Action, *see* Howitt (1869).

76 Sunderland (1915) 23.)

77 *Ibid.*

78 Thornbury & Walford **v** (1879-85) 434.

79 Sunderland (1915) 53.

80 Dunkling & Wright (1994) is useful on pub names.

81 Thornbury & Walford **v** (1879-85) 443.

82 Pepys **ii** (1953) 28.

83 *Ibid.* **iii** 34.

84 Sunderland (1915) 106.

85 Field (1652) June.

86 Childrey (1661).

87 Decisive engagement (1471) in the Wars of the Roses, when the Yorkists defeated the Lancastrians, prior to the subsequent (and extremely bloody) Battle of Tewkesbury in the same year.

88 Fuller (1662).

89 *ODNB* **lix** (2004) 910-11.

90 Witty (1660).

91 'Poet and Tragedian'.

92 Witty (1660) and *see* also Foorde (1910) 154; Sunderland (1915) 107.

93 Chauncy (1700).

94 Thorne (1876).
95 Sunderland (1915) 107.
96 Foord (1910) 155.
97 Monro (1770).
98 Rutty (1757).
99 Foord (1910) 156.
100 Morant (1768).
101 Walker (1685).
102 Probably a corruption of 'Rough'.
103 Walford **i** (1884) 458.
104 Ogborne (1814): the study, though impressive, is incomplete and it seems the date of publication was actually 1817. *See ODNB* **xli** (2004) 557.
105 Sunderland (1915) 108.
106 *See* Anonymous (1774), but the edn. in question here was 1793.
107 Walford **i** (1884) 463.
108 Trinder (1783).
109 *Ibid*.
110 Sunderland (1915) 58.
111 Fold of the peritoneum, keeping the intestines in place, but also applied (loosely) to the gut in general. For *Gidea Hall see* Mason (1975) and Trinder (1783).
112 Invigorating, a tonic.
113 Something that removes obstructions by opening up the passages and pores.
114 Sunderland (1915) 58.
115 Trinder (1783) is revealing on these matters.
116 Sunderland (1915) 59-60.
117 *Ibid*. 60.
118 Sunderland (1915) claimed *Witham Well* was in 'grounds adjoining Witham Place', but this was, in fact, Powers Hall End.
119 Trinder (1783).
120 Taverner (1737).
121 Morant (1768). *See* also Bettley & Pevsner (2007) 157, 846.
122 For which the Author is indebted to the late Cecil Hewett, who first alerted him to the delights of Essex.
123 Rutty (1757).
124 Trinder (1783).
125 Timbs (1867) 745 states it was 'situate on the north-western verge of St. James's Park'.
126 Davis (1859) 149 ff.
127 Thornbury & Walford **v** (1879-85) 21.
128 Wroth & Wroth (1896) 221.
129 *Daily Advertiser* (17 March 1764).
130 *See* Faulkner **ii** (1829) 354-6 and Davis (1859) 264. The factory was that opened (1801) by Rudolph Ackermann (1764-1834) for the waterproofing of cloth.
131 Sunderland (1915) 29-30.
132 For the name *see* Larwood & Hotten (1868).
133 Thornbury & Walford **v** (1879-85) 45.
134 *The Post Man* (3-6 October 1702).
135 Anonymous (1764) on *Stepney Spring Gardens*.
136 Sunderland (1915) 31.
137 Formerly Vine Tavern Fields.
138 Linden (1749).
139 Sunderland (1915) 52.
140 Stow **i** (1908) 15.
141 *See* Fitzstephen (1772) and Stow **ii** (1908) 220, *De Fontibus*.
142 Maitland (1756) for this and other matters. *See* also Stow **ii** (1908) 273.
143 Foord (1910) 111.
144 *Ibid*. 110.
145 Sunderland (1915) 41.
146 Foord (1910) 110-12.
147 *See* Childrey (1661).
148 Stow **ii** (1908) 272.
149 *Ibid*. 31.
150 *Ibid*. **i** 15-16.
151 *Ibid*. 95.
152 Hassall (1938, 1939), Hassall (*Ed*.) (1949) for St Mary's Convent, Clerkenwell.
153 Stow **ii** (1908) 272-3.
154 *Ibid*. **i** 11, 16; **ii** 86, 272.
155 Saint (*Gen.Ed*.) (2008*a* & *b*) *passim*.
156 Hassall (1938, 1939); Hassall (*Ed*.) (1949).
157 Recorded in 1205 as *vico Sancte Brigide*.
158 Hone **i** (1835) 325.
159 St Giles (d. *c*.710), hermit, Patron Saint of cripples, lepers, nursing mothers, and smithies. Feast-Day 1 September. *See* Baring-Gould **x** (1914) 8-10.
160 *Vicus Judeorum* mentioned in the twelfth century.
161 Foord (1910) 325-41.
162 *ODNB* **ii** (2004) 495-8. His findings were published in 1855 as *On the Mode of Communication of Cholera* (London: John Churchill).

PART II

SPAS, WELLS, AND PLEASURE-GARDENS SOUTH OF THE THAMES

'The knowledge of man is as the waters, some descending from above, and some springing from beneath...'
FRANCIS BACON (1561-1626): *The Twoo Bookes of Francis Bacon: of the Proficience and Advancement of Learning*, etc.
(London: Henrie Tomes 1605) ii Ch. 5 Sect. 1.

'The chalybeate waters form the best tonics'.
JAMES SMITH (1759-*c*.1828): *The Panorama of Science and Art*
(Liverpool: Nuttall, Fisher, & Dixon 1816) ii 385.

CHAPTER X

NEAR THE THAMES

Introduction; Bermondsey Spa; St Helena Tavern and Gardens, Rotherhithe; Finch's Grotto Gardens; Restoration Spring Gardens; St George's Spaw; Lambeth Wells or Spa; Cuper's Gardens; Belvedere House and Gardens; The Flora Tea-Gardens; The Temple of Flora; Temple of Apollo and Apollo Gardens

'We never know the worth of water till the well is dry'.
THOMAS FULLER (1654-1734): *Gnomologia: Adages and Proverbs, Wise Sentences, and Witty Sayings, Ancient and Modern, Foreign and British* (London: T. & J. Allman 1819) 5451.

INTRODUCTION

The fashion for, and success of, some Spas north of the Thames in the eighteenth century led to the exploitation of the craze south of the River, and these concerns resembled in many ways their northern counterparts, especially those of Islington and Clerkenwell. This Chapter will concentrate on several Pleasure-Gardens that enjoyed fame and favour, albeit for a relatively short time. Some could be described as Spas, some had Wells, and others had only a tentative connection with waters, but all the establishments mentioned here had many aspects in common. The area in which these Gardens once provided many delights has undergone such a transformation over the last 150-200 years that one has great difficulty imagining what they were like: to judge from surviving documentary evidence the change has definitely not been an improvement.

BERMONDSEY SPA

Thomas Keyse (1721-1808)[1], still-life painter, whose representations of legs of mutton and rumps of beef 'in the true Dutch style'[2] were greatly admired during his lifetime, purchased a Tavern, *The Waterman's Arms*, in 1765, and there laid out a Tea-Garden on the adjoining waste ground. He also opened a permanent Gallery for the exhibition of his own works[3] there, the site being near the River Neckinger and the remains of the mediaeval Abbey of Bermondsey *(Plate 133)*. In *c.*1770 a chalybeate Spring, happily, was discovered, and Keyse re-named his establishment the *Bermondsey Spa*, the existence of which is recalled by the name *Spa Road*, SE16[4]. The *Spa* appears to have been situated on the north side of what is now Grange Road, where Spa Road and Keyse Road run off it, but these names, unfortunately, are all that remain to remind us of what was once a lively place of recreation.

The Spring had the added attraction of a cascade, but even so, as with many other such places of the time, the waters appear to have been only a catalyst, the main 'draws' being music and a vast picture-model by Keyse himself representing the *Siege of Gibraltar* (1779-83 – such patriotic allusions to victories, as previously noted, were very much a part of popular entertainment at the time). Although the Gardens only appear to have been about four acres in extent, they included the usual arbours and benches for tea-drinkers, a lawn, an avenue of trees leading from the entrance to the Picture-

Plate 133: *Bermondsey Spa* was situated in the grounds of *The Waterman's Arms*, a Tavern near the ruins of the ancient Abbey of Bermondsey, shown here in an impression by William Henry Prior *(From Thornbury & Walford* ***vi*** *[1879-85] 120: Collection JSC).*

Gallery, and a space before the Orchestra. Hanging from the rows of trees were lamps fitted with coloured glass, in imitation of both *Marylebone* and *Vauxhall Gardens*. Keyse's famous cherry-brandy was a celebrated beverage, enjoyed, it seems, in prodigious quantities.

Admission was gained on payment of sums that varied from sixpence to three shillings, and metal tokens were exchanged for the money (a common arrangement in London Pleasure-Gardens): these tokens could then be traded in for refreshments. Jonas Blewitt (1757-1805), one of the most celebrated organists of his time, composed numerous works for *Bermondsey Spa* from around 1780, and indeed performed there himself[5]. Among the Spa poets was John Oakman (*c*.1748-93 – who was also an engraver and a writer of bawdy novels[6] based on his own itinerant experiences): his works included *Cupid's Revenge, Damon and Cleora, The Macaroni, The Maid of the Mill, The Rover Reclaim'd, Taste a-la-mode,* and other material set to music by various composers[7]. Songs on offer varied from the sentimental to the mawkish, though they often embraced topics such as drinking, hunting, and seafaring, and there were *Burlettas*, duets, and various arrangements of popular airs. One of the *Burlettas* strayed into the familiar Gothick territory of reluctant nuns, wicked guardians, and humanely humorous friars. Various poems and *Burletta* libretti were printed and sold at the *Spa* at sixpence a time[8].

As with the northern Pleasure-Gardens, *Bermondsey Spa* did not eschew fireworks and illuminations[9]. The *Siege of Gibraltar* was engulfed with fireworks, projections, and even bomb-shells: the floating batteries were blown up and ships were sunk in 'fictitious' water[10]. Keyse's Gallery, though, was a perennial attraction: among his most admired works were a picture of Vesuvius erupting and another of a candle which looked so real that viewers thought it was alight.

Surprisingly, given its position, *Bermondsey Spa* does not appear to have developed a *louche* reputation: although never fashionable, it was patronised by the respectable middle classes, and it provided its proprietor with a reasonable and gratifyingly steady income. Keyse was keen to point out that his *Spa* was safe: the 'Spa Gardens in Grange Road, Bermondsey, one mile from London Bridge' could be approached by a road 'lighted and watched by patroles every night at the sole expense of the proprietor'. This is probably a somewhat exaggerated claim, for it is highly doubtful if the owner of *Bermondsey Spa* could have afforded either 'patroles' or adequate lighting over such a distance as a mile.

In 1795, however, the *Spa* was declining in popularity, and John Thomas Smith (1766-1833) described it as having 'idle waiters' and virtually no custom, but he greatly admired Keyse's paintings in the Gallery. His experience of the music, sung by a 'handsome, most dashingly dressed, immensely plumed, and villainously rouged' woman, was rather sad, for there was no audience[11], apart from Keyse and himself.

After Keyse's death in 1800 the *Spa* tried pony-racing, but it was of no avail: it closed around 1805, the pictures were sold off, and the site built over. The buildings shown in a wash drawing by John Chessell Buckler (1793-1894) dated 1826, and identified as 'Spa Place, Bermondsey', probably show the site of the Spa *(Plate 134)*. It seems that the waters of the *Bermondsey Spa*, like those of the *Marybone Spa*, were really fashionable extras, added to concerns that were already established: Sunderland, therefore, labelled Bermondsey a 'spurious' Spa because he found no evidence to suggest that many of the visitors were attracted by any supposed virtues of the water[12].

New homes being built in the area at the time of writing, described as 'modern living in the heart of historic, vibrant Bermondsey', are optimistically called Bermondsey Spa.

ST HELENA TAVERN AND GARDENS, ROTHERHITHE

Further east, beyond *Bermondsey Spa*, was *St Helena Gardens*, situated to the south-east of the junction of what is now Raymouth Road and Rotherhithe New Road: it was just west of St Helena Road, and part of the grounds lie under the Church of St Katharine, Eugenia Road (1960 – by Covell Matthews & Partners, replacing a Church of 1884 designed by William Oswald Milne [1847-1927]).

The *Gardens* opened in 1770: by 1776 music was being performed there, and dances took

Plate 134: View of *Spa Place*, Bermondsey, by John Chessell Buckler (1826) *(LMA SC/GL/PEN 21/Ce24046/cat.no.p5353565).*

Plate 135: The *St Helena Tavern and Tea Gardens* shown in a water-colour by 'R.B.' dated 7 June 1839. *Eastern Vaux Hall* is visible on the upper frieze above the large bay-window *(LMA SC/GL/WAK/B1-D/Ce20094/cat.no.p5958953).*

place. Although essentially a Tavern with a large Garden, the establishment seems to have had its attractions, and even the Prince of Wales is supposed to have visited, together with several other Persons of Quality. From the few surviving views of it, it seems to have been quite pretty *(Plate 135)*. In the early decades of the nineteenth century it was favoured as a Tea-Garden, and although much used by the neighbouring populace, it became known for a time as *The Eastern Vauxhall*. The establishment acquired an Organist and Director of Music, and there were vocalists and a performer on musical glasses, but these activities ceased around the end of the 1860s, although there were attempts to revive them from *c*.1874 when new proprietors built an Orchestra and dancing-platform, beautified the Gardens, provided supper-boxes, and laid on music, fireworks, illuminations, and other familiar draws, but the venture failed by 1881 and shortly afterwards the Gardens were developed for building. Fortunately, John Drayton Wyatt (1820-91), the architect, made some drawings of the *St Helena Gardens* in 1881, just before they disappeared, which help an understanding of much detail found in similar establishments *(Plates 136 & 137)*. Two more views appear on a steel engraving of *c*.1840s: they show the entrance to the *St Helena Tavern and Tea Gardens (Plate 138)* and an enticing view of walks around a pond, so there is no doubt that, at least in its earlier days, the establishment had many things in its favour. Its sale for building was advertised as four acres of building land together with the pub and fourteen cottages, so it was not a small place: the auction was carried out by Messrs Glasier & Sons on 28 July 1881 *(Plate 139)*.

The *St Helena Tavern and Gardens* does not appear to have had any ambitions to offer water, medicinal or otherwise, although tea, coffee, and the inevitable rolls were available every day.

Plate 136: The *Tavern & St Helena Gardens,* Rotherhithe, as seen from St Helena Street, drawn by J. Drayton Wyatt in 1881 (*LMA SC/GL/NOR/TEA & MUSIC vol. 9 p.29*).

Today, the proximity of the Bermondsey Trading Estate, main roads, railway, and other unpleasantnesses leave no suggestion of what must once have been an agreeable retreat which never really attained more than local celebrity despite the *Eastern Vauxhall* affectation[13].

FINCH'S GROTTO GARDENS

Another painter, Thomas Finch (d. 1770), this time one who painted Coats of Arms on Escutcheons, Boards, Tables, Hatchments, and the like, inherited a house and garden (well stocked with lofty trees, evergreens, and shrubs) on the western side of St George's Street, Southwark, near St George's Fields (its site seems to have been approximately where Southwark Street joins Southwark Bridge Road), and opened both to the public in 1760. In the centre was a medicinal Spring over which Finch caused a grotto and fountain to be constructed. This fountain played over artificial embankments and formed an attractive cascade.

The waters received the *Imprimatur* of a medical man named Townshend, and for a brief period they were held in some esteem, but, like many other establishments, the customers went thither for reasons other than the water. We know that the supposed 'scientific' analyses of water in the eighteenth century were anything but reliable, and William Rendle (1811-93), the historian of Southwark, was of the opinion that the water was merely the filtered 'soakage' of a super-saturated soil which occurred almost everywhere in Southwark[14].

Finch introduced the usual entertainments and adopted the token system for entry and

Plate 137: View in *St Helena Gardens, Rotherhithe,* drawn by J. Drayton Wyatt, looking east towards the 'dancing-platform' and Tavern in 1881. The platform was surrounded by fluted columns supporting an entablature, painted and enriched, surmounted by a row of lights *(LMA SC/GL/NOR/TEA & MUSIC vol. 9 p.29).*

refreshments (which included tea, wine, cakes, cider, and so on). An Orchestra, an organ, an octagonal Music-Room (decorated with paintings), and other facilities were provided. The Octagonal Room was used for dances, promenades, and concerts (of which there were many, given every evening from May to September). Benefit-nights were given for performers, and the Freemasons appear to have had dinners there too. Robert Hudson (1732-1815) played the organ, and among the singers were Sophia Baddeley (*née* Snow [*c*.1745-86]), whose putative father, Valentine Snow (d.1770), was the trumpeter for whom Händel wrote virtuoso parts (e.g. *The Trumpet Shall Sound* in *The Messiah*). Baddeley sang at *Vauxhall* and *Ranelagh Gardens* as well as at *Finch's*, and was a considerable beauty (she was painted by the great Johan Joseph Zoffany [1733-1810], for example), but her intrigues with an impressive regiment of dissolute aristocrats and wealthy drones turned her head, and she eventually died in reduced circumstances, having been over-generous and wildly extravagant in her days of youthful loveliness and heady success. Thomas Lowe (we have encountered him previously in connection with *Marylebone Gardens*) accepted engagements to sing at *Finch's* after he became bankrupt, and his name recurs in connection with the Freemasons' concerts.

When Finch died, the *Grotto Gardens* were taken over by one Williams, who pulled down the Grotto and formed a skittle-ground over the site of the Spring. Concerts continued; firework-displays took place; and there were balls, illuminations, and music in the Gardens as well

Plate 138: Steel engraving of the 1840s showing *(top)* the entrance to *St Helena Tavern and Tea Gardens,* and *(below)* the pretty Gardens around a pool *(LMA SC/GL/NOR/TEA & MUSIC vol. 9 p.29).*

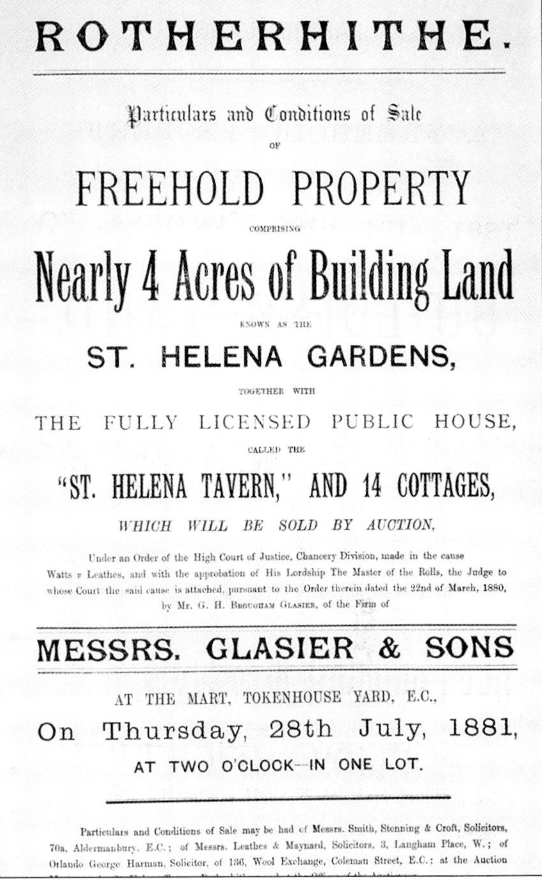

ROTHERHITHE.

Particulars and Conditions of Sale
OF

FREEHOLD PROPERTY
COMPRISING

Nearly 4 Acres of Building Land
KNOWN AS THE

ST. HELENA GARDENS,
TOGETHER WITH

THE FULLY LICENSED PUBLIC HOUSE,
CALLED THE

"ST. HELENA TAVERN," AND 14 COTTAGES,

WHICH WILL BE SOLD BY AUCTION,

Under an Order of the High Court of Justice, Chancery Division, made in the cause Watts v Leathes, and with the approbation of His Lordship The Master of the Rolls, the Judge to whose Court the said cause is attached, pursuant to the Order therein dated the 22nd of March, 1880, by Mr. G. H. Brougham Glasier, of the Firm of

MESSRS. GLASIER & SONS

AT THE MART, TOKENHOUSE YARD, E.C.,

On Thursday, 28th July, 1881,

AT TWO O'CLOCK—IN ONE LOT.

Particulars and Conditions of Sale may be had of Messrs. Smith, Stenning & Croft, Solicitors, 70a, Aldermanbury, E.C.; of Messrs. Leathes & Maynard, Solicitors, 3, Langham Place, W.; of Orlando George Harman, Solicitor, of 136, Wool Exchange, Coleman Street, E.C.; at the Auction

Plate 139: *Particulars and Conditions of Sale* relating to the *St Helena Gardens,* 1881 *(LMA SC/GL/NOR/TEA & MUSIC vol. 9 p.31).*

as plays. Performers included the singer John Barnshaw (*fl.*1768-83 – who rendered works such as *A New Hunting Song* [*c.*1776]) and Fredericka Weirman (d. 1786 – who gave pieces by composers such as Henry Brewster [*c.*1747-88])[15]. Musical tastes of the period ensured that Händel's festive Coronation Anthems were often performed, together with less elevated numbers, such as *Thro' the Wood, Laddie, O What a Charming Thing is a Battle, British Wives,* and *Cupid's Recruiting Sergeant* (the last with suitable drum-and-fife accompaniments)[16].

Other attractions included 'grand transparent paintings': featured were Neptune supported by Tritons with serpents spouting water, Neptune drawn by Hippocamps, Venus rising from the sea, and another picture represented a waterfall in Wales. However, the *Grotto Gardens,* despite their curious entertainments, did not pay their way, and in 1777 the grounds were bought for the Parish of St Saviour, Southwark, part of them for the erection of a Workhouse (designed by George Gwilt, Senior [1746-1807][17]) and part for use as a burial-ground. The Tavern, however, continued as a public-house under the sign of *The Grotto,* but burned down in 1795: a new pub was erected called at first *The Goldsmith's Arms* and then *Old Grotto Reviv'd,* and on its front was a stone inscribed

'Here Herbs did grow
And Flowers sweet,
But now 'tis call'd
Saint George's Street'[18].

The Workhouse did not flourish for long: it was sold in 1799 to become a manufactory and a residence, and the remains of the Octagon Room were used as a mill and then as an armoury. The timber tea-rooms became poor cottages and in the 1820s a very old mulberry tree still stood in the remains of the Gardens. Even the pub was demolished when Southwark Bridge Road was formed, and another establishment called *The Goldsmith's Arms* was erected on the western side of the new road on the site of the former Gardens. Gwilt's Workhouse partially survived: it was incorporated within the premises of the London Fire Brigade (later the Fire Brigade Training Centre, Winchester House)[19].

Sunderland's opinion that claims for the *Grotto Gardens* as a Spa were spurious would be hard to refute: the water seems to have been only a kind of advertisement to attract custom.

RESTORATION SPRING GARDENS

These Gardens were a going concern in the reign of Charles II (reigned 1660-85), and were situated in St George's Fields, about half-way between what is now Blackfriars and Waterloo Roads, near The Cut. Tokens[20] were issued for admission to 'ye Restoration in St George's Feilds', and the Gardens were originally attached to a Tavern called *The Restoration* (referring, of course, to the Restoration of the Monarchy in 1660). By 1714 a new cock-pit had been constructed, and huge sums were wagered: two guineas per battle represented an enormous sum of money then, and cock-fights took place all week, beginning at four o'clock in the afternoons. The Tavern also attracted custom from those who attended the races and other popular sports in St George's Fields.

By 1733, when the Spring in the Gardens was advertised as 'well known for the cure of all cancerous and scorbutic humours'[21], and referred to as a 'Purging Spring', another Spring was discovered: this produced chalybeate water similar in nature to that of 'Piermont', 'but superior', and was readily available at 'Mr Lewis's, commonly called the Restauration Gardens' as well as in bottled form in a shop in The Strand[22]. Rendle, however, doubted if the water had any medicinal properties[23] whatsoever, regarding it, like *Finch's* water, as soakage. Sunderland classified the place as a 'spurious' Spa[24], and the benefits (if any) conferred were soon eclipsed by the attractions of the *Dog and Duck* near by, of which more anon.

In 1771 the Garden, or part of it, was taken by William Curtis (1746-99), the botanist and entomologist, who formed the *London Botanic Garden* at Lambeth Marsh there: it remained until 1789 when Curtis moved it to a larger and more salubrious site at Brompton[25]. Curtis gave lectures at his *Botanic Garden* in Lambeth, published and beautifully illustrated after his death[26]. The *Botanic Garden* was supported by subscriptions.

ST GEORGE'S SPAW

The *Dog and Duck* Tavern was situated in St George's Fields conveniently near several ponds used for the 'sport' of duck-hunting with dogs, and appears to have been in existence in 1642 and probably earlier *(Plate 140)*. An aperient Spring there was first mentioned in 1695, the waters of which were claimed to be useful for the treatment of various 'Distempers' including Gout, Gravel, Stone, Ulcers, Fistulas, King's Evil, Blotches, Sore Eyes, all 'salt and sharp Humours',

Plate 140: Carved inn-sign of the *Dog and Duck* Tavern, St George's Fields. Hunting ducks with dogs was a popular pastime well into the nineteenth century *(From Thornbury & Walford **vi** [1879-85]344: Collection JSC).*

Plate 141: Interior of the Long-Room of *St George's Spaw*, otherwise known as the *Dog and Duck*. One of the central characters on the right appears to be a young woman dressed as a man, but wearing a fashionable hat usually donned by females. Anonymous stipple engraving, July 1789 *(LMA SC/GL/PR/S2/CHR-S2/GEO/FIE/Ce17671/cat.no.p5400419)*.

and Inveterate Cancers. Dr John Fothergill (1712-80)[27] is supposed to have recommended them for the 'cure of most cutaneous disorders', for 'keeping the body cool', and for 'preventing cancerous affections'[28]. By 1731 the establishment had assumed the title *St George's Spaw*, and the water was advertised for sale for four pence a gallon at the pump or a shilling for a dozen bottles[29].

The *Spaw*'s water seems to have been in some demand, and the proprietor erected a Long-Room with tables, benches, and an organ *(Plate 141)*, a bowling-green, and a swimming-bath (1769). Breakfasts were served in the Long-Room, and some Persons of Quality seem to have patronised the *Spaw* for the sake of their health, including Mrs Hester Lynch Thrale[30] (if Samuel Johnson's recommendations were followed) and Catherine Talbot (1721-70 – who wrote to her friend Elizabeth Carter [1717-1806] recommending the waters[31]). Various puffs compared the *Spaw* waters favourably with those of Buxton, Cheltenham, and Tunbridge Wells. Walter Besant (1836-1901), in his novel *The Orange Girl*[32], made several references to the 'Dog and Duck Spa', and there was even an attempt to connect the *Spaw* with Lazare Rivière (1589-1655), the celebrated French doctor: his portrait was struck in silver on admission-tickets (1760) for subscribers[33].

In the 1770s the *Spaw* attracted custom from a Circus in St George's Fields, and the equestrian Sampson, of *The Three Hats*, Islington, performed there. By the 1770s, the landlady, a Mrs Hedger, called in her son who had been a stable-boy at Epsom, and young Hedger (who was clearly no slouch) improved the property and its Tea-Gardens, making much of a 'pretty piece of water', and enhancing the quality of musical performances. Lighting, too, was improved, but, with attempts to pull in more custom, tone degenerated, and by the mid-1770s, the place was somewhat raffish:

'St George's Fields, with taste and fashion
struck,
Display Arcadia at the 'Dog and Duck',
And Drury misses here in tawdry pride,
Are there "Pastoras" by the fountain side;
The frowsy bowers they reel through
midnight damps,
With Fauns half drunk, and Dryads breaking
lamps'[34].

By the mid-1780s the *Dog and Duck* or *St George's Spaw* appears to have sunk rather low. Carington Bowles, in one of his series of humorous mezzotints featuring London Spas, showed two overweight persons in the rural setting of *St George's Spaw*, hardly suggesting an elevated tone *(Plate 142)*. Bowles's characters, though, look harmless, but others who went to the *Spaw* were nothing of the sort: one infamous strumpet, Charlotte Shaftoe, is supposed to have lurked there and betrayed several of her intimates to the tender mercies of the Georgian gallows. By 1792 the *Spaw* was closed on Sundays. Nineteenth-century opinion held that the *Dog and Duck* grounds were 'unworthy of patronage' and that the audience for 'popular concerts' was 'composed of the riff-raff and scum of the town'[35].

Plate 142: *Labour in Vain, a Fatty in Distress* 1782: one of Carington Bowles's humorous mezzotints of the humours of the day, showing two 'elephants' attempting to struggle through an opening in a fence, a young gallant and spaniel (presumably to chase the ducks) in attendance. The rural setting of St George's Fields is clearly shown, and in the background is the considerable extent of *St George's Spaw* attached to the *Dog and Duck* Tavern *(LMA SC/GL/PR/S2/GEO/FIE/Ce17672/ cat.no.p5400402)*.

However, in 1795 the Bath and bowling-green were advertised, and the waters were again being promoted, but tone was dubious: the anonymous author of *A Sunday Ramble* found bankrupts, strumpets, and other curiosities there. Very soon the patrons of the *Dog and Duck* could be described as 'children of poverty, irregularity, and distress', and the Gardens 'were at length put down by the magistrates'[36]. Nemesis came, first in the form of a public soup-kitchen, and then in the form of a School for the Indigent Blind, which remained there until 1811[37].

Then the site was redeveloped from 1812 as the Bethlehem Hospital to designs by James Lewis (*c*.1751-1820), a truncated and altered part of which is now the Imperial War Museum[38].

LAMBETH WELLS *OR* SPA

Situated in Three Coney (now Lambeth) Walk, there were two Springs (called the Nearer and Farther Wells), both known in the late seventeenth century, and protected by a Pump-House surmounted by a gilded ball. The *Wells* is shown in Rocque's *Plan* of 1746 as a large establishment on the east side of Three Coney Walk near the junction with Paradise Row *(Plate 143)*. An advertisement of 1696 referred to the 'Lambeth purging waters in Langton Gardens, Lambeth Fields, near the "Three Coneys",... fitted for the entertainment of persons of all Qualities'[39].The usually sceptical Sunderland regarded *Lambeth Wells* as a genuine Spa, amply provided for with purging waters. As usual, musical entertainments were provided, with 'consorts of very good musick, with French and Country Dancing'. Attendance was given every morning to any gentleman or lady who had 'occasion to drink the waters'. The *Wells* supplied St Thomas's Hospital with water for relief of 'affections' of the liver and stomach[40].

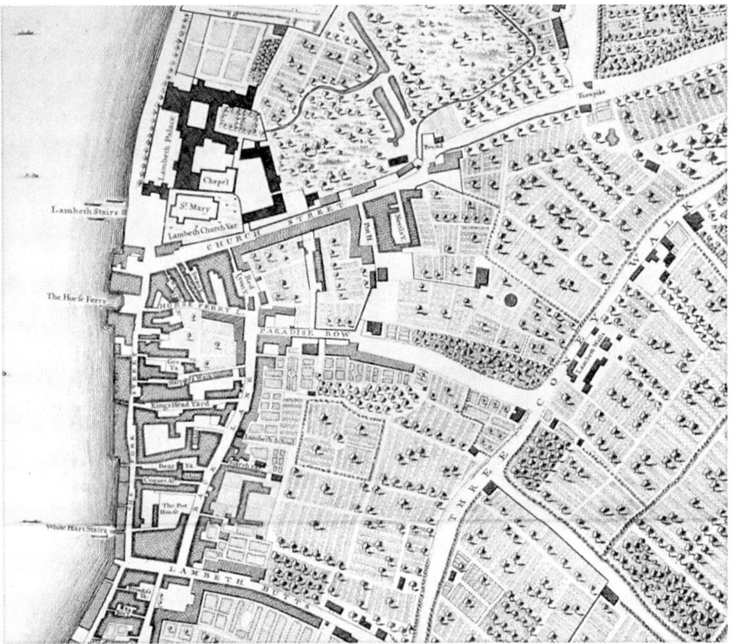

Plate 143: Detail from the *Plan of the Cities of London, Westminster, and the Borough of Southwark* (1746) sheet 3C, by John Rocque (*c*.1704-62), engraved by John Pine (1690-1756), published by John Tinney (*c*.1706-61), showing *Lambeth Wells* in Three Coney Walk, set among market-gardens and orchards *(LMA GL/PR/Ce33544/cat.no.q8972932).*

From about 1700 the place was open for drinking the waters from seven in the morning, and the charge for admittance was three pence. Entertainments went on until sunset. There was a Great-Room in which concerts and dancing took place. 'Consorts' were given every Wednesday consisting of 'vocal and instrumental musick' performed by about thirty persons, an impressive number. The charge for these 'Consorts' was a shilling, and they began at 2.30 pm, and later on at six in the evening, after which nobody was admitted in a mask[41].

Around the beginning of the eighteenth century the shilling concerts appear to have ceased, but the *Wells* continued to attract custom until the rival establishment of the *Dog and Duck* began to be patronised by a fickle public. In the mid-eighteenth century a music-society gave monthly concerts at the Spa, directed by the organist of St Saviour's, Southwark, Sterling Goodwin, and programmes seem to have been reasonably edifying[42]. There were also lectures on Natural Philosophy given by Erasmus King (d. 1760), who appears to have been coachman at one time to the great John Theophilus Desaguliers (1683-1744), Natural Philosopher, promoter of Newtonian principles, and Freemason: clearly King absorbed many of Desagulier's ideas, and probably used the great man's own works in his lectures. King seems to have had pretensions as an expert on Mineral-Waters, as a Catalogue of his experiments demonstrates[43]. Apart from lectures of an Improving Nature (entrance-fee six pence), 'Consorts', and so on, there were gala dances and even (in 1752) a 'wedding in the Scotch manner'.

Some time after 1755 the magistrates refused to allow any more dancing, and the Great-Room became a Methodist meeting-house, the preacher delivering his harangues from the music-gallery (to not always appreciative audiences) and during the latter part of the eighteenth and beginning of the nineteenth century the building became what was really a common ale-house called *The Well*[44]. The *Wells* seem to have existed as late as 1829, but were built over after then, and the public-house (by then called *The Fountain*) was pulled down: during the preparation of the site for a new Tavern, many glass bottles or flagons were discovered with the initials 'P.K.' on them, presumably referring to the proprietor, one Keefe or Keeffe (*fl.*1740s). The newly-built *Fountain* was in Lambeth Walk, almost opposite what is now Old Paradise Street. Despite these vicissitudes, part of the grounds of *Lambeth Spa* continued to be used as a Tea-Garden until about 1840[45].

CUPER'S GARDENS

These were laid out on a long, narrow strip of meadow-land on what had been Lambeth Marsh, opposite Somerset House. The property was surrounded by water-courses: its long axis coincided with what became Waterloo Bridge Road, and it was later bisected by Stamford Street and its approaches (the large roundabout at the west end of Stamford Street is on top of part of the Gardens) *(Plate 144)*.

The place got its name from Abraham Boydell Cuper (a former employee of Thomas Howard [1585-1646 – 14th Earl of Arundel from 1595]), who obtained a lease of the ground and there he or his son opened a public Pleasure-Garden, with walks, arbours, and bowling-greens, enhanced by statues from Arundel House in The Strand when it was demolished in *c.*1678. The Gardens were extended by Cuper from 1686 when he obtained a lease of a further seven acres of ground from the Archbishop of Canterbury[46].

Edward Hatton (*c.*1664-?) described the 'pleasant Gardens and Walks with Bowling greens... whither many of the Westerly part of the Town resort for Diversion in the Summer Season'[47]. The statues, known as the 'Arundel Marbles', were sold by John Cuper in 1717 for all of £75[48]. A public-house by the river-bank, *The*

Plate 144: *A Plan of Cuper's Gardens with Part of the Parish of Lambeth In the Year 1746 Shewing also the Site of the Waterloo Bridge Road and the New Roads adjacent*, published by Robert Wilkinson (*fl.*1785-1825), 1825. The rectangular building (A) to the east of the inscription WATER is the *Old Feathers*, and the *New Feathers* (C) stands at the top of the Gardens where the THE of COMMERCIAL ROAD sweeps round in a quadrant. The Royal Universal Infirmary for Children (D) stands in the Gardens just to the right of the long pond or canal on the line of what was to become Waterloo Road. On the same alignment is the handsome Greek Doric hexastyle portico of the Church of St John the Evangelist (1822-4) designed by that under-rated master, Francis Octavius Bedford (1784-1858) *(LMA SC/GL/PR/L1/BEL-L1/CUT/Ce17602/cat.no.q9513818)*.

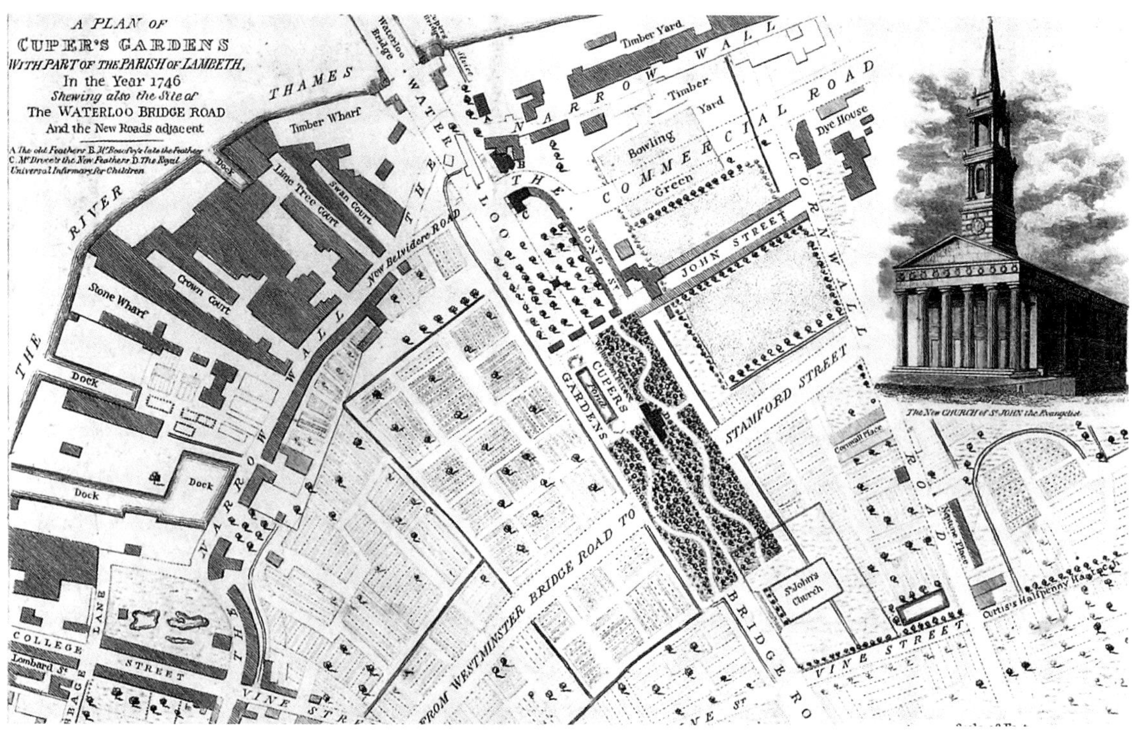

Feathers, was connected with the grounds, and it and the Gardens were popular during the summer months. In 1738 both Tavern and Gardens were taken over by Ephraim Evans, who improved them, erected an Orchestra, and installed an organ by Richard Bridge (or Bridger) (d. 1758).

It was not long before *Cuper's* became known as *Cupid's Garden*, as the following verse shows:

''Twas down in Cupid's Garden
For pleasure I did go,
To see the fairest flowers
That in that garden grow:

The first it was the jessamine,
The lily, pink and rose,
And surely they're the fairest flowers
That in the garden grows'[49].

Cuper's was most usually approached by water, and there was a landing-stage, east of where Waterloo Bridge is now, at Cuper's Stairs *(Plate 145)*. Those who came across St George's Fields were given some protection by night-watchmen, but even so such parts could be dangerous in the dark.

When Evans died in 1740, his widow took over, and the Gardens flourished. 'Musick' included works by Händel, Arne, Johann Adolph Hasse (1699-1783), and others: Händel's 'celebrated Fire-Musick'[50] was performed with fireworks 'consisting of Fire-Wheels, Fountains, large Sky-Rockets, with the Addition of the Fire-Pump, etc., made by the ingenious Mr Worman... play'd off from the Top of the Orchestra by Mr Worman himself'[51].

Patronage from fashionable Society was undoubtedly present at *Cuper's*, but well-dressed card-sharpers, pickpockets, and strumpets could be found there as well. No lady would venture there alone as it was a place of resort for the 'gay and profligate' and the 'abandoned of either sex'. Nevertheless, music by almost forgotten names such as 'Henry Burgess Junior' was performed, together with works by Arcangelo Corelli (1653-1713) and other still celebrated composers, so it cannot have been as bad as was claimed. Lavish celebrations took place in 1746 after the 'glorious victory obtained over the rebels' by the Duke of Cumberland, and there were more in 1750 to commemorate the General Peace.

In 1751 the Act of Parliament 'for the better preventing thefts and robberies, and for

Plate 145: *View of the Savoy, Somerset House and the Water Entrance to Cuper's Garden.* Aquatint after a painting by Samuel Scott (*c.*1702-72), engraved by William M. Fellows (*fl.*1792-1825) published (1808) by John Thomas Smith (1766-1833), from Smith's *Antiquities of Westminster* *(LMA SC/GL/NOB/B/W2/REG-W2/SOH).*

Plate 146: *View in Cuper's Gardens, Lambeth*, drawn by Ravenhill and engraved by Bartholomew Howlett (1767-1827). It shows the former Orchestra *(LMA SC/GL/PR/L1/BEL-L1/CUT/Ce17602/ cat.no.q9513818).*

regulating places of publick entertainment and punishing Persons keeping Disorderly Houses', otherwise known as the *Disorderly House Act* (25 Geo. II *c.* 36) by which every house, room, garden, or other place kept for public dancing or music within the Cities of London and Westminster, or twenty miles thereof, had to be licensed. The Act came into effect at the end of 1752, and the necessary licence for *Cuper's Gardens* was refused, for by that time the place had acquired a reputation for dissipation and raffishness. This spelled the end of the heyday of *Cuper's*, even though the Widow Evans continued to run the place as an unlicensed 'Tea-Garden' in close association with *The Feathers* public-house: occasional concerts and firework displays were given for subscribers only, but *Cuper's* finally closed in 1760, as the 'subscription' device was soon rumbled. The buildings seem to have included several substantial structures, some of which were recorded *(Plate 146)*. Illustrations also survive which give some idea of what the place (including *The Feathers*) *(Plates 147 & 148)* looked like. However, it is worth noting that there was a large pond or canal in the Gardens in its glory-days, and that water featured in several of the displays. Although waters for drinking do not seem to have been exploited, the Gardens were

Plate 147: *View in Cuper's Gardens, Lambeth*, published by Robert Wilkinson, 1825, showing the Orchestra at the time it was occupied by Messrs Beaufoys for the British Wine Manufactory. Drawn by George Sidney Shepherd (1784-1862) and engraved by Dale *(LMA SC/GL/NOR/TEA & MUSIC vol. 9 p.13).*

Plate 148: View of the *Feathers Tavern, Cupers-Bridge, Lambeth,* published by Robert Wilkinson, 1825, with a view over the Thames to Hungerford and The Strand. To the left of the public-house is a chandler's shop, and on the left is the sluice. Drawn by Henry Francis De Cort (1742-1810) and engraved by Bartholomew Howlett (1767-1827) *(LMA SC/GL/NOR/TEA & MUSIC vol. 9 p.27).*

certainly well-supplied with water, and this was used by the firm of Beaufoy which took over the establishment to distil wine and vinegar.

Construction works for the approaches to Waterloo Bridge and the laying out of Waterloo Road cut through what was left of the Gardens, and the Royal Hospital for Children and Women was erected in 1823 at the north-eastern corner of Waterloo Road and Stamford Street (entirely rebuilt 1903-5 to designs by M. S. Nicholson)[52].

BELVEDERE HOUSE AND GARDENS

This establishment, a well-known place of amusement, in existence from the reign of Queen Anne (1702-14), was not far from *Cuper's Gardens*, but up-river, more or less opposite York Buildings in The Strand, and extended from the present Belvedere Road to the bank of the River. It was a private house, but in 1781 it became an Inn with Gardens and fish-ponds, offering choicest wines and good food, especially 'river-fish' which could be caught on the premises. However, in 1785 the place became a timber-wharf, and part of the Gardens were taken for the machinery of the Lambeth water-works. Apart from the fish-ponds, there does not appear to have been any exploitation of 'waters'[53].

THE FLORA TEA-GARDENS

This short-lived (1796-7) concern on Westminster Bridge Road was patronised by 'ordinary' persons at first, who presumably viewed the 'genteel paintings' having paid the sixpence entrance-fee, but tone rapidly changed for the worse, and many 'dissolute' characters ensured the demise of the venture. The grounds were built over in the 1820s and called 'Mount Gardens'. There appears to have been a Well there, but the 'waters' were never, it seems, exploited as such[54].

THE TEMPLE OF FLORA

This establishment, also on Westminster Bridge Road, prompted by a similar structure at *Ranelagh*, was 'fitted up with alcoves and exotics' and had a hot-house graced by a statue of Pomona. There were also a transparency of Flora, a 'natural cascade', and a fountain. Illuminations, fireworks, water-works, and imitations of singing-birds were also given. Refreshments included lemonade, strawberries and cream in season, confectionery, and orgeat[55].

In its early manifestation (1788-91) it appears to have been reasonably respectable, and the boxes in the gardens were 'neatly painted'[56]. However, the proprietor was imprisoned for keeping a disorderly house, and it appears that Jeanne de Saint-Rémy de Valois, *soi-disant* Comtesse de Lamotte, one of the protagonists of the curious Affair of the Diamond Necklace (in which Louis-René-Édouard, Cardinal de Rohan [1734-1803], and Marie Antoinette, Queen of France [1774-93], had been implicated) had a fatal fall near the Temple of Flora in 1791.

Although there was obviously plenty of water on the site, it does not appear to have been used for medicinal or commercial purposes[57].

TEMPLE OF APOLLO AND APOLLO GARDENS

Another establishment on the left-hand side of Westminster Bridge Road when travelling from Westminster towards St George's Circus was the *Apollo Gardens* with a Concert-Room having a 'kind of orrery in the dome, displaying a pallid moon behind two brilliant transparencies': within this room was a fine organ, and in the opening concert (1788) an audience of nearly a thousand heard about seventy instrumental and vocal performers give a rousing performance. As usual, the Gardens contained 'elegant pavilions' or alcoves in which refreshments could be taken, and these were decorated with painted scenes. In 1792 there were musical performances throughout the Season in what was described as the 'Grand Apollonian Promenade', and another room was made available for dinner-parties. There were also exhibitions of 'Fantoccini' (i.e. marionettes or puppets). 'New Overtures' were played: these were composed by Franz Joseph Haydn (1732-1809 – then on his first visit to London) and the latter's gifted pupil, Ignaz Joseph Pleyel (1757-1831 – then also in London)[58].

The *Apollo Gardens* was favoured for hot suppers, and the grounds were attractively illuminated. Fine music and wines went with what the proprietor was pleased to call the 'chastity and dignity' of the establishment. However, persons arriving from other places of public resort for suppers, invariably well-oiled by the time they arrived, began to give the place an unenviable reputation for rowdiness: in addition, it became a haunt of thieves, confidence-tricksters, and strumpets of varying degrees of notoriety, all out for rich pickings. Well-dressed and handsome young women, delectable to look at but as hard as nails, were given to 'trepanning' (ensnaring, luring, or decoying) the unwary and gullible, even relieving children of fine sashes and other ornaments by employing soothing blandishments and fake charm.

Even Haydn and Pleyel could not rescue the Gardens from suppression by the magistrates in 1793, and the proprietor (the Irish musician, Walter Clagget [1742-98]) went bankrupt. Not long afterwards the Temple and its grounds became ruinous, and the site succumbed to development. Again, although the Gardens shared many attributes with places that aspired to be Spas or had Wells, there does not appear to be any evidence that waters on the site were used for drinking neat or with syrups, or that they featured in advertisements to attract custom[59]. One description was damning:

> 'A want of the rural accompaniment of fine trees, their small extent, their situation, and other causes, soon made them the resort of only low and vicious characters; and after an ineffectual struggle, lasting through two or three seasons, they were finally closed, and the site was built over. The old orchestra of the gardens, when taken down, was removed to Sydney Gardens, at Bath, to be re-erected there'[60].

Like their competing establishments, the *Temple of Apollo* and *Apollo Gardens*, with their snug boxes, paintings, and sculptures, proved to be ephemeral: they were a passing craze, as insubstantial as a discarded tumbler of water.

Chapter X References: Near the Thames

1 *Burlington Magazine* **lix** (1931) 75. *See* also Keyse (1986).
2 *Gentleman's Magazine* Series I **lxx**/1 (1800) 284.
3 *See* Lysons **i** (1792-6) 558.
4 For Keyse *see ODNB* **xxxi** (2004) 501.
5 *ODNB* **vi** (2004) 209. One of his popular efforts, 'sung by Mrs Thompson, with universal applause', was the ballad, *The Lass of Humber Side*, published by Longman & Broderip in 1787. 'Mrs Thompson' was probably Jane Henrietta Thompson (*née* Poitier – 1736-c.1788). *See ODNB* **xliv** (2004) 681-2.
6 *See The Life and Adventures of Benjamin Brass. An Irish Fortune-Hunter* (London: W. Nicoll 1765), for example.
7 It is pretty dull stuff.
8 *See* such delights as *The Quack Doctor*, *The Fop*, and *The Auctioneer*, none of which would really work today.
9 In the 1790s Rossi and Tessier designed the firework-displays.
10 Anonymous (1797) gives descriptions of the 'picturesque prospect' of the Siege. For pyrotechnics *see* Brock (1922, 1949) and Dixon (1987).
11 Smith (1861) 135 ff. *See* Hughson **v** (1805-9) 60; Ledger (*Ed.*) (1870) 18; Phillips (1841) 84-5; Thornbury & Walford **vi** (1879-85) 128-9.
12 Sunderland (1915) 110.
13 Feltham (1802, 1829); Gaspey (*Ed.*) (1851-2); Ledger (*Ed.*) (1868-92) issue (1871) 6; Thornbury & Walford **vi** (1879-85) 138; Wroth & Wroth (1896) 238-40.
14 Rendle & Norman (1888) 360-4.
15 *See* Henry Brewster (1771): *1771 Vauxhall and Grotto Songs with an Ode to Summer: sung by Mrs Weichell* [sic], *Miss Dowson, Miss Cantrell, Mr Barnshaw, & Master Suett* (London: Longman, Lukey, & Co.).
16 A typical concert programme from 1771 is reproduced in Wroth & Wroth (1896) 244.
17 Colvin (2008) 457.
18 Wroth & Wroth (1896) 246, also quoted in Thornbury & Walford **vi** (1870-85) 64.
19 *See* Brayley, Britton, Brayley, & Mantell **v** (1841-4) 371; Manning & Bray **iii** (1809-14) 591; Rendle & Norman (1888) 360-4; Sunderland (1915) 112-3; Thornbury & Walford **vi** (1879-85) 64; Wilkinson **ii** (1819-25) on *Finch's Grotto Gardens*; Wroth & Wroth (1896) 241-6. *See* also Cherry & Pevsner (1983) 589.
20 Boyne (1889-91) 1036.
21 *Country Journal or The Craftsman* (31 March 1733).
22 Wroth & Wroth (1896) 263.
23 Rendle & Norman (1888) 367-8.
24 Sunderland (1915) 113.
25 *ODNB* **xiv** (2004) 780-1.
26 Curtis (1805). *See* also Nichols (1786) 84.
27 *ODNB* **xx** (2004) 534-6.
28 Quoted in Sunderland (1915) 114.
29 *See The Country Journal or The Craftsman* (12 and 26 August 1732). *See* also Wroth & Wroth (1896) 271. *See* also a notice in LMA (D1.12), kindly drawn to the Author's attention by Jeremy Smith.
30 Hester Lynch Piozzi (1741-1821). *See* Johnson **xii** (1816) Letter **viii**.
31 Wroth & Wroth (1896) 272.
32 Besant (1899).
33 *See* Rudolph (1862) 45.
34 Garrick (1777): *Epilogue*. *See* also Baker (1782).
35 Thornbury & Walford **vi** (1879-85) 343.
36 *Ibid*.
37 Castro (1824) 124, 134; Wroth & Wroth (1896) 276.
38 *See* Allen **iv** (1827-37) 470, 482, 485; Allen (1827) 7, 347; Anonymous (1797) Ch. viii; Fores (1789) vi; Humphreys (*Ed.*) (1824) 126 ff; Larwood & Hotten (1868) 196-7; Manning & Bray **iii** (1809-14) 468, 554, 632, 701; Rendle & Norman (1888) 368 ff; Thornbury & Walford **vi** (1879-85) 343-4, 350-2; Trusler (1786) 124, 164; Wheatley (1891) on St George's Fields and the *Dog and Duck*.
39 *London Gazette* (27-30 April 1696).
40 Sunderland (1915) 116. *See* also *Daily Courant* (8 March 1721).
41 Wroth & Wroth (1896) 279.
42 *See* the paper 'Music at the Public Pleasure Gardens of the Eighteenth Century' by T. Lea Southgate in the *Journal of the Royal Musical Association* **xxxviii**/1 (1911) 141-59. *See* also Nichols (1786) 65.
43 King (1741).
44 Manning & Bray **iii** (1809-14) 468, for these matters.
45 *See*, for further information, Allen (1827) 346 ff; Brayley, Britton, Brayley, & Mantell **iii** (1841-4) 399 ff; Foord (1910) 193-5; Manning & Bray **iii** (1809-14) 468; Nichols (1786) 65 ff; Sunderland (1915) 116-17; Thornbury & Walford **vi** (1879-85) 389; Timbs (1867) 498; Wroth & Wroth (1896) 279-80.
46 Roberts & Godfrey (*Eds.*) (1951) 25-31.
47 Hatton **ii** (1708) 785.
48 Michaelis (1882) 35-37; Nichols (1786).
49 Chappell **ii** (1855-9) 727-8.
50 This appears to have been the Fire Music from the opera *Atalanta*, first given at Covent Garden 12 May 1736, not the better-known work of 1749.
51 Newspaper cutting (30 June 1741) quoted in Roberts & Godfrey (*Eds*) (1951) 25-31. *See* Brock (1922, 1949).
52 Hatton **ii** (1708) 785; Hone **i** (1835) 603; Lysons **i** (1792-6) 319-20; Pennant (1793) 32-4; Roberts & Godfrey (*Eds.*) (1951) 25-31; Thornbury & Walford **vi** (1879-85) 388-9; Wilkinson **ii** (1819-25) on Cuper's Gardens; Wroth & Wroth (1896) 247-56.
53 Brayley, Britton, Brayley, & Mantell **iii** (1841-4) 393; Manning & Bray **iii** (1809-14) 467; Nichols (1786); Wroth & Wroth (1896) 261-2.
54 Allen (1827) 335; Anonymous (1797) Ch. viii
55 Orgeat was a syrup drink made from almonds, sugar, and barley.
56 Anonymous (1797) Chapter VIII.
57 Allen (1827) 321; Brayley, Britton, Brayley, & Mantell **iii** (1841-4) 399.
58 Pleyel established the distinguished firm of pianoforte makers in Paris in 1807.
59 Allen (1827) 319; Anonymous (1797) mentions the Temple as becoming ruinous; Kearsley (1791) referred to a 'resort of company in the evenings'. *See* also Brayley, Britton, Brayley, & Mantell **iii** (1841-4) 399.
60 Thornbury & Walford **vi** (1879-85) 343, 389.

CHAPTER XI

VAUXHALL AND ITS NEIGHBOURS

The Black Prince; The Surrey Gardens: Vauxhall Well; Marble Hall, Vauxhall; Cumberland Tea-Gardens, Vauxhall; The New Spring, or Spring Gardens, Vauxhall

'A garden is like those pernicious machineries we read of, every month, in the newspapers, which catch a man's coat-skirt or his hand, and draw in his arm, his leg, and his whole body to irresistible destruction'.
RALPH WALDO EMERSON (1803-82):
The Conduct of Life (London: Smith, Elder 1860) on *Wealth* 50.

THE BLACK PRINCE

Not much is known about this Tavern with its Gardens, probably situated at Newington Butts, near the convergence of Kennington Lane, Kennington Park Road, and Newington Butts. Carington Bowles, however, illustrated it in a view dated 22 September 1788 *(Plate 149)*. Trap-ball was played there, and Bowles showed a lantern on a table where refreshments were taken, but the place seems to have had a short life and made little impression on contemporary society. It was a different story to the south-west, near the river at Vauxhall, where there were establishments that enjoyed a certain *cachet* in the Georgian period, and these will be mentioned below.

THE SURREY GARDENS

Situated on the east side of Kennington Park Road, near the junction of that thoroughfare with Kennington Lane and Newington Butts, is Penton Place, which provided one of the main approaches to these short lived (1831-62) Gardens, once known as the *Surrey Zoological Gardens*, for it was there, on some fifteen acres of land formerly attached to the Manor House of Walworth, that Edward Cross (1774-1854)[1] moved his menagerie from the King's Mews at Charing Cross thither under the aegis of the Surrey Literary, Scientific, and Zoological Society. *The Zoological Garden* was laid out, the patrons being Queen Adelaide and the Archbishop of Canterbury. There was a three-acre lake, and a circular glass-house, 300 feet in diameter, was built, first as a conservatory, and then adapted to house the big cats: this was, at the time, the largest building of its kind in

Plate 149: *Trap Ball Played at the Black Prince, Newington Butts,* by Carington Bowles, 1788 *(Collection JSC).*

TRAP BALL, Played at the Black Prince, Newington Butts.

Plate 150: *Surrey Zoological Gardens (Collection HP/4848).*

England. So spacious and ambitious was the layout that the Gardens were said to be more imposing than those of Regent's Park. Various other animals were added to the collection, and sundry attractions were laid out to draw the public, including firework-displays (which must have distressed the animals) and balloon-ascents. Cross established good relations with the painters Edwin Henry Landseer (1802-73)[2] and Jacques-Laurent Agasse (1767-1849)[3], who made celebrated studies of various animals that established them among the foremost animal-painters in the country. However, the zoological collections were auctioned just over a year before Cross died.

As with other Pleasure-Gardens in London, there were various themes in the painted panoramas and pyrotechnic displays, including the 'Eruption of Vesuvius' (1837-9), 'Iceland and Mount Hecla' (1839), the 'City of Rome' (1841), the 'Great Fire of London' (1844), the 'Storming of Badajoz' (1849), and other spectacles, among them 'Napoleon's Passage over the Alps' (1850), using optical illusions and living men to suggest an army of 50,000. Promenade concerts were also given under the direction of Louis Jullien (1812-60) from 1845-57: his performances were distinguished by vast forces and extra effects, including cannon-fire and dried peas rattling in metal containers to simulate hailstones during the Storm episode in Beethoven's *Pastoral* Symphony[4].

The Gardens were planted with every kind of native and exotic fruit-trees, and the lake was arranged with islands, shrubberies, and rich plantations. The Garden-buildings were also varied in style *(Plate 150)*. The designer of the Gardens was Henry Phillips (1779-1849), remembered today as the author of an important book on shrubberies entitled *Sylva florifera: the Shrubbery Historically and Botanically Treated* (1823), among other substantial works[5].

John Claudius Loudon (1783-1843) the celebrated writer on horticulture, glass-houses, and many other matters, waxed lyrical about these Gardens in *The Gardener's Magazine*, and described the layout of the gigantic conservatory: the big cats were kept in separate compartments in the centre of the structure, and around these was a colonnade supporting the glazed roof and cages for birds. Within the colonnade were hot-water pipes to heat the whole, and around the colonnade was a paved area for spectators surrounding which was a channel for water containing fish. The perimeter of the interior had a border from which climbing-

Plate 151: The Music-Hall at *Surrey Gardens* with the lake in the foreground *(From Thornbury & Walford* ***vi*** *[1879-85] 265: Collection JSC).*

plants rose, trained on wires under the roof.

Phillips also planned several cages and aviaries in the grounds, as well as a dam for beavers. A huge structure of poles and boards, some eighty feet in height, provided the framework for the machinery necessary for the pyrotechnics: the social reformer, Henry Mayhew (1812-87), noted in 1850 that 'Mount Etna, the fashionable volcano of the season, just now is vomiting here its sky-rockets and Roman Candles'[6].

After Cross's death in 1854, the management of the Gardens passed to his assistant and secretary, one Tyler, and the property became vested in a Limited Liability Company. In 1856 the Gardens were sold by auction, and, in order to accommodate Jullien's Monster Concerts, a vast Music-Hall was erected in that year at a cost of £18,000 *(Plate 151)* to hold 12,000 persons. In 1857, however, mismanagement of the *Surrey Gardens* led to failure of the venture, and all Jullien's scores and personal property were seized, causing a loss of £6,000 and his second bankruptcy[7]. The Music-Hall had octagonal towers containing the staircases at each of its corners, and elegant galleries faced the Gardens, providing access to its interior. This building was used for a religious service conducted by the Baptist preacher, Charles Haddon Spurgeon (1834-92) in October 1856, but a false fire-alarm caused a stampede in which seven persons died and twenty-eight were badly injured. In spite of the disaster, Spurgeon continued to draw the crowds (and several well-known personages) to his meetings until in March 1861 he moved to his purpose-built Metropolitan Tabernacle at Newington Butts, designed by William Willmer Pocock (1813-99). Shortly afterwards, in June 1861, the Music-Hall really was destroyed by fire, and the Tabernacle also burned down in 1898 (only the hexastyle Corinthian portico survives).

There were attempts to revive the fortunes of the Gardens with spectacles that included 'The Bay of Naples' in 1862, but public interest in such things had waned, and no other efforts at revival met with better success. The Gardens were closed and the land sold off for building. Although refreshments were provided in these Gardens, the establishment never became a Spa, and water for human consumption does not appear to have played any part, although the lake, channel of exotic fishes, fountains, and beaver-dam proved popular sights for a time[8].

VAUXHALL WELL

Where the Wandsworth Road led from the Vauxhall Turnpike to Wandsworth, was a Well with water that was never known to freeze: it was prized in the treatment of eye troubles[9]. Sunderland considered it as having 'slight medicinal properties'[10], although it never became a Spa or developed in the way in which so many commercial enterprises evolved at the time.

MARBLE HALL, VAUXHALL

This was situated by the river, at a place later occupied by the southern abutment of Vauxhall Bridge: much of the site is now covered by the roads leading to and from the Bridge.

Presumably there must have been some Well on the site, for *Vauxhall Well* had a reputation for the medicinal quality of its water, and the latter was very near *Marble Hall*. In 1740 the Gardens were enlarged, beautified, and illuminated, and acquired the obligatory Long-Room where dances were held. In the 1750s the establishment was taken over by Naphthali (*or* Nathan) Hart, a Jewish teacher of music and dancing, who had an Academy at Essex House, Essex Street, The Strand, where 'gentlemen' were taught to 'dance a minuet and country dances in the Modern Taste, and in a Short Time'. Hart's Academy also taught 'Musick, Fencing, French, Italian, Spanish, Portuguese, High German, Low Dutch, Navigation, or any other part of the Mathematicks': as well as teaching gentlemen to 'play on any instrument', the school provided instruction in the 'use of the small Sword and Spedroon'. A small-sword was a light sword, tapering gradually from the hilt to the point, used especially in fencing; 'Spedroon' must be a misprint for 'Spadroon', meaning a light sword, made both to cut and thrust, but much more elegant than a broadsword.

The place seems to have had an undistinguished career as a coffee-house and Tavern, and existed until *c*.1813, when it was demolished to make way for the construction of the approach to the Bridge[11].

CUMBERLAND TEA-GARDENS, VAUXHALL

Slightly larger than the Gardens of *Marble Hall* situated to the south of the latter, they were originally called *Smith's Tea-Gardens*, where a 'Grand Rural Masked Ball' or '*Fête Champêtre*' was advertised for 22 May 1779, starting at ten in the evening at a charge of a guinea. The establishment was taken *c*.1784 by Luke Reilly, who ran *Freemasons' Tavern*, Great Queen Street, himself a Freemason: under his management *Smith's* became the *Cumberland* (or *Royal Cumberland*) *Gardens*[12], which were laid out with the usual arbours, and had a tea-room which also served suppers, and were open in the afternoon and evenings[13]. Until 1825 the Gardens and Tavern were favoured by persons living south of the River, but a huge conflagration that year destroyed the public-house, ball-room, and much of the plantations and arbours. Thereafter it ceased to function, and was redeveloped. Timbs declared that the site became 'Price's Candle Company's Works'[14], but Price's factory was actually further to the south, beyond the little Vauxhall Creek which defined the southern boundary of the Gardens. It seems that the South Lambeth Water Works actually took over the site, followed by the South Metropolitan Gas Company, after which any chance of unpolluted waters, let alone medicinal ones, would have receded[15].

THE NEW SPRING *OR* SPRING GARDENS, VAUXHALL

This celebrated establishment's western boundary coincided with what is now Goding Street, its eastern extent with St Oswald's Place, and its southern limit by Kennington Lane: the twelve acres of the *Spring Gardens* are now occupied by parts of Tyers Street and Vauxhall Walk, and the most distinguished buildings on them are the Church and ancillary buildings of St Peter, Vauxhall, robustly designed by John Loughborough Pearson (1817-97), built 1859-65, a fine essay in the early French First Pointed style.

Shortly before the Restoration of the Monarchy in 1660 there appear to have been two *Spring Gardens* at Vauxhall: Pepys referred to the *Old Spring Garden*, where he was somewhat put out by the expensive fare on offer, so he and his party went to the *New Spring Garden* where they had 'cakes and powdered beef and ale, and so home again by water, with much pleasure'[16]. Pepys referred to the place as 'Fox-Hall', and it soon became a favourite haunt of his, where he enjoyed lobster, syllabub, and other delights[17].

There is a vast literature on *Vauxhall Gardens* from which the reader may glean information about its raffishness: there are many tales of gallants pouncing on ladies in arbours, and clearly the place was not a little notorious for intrigue. Even Pepys admitted to eating, drinking, and more with the singer and actress, Elizabeth Knipp (d. 1680 x 82)[18], at 'Fox-Hall', it 'being darkish'[19]. In their characters of 'Bab Allen' and 'Dapper Dicky' they conducted a liaison until Mrs Pepys insisted it should stop in around October 1668. Thomas Brown (1663-1704) observed that at the *Spring Gardens* both sexes met, to 'eventually serve one another as guides to lose their way, and the windings and turnings in the little Wildernesses' were so intricate that 'the most experienced mothers' often lost themselves when looking for their daughters[20].

Vauxhall Gardens were famous for the fragrant walks and bowers, choirs of birds, and nightingales, and became one of the sights of London[21], but a reputation for naughtiness demanded an antidote, and new attractions had to be provided[22]: these came about under the proprietorship of Jonathan Tyers (1702-67), who obtained a lease of the *Spring Gardens* for thirty years from Elizabeth Masters in 1728. Confronted with what had become a 'rural brothel'[23], Tyers transformed the *Spring Gardens* into a fashionable place of evening entertainment, open to all who could pay a shilling a head. There were many choices of promenades, illuminated by means of small lanterns, a crescent of supper-boxes, an Orchestra next to the Grand Walk, opportunities to listen to smaller ensembles strategically placed throughout the grounds, or to sit, to be seen, and to watch the Exquisite Mob go by.

Tyers[24] was cultivated: he had a large art-collection and he brought in many persons he knew to contribute to the visual and musical delights of the place. Among the artists involved

Plate 152: *The Inside of the Elegant Music-Room at Vaux Hall Gardens*, drawn by Samuel Wale (*c*.1721-86), engraved by Henry Roberts (*c*.1710-*c*.1790), published (1752) by Thomas Bowles (*c*.1712-62), showing the extraordinary mixture of Baroque, Rococo, and Gothick *(Collection JSC).*

with the Gardens were William Hogarth (1697-1764), Hubert-François Gravelot (1699-1773), Louis-François Roubiliac (*c*.1705-62) and the Drury Lane scene-painter, Francis Hayman (1707/8-76), whose decorations for the boxes and pavilions were spectacular[25].

Music at Vauxhall was of a somewhat higher calibre than in many Pleasure-Gardens and included works by Thomas (1710-78) and Michael (1740/1-86) Arne, James Hook (1746-1827), and John Worgan (1724-90). Many, indeed, sailed across the Thames in order

'To hear the fiddlers of Spring Gardens play,
To see the walks, orchestra, colonnades,
The lamps and trees in mingled lights and
shades,
The scene so new, with pleasure and
surprise,
To feast awhile their ravish'd ears and eyes'

and to survey the 'motley crowd', the 'old, the splenetic' the 'gay' the 'fop emasculate' and 'the rugged brave'[26]. It was all rather wonderful, and the décor charming in that extraordinarily inventive admixture of styles we associate with Georgian Eclecticism, perfectly suited to pleasure, and not to be taken mightily seriously: jokey Gothick, Chinoiserie, Rococo, and Baroque all fizzed together in a heady brew as strong as the powerful drinks provided *(Plate 152)*.

In 1758 the Orchestra was replaced by a splendid Gothick structure, painted white and 'bloom', and surmounted by a dome crowned with a plume of feathers. Persons of Quality flocked thither, including the Prince of Wales, and at no other London Pleasure-Garden could the 'humours' of every class be observed in such profusion. Even Bishops could be seen there without any injury being done to their characters.

The fine pavilions, shady groves, and charming walks illuminated by means of a

Plate 153: So-called 'Chinese' Pavilion at *Vauxhall Gardens* (really Rococo Gothick) *(From Thornbury & Walford* ***vi*** *[1879-85] 462: Collection JSC).*

thousand lanterns, could only delight, while statuary (including a representation of Apollo, and one of Händel) embellished the place, and fountains played. Most visitors arrived by water from Westminster and the City, some in boats with servants bearing provisions. There were barges conveying parties of revellers attended on by musicians playing French horns, and people arriving in the Gardens for the first time were dazzled by the scenes: there were high hedges and trees, gravel paths, pavilions, lodges, groves, grottoes, lawns, temples, cascades, porticoes, colonnades, rotundas, statues, ornaments, and much else, and then there was the company, supping on cold collations, enlivened with mirth and good humour, and much pleased and animated by the excellent music (although some critics found the songs 'abjectly sentimental'). Groups would find accommodation in the 'supper-boxes', listen to the music, chatter, eat, and drink, and fruit-girls would offer hampers of strawberries and cherries. The establishment provided Burgundy, Champagne, Frontiniac (Muscat wine made at Frontignan, Hérault, in France), Claret, 'Old Hock, with or without Sugar' (the Georgians had a Sweet Tooth), ice, Rhine wine with sugar, Mountain, red Port, Sherry, 'Cyder', table beer by the quart, chicken, ham, beef, salad, oil, oranges and lemons, sugar for adding to food or drink, bread, butter, cheese, tarts, custard, cheesecake, Heart Cake, Shrewsbury Cake, and 'Arrack'[27] by the quart[28].

Plate 154: William Henry Prior's impression of the Triumphal Arches at *Vauxhall Gardens (From Thornbury & Walford* ***vi*** *[1879-85] 457: Collection JSC).*

The ham at Vauxhall was cut so thinly it was said one could read a newspaper through a slice of it, and the chickens were no bigger than sparrows. Early in the nineteenth century 'Vauxhall Nectar' became a popular beverage: it was a mixture of rum, syrup, and benzoic acid or 'flowers of benjamin', and was diluted with water from the Wells. But Vauxhall was important, not for its transparent ham, miniature chickens, or Arrack, but because Tyers transformed it into the epitome of the Continental Rococo style (albeit modified with Gothick to suit English Taste): at Vauxhall, the flimsy Rococo-Gothick architecture *(Plate 153)*, the lofty avenues with their Triumphal Arches *(Plate 154)*, the open-air supper-boxes with their painted decorations, and the standards of entertainment raised the place a cut above most other establishments of the period and kind. These wood-and-canvas painted 'Triumphal Arches' (*c*.1749), and perhaps some other *fabriques* at Vauxhall, were probably designed by Giovanni Niccolò Servandoni (1695-1766[29]) *(Plate 155)*. The choice spots by the Orchestra enabled strollers, diners, drinkers, and so on to enjoy the musical and other fare on offer, all splendidly illuminated *(Plate 156)*.

On Tyers's death, Vauxhall was taken over by his sons, and musical entertainments seem to have become even more numerous, although there were rowdy and destructive elements which created uproar on occasion. In 1774, for example, 'upwards of fifteen foolish Bucks' amused themselves by smashing lamps, and Fanny Burney's 'Evelina' had a scary experience in the Dark Walk and Long Alleys[30]. There was the occasional affray: one of the most celebrated involved Sir Henry Bate Dudley, Bart. (1745-1824), known as the 'Fighting Parson', who defended the honour of the actress, Mrs Elizabeth Hartley (1750/51-1824 – the 'finest figure on the London Stage'[31]), from the attentions of a group of 'macaronis'[32] at Vauxhall in 1773. The ringleader of this crew was George Robert Fitzgerald (*c*.1746-86), a thoroughly disreputable character, who got his footman to fight Dudley (who easily defeated the unfortunate fellow[33]) rather than face the formidable fists of the Baronet himself. However, if Fitzgerald was little better

Plate 155: *A General Prospect of Vaux Hall Gardens Showing at one View the disposition of the whole Gardens,* drawn (1751) by Samuel Wale, engraved by Johann Sebastian Müller (1715-*c.*1785), and published by Thomas Bowles. In the *centre* is the Orchestra; *right* and *left* are the circles of boxes for partakers of refreshments; and on the *left* is the conical roof of the Rotunda, and beyond it is the Picture-Gallery. The series of 'Triumphal Arches' should be noted over the Walk, as should the remarkably pretty Gothick detailing of various pavilions *(Collection JSC)*.

than a desperado, Dudley was described as

' A Canonical Buck, Vociferous Bully
A Duellist, Boxer, Gambler & Cully...
A Government Runner of Falsehood a Vender
Staunch Friend to the Devil, the Pope & Pretender
A Managers parasite, Opera Writer[34]
News paper Editor, Pamphlets Indictor'[35].

Dudley was no ornament to the Anglican Church, and perhaps the only constant in his life was his pursuit of personal advantage[36]: he was, however, more civilised than Fitzgerald, who would quarrel with anyone, and whose enmity was of an implacable, sanguinary, and revengeful nature. Indeed, Fitzgerald (whose mother was Lady Mary Hervey [1725-1815]) seems to have been a wild character, possibly at least half-mad, and was hanged in 1786 outside the new Gaol at Castlebar, County Mayo, for his part in the murder of Colonel Patrick Randal McDonnell[37].

Vauxhall seems to have enjoyed spectacular displays of illuminations, but fireworks (which had been usual in many other Pleasure-Gardens) were not introduced until 1798. Celebratory banquets and illuminations were given after various victories during the Napoleonic Wars, and throughout its existence, Vauxhall put on numerous concerts featuring competent singers of the day. In 1816 'Madame Saqui' (Marguerite-Antoinette Lalanne [1786-1866]), the tight-rope walker, appeared, and was the main attraction for several seasons thereafter: of 'muscular and masculine' appearance, wearing a curious garment embellished with spangles, and wearing a somewhat Camp helmet from which plumes sprouted, she provided a peculiar, almost supernatural appearance, as she descended in a shower of 'Chinese Fire' in a 'tempest of fireworks' *(Plate 157)*. Indeed,

Plate 156: *Vauxhall*, a scene by the re-vamped (post-1758) Orchestra, with a female singer in full voice and the musicians (in three-cornered hats) accompanying her. The scene on the right must have been fairly typical of uninhibited Georgian enjoyment. In the centre, between the trees, is a Scotsman in a kilt, which points to a late date, for prohibition of Highland dress was not formally repealed until 1782 under 22 Geo. III *c.* 63, and the lamps look rather like gas-lamps which were not installed until 1846, so the illustration may be partly imaginary, although, from the style of dress it would appear to date from the 1780s, and indeed it is dated 1785. Drawing by Thomas Rowlandson (1757-1827), engraved by Robert Pollard (1755/6-1839) and aquatinted by Francis Jukes (1745-1812) *(Collection JSC).*

'Amid the blaze of meteors seen on high
Etherial Saqui seems to tread the sky'[38].

By the time of 'Madame Saqui's' extraordinary appearances, the old *Spring Garden* had been transformed. In 1786 a large rectangular Supper-Room had been added next to the Rotunda, and two sides of the so-called Grove were covered in by colonnades with cast-iron columns in *c.*1810. Many trees were sacrificed in the process. These colonnaded walks were brightly lit, but much of the pleasant, rural-garden atmosphere was lost.

After the Napoleonic Wars and the accession of George IV (who, as Prince of Wales had regularly enjoyed the pleasures of the Gardens) in 1820, the place was renamed 'The Royal Gardens, Vauxhall' in 1822, and, with thousands of extra lamps, took on a suitably flashy appearance, reflecting 'Prinny's' own exotic tastes. The Rotunda became an Indian Garden-Room and later was used for equestrian shows. The Picture-Room acquired plates of glass on which were reflected revolving columns, palm-trees, entwined snakes, and a fountain, and elaborate exhibitions of water-works were added. At the far end of the Garden stood the Firework Tower, and, in an isolated corner was a timber-and-canvas Hermit's Cottage, where the Hermit could be observed deep in study. The

Plate 157: Madame Saqui the celebrated Performer on the Rope, at *Vauxhall Gardens*. Engraved by J. Alais from a painting by Joseph Hutchisson (*fl.*1790-*c.*1810) published by J. Bell, 1820 *(Collection JSC).*

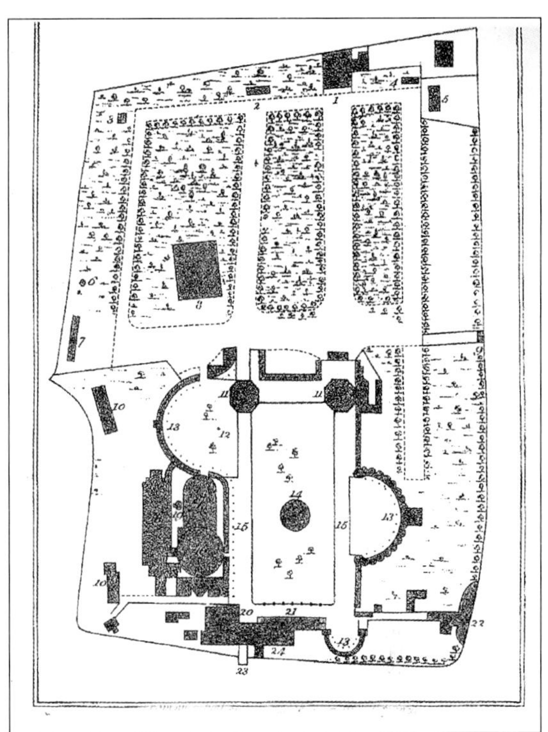

Plate 158: *Vauxhall Gardens*, from a survey (1826) by Thomas Allen (1803-33). The Firework Tower is at the top (1), the Theatre is the large, isolated, almost square building (8), the Orchestra is the circular building in the centre (14), the Circles of Supper-Boxes (13) are clearly shown, and the complex of buildings on the left contains the Rotunda, Picture-Gallery, Supper-Room, and Ice-House. Access from the Thames was by the Water-Gate at the bottom (23), the Main Entrance (22) is bottom right, and the Hermitage is the small, isolated building (3 – *top left*). *See* Allen (1827) *(Collection JSC).*

Triumphal Arches were removed and a new cockle-shell sounding-board was placed over the Orchestra. Indeed, the place required so many alterations to keep up with fashion that there had to be constructed special Artificers' Workshops which must have been permanently busy *(Plate 158).*

During the 1820s the tone of the place became somewhat vulgar: there were jugglers, sword-swallowers, performances of comic songs (none of which seem very amusing today), and in 1826 Braham sang there (his *Death of Nelson* remained hugely popular), and Madame Vestris (Lucia Elizabeth Vestris, *née* Bartolozzi [1797-1856]) performed her celebrated 'signature-tune', *Cherry Ripe*, composed by Charles Edward Horn (1786-1849), who for a brief period directed the music at Vauxhall.

Further clearances of shrubs in front of the Firework Tower took place in 1827, and on the ground a spectacular re-enactment of the Battle of Waterloo, involving a thousand horse- and foot-soldiers, was given. This area was subsequently used for other displays such as the 'Polar Regions' (1834) and 'View of Venice' complete with 'imitation water'[39]. Andrew Ducrow (1793-1842) performed there (1828) with his equestrian shows, and, when that palled, ballets were given. In 1830 Henry Rowley Bishop (1786-1855)[40] became Director of Music (he had earlier written his Cantata, *Waterloo* [1826], for performance at Vauxhall) and composed several operettas to be given there, including *The Sedan Chair*, *The Magic Fan*, *The Bottle of Champagne*, and *Under the Oak*, none of which seems to have stood the test of time. John Alexander Fuller Maitland

Plate 159: Balloon ascent at *Vauxhall Gardens*, 1849 *(From Thornbury & Walford **vi** [1879-85] 463: Collection JSC).*

Plate 160: Engraving by Benjamin Cole (1695-1766) above *The Farewel* [sic] *to VAUX HALL*, a song set to music by J. F. Lampe *(Item XXXIII from Lampe [1739], also found in Bickham [1737-9]: Collection JSC).*

(1856-1936) dismissed Bishop's 'so-called operas', stating that the 'low taste of the public was pandered to in each and every one of them'[41], and Grove described his music as 'thin and tame'[42], a diagnosis with which it would be difficult to disagree. Nevertheless, in 1833, when admission to the Gardens at a shilling a head was re-introduced as a trial, more than 27,000 flocked there, a formidable number by any standards.

Balloons featured as entertainments at Vauxhall *(Plate 159)*: in 1802 André-Jacques Garnerin (1769-1823) made an isolated ascent from the Gardens[43], but in 1835 Charles Green (1785-1870) made an ascent in a balloon, remaining up in the air all night, and in 1836 he constructed the *Royal Vauxhall* balloon for the proprietors of the Gardens. In that year he made several ascents, on one of which he was accompanied by Thomas Monck Mason (1803-89 – the musician) and Robert Hollond (1808-77 – Liberal Member of Parliament for Hastings): the journey ended at Weilburg, near Nassau, Germany, a record of 500 miles in 18 hours which stood until 1907. The balloon was renamed *The Great Nassau*, and again ascended from Vauxhall in 1837 accompanied by Edward Spencer (1799-1849) and Robert Cocking (1776-1837 – suspended in his own design for a parachute below the balloon, but his parachute broke up and he was killed at Burnt Ash Farm, Lee: his was the first British parachute fatality[44]).

Under new management in 1841 Ducrow made one of his last appearances, but this was insufficient to save the Gardens. Furniture and fittings were sold, including Hayman's paintings. Certainly there were many galas, masquerades, and other entertainments, but in the new atmosphere of Victoria's reign (from 1837) taste was changing, and the kind of raffish Regency diversions previously enjoyed there would no longer do. Attempts were made to continue the musical tradition, and in 1845 Philippe Musard (1793-1859) conducted Promenade Concerts there. In the French musician there was

> 'No trace of your Macaroni;
> But looking at him,
> So solemn and grim,
> You think of the Marshals who served under
> Boney'[45].

1846 saw the installation of gas-lamps at Vauxhall and three years later there was a Grand Venetian Carnival, illuminated by 60,000 lamps. Complaints were made about rowdiness,

Plate 161: William Henry Prior's impression of the old village of Vauxhall, with the entrance to the Gardens on the left, 1825 *(From Thornbury & Walford* ***vi*** *[1879-85] 456: Collection JSC).*

however, and renewed licences restricted the times when fireworks could be let off. Advertisements for Green's ascent by balloon *on horseback* were issued in 1850; a platform was laid down for dancing, 'but there was no music worth the name'; and the quality of just about everything declined[46]. Even 'monster galas' 'positively last nights', and other tricks failed to restore the glories of Vauxhall, and one gets the impression of seediness, like some once-grand hotel gone to pot under incompetent management. In 1859 the place was closed, all the trees were felled, everything was demolished and sold, and the site handed over to the builders.

'Farewel dear Scenes of gay Delight,
Adieu ye ever-pleasing Shades,
Since now no more my ravish'd Sight
Surveys ye lovely tuneful Glades:
Sweet Philomel no more complains,
Nor chants her soft love labour'd Song
Nor round ye Muse's warbling Fanes
Attend y^e in-raptur'd list'ning Throng.

No more ye fragrant Zephyrs spread
Their Sweets along th' illumin'd Groves,
Nor *Cynthia* glimmers thro' ye Shade
That witness'd to a thousand Loves;
No longer each sweet thrilling Sound,
Lulls the forsaken Lover's Care,
Nor Airs melodious help to wound,
The Bosoms of the lovely Fair.

But Oh! Thou beaut'ous *Source of Day*,
Quickly thy Winter's Journey run,
With hast restore the blooming *May*
And thy own Choir once more attune
Then soon as *Vesper* gilds the West
Let me with dear *Corinna* move
Along y^e *Thames*, fair dimply Breast,
To Scenes of Harmony and Love'[47].

Although those conventional eighteenth-century pastoral verses were set to music by John Frederick Lampe (1702/3-51 – whose funerary monument in the Canongate churchyard, Edinburgh, optimistically predicted that his 'harmonious compositions' would outlive 'monumental registers, and, with melodious notes,... perpetuate his fame') they, and the charming engraving above the song *(Plate 160)* showing musicians departing, seem curiously appropriate to the decline and end of the Gardens.

It is impossible, when visiting this less than inspiring part of London today, to even imagine the 'lustrous long arcades' of Vauxhall, let alone the old village of Vauxhall *(Plate 161)* for squalid developments engulfed it in the second half of the nineteenth century, and the shades of Braham, of Mrs Billington, of Madame Vestris, and of Horn, must have looked on with anguish at the changed and ruined place. Those green retreats where 'fair Vauxhall' once bedecked her 'sylvan seats' were no more. Nothing remains of what, in the eighteenth century, must have been a charming place, one of the most amazing Rococo[48] Gardens in England, with music to delight and settings to please[49].

Chapter XI References: Vauxhall and its Neighbours

1 *ODNB* **xiv** (2004) 421. For lost Zoological Gardens *see* Keeling (1984).
2 *ODNB* **xxxii** (2004) 405-12.
3 *ODNB* **i** (2004) 453-4.
4 For pyrotechnics *see* Brock (1922, 1949), and for panoramas *see* Altick (1987); Hyde (1980); Oettermann (1980).
5 *ODNB* **xliv** (2004) 114. *See* Phillips (1823).
6 Thornbury & Walford **vi** (1879-85) 267. For pyrotechnics *see* Brock (1922, 1949).
7 *ODNB* **xxx** (2004) 826-7.
8 Thornbury & Walford **vi** (1879-85) 265-8.
9 Sunderland (1915) 54.
10 *Ibid*. 52.
11 Allen (1827) 368; Manning & Bray **iii** (1809-14) 484, 526; Wroth & Wroth (1896) 281-2.
12 Trusler (1786) called the place *Riley's Gardens*, Vauxhall, which is clearly inaccurate.
13 Feltham (1802, 1829).
14 Timbs (1867) 18.
15 Allen (1827) 379; *The Courier* (25-26 May 1825); Feltham (1802, 1829); Thornbury & Walford **vi** (1879-85) 389, 449; Wroth & Wroth (1896) 283-5.
16 Pepys **i** (1953) 258-9.
17 *See* Manning & Bray **iii** (1809-14) 526 for other descriptions.
18 Her second name may have been Mary, and her maiden name could have been Carpenter. She often sang *Barbara Allen* to Pepys while he was paying attention to her person.
19 Pepys **iii** (1953) 215.
20 Brown (1700) 54.
21 Anonymous (1726).
22 Anonymous (*c*.1750).
23 *Ibid*. 28.
24 *ODNB* **lv** (2004) 759-61.
25 Two examples are now (2009) in the Victoria & Albert Museum. *See Burlington Magazine* **cv** (January 1953) 4-19.
26 Mac-Sturdy (1737) *passim*.
27 Sweet Punch.
28 This from Hooper (1762).
29 *See* Allen (1981); Bonnemaison & Macy (*Eds*.) (2008); Edelstein (1983); Grove **viii** (1966) 709-11; Hunt (1985); Rogers (1896); Scott (1955); Snodin (*Ed*.) (1984); Southworth (1941); Surel (1977); and Wroth (1898).
30 Burney (1778) is illuminating on such misadventures. *See* Letter **xlvi**.
31 *ODNB* **xxv** (2004) 611.
32 An Exquisite of a class which arose in the 1760s, consisting of young men who had travelled and who affected the tastes and fashions prevalent in Continental Society: they often used spy-glasses to ogle young women. This class talked 'without meaning', ate without appetite, rode without exercise, and wenched without passion, it would appear from contemporary opinions.
33 The footman had his face smashed to a 'perfect jelly', according to the *Morning Chronicle* (26 July 1773).
34 He produced at least eight comic operas.
35 *A Baite for the Devil*, satirical print of 1779.
36 *ODNB* **xvii** (2004) 71-3.
37 *ODNB* **xix** (2004) 797-8.
38 Bayley (1821) 216.
39 Wroth & Wroth (1896) 319.
40 He was knighted in 1842.
41 Sadie (*Ed*.) **i** (2002) 483.
42 Grove **i** (1966) 723.
43 *Ibid*. **viii** 711.
44 *ODNB* **xxiii** (2004) 498-500.
45 Grove **v** (1966) 1011.
46 Grove **viii** (1966) 711.
47 Lampe (1739) **xxxiii**, also published in Bickham (1737-9).
48 *See* Symes (2005).
49 *See* Edelstein (1983); Hooper (1762); Kearsley (1791); Scott (1948,1955); and Select Bibliography.

CHAPTER XII

SPAS AND WELLS FURTHER SOUTH

Sydenham Wells; Dulwich Wells; Streatham Spa; Richmond Spa or Wells; East Sheen Well; Epsom Spa; Shooter's Hill; Ladywell; Bromley Wells; Camberwell and Stockwell

'This was in my prayers: some land not very large, where there would be a garden, and near the house a spring of ever-flowing water, and above these some woods as well'.

(Hoc erat in votis: modus agri non ita magnus,
Hortus ubi et tecto vicinus iugis aquæ fons
Et paulum silvæ super his foret)
QUINTUS HORATIUS FLACCUS (65-8 BC): *Satires* ii/6 l.1 .

SYDENHAM WELLS

This source of water was mentioned by John Evelyn (1620-1706) in his famous *Diary*[1], and Nicholas Culpeper (1616-54), in his celebrated *English Physitian* (1652) also referred to it. Sydenham was once a hamlet in the County of Kent, but its Wells were sometimes referred to as 'Dulwich' or even 'Lewisham' Wells.

The waters were known for some time, but appear to have been publicised around the beginning of the seventeenth century: there were about a dozen Wells in all, and there were two late-seventeenth-century publications dealing with them. The first was John Peter's *Judgement, or Dullidge or Lewisham Water*[2]: therein, we learn that the 'gushings' of waters attracted 'multitudes of pigeons' which delighted in 'tippling' the 'saline aluminous liquor'. Peter advised that the Sydenham waters should be warmed and taken either as a 'posset'[3] or mixed with boiling milk in the ratio three pints of water to a quarter-pint of milk. The second was by Benjamin Allen (1663-1738), who described[4] the waters as 'medicated with a salt of the nature of common salt, but with a nitrous quality and a little more marcasitical'[5].

Allen noted that the Wells were at the foot of a heavy 'claiy' hill and that they were 'discovered' about 1640. They were nine feet deep, and the 'petrif'd incrusted' stones, when fractured, glittered with 'Ferreous Parts, as Sulphurous Marcasites produce'. He observed that the water was heavier than 'common' water, and that it contained common salt[6]. The medicinal qualities of the water were first recorded in the 1640s, when a woman, suffering from some terrible and unspecified disease, took them and was cured[7]. Dr Donald Monro (1727-1802) claimed that the waters were 'impregnated' with 'Calcareous, Glauber, and Sea Salt', but mostly with the first[8]. Monro was a military physician, and published important studies of diseases in military hospitals and on the means of preserving the health of soldiers: his work on *Materia Medica* was also important, and he clearly recognised that certain waters had properties which could be beneficial. Lysons observed that Sydenham was a hamlet in the Parish of Lewisham lying to the south-west of the town 'on the borders of Surrey', and that it was 'celebrated for its Mineral Springs' of a 'mild cathartic quality' which nearly resembled 'those of Epsom'[9].

Sydenham waters were bottled and sold in London: in 1729 the Parish of Lewisham ordered in Vestry that 'no water shall be carried from the Wells on Sidenham-Common, in the said Parish, for Sale', and gave 'the Publick Notice, thereof, that for the future no Persons may be imposed upon, by any that pretend to sell the said Water' although 'Any Person may send as usual for any Quantity not exceeding Two Gallons for private Use'[10]. The proprietors of the Wells, unusually, made no efforts to provide amusements, and the place remained a simple rural Spa, the Wells House being a cottage, known as the *Green Dragon*, Wells Road *(Plate 162)*[11]. However, despite the 'simple rural' ambience *(Plate 163)*, there was often committed 'a very great abuse occasioned by a rabble of Londoners and others' frequenting the Wells on Sundays: under the 'pretence' of drinking the waters, they spent the day 'in great profaneness, drinking excessive quantities' of Brandy ('that bane of Englishmen') thereby becoming 'greatly prejudiced in their health', and, to 'add to their folly' were not 'ashamed to impute their indisposition' to the waters[12].

The little house from which the waters were dispensed was purchased in the 1720s by one Alexander Roberts, whose daughter, Elizabeth (d. 1791), married a John Fairman. The Fairmans' daughter, Elizabeth, married a William Evans[13], whose daughter's son was still running the place before the 1914-18 War. Clark's *Sydenham and Forest Hill Directory* for 1859 records an Elizabeth Evance, Laundress, of Sydenham Wells, Wells Road, which suggests that the Wells were still functioning as such at that time. Some doggerel records the Evans connection:

'Those who wish all the beauties of Nature to know,
Must around Dulwich hill towards Rockels repair,
Where the bright summer Sun warms the landscape below,
And the dog rose and briar perfume the sweet air.

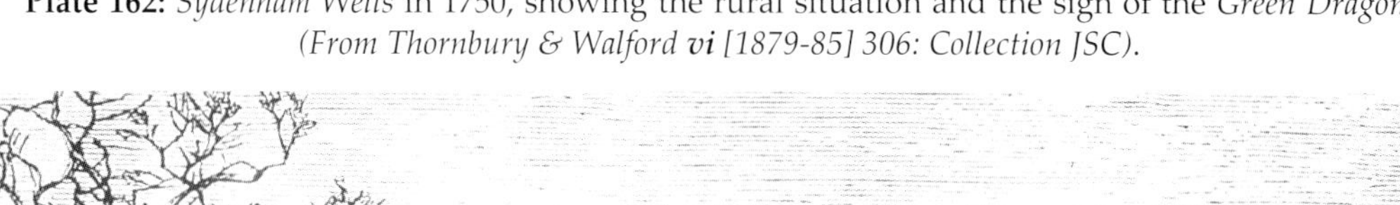

Plate 162: *Sydenham Wells* in 1750, showing the rural situation and the sign of the *Green Dragon* *(From Thornbury & Walford **vi** [1879-85] 306: Collection JSC).*

And there you will find a wild rural retreat,
From Time immemorial call'd *Sydenham Wells*,
With old Betty Evans, complacent and neat,
And a Gipsy, if wish'd who your fortune
foretells.

Then go ye fair Maidens and amorous
swains,
And list where for Sixpence the Sybil decides,
Whether truly or not never trouble your
brains,
But take the good cheer which your basket
provides.

Escap'd from the Town in gay holiday clothes,
O'er hedges you trespass, o'er furzes you
roam,
Or stretch'd on the grass, seek a transcient
repose,
Till the dull mists of Night give the sign to go
home'[14].

A document entitled *The Original Old Well kept by Alexander Roberts* printed 'Dr Peter's Judgment of Sydenham Water', stating the water was 'taken notice of' in 1648: its 'Virtues' included abilities to open 'all obstructions of the Liver, Spleen, Mesaraick Veins, Pancreas, the Billiary, Uterine, & Urinary Passages by which means such ling'ring Disorders are bred, Viz, Tumours of the Liver & Spleen, Hypochondriacks, Jaundice, Gravel & Stone, Hæmorrhoides, Dropsy, Green-Sickness, &c.' Among other benefits, the waters prevented 'Barrenness' and 'sharp Humours', strengthened the 'Brain and Nerves', destroyed 'Worms', and helped the 'Stomach and Digestion'. They opened 'Obstructions', evacuated 'Superfluous Humours', allayed the 'Vapours', and cleansed and strengthened 'all parts of the Body'. They were also useful if applied externally to cure 'Itch, Pimples, Ring-Worms, & Scurvy' as well as the ubiquitous 'cutaneous Distempers', 'the Gout', and even 'Rheumatism', or so Dr Peter declared[15].

Thornbury and Walford inform us that 'Dr Webster, who had been considered a high authority on the subject', stated that

> 'the saline spring was, and is, situated on Sydenham Common, in Wells Lane, on the slope of the hill between Dulwich and Sydenham. The little old cottage *[**Plate 164**]* and garden where the "Sydenham Wells" are, belongs to two elderly women of the name of Evans, and on my expressing surprise that they had not been "bought out' for building, as the spot is surrounded by modern mansions and good houses, they replied, they kept

Plate 163: *A View of Sydenham Wells, Kent*, showing the very simple clap-boarded buildings and openness of the country site *(LMA SC/GL/NOB/C/001/12-003/2)*.

Plate 164: Wells Cottage, Sydenham, in *c.*1903. The Well lay to the left of the house behind the palings *(From Foord [1910] facing p.218: Collection JSC).*

> possession, as the little property would be beneficial to their deceased brother's children. It is not at all resorted to now for medicinal purposes; but the water is strongly saline, similar to that of the quondam "Beulah Spa", at Streatham Common, and at Epsom. It is situated in the parish of Lewisham, Kent'[16].

'Dr Webster' seems to have been Dr George Webster (d. 1875), who practised in Dulwich from *c.*1815.

Sydenham Wells is supposed to have been honoured by the presence of King George III[17] who spent some time there taking the waters and discoursing with the proprietors. Around 1895 the last of the Wells was filled up: others lay under a row of cottages, opposite Wells Cottage, one was covered by 'Wells Road' (now Wells Park Road), and one was said to be beneath the Church of St Philip, Taylor's Lane (1864-7 – designed by Edwin Nash [1814-84] and J. N. Round [*fl.*1850-67] – demolished 1982).

In 1901 the remaining ground was taken over by the London County Council and became Sydenham Wells Park, bounded by Longton Avenue, Taylor's Lane, and Wells Park Road[18].

DULWICH WELLS

Dulwich Spa or *Wells*, a chalybeate Spring, was about a mile south-east of Dulwich College near where Lordship Lane joins Dulwich Common. It started life when the landlord of the *Green Man* Tavern sank a Well in the grounds. The waters were analysed by John Martyn, FRS (1699-1768), in 1740: he found that they had a 'sulphurous' taste and smell and possessed purging properties 'being drank fresh in the quantity of five half-pint glasses'[19]. It was also noticed that the 'sulphurous' smell abated if the Well had been left uncovered for a few days. Martyn noted that there had not been 'any medicinal spring observed in Dulwich before'. Martyn published his findings in *Philosophical Transactions* of the Royal Society[20], and pointed out that the Dulwich waters should not be confused with those of *Sydenham Wells* in the Parish of Lewisham, Kent, for Dulwich lay in the Parish of Camberwell in Surrey, and that the well had to be dug 'pretty deep' to reach water at all through some twenty feet of clay mixed with 'Pieces of Root and Leaves' and with other fragments of vegetable matter. Martyn specifically noted that there was 'no Spring of good Water' near the 'well-known House of Entertainment' before that time.

Sundry advertisements appeared that announced the 'purging waters' were in their 'proper season for drinking', and the landlord opened a 'Great Breakfast-Room' at a charge of a shilling a head. These 'Spa' or 'Wells' waters were drunk on the premises, sold in London, and supplied to St Bartholomew's Hospital. For about forty years the waters were fashionable, but by 1814 they were no longer esteemed or (apparently) drunk[21].

The *Green Man* ceased to be a Tavern and was converted into a private house for Edward Thurlow (1731-1806), 1st Baron Thurlow of Ashfield, Suffolk (from 1778), and Lord Chancellor. The establishment was re-named 'Dulwich Grove', and Thurlow lived there while his permanent residence, 'Knight's Hill', Norwood, was being built to design by Henry Holland (1745-1806): as 'Knight's Hill' was completed in 1787, 'Dulwich Grove' must have ceased to be a Tavern some time in the 1780s. 'Knight's Hill' did not survive either Holland or Thurlow: it was demolished in 1810.

'Dulwich Grove', however, became a private school run by an Aberdonian, William Glennie (1761-1828), and was certainly in existence as a school by 1799 when George Gordon Noel, Lord

Plate 165: Dr Glennie's Academy, Dulwich Grove, in 1820
(From Thornbury & Walford vi [1879-85] 294: Collection JSC).

Byron (1788-1824), became a pupil there, remaining until 1801 when he went on to Harrow. Glennie seems to have been a civilised man, and established regular concerts at Dulwich Grove which were attended by his fellow-Scots, the poet Thomas Campbell (1777-1844), the artist David Wilkie (1785-1841), and the painter of panoramas, Henry Aston Barker (1774-1856).

Webster knew 'Dulwich Grove' when it was 'Dr Glennie's well-known academy' in 1815, and managed to taste the waters, which he pronounced as 'decidely chalybeate'. He also noted that there were 'two distinct spas within a mile' of each other, 'but in different parishes and counties' (Dulwich was in Surrey and Sydenham in Kent – both are now in Greater London, of course)[22]. Glennie's establishment was a very substantial, handsome building *(Plate 165)*, but was demolished *c.*1825[23] when one Bew opened an ale-house on the site, making use of some of the outbuildings and converting the grounds into a Tea-Garden. He appears to have called his ale-house 'Grove Cottage' *(Plate 166)*, and it remained until *c.*1860-3, when a much grander establishment, the *Grove Hotel*, was erected, in the Gardens of which open-air concerts and other entertainments took place, although no trace of the Spring appears to have remained[24]. The pub was rebuilt yet again in 1923 in a vaguely Domestic Revival style (subsequently much altered).

Plate 166: *Grove Cottage ale-house* as it was when Bew ran it *(From Thornbury & Walford **vi** [1879-85] 295: Collection JSC).*

STREATHAM SPA

According to Sunderland, this was 'one of the most important of the London spas'[25], and in 1915 was 'probably the only one of the medicinal springs of the environs of London' where the waters remained 'uncontaminated' and could be drunk with beneficial effect.

The original Springs were discovered in 1659 in grounds 'East of the Green'[26]. Wells were sunk, three in number: one had water that was emetic and another was 'useful in expelling intestinal worms'. The main constituent of *Streatham Spa* waters was magnesium sulphate[27]. One of the first accounts of *Streatham Wells* was given by the antiquary and biographer, John Aubrey (1626-97), who noted that the ground below Wellfield House was 'cold, weeping, and rushy clay' that in hot weather 'shoots a kind of salt or alum on the clay;... and... turns milk for a posset'. Five or six cups of water were recommended, the commonest dose being three, 'held equivalent to nine at Epsom'[28]. Monro recommended a dose of three pints or more[29], and the waters were also recommended for bathing of eyes.

It appears that the discovery of the waters came about when the land was being ploughed: the horses got stuck in a quagmire, and this suggested the existence of a Spring or Springs. When the ground was being weeded later in the year, the weeders drank some of the water, which purged them, 'by which accident its medicinal virtue was first discovered'[30]. Rutty, in his account, described the *Streatham Spa* waters as 'a weak solution of salt, partly like sea-salt and partly nitrous, with a little sulphur, and a greater proportion of absorbent earth than Acton water and some others'[31]. Rutty found two Wells 'situated on the declivity of a pleasant hill, about one hundred yards from a house on Streatham Green', some fifteen yards apart, and both 'arched, secure from rains'. A pump was erected over them 'to prevent decomposition of the water'[32]. Aubrey mentioned three Wells, each with a different kind of water: one was emetic, one was useful for 'worm complaints', and the other was purgative[33].

Frederick Arnold (*fl.* 1880s) provided a full description of *Streatham Spa*[34]. At the beginning of the eighteenth century the reputation of the place stood high: the Common became a fashionable promenade, concerts were given at the Wells, and it seems that the Spa was a 'scene of much gaiety'[35]. The waters were sold at several London coffee-houses, and by 1744 the Streatham products, with those of Acton and Dulwich, were very much in vogue[36]. During the last two decades of his life Dr Johnson patronised the Spa and waxed enthusiastic about the waters. The Spa was not far from the Thrale house at Streatham Park, where Johnson was a regular (if exhausting) guest (from 1766) and close friend of Hester Lynch Thrale (*née* Salusbury [1741-1821]), and who later became (1784) Mrs Piozzi, the wife of the Italian musician, Gabriel Mario Piozzi (1740-1809), much to the Great Cham's chagrin.

Arnold held that around 1792 the Spring was closed, but it appears that a small building covered the pump over one of the Wells in the kitchen-garden of *Streatham Spa* house, and this pump still existed in the years before 1914. According to information published by Foord[37], the pump was housed in a circular building in which was a large lead-lined bath, but by 1907 the water was no longer fit for human consumption.

However, Nathaniel (sometimes given as Nathanael) Salmon (1675-1742) stated that all the waters of the village of Streatham were 'medicated' apart from one Spring 'in the road to Brixton Causeway'[38]. Lysons declared that the main Wells were on Lime Common, in the Manor of Leigham, 'still used by country people' and sent to the hospitals in London. There was also, according to an advertisement of 1717, 'good entertainment' to be found by 'All Gentlemen & Ladies' at the Well: the same source mentioned that 'True Streatham Water fresh every morning' was available at several coffee-houses in London, and that it was 'judged to be the best for purging in England'[39]. The Wells establishment is also mentioned[40] in *The Album of Streatham*, a work attributed to Joseph Richardson (1755-1803).

Matters were complicated by the discovery of another Well in the 1790s, and this has caused some confusion. There was a Well situated at The Rookery, Streatham Common, just east of Covington Way by Copgate Path, but, as Lysons specifically states the Wells proper were at Lime (Leigham) Common, and identified as being at the end of Wells Lane, later Wellfield Road, SW16, that is, where it joins Valley Road. Foord, relying on Arnold and Wakefield, firmly states that it was the later Spring, discovered in the 1780s, which was situated at Lime Common[41]. One extraordinarily interesting writer, Priscilla Wakefield (*née* Bell [1750-1832]), in her 1809 *Perambulations*[42], stopped at Streatham and tasted the waters: Foord wrote that this must have been the Lime Common site, and that 'a proper distinction' between the 'original well on Streatham Common and its successor on Lime Common' was not made until Edward Walford (1823-97) undertook his revisions of Brayley's *History of Surrey*[43]: the 'original' Well was in the Manor of Vauxhall in Lower Streatham, and the later one at Lime Common was described as being in the Manor of Leigham (the name of which is perpetuated today in Leigham Avenue, Leigham Court Road, Leigh Orchard Close, and Leigham Vale). Sunderland, however, says the later Spring was 'at the bottom of Wells Lane, in Streatham Common', which is a mis-reading of the matter[44].

The 'Old Well House' was shown in an advertising brochure issued by the proprietors, Curtis Brothers, as dating from 1659, but this is clearly nonsense because the building was obviously a structure of the late-eighteenth century or Regency period, with a symmetrical front, a low-pitched roof, and a bust of Æsculapius in a round-headed niche in the centre between two first-floor windows. It was rendered with stucco, and to the north of the building, attached to it, was a single-storey Pump-Room where the waters could be drunk on the premises at a penny a glass *(Plate 167)*. Water was also sold on the premises in bottles at one shilling and sixpence per dozen or delivered 'to all parts of London daily' at two shillings and sixpence[45]. The waters were also exported to all parts of the United Kingdom, and also to 'Delagoa Bay and Buenos Ayres'.

Plate 167: Drawing of the house at *Streatham Spa*, with the single-storey Pump-Room on the left. In the central niche at first-floor level is a bust of Æsculapius *(LMA SC/GL/NOB/C/001/12-003/2)*.

An analysis of the water showed it contained magnesium sulphate, sodium chloride, ferrous carbonate, potassium chloride, calcium carbonate, sodium carbonate, and that it was 'naturally charged' with carbonic acid. Even in the 1890s (and presumably until the 1914-18 War) it was 'strongly recommended' for its 'efficacy in renovating the impaired functions of life' and for 'all obstinate Diseases of the skin and Lymphatic Glands, especially in that afflicting disease called Scrofula'. In addition, the waters were perceived as valuable for 'Liver Complaints, Indigestion, Jaundice, and Bilious Attacks' which sounds like tautology. They were supposed to have 'effected permanent cures' in cases of 'Eruptions, Scrofula, Jaundice, Indigestion, Worms, Eczema, Acne (or Blotched Face), Chlorosis, Rheumatism, Gout, Shingles, Gravel, Palpitations, and Giddiness' as well as 'most Diseases arising from an impaired state of the Digestive Organs'[46]. *Streatham Spa* water restored 'Strength and Vigour to the weakened Frame by a Direct Operation on the System in General, and by improving the Quality of the Blood'. Its 'aperient property', we are assured, which was 'owing to the quality of Sulphate of Magnesia' it contained, was capable of 'evacuating irritating matter from the Intestines, without producing any constitutional disturbance', while the 'Soda' corrected 'any acidity which might remain in the primæ viæ'. It was a 'valuable remedy' in cases of 'Nervous Debility'[47]. The waters appear to have received the *Imprimatur* of Mathew Baillie (1761-1823), the anatomist and physician[48].

The pretty little Wells House had a Tea-Garden attached to it, but this seems to have fallen from favour by the 1860s, and the place became a dairy-farm owned by the Curtis Brothers, who still provided the waters until well into the twentieth century, when the establishment was referred to as the only Mineral-Spring

Plate 168: View of *Streatham Spa Wells House* from a photograph of *Streatham (New) Wells* in *c*.1902. *(From Foord [1910] facing p.226: Collection JSC).*

remaining open of the several 'once noted ones' in London[49]. A photograph of around 1901-2 *(Plate 168)* shows the building as it was then, with a much-altered Pump-Room to the left and a large clap-boarded structure to the rear. Hanslip Fletcher (1874-1955) made a drawing of the 'Well-House of Streatham Spa' for the 'Where London Sleeps' section of *The Sunday Times*. The building appears in a murky photograph in a pamphlet advertising *Streatham Mineral Wells*, probably of *c*.1890s vintage *(Plate 169)*.

Plate 169: *Streatham Mineral Wells, Valley Road, Streatham, S.W.*, showing *The Old Well House*, purported to be of 1659, but is clearly of early-nineteenth-century date *(LMA SC/GL/NOB/B/W1/GRA-W2).*

RICHMOND SPA *OR* WELLS

Richmond Spa owed its existence to the discovery of a saline Spring *c*.1689 in grounds subsequently the gardens of Cardigan House, Richmond upon Thames. Benjamin Allen described the water as a 'level Spring' feeding Wells 'on the side of the hill a few rods from the River Thames, in a brown loamy clay' about nine feet deep. 'This water purgeth well, but... scarce as much as Epsom and Acton', although it did so, we are relieved to read, 'more smoothly'[50]. It would therefore appear that the water was impregnated with magnesium sulphate at least.

A few years after the discovery of the Spring a 'House of Entertainment' was erected, with Assembly-, Card-, and Raffling-Rooms, and the so-called *Richmond Wells* was in business. 'The New Wells on Richmond Hill' were 'compleated' for the 'Reception of Company', and could boast a large, high dining-room, broad walks some three hundred feet long, 'open and shady', from which an agreeable 'Prospect' of the country could be enjoyed[51]. 'Consorts of Musick' were performed, 'both Vocal and Instrumental', with new works composed especially by 'Mr Frank'; the songs performed were also printed and sold at the Wells. 'Mr Frank' was Johann Wolfgang Franck (1644-*c*.1710) who had arrived in London in *c*.1690, and was later murdered in Spain[52].

The place seems to have been an instantaneous success, the price of admission was doubled in order to exclude the riff-raff, and concerts were advertised at five shillings a ticket (no small sum then). Curiously, the *Wells* was put up for sale in 1697[53], but musical performances seem to have continued well into the eighteenth century, including dances. Gambling was also a feature for several years. In 1701 a concert was advertised to be held in the Great Room, during which 'Mr Abel' would sing alone to the harpsichord[54]. This was probably John Abell (1653-*c*.1716), who was born in Aberdeenshire and had been admitted a 'gentleman of his majesty's chapel extraordinary' in 1679. This Abell should not be confused with the German composer, Karl Friedrich Abel (1723-87), friend and colleague of Johann Christian Bach (1735-82). The Richmond 'Consorts' usually ran from five until seven p.m., after which there was dancing.

Many surviving advertisements for *Richmond Wells* give information about the tides on the River Thames for the convenience of visitors. This is because during the seventeenth and eighteenth centuries the River offered a faster, easier, convenient, and *safer* means of travel than did the roads, which were not only very rough, but dangerous, thanks to the presence of footpads, highwaymen, and other ruffians. The Balls which were held at *Richmond Wells* every Monday and Thursday evening during the Summer months attracted plenty of custom[55], and ladies and gentlemen were invited 'either to raffle for gold chains, equipages[56], or any other curious toys, and fine old china; and likewise play at quadrille[57], ombre[58], whist, &c.'[59] One imagines that the company, well-oiled and carrying cash and gold, would have provided rich pickings for unscrupulous Georgian thieves, so it is little wonder that travel by boat was preferable.

For something like fifty years *Richmond Spa* or *Wells* enjoyed success: the usual refreshments, including breakfasts, teas, and dinners (not to mention phenomenal quantities of alcohol), were available at a price (very few Georgian pleasure-grounds were cheap). The fashion for the 'Publick Breakfast' introduced to London from places like Bath and Tunbridge Wells had quite a run, and involved the consumption of prodigious amounts of coffee and tea. The waters do not appear to have played a major part in the commercial fortunes of *Richmond Wells* as they seem to have been taken for granted as part of the establishment. By the 1750s card-playing and dissipation seem to have gained the upper hand, and, as tone declined so did attendance by Polite Society. To attempt to recoup losses, prices of admission were lowered, which attracted a lower class of customer, with the inevitable increase in bad publicity. In 1775 the estate was purchased by the Misses Houblon, two ladies of a Walloon Protestant family originally from Lille, who caused the erection of the Houblon Almshouses (1757 and 1758) in Worple Way, Sheen Road, Richmond.

It appears that the buildings associated with the medicinal Well were demolished in the 1860s, for around 1780 *Richmond Wells* as a place of entertainment had ceased to exist[60]. The 'chalybeate' Spring has apparently disappeared, although John Evans (1767-1827), in his useful book[61], mentioned that at the top of the hill, in 'the New Park' (i.e. Richmond Park) there was a 'bubbling up of water, which running down into the adjacent vale, exhibits indications of an ochreous description, which might be gathered into a basin, and become subservient to the health of visitants'.

It would seem that no trace could be found of the Wells in the grounds of Cardigan House, and Foord failed to find any images, but Sunderland published a photograph of the Grotto in the grounds of Cardigan House 'showing one of the original wells' in 1915[62]. Cardigan House, of 1777, designed by the little-known William Eves, has been replaced by a nondescript block of flats[63].

EAST SHEEN WELL

At East Sheen on what was Palewell Common (known locally as 'Donkey Common'), due east of Richmond, was a chalybeate Well once used for bathing eyes and legs, probably to alleviate skin complaints. London's expansion seems to have killed it off, although there is still a Palewell Common Drive in existence.

EPSOM SPA

The waters of *Epsom Spa* contained magnesium sulphate, and seem to have been discovered around 1618 on Epsom Common. The salt was first extracted by Nehemiah Grew (1641-1712)[64], who made a special study of the waters, and published a Latin account in 1695[65]. He pioneered the production of Epsom Salts, which were sold at the astronomical price of five shillings an ounce. An unauthorised English translation of

Plate 170: *Epsom Wells* in its rural state *(From Walford **ii** [1884] 246: Collection JSC).*

his *Tractatus* was published in 1697 by the apothecary, Francis Moult[66]: this prompted an almost immediate riposte in another English translation by Dr Joseph Bridges, with 'Animadversions on a late Corrupt Translation publish'd by Francis Moult, Chymist'[67]. This row went on until Grew was vindicated by Josiah Peter's *Truth in Opposition to Ignorant and Malicious Falsehood*[68], which put Moult and his associates firmly in their places.

The story of Epsom Salts appears to begin when one Henry Wicks, who kept cattle *(Plate 170)*, found a pool of water on Epsom Common, and enlarged it so that the cows could drink there. The animals, however, would not drink the fluid, which aroused Wicks's curiosity, so he drank the water and discovered it had a powerful purging action, a fact which soon became widely known: by the middle of the seventeenth century the Epsom waters were resorted to by the Court and Quality, and there were regular coaches from London to facilitate visits. Soon a Wells House was erected, with ballroom, gaming-room, and other accommodation, and bowling-greens were laid out near by. Inns, coffee-houses, and Taverns were enlarged or newly built, and flourished. A large pub, called *The New Inn*, was built (supposedly the first of its kind in England at that time) on the High Street *c.*1690 *(Plate 171)*, later called Waterloo House when it ceased to be an inn: on the first floor was an Assembly-Room, an early example of the type, and a model for later exemplars. It was the scene of cock-fights on Sunday afternoons until around the middle of the nineteenth century. Pepys visited Epsom 'to the Well', where he found 'much Company': he seems to have made a bee-line for Spas and Wells when he could, more for the sake of being 'merry', one suspects, than for medicinal purposes.

Epsom offered breakfasts, music, dancing, equestrian exercise on the Downs, horse-racing, wrestling, and boxing (with regard to the last three activities wagers were very much a part of the fun). During the evenings there were assemblies, private parties, card-games (again with bets), and musical diversions as well as dances. The place doubtless gained in kudos when it was included in the visits of George, Prince of Denmark and Duke of Cumberland (1653-1708) to various watering–places for the sake of his health. As husband of Queen Anne (reigned 1702-14), his presence drew Persons of Quality, but there was a very real reason for Prince George's attempts to seek relief for his debilitating condition at Spas such as Bath and Tunbridge Wells: he had chronic asthma, but unfortunately no waters, not even those of Epsom, had any beneficial effects on his weakened constitution.

One John Livingstone (or Levingstone, d. 1727), apothecary, purchased land in Epsom, sank a Well, built a ballroom, and a room for gambling, and put up shops and houses, in order to attract custom from the Wells on the Common. Furthermore, he purchased a lease of the old Wells, which he closed, and these were not re-opened until after his death. The 'New Wells', however, do not appear to have had any medicinal properties, and they rapidly fell from favour.

In 1735, Sarah Mapp (*née* Wallin – 1706-37)

Plate 171: *The New Inn* at Epsom, from a watercolour reproduced in *A Pilgrimage in Surrey* **ii** 322, by James S. Ogilvy (also the artist), in 1914 *(Collection HP).*

settled in Epsom, by then a place with established Royal connections, and much-favoured by fashionable society. However, the horse-racing, pugilism, and even canters on the Downs produced a fair amount of broken bones, and Mrs Mapp (called 'Crazy Sally'), who was unusually strong and beefy, gained a useful reputation as a bone-setter, not only when attending to fractures, but putting right dislocated limbs. Even persons who had suffered pain for years were soon sorted out by the powerful muscles of Sarah Mapp, who, despite her unappetising appearance (she was slovenly and none too clean), was very neat in her work, and could roll bandages with consummate professionalism. She was earning something like twenty guineas a day, an enormous sum then, as well as collecting presents and gratuities from the well-to-do. She purchased a four-horse chariot, and took herself off to London every week, where, at a coffee-house near the Temple, she carried out bone-setting, straightening of bent backs, and manipulating hips, some of which feats were witnessed by Sir Hans Sloane (1660-1753), no less.

Although the *Haut Ton* took Sarah Mapp to its fickle heart, like any 'celebrity' of the tabloids today, she began to behave in a more eccentric manner, then rapidly fell from grace, took spectacularly to drink, died, miserably poor, in Seven Dials, and had to be buried at the Parish's expense[69]. Georgian London could be just as cruel as the capital is today. Nevertheless, she did show more understanding of bones than did the general run of quacks of the period. A contemporary verse said as much;

> 'You doctors of London, who puzzle your pates
> To ride in your coaches and purchase estates;
> Give over, for shame, for your pride has a fall,
> And the doctress of Epsom has outdone you all'[70].

John Toland (1670-1722) claimed that the waters of Epsom were 'beneficial in gently cleansing the body, in cooling the head, and purifying the blood; the salt, that is chymically made of 'em, being famous all over Europe'[71].

From a high vantage-point on the Downs Toland recorded that he had counted above sixty coaches on a Sunday evening, and, as no part of England was 'supplied with more diversity of the best of provisions' than Epsom, the place, thanks to the 'nearness of London', could provide 'all the exotic preparatives and allurements to luxury' when ever anyone was 'disposed to make a sumptuous banquet, or to give a genteel collation'. He went on to describe how the 'choicest fruits, herbs, roots, and flowers, with all sorts of tame and wild fowl, with the rarest fish and venison, and with every kind of butcher's meat, among which Bansteaddown mutton' was the 'most relishing dainty', could be obtained there[72].

From *c.*1728 the original Well on the Common was revived, and the facilities were improved, but the Spa never regained its previous popularity. When Richard Russell (1687-1759) began to promote bathing in sea-water (and drinking it)[73], custom further deserted Epsom, and enthusiasm for the pleasures of Bath also damaged its fortunes. Dale Ingram (1710-93), surgeon and male midwife, visited Epsom in the 1760s, and published a book on the principal saline ingredients of the Epsom waters[74]. Ingram advertised preparations of magnesium obtained from the Mineral-Water, and attempted to revive the public breakfasts, but without a great deal of success. The site of the Well is still visible today.

Not far from once-fashionable Epsom were several other Wells, including the *Scouring Well*, Ashtead Oaks, *Jessop's House* at Stoke (*Jessop's* waters were brought to London for sale), and the *Purging Well* at Ewell, where names such as the Spring Hotel, Spring Street, Spring House, and Bourne Hall are reminders of a watery history. Macpherson observed that a 'neglected' Pump-Room survived over *Jessop's Well* in 1871[75]. Other Springs in Surrey that enjoyed brief fame included *Cobham Spring*, Cobham, on the Guildford Road, which produced a strong and, for a time, celebrated chalybeate water. Just over the County boundary to the north, in Berkshire, were *Sunninghill Wells* near Ascot (again with chalybeate water – it survived until 1871 at the Wells Hotel) and *Windsor Forest Spring* (with mild purging waters, much less ferocious than those of Epsom and certain other localities).

SHOOTER'S HILL

There were several purging Wells at Shooter's Hill, Kent, not far from Greenwich, and these gained a reputation in the 1670s, having a 'brisk' and 'bitterish taste', and were valued as 'medicinal, for internal and external griefs'[76]. John Evelyn resorted to these waters, and it appears Queen Anne also drank them. A Wells House was built over one of the Wells, but none of the Shooter's Hill Wells seems to have acquired buildings for entertainment: they were solely used as supplies of Mineral-Water impregnated with magnesium sulphate which was extracted from the waters by evaporation and sold dry.

Walford stated that a Mineral-Well, 'still visited by invalids of the neighbourhood', could be found in the 1880s on the north-west side of Shooter's Hill, 'a little above the Royal Military Academy', and was 'celebrated for its curative properties'[77]. Thus the Wells were properly in Woolwich. Shooter's Hill, a large spur of London Clay, is in marked contrast with the alluvial flats that stretch along the River at its base. Capped with gravel, it is a classic example of the geological structure from which Springs and Wells derive. The Shooter's Hill waters possessed a 'nitrous and bituminous'[78] scent, and apparently, during the late 1670s, two of the Wells were 'steined' (i.e. lined) with brick, but the water was extracted using basic methods rather than pumps. Early in the nineteenth century, one source stated that the Spring at the top of Shooter's Hill constantly caused its Well to overflow, and did not freeze, even when extremely cold[79]. However, this may not be correct, for Vincent, in his *Records*, identified the site of the most important Mineral-Well as on the eastern side of the waste ground behind the Royal Military Academy which could still be seen under a shed in the garden of a cottage at the rear of the *Eagle Tavern*[80]. Foord[81] noted that the Ordnance Survey Map of the 1894-6 edition showed the position of the Well, which agreed with Vincent's account.

On the south side of Shooter's Hill Road there was a Well in the south-east corner of the approach to Severndroog Castle, but this was not a medicinal, but a 'dipping' Well approached down a few steps[82]. Severndroog is a triangular Gothic tower with hexagonal corner-turrets, used as a belvedere, and erected in 1784 by his widow to commemorate the taking of the stronghold of Savanadrug on the coast of Malabar in 1755 by Sir William James, Bt. (1722-83). It was designed by Richard Jupp (1728-99), who was also responsible for the James residence, Park Farm Place, Eltham, and who was Surveyor (1768-99) to the East India Company.

LADYWELL

Other Wells included *Ladywell*, between Brockley and Lewisham in what was Kent, which seems to have had at least two Springs, one of which was chalybeate, and may have been (though this is doubtful), as the name suggests, a Holy Well. Lysons[83] mentioned it, and observations by John Warkworth (*c*.1425-1500) concerning the 'abundance' of water at 'Levesham' were quoted by numerous writers on Kent, including Hasted[84] and Kilburne[85]: the position of the main Well was given as 'exactly in front of' *The Freemason's Arms* inn, situated under the middle of the road leading to the railway-station, but it was filled in and covered up when a sewer was formed in *c*.1865. The Mineral-Spring was on the southern side of the road at 'Ladywell Cottage, before the cemetery is reached'. This will be Ladywell Cemetery in Brockley. Apparently the Mineral-Spring was valued for the treatment of eyes[86]. Two sources are useful on the Ladywell waters: the correspondence in the *Kentish Mercury* in 1896[87] and the summaries collated by Charles Angell Bradford (*fl*.1890-*c*.1935)[88]. Bradford suggested that the name 'Ladywell' appears to have been of comparatively modern origin, for neither name nor Well was marked on Rocque's 1745 Map, nor on Hasted's Map of 1778. A Well *was* marked on the 1799 Ordnance Survey Map, but the *name* does not appear to have been used by the Ordnance Survey until the one-inch map of 1841. However, Cruchley[89], in his *New Map* annexed to his *Picture of London* in the 1831 edition, gave both the Well and the name: Cruchley identified the site of the Well as west of the Ravensbourne on the south side of Brockley Lane, which was afterwards bridged over for the railway. A more mundane origin of the name was that ladies sent their servants to obtain water to make 'tay'. Foord set out the main arguments in his book[90].

BROMLEY WELLS

Also in Kent, two Wells at Bromley should be mentioned: these are *St Blaise's* or *St Blaize's Well* (supposedly a Holy Well, 'rediscovered' in 1756 at the height of the craze for Mineral-Waters, which attracted the public for a time) and *Caesar's Well*, the main source of the Ravensbourne, also once known as *The Bath*, and said to possess medicinal properties. It appears on Hasted's plan of the camp at Holwood[91] which is in Keston. 'Caesar's Well' is supposed to have been where Julius Caesar found water for his legions, but 'Caesar's Camp' in Holwood Park is actually an Iron Age Fort, greatly predating the arrival of the Romans[92].

St Blaise's Well is commemorated by St Blaise Avenue, Bromley, in which is the former Palace of the Bishops of Rochester, later (1933) Stockwell Teachers' Training College, and more recently (1982) Bromley Civic Centre. 'In a shady dell in the grounds, about a hundred yards eastwards of the house', was the chalybeate Well 'long celebrated in connection with Bromley'[93]. Because of its situation, this Well was also called the *Bishop's Well*, and is supposed to have had a small oratory near by during the Middle Ages. The indefatigable William Hone declared that the water of the *Bishop's Well* was a 'chalybeate, honoured by local reputation with surprising properties', and that it was 'of the same nature as the mineral water of Tunbridge Wells'[94].

The Reverend James Edward Newell, Vicar of Bromley (1819-65), published a slim volume of poetry in which he mentioned St Blaise's Well:

'The morning dew hangs on the flower
Around thy blessed spring,
St Blaise! untrodden now! The hour
Of thy renown
Is past away and gone.

Erst to thy fount the baron went;
The sandal'd pilgrim lowly bent
Before the sacred shrine.
The warrior bowed his plumed head,
His hasty prayer the friar said,
And many a gay and gallant knight,
And many a gentle lady bright,
Implored thy aid divine.

Where are they now? The warrior's tread,
The orison the sick man said,
The lover's vow to lady fair,
The palmer's reverential prayer,
The poet's lay, the minstrel's shell,
Are silent – all are gone!
Hangs o'er thy desecrated well
One rugged thorn alone'[95].

Charles Williams (1797-1830) recorded the appearance of the Well for Hone in the late 1820s *(Plate 172)*. At the end of the twentieth century the Spring was landscaped, and the waters still issue forth into a pool with the outfall to a lake in the centre of which is a fountain.

CAMBERWELL AND STOCKWELL

This Chapter ends with a brief consideration of two places, the names of which suggest there were indeed Wells there at some time.

Two Wells appear to have existed in Stockwell, one just south of Clapham Road near the present Edithna Street, and the other west of Stockwell Road where Stockwell Green is today. Neither location now gives much indication that once there were important Wells there. At Camberwell, however, there appear to have been several Wells, one at Milkwell Manor, now only recalled by Milkwell Yard, an unprepossessing space south of the junction between Camberwell New Road and Camberwell Road (west of Denmark Hill). There seems to have been a Well in the grounds of Grove Hill, the villa once the home of John Coakley Lettsom (1744-1815), the physician and philanthropist, and Sunderland mentioned three more[96]. Various writers[97] confirmed the location of an important Well in Lettsom's garden, even suggesting it was this which gave Camberwell its name, but not all have been of the same opinion. Salmon stated that the place 'seems to be named for some mineral water which was anciently in it'[98], and Manning & Bray followed this line[99]. Some opined that the Well was important in ancient times, so much so that when the property in which it was situated changed hands the vendors reserved rights over the waters to themselves, their heirs, and assigns[100]. Others, however, were more sceptical, and doubted if Dr Lettsom's Well was the same as that which gave its name to Camberwell[101]. There have been other speculations: the Patron of the Parish-Church of Camberwell is St Giles (d. *c.*710), also Patron of cripples, lepers, and nursing mothers, and the old word *cam* means crooked, bent, bowed, twisted, askew, or blind in one eye, which may mean that the place-name was associated with a medicinal Well resorted to by cripples. Credence is given to this by the fact that for many years it was called 'Camwell', 'Cammerwell', or 'Camerwell', the 'b' only creeping in during the seventeenth century[102].

It is extraordinary that a Spring in Camberwell was discovered as late as 1906, and was reported in the Press[103]. Analysis showed that the water was unusually rich in iron, and was therefore comparable with *Tunbridge Wells* water[104]: this was carried out by Dr Edward Collins Bousfield (1855-1921), Bacteriologist to the Metropolitan Boroughs of Camberwell and Hackney, and Director of the Camberwell Research Laboratories[105]. Thornbury & Walford

Plate 172: *Bishop's* or *St Blaise's Well*, Bromley, in the 1820s, from a drawing by Charles Williams *(From Hone **iii** [1835] 65-6: Collection JSC).*

reported that 'within the last century or so three ancient wells were discovered in a field' in the Parish of Camberwell, but 'they were covered in again by the owner of the land'[106].

This seems to have been a common fate, for, with a few exceptions, most ancient Wells are but a memory nevertheless, nearly all of them have histories worth knowing.

Chapter XII References: Spas and Wells further South

1 *See* 2 September 1675 and 5 August 1677.
2 Peter (*c.*1680).
3 Drink composed of hot milk curdled with ale, wine, or other liquor, often with sugar, spices, etc.
4 Allen (1699, 1711).
5 Pertaining to or containing marcasite (iron pyrites or disulphide).
6 Allen (1699).
7 Foord (1910) 217.
8 Monro **i** (1770) 138-9.
9 Lysons **iv** (1792-6) 536.
10 Notice in LMA: I am grateful to Jeremy Smith for drawing this to my attention.
11 Sunderland (1915) 121.
12 *Ibid.*
13 Given in some sources as 'Evance'.
14 The Print Depôt &c. No 63½ Red Lion Street, Clerkenwell. For further information *see* Read (1977).
15 The document is illustrated in Sunderland (1915) opposite 122.
16 Quoted in Thornbury & Walford **vi** (1879-85) 294.
17 Foord (1910) 219-20.
18 London County Council (1901).
19 Foord (1910) 213; Sunderland (1915) 118.
20 Martyn (1741).
21 *See* Manning & Bray (1809-14).
22 Thornbury & Walford **vi** (1879-85) 294.
23 *Ibid.*
24 Sunderland (1915) 119.
25 *Ibid.* 127.
26 Aubrey **i** (1718-19) 215.
27 Rutty (1857).
28 Aubrey **i** (1718-19) 215, but *see* the Streatham section reprint (1989).
29 Monro **i** (1770) 135.
30 Aubrey (1718-19).
31 Rutty (1757) on Streatham.
32 Foord (1910) 231.
33 Aubrey **i** (1718-19) 215.
34 Arnold (1886).
35 Foord (1910) 231.
36 Rutty (1757).
37 Foord (1910) 233.
38 Salmon (1726), an under-rated source of material.
39 *Post-Boy* (28 May 1717) cited by Lysons (1811) 89. *See* also Manning & Bray **iii** (1809-14) 381, 701, and Anonymous (1760).
40 Richardson (1788).
41 Foord (1910) 234.
42 Wakefield (1809). For Wakefield *see ODNB* **lvi** (2004) 740-3.
43 Walford (*Ed.*) (1878-81) on Streatham.
44 Sunderland (1915) 130.
45 Curtis Bros. (*c.*1895), a rare booklet held in GLCL ref. B WI/STR.
46 *Ibid.*
47 *Ibid. See* also Anonymous (1760), possibly by M. Kingman.
48 *ODNB* **iii** (2004) 294-6. Baillie's interest in post-mortem investigations of organs led him to make one of the first connections of cirrhosis of the liver with alcoholism, which probably accounted for his interest in the curative properties of Mineral-Water.
49 Arnold (1886) 95-104.
50 Allen (1699) on Richmond.
51 *London Gazette* (20-23 April 1696).
52 Sadie (*Ed.*) **ii** (2002) 282-3.
53 *London Gazette* (5-8 April 1697).
54 *Postman* (9 August 1701).
55 Macky (1724).
56 Small articles of domestic furniture such as glass or earthenware.
57 Card game played by four persons with 40 cards, the eights, nines, and tens of the ordinary pack being discarded. It superseded *ombre* in popularity *c.*1726, and was in turn superseded by whist.
58 Card game played by three persons with 40 cards, the eights, nines, and tens of the ordinary pack being discarded.
59 *Craftsman* (11 June 1730).
60 Crisp (1866).
61 Evans (1825).
62 Sunderland (1915) opposite 134.
63 Cherry & Pevsner (1991), whose only comment is 'alas'.
64 *ODNB* **xxiii** (2004) 797-9.
65 Grew (1695).
66 Moult (1697)
67 Grew (1697).
68 Peter (1701)
69 *ODNB* **xxxvi** (2004) 589-90. *See* also *Grub Street Journal* (19 April 1736).
70 Quoted in Walford **ii** (1884) 250.
71 Toland (1711).
72 *Ibid.*
73 Russell (1753).
74 Ingram (1767).
75 Macpherson (1871).
76 Quoted in Sunderland (1915) 143.
77 Walford **ii** (1884) 33.
78 Foord (1910) 204.
79 Hughson (1805-9).

80 Vincent (1888-90).
81 Foord (1910) 204-5.
82 Vincent (1888-90); Foord (1915) 205.
83 Lysons **ii** (1811 edn.) 572.
84 Hasted (1778-99).
85 Kilburne (1659) 168.
86 Butts (1878). For the sewers *see Kentish Mercury* (12 January 1866).
87 *See* especially 12 June 1896.
88 *The Home Counties Magazine* **i** (1899) 305-10.
89 Cruchley (1831).
90 Foord (1910) 201-2.
91 Hasted (1778) on Holwood.
92 Walford **ii** (1884) 111.
93 Walford **ii** (1884) 90.
94 Hone **ii** (1835) 66-7.
95 Quoted in Walford **ii** (1884) 91, where 'Well' is given as 'Wall'.
96 Sunderland (1915) 32.
97 *See*, for example, Allport (1841).
98 Salmon (1736).
99 Manning & Bray (1804-14).
100 Heckethorn (1899).
101 Brayley, Britton, Brayley, & Mantell (1841-4) and 1878-81 edn. edited by Walford.
102 Thornbury & Walford **vi** (1879-85) 270. *See* also Blanch (1875).
103 *Daily Telegraph* (5 June 1906).
104 Foord (1910) 210.
105 *British Medical Journal* **i**/3135 (29 January 1921) 77-8.
106 Thornbury & Walford **vi** (1879-85) 269, an invaluable but undervalued source.

CHAPTER XIII

BEULAH AND BIGGIN HILL

Beulah Spa; Biggin Hill Spring

'The water that comes from the same spring cannot be fresh and salt both'.
THOMAS FULLER (1654-1734): *Gnomologia: Adages and Proverbs, Wise Sentences, and Witty Sayings, Ancient and Modern, Foreign and British* (London: B. Barker, A. Bettesworth, & C. Hitch 1732) 4817.

BEULAH SPA

This was the 'last of the Springs in the environs of London to be inaugurated' as a Spa[1]. On Rocque's 1746 Map Bewly Wood and Bewly's Farm are shown at Norwood, and by 1808 plans of Norwood show 'Beaulieu Hill'. During the 1820s the Whitehorse Manor at Norwood was sold by the Cator family to one John Davidson Smith (d.1844) who acquired the Bewly or Bewlye Coppice in which there were known Mineral-Springs, impregnated, like those of Dulwich, Streatham, and Sydenham, with sulphate of magnesia. Smith began work on the transformation of his estate into a salubrious place of recreation in the 1820s, and called in the great architect, Decimus Burton (1800-81), to design the Pump-Room and lay out the grounds (1828-31)[2] as a genteel Spa. It was a curious commercial decision, for, by that time the vogue for such health-resorts was in decline. Smith obviously thought that, backed by up-to-date medical opinion, with sound architectural and landscape advice, and a marvellously favoured naturally rolling site, he could combine park, watering-place, and tea-garden all in one. Burton, of course, was also involved in the design of St Leonard's, Hastings, Sussex (1828), and at the Calverley Estate, Tunbridge Wells, Kent (also 1828), and had already designed numerous private houses, gardens, and public buildings (including the Ionic screen at Hyde Park Corner [1824-5], the Gardens of the Zoological Society, Regent's Park [1826-41], the Athenæum Club, Waterloo Place [1827-30], and The Grove, Penshurst, Kent [1828-33], the last in a *cottage orné* style).

It is clear that Smith intended to promote his Spa not only to obtain an income from ticket-sales and refreshments, but to establish the newly-named *Beulah Spa* as such a fashionable and delightful spot that the public would become so enamoured with it they would wish to acquire property there when he developed it as a 'new town' to designs by Burton, who was no slouch when it came to landscape either: Smith intended from the very beginning that the tone would be elevated and would appeal to a respectable middle-class *clientèle*. In order to make this 'earthly Elysium' possible, Bewly's Farm at the foot of Spa Hill was demolished, and the farm-lands were combined with the Coppice, providing about thirty acres of attractively varied landscape to be enhanced and beautified. The site lay between Leather Bottle Lane (now Spa Hill) and Grange Wood, Upper Norwood, and the Spa is remembered in the names of streets like Beulah Hill, Upper Beulah Hill, and Spa Close.

The next essential move was to get a medical man to promote the waters. George Hume Weatherhead (*c*.1790-1853 – who published several works on Spas and Mineral-Waters in the course of his career, but, curiously, died of kidney disease at his home, The Cottage, Foots Cray Park, near Bromley, Kent[3]), prepared *An Account of the Beulah Saline Spa*[4] intended as a puff

Plate 173: View of the entrance-lodge of *Beulah Spa*, Norwood, by John Preston Neale, engraved by R. Martin, 1831. In the background, on the right, can be seen the chimneys of the *Beulah Spa Hotel* *(LMA SC/GL/PR/VI/GUI-VI/NOR/CRY/Ce28995/cat.no.p7494258).*

for Smith's venture. He described the Spring as rising about fourteen feet 'within a circular rock-work enclosure', the water drawn 'by a contrivance at once ingenious and novel'. This was an urn-shaped vessel of glass 'terminating with a cock of the same material': the urn had a 'stout rim and cross handle of silver' and was attached to a thick 'worsted rope' by which it was let down into the Spring by a pulley, and when the vessel was 'taken up full', the water was drawn off by means of the cock.

Michael Faraday (1791-1867) analysed the *Beulah Spa* waters, and, according to various sources[5] found them strongly impregnated with magnesium sulphate, sodium chloride, 'muriate[6] of magnesia', carbonate of lime, and carbonate of soda. Indeed, the Spa waters were among the strongest of all produced by saline Spas in the country, and compared favourably with those of Bath, Cheltenham, and Wells. Charles Scudamore (1779-1849) included the *Beulah Spa* waters in his *Treatise*[7], and there were several other publications that described the waters as well as the physical surroundings, among them works by Archibald Maxfield (*fl.*1825-42 – of St Bartholomew's Hospital and Southampton)[8] and James Wyld (1812-87)[9], the publisher of numerous guide- and travel-books.

Burton laid out a road through Whitehorse Wood to give access to visitors from the Croydon direction: this was once called Decimus Burton Road, but, in conformity with the obliteration of anything perceived as 'different' or 'cultural', this is now that stretch of Grange Road between Thornton Heath High Street and Grange Hill. He also designed a suitably 'rustic' cottage which doubled as the entrance-lodge and ticket-office, with thatched roof, ferociously tortured barge-boards, dormer-window, spiky finials, hood-moulds over vaguely seventeenth-century style windows, and elaborate chimneys. This building is shown in a *View* drawn by John Preston Neale (1780-1847) engraved by R. Martin (*fl.*1820-40) and published in 1831 *(Plate 173)*, but it was extended upwards in the nineteenth century and became *Tivoli Lodge* with a slate roof: some of Burton's decorative barge-frets were retained *(Plate 174)*[10].

Plate 174: Burton's entrance-lodge extended upwards, re-named *Tivoli Lodge* *(CLSLAS/PH-95-1789).*

Plate 175: *Beulah Saline Spa Norwood, the Estate of J. D. Smith Esq^{e}.*, published in November 1832 by R. Havell *(LMA SC/GL/NOB/C/001/1-12).*

The outlay on planting must have been very considerable, and of course there were the lakes with their inevitable islands and bridges and the buildings, including a circular or octagonal structure with external rustic columns and embellishments used as a room for Swiss confectionery and as a reading-room, various booths, alcoves, and grottoes in which visitors could take rest and refreshment, and the conical thatched protective cover over the Spring ('built in the form of an Indian Wigwam'). The Spa is shown in a charming prospect of *Beulah Saline Spa* published by the firm of R. Havell of 77 Oxford Street and dated November 1832: as Robert Havell Senior (1769-1832) died on 21 November of that year, the Havell responsible for the fine engraving must have been Robert Junior (1793-1878), who was to emigrate to America in 1839. This splendid view, described as 'The Estate of J. D. Smith Esq^{e}', shows the octagonal building, the conical cover of the Spring, and several tent-like structures, but no colonnades or arcaded elements: those were to come later *(Plate 175)*.

As with eighteenth-century Pleasure-

Gardens, *Beulah Spa* had a space for musical performances, and with its band, ballad-singers, 'gipsy' fortune-tellers, maze, rosary, camera obscura, archery-ground, spectacular views, and facilities for visitors who wished to enjoy picnics, it was a place of considerable attractiveness. The Spa was opened in August 1831 by Sarah, Countess of Essex, who had married George Capel-Coningsby (1757-1839 – 5th Earl of Essex from 1799) in 1786. One of the garden-seats in a choice position in the grounds of *Beulah Spa* was called 'Lady Essex's seat' as she was a frequent visitor to the establishment, and her presence would have helped to improve the social standing of the Spa. Lady Essex, *née* Bazett, was the widow of Edward Stephenson, and was to die in January 1838. This Lady Essex has been confused with Catherine ('Kitty') Stephens (1794-1882), the soprano and actress who sang Susanna in the first performance of Mozart's *Figaro* in English (1819)[11], Agnes (Agathe) in the English version of *Der Freischütz* (The Freeshooter) by Carl Maria Friedrich Ernst von Weber (1786-1826) in 1824, and Zerlina in *The Libertine* (1817), which counts as the first performance in English of Mozart's *Don Giovanni*[12]. Weber, who greatly admired Stephens, composed for her 'From Chindara's warbling fount I come', the words of which she selected from the 'Oriental Romance', *Lalla Rookh* (published 1817), by the Irish poet, Thomas Moore (1779-1852): Weber himself accompanied her when she sang it at his own Benefit Concert in 1826, only a few days before his death. She retired from the stage in 1835 (her voice had become thin and her intonation unsteady), having amassed a considerable fortune, and in 1838 at the age of 44 she married the Earl of Essex (a distinguished Patron of Drama) less than three months after his estranged Countess's death[13]. Unlike many of her fellow-performers however, Kitty Stephens's reputation was anything but disreputable, and to suggest she 'entrapped' the elderly Earl or had a 'loucheness' about her is as unfair as it is inaccurate to suggest she opened the Spa in 1831, because in that year she was *not* the Countess of Essex[14]. Had any whiff of scandal hung about her person, it is highly unlikely Queen Victoria would have 'called up' Lady Essex and spoken to her at a Ball, nor would the young Queen have agreed with Lord Melbourne that Kitty was a 'very nice person'[15].

One shilling was charged on 'ordinary' days for admission to *Beulah Spa*, and half-a-crown on special (or *fête*) days: the yearly subscription for a family was three guineas, and for a single person one and a half guineas. The waters could be consumed on the premises or purchased to take away, and they were delivered to addresses in London for two shillings a gallon. There were coaches plying from Charing Cross to *Beulah Spa* several times a day. During the season a military band played from eleven in the morning until sunset, and there were areas for dancing. Various organisations were invited to hold fêtes at the Spa in aid of their fund-raising activities[16], and in July 1834 around 3,000 persons attended one such event. As with today, however, the success or failure of such open-air activities was dependent on the vagaries of the weather: in 1838 one such fête organised for the relief of Polish refugees was washed out, and ran at a catastrophic loss.

In its early days the Spa gave *Burlettas* (an entertainment, as previously noted, that featured at places such as *Vauxhall*, *Marylebone*, or *Ranelagh Gardens*). Charles Dance (1794-1863) wrote one such, a farce called *The Beulah Spa*[17], which was performed at Madame Vestris's new Winter season: two ballads included in this piece were always warmly encored, and became widely popular[18]. The Irish biographer and writer, Richard Ryan (1796-1849 – whose name is virtually forgotten today), wrote numerous poems and ballads, several of which were set to music by eminent Victorian composers, and some by composers who have passed into obscurity. In the latter category is E. Solis (*fl.*1820s-1830s – who was also a music-publisher and music-seller, of Greenwich and Clapham [presumably of Spanish extraction]), the 'arranger' of Ryan's ballad *I met Her at the Beulah Spa*, advertised as sung by 'Mr Anderson', lithographed by George Edward Madeley (*fl.*1830-59), and sold at two shillings. It had a pretty frontispiece showing a somewhat fanciful Spa, much grander than the reality *(Plate 176)*. The third edition of this ballad was also available from three principal London music-publishers (Goulding & D'Almaine of Soho Square; Cramer, Addison, & Beale of Regent Street, and Collard &

Plate 176: Title-page of Ryan and Solis's *I met her at the Beulah Spa (Photograph by GB, from the Collection of John Earl, with kind permission).*

Plate 177: Title-page of Ryan and Solis's song, third edition, re-titled *The Maid of Beulah Spa (Photograph by GB, from the Collection of John Earl, with kind permission).*

Collard of Cheapside), and the vignette of the title-page was different *(Plate 177)*. The 'lyric' is reproduced here:

'I met her at the Beulah Spa,
So beautiful and fair;
The sweetest maid I ever saw,
Bright eyes and flowing hair.

Her fairy form flew graceful round,
The envy of the throng;
Each fleeting hour with Joy was crown'd,
And mov'd with speed along...

I met her at the Beulah Spa, etc...

She sang and all who heard admir'd
Her soft and dulcet tone;
And each gay youth entranc'd aspir'd
To woo her for his own.

My heart was gone, I left the spot,
And in my dreams I saw;
A form that ne'er can be forgot,
The maid of Beulah Spa...

I met her at the Beulah Spa'... etc.[19]

If the words of what is described on page 1 of the song-sheet as *The Maid of Beulah Spa* are banal, the music is no better, and it has to be admitted that the subtleties of a Beethoven, a Schubert, or a Mozart do not seem to have impinged on E. Solis's skills to any extent whatsoever. An inspection of the scores of many ballads of the period suggests that musical and public taste of the 1820s, 1830s, and 1840s, intimately associated with popular entertainments given in Pleasure-Gardens and elsewhere, was hardly of an elevated kind, and that it is little wonder that attempts at musical composition by men such as E. Solis are now hidden in decent obscurity.

Beulah Spa received plenty of publicity when it first opened, and under the management of James Fielding it attracted many Persons of Quality, among whom were Maria Anne Fitzherbert (1756-1837 – *née* Smythe, who had married Edward Weld [1741-75] and then Thomas Fitzherbert [1746-81] before becoming (1785) the unlawful[20] wife of George Augustus Frederick [1762-1830], Prince of Wales and later [1820] King George IV), who visited numerous watering-places in her old age for the sake of her health. This was in 1833, the year in which George Augustus Frederick FitzClarence (1794-1842 – 1st Earl of Munster from 1831) and his Countess (d. 1842) also visited *Beulah Spa* seeking solace in the waters[21]. As the eldest, illegitimate son of William Henry, Duke of Clarence (1765-1837 – King William IV from 1830) and 'Mrs'[22] Dorothy Jordan (1761-1816 – the actress), the Earl felt his illegitimacy very acutely: his wife, too, was illegitimate (she was Mary Wyndham, daughter of George O'Brien Wyndham [1751-1837 – 3rd Earl of Egremont from 1763]), and their marriage was unhappy. Fitzclarence shot himself in his Library in Belgrave Square. In 1834 Prince William Frederick, 2nd Duke of Gloucester and Edinburgh (1776-1834), came to the Spa in a vain attempt to resurrect his failing liver[23]. In 1832 there was a laconic notice published to the effect that 'Lord Dudley' was 'so much recovered as to be frequently seen among the promenades at the Bulah [*sic*] Spa, where he often' entered into conversation with the 'visiters', in 'the most collected and rational manner'[24]. This was John William Ward (1781-1833), Earl of Dudley, who recorded in pornographic detail his remorseless and joyless couplings with women 'both in high and low life'. His later years were marked by peculiarities of behaviour, including obsessions about apple-pies and holding tormented dialogues with himself in different voices, with the result that he was placed under restraint at Norwood. It was presumably when he was allowed out for exercise that he was heard to converse in a 'collected and rational manner', but his 'harmless derangement' was symptomatic of a serious condition (possibly Syphilis), and he died at Norwood in March 1833 having suffered a series of strokes[25]. The deference shown to the gentry and nobility, even if they were mad (as Ward undoubtedly was, by 1832), speaks of a lost world, and seems very strange when viewed from times when all deference has been jettisoned. There is no doubt that titled 'visiters' were seen as of great commercial benefit, and Royal patronage must have occasioned ecstasies of joy in the bosoms of the proprietors.

Despite these gratifyingly illustrious visitors, the promoters of the Spa had made a fatal mistake: they had not provided accommodation for visitors, so William Goodwin, who owned land adjacent to *Beulah Spa*, joined forces with Fielding to build the *Beulah Spa Hotel* which went up rapidly opposite the main entrance to Smith's Spa, and it was ready to receive the first guests only two months after the Spa itself had opened. A handsome, grandly symmetrical Italianate composition, it was certainly an ornament to the locality *(Plate 178)*.

In the same year as the Duke of Gloucester attempted a cure, the poet Thomas Campbell (who, as noted above, had attended concerts at Dr Glennie's educational establishment at Dulwich) stayed at the *Spa Hotel* in order to take the waters and flush himself out: after three days he felt 'rather better' for the experience[26]. Campbell had concerned himself with support for the Polish cause, and it may have been his influence that brought about attempts to raise money for Polish exiles at *Beulah Spa* (thousands of Poles had emigrated after the Russians crushed the insurrection of 1830-1, and many ended up in London). However, unfortunately for Campbell, his liver (like the Duke's) was rather too far gone after years of dissipation (exacerbated by a severe venereal infection he had acquired in Altona in 1801 [probably Syphilis]), and his abused internal organ finally gave up the unequal struggle in Boulogne.

Sundry adverts concerning *Beulah Spa*, Norwood, survive from 1832-3 from which it is

Plate 178: *Beulah Spa Hotel* as it was in *c.*1860, by which time it had acquired a large billiard-room and *(right)* Turkish and Electro-Chemical Baths, complete with Islamic cupola *(CLSLAS/PH-95-1782).*

clear that attractions such as 'the celebrated BANDS of the three Regiments of Foot Guards' would be provided for the 'amusement of visiters [*sic*] to the Spa, when it was expected that 'a numerous and distinguished party of the nobility and gentry' would 'grace with their presence this fashionable resort,... equally esteemed for its beautiful sylvan scenery and salutary waters'. James Fielding, the 'Proprietor of the Beulah-spa House and Hotel' informed the 'nobility and gentry' that on the occasion of the attendance of the bands of the Foot-guards he had made 'extensive preparations for the accommodation of visiters [*sic*]' 'Refreshments and wines of the very best quality' were always provided 'for large and small parties, either in the hotel or in separate marquees on the lawn attached to the hotel'. There was also 'accommodation for horses and carriages'[27].

In 1833, too, the 'celebrated BAND of the Grand Duke of Hesse Darmstadt', 'by permission of the proprietors of Vauxhall', were advertised to PERFORM 'several of their most admired PIECES OF MUSIC, at the Grounds, on Sunday, July 6, and on Tuesday, July 9. To commence at 1 o'clock each day'[28]. The German band is a reminder of a time when, until 1837, the United Kingdom of Great Britain and Ireland shared a King with Hanover (under Salic Law no woman could succeed to the Throne of the German State, so when William IV died, his brother, rather than his niece, became King of Hanover), and of when the United Kingdom was not only on friendly terms with several German States (which had been Allies during the Napoleonic Wars), but shared ties of blood with numerous ruling Houses.

By 1835 considerable efforts had been made to improve *Beulah Spa*. The flower-beds were enlarged and beautified, and a vast tent was put up to protect the band, but nevertheless the Whitehorse Estate (as it was known) was advertised for sale by auction, to include the Ornamental Grounds, Pump-Room, Music-Room, and Gothic and other buildings attached to the Spa. Under the proprietorship of one Atkinson (of whom more anon) considerable improvements were then made, and by May 1836 these were judged to have been 'conducted with much judgement and taste', including the

Plate 179: *The Beulah Spa, Norwood.* Engraving of *c.*1835 showing the octagonal building with its 'rustic' colonnade and flanking structures *(LMA SC/GL/PR/VI/GUI-VI/NOR/CRY/Ce28994/cat no.p7494241).*

formation of new paths, the creation of 'pleasing glimpses of the neighbouring country', enlargement of the lawns, the erection of 'a number of log-houses, ingeniously constructed... in various parts of the wood', and 'a kind of rustic colonnade' was put up for 'the convenience of invalids and other visitors'[29]. An engraving, probably of *c.*1835, shows what appears to be some sort of colonnaded or arcaded arrangement on either side of the octagonal structure, the colonnade around which is most definitely of the 'rustic' variety *(Plate 179)*. A more detailed illustration of the buildings is clearly delineated in an engraving by Henry Wallis (1806-90) after a drawing by John Salmon (*fl. c.*1814-*c.*1875), published in London by Thomas Fry (*fl.*1830s), which gives a better idea of the 'rustic' character of the architecture, with tree-trunk columns in the *cottage-orné* style, trellis-work, thatched roofs, covered arcaded walks, and various sheltered areas in which visitors could sit, relax, talk, and enjoy refreshments *(Plate 180)*. These arcaded additions were constructed 1835-6.

Such improvements led the proprietor to advertise the place as 'Royal Beulah Spa' (on account, no doubt, of the visitors who included members of the Royal House), to claim that 'Meichel's German Band' would be in 'constant attendance', and extol the establishment as a 'favourite resort of fashion having undergone extensive improvements'[30]. A more extensive report referred to the 'former proprietor' having 'been necessitated' to give up ownership, 'Mr Atkinson, a man of property', intended to 'carry out with vigour, tempered by discretion', a 'scheme of attraction and amusement'. Unfortunately, 'one class of improvement' did not meet with approval: this was effected by 'cutting off the heads and arms of a beautiful avenue of young elms, and condemning them to the fate of the ancient Persian captives termed caryatides – i.e. to bear a roof upon their trunks as long as they shall continue to stand'[31]. In other words the critic disapproved of using tree-trunks and

Plate 180: *Beulah Spa, Norwood*, engraved by H. Wallis after a drawing by John Salmon. It should be noted that the main building, shown as octagonal on earlier illustrations, appears to be circular in this one, and is thatched *(LMA SC/GL/NOB/C/001/1-12)*.

branches as columns, even though the octagonal building is shown surrounded by them in the 1832 view. He also complained of the cost of sandwiches which he estimated at 'sixpence a mouthful'.

Nevertheless, the 'Royal Beulah Spa' waters were praised for their medicinal properties, while the 'natural attractions', 'beauty of locality', and 'convenience of access' were trumpeted. The author of these improvements was Thomas Witlam[32] Atkinson (1799-1861), who was referred to as 'a gentleman combining the knowledge of an architect with a great natural facility for landscape gardening'. Furthermore,

> 'Under the tasteful eye of this gentleman, new walks have been opened, affording different and varied views of the surrounding scenery and country. The lawn in the centre of the Spa has been enlarged, and beautified, by the intermixture of rustic flower beds, planted with geraniums, fuchsias, and other exotics; an arcade in the same style has been thrown up, communicating with a refreshment room, and within a step of the well, and it is in contemplation to erect another well at the back of the arcade, as the mineral water is very abundant, and the increased popularity of the Beulah Spa, has created a great additional demand for it'[33].

Then we read on:

> 'Mr Atkinson has also projected a terrace formed of convenient and elegant residences, for the visiters [*sic*], as such are now greatly wanted. The site of this terrace is a platform standing so high as to command nearly a perfect view of the horizon, which is a desideratum, and already have several of the Nobility and Gentry become parties to this scheme, which is to be based on the novel principle of making the annual rent for a limited number of years serve as the purchase money of the house itself, so that after a man has paid his rent for 15 or 20 years, his house becomes his own property'.

Plate 181: *View of the Crescent proposed to be erected on the Terrace, Beulah Spa, Norwood,* showing Atkinson's design drawn by George Hawkins and lithographed by William Day (1797-1845) & Louis Haghe (1806-85). Note the Spa buildings on the left, with clearly delineated colonnades and (to the right of the octagonal building [which looks as though it is circular by then, confirming Salmon's drawing]) and conical cover to the Spring *(CLSLAS/PH-07-1538).*

Now this (1836) description clearly refers to a terrace of houses, which must be the handsome building shown in the seductive lithograph entitled *View of the Crescent proposed to be erected on the Terrace, Beulah Spa, Norwood* by George Hawkins (1809-52) *(Plate 181)*. This also shows the conical Pump-Room and the octagonal building with the new arcades and colonnades as well as the extended lawns.

We also learn that a

> 'piece of marshy ground, of some extent, and of unsightly appearance, has been converted into a lake, divided into two compartments, separated by a bridge and waterfall, on which workmen are now engaged. This little sheet of water forms a beautiful feature in the landscape when seen from some stations in the grounds, and if interspersed with water plants, as is proposed, it will be rendered still more pleasing'[34].

These improvements to the landscape, with bridges and lake, are suggested in the delightful *View* of the grounds from the Upper Lake by George Hawkins which shows a place of considerable beauty and charm, with Burton's entrance-lodge clearly visible at the top of the picture *(Plate 182)*.

This piece continues to describe how the Spa was 'conducted upon the scale of a subscription... which now contains the names of a great number of the surrounding gentry', and that 'many of the nobility and upper classes resident in London are amongst its constant visiters [*sic*] and subscribers'. Amusements were 'light and varied', and included 'agreeable' dances 'got up on the lawn' accompanied by 'Miechel's German band'[35]. 'We observed', the notice continued, 'the Countess of Essex looking at the animated groups with apparent satisfaction'[36]. This, of course, was Sarah, Countess of Essex, who opened the Spa in 1831, and often visited the place. However,

Plate 182: *View from the Upper Lake, Beulah Spa,* drawn by Hawkins and lithographed by Day & Haghe, showing Atkinson's improvements to the landscape. Burton's entrance-lodge is shown at the top of the hill *(CLSLAS/PH-95-1805).*

Smith's original vision, and Atkinson's plans, could not be realised. The vast and handsome unified Classical terrace imagined by the architect was 'old hat' by then, and potential house-purchasers and -renters began to seek Picturesque detached residences in gardens in the country and in suburbia.

Grand galas took place, with several bands of musicians performing in the grounds, and festivals were held in aid of various charities. In 1839, for example, a *fête* for the Freemasons' Girls' School was given under the Special Patronage of the Queen Dowager, the widow of William IV, Queen Adelaide[37], with vocal and instrumental music provided for the occasion. Such *fêtes* were lampooned by William Makepeace Thackeray (1811-63) as the 'British Washerwoman's Orphans' Home' in *Barber Cox and the Cutting of His Comb*[38]: the event was organised by 'Lady de Sudley at *Beulah Spa*'[39]. Nevertheless, the *fête* for the School had the attractions of performers of the calibre of Giulia Grisi (1811-69), Nikolay Kuz'mich Ivanoff (1810-80), Giovanni Battista Rubini (1794-1854), and Fanny Tacchinardi-Persiani (1812-67), wife of the composer Giuseppe Persiani (*c*.1799-1869), all of whom had enjoyed operatic success in London.

Atkinson moved to Manchester in 1836 where he designed several important buildings, including the Manchester & Liverpool District Bank in Spring Gardens, Manchester (1834 – demolished, like most of the rest of his work), but became bankrupt in 1838, after which he returned to London and subsequently became a successful topographical artist. After sundry travels he returned to England and died in Kent. Despite these vicissitudes, the Spa and Gardens were advertised in 1839 as having 'various new Promenades, Rustic Edifices' added, and that the 'arrangements for the accommodation of Pic-nic and Gipsy Parties' had been 'much improved and extended' since the previous season. In addition, the 'splendid marquee used by Marshal Soult, and other tents and marquees', could be 'engaged

THE NORWOOD GIPSEY; OR, SECRETS WORTH KNOWING AT BEULA SPA

Plate 183: *The Norwood Gipsey: or, Secrets worth knowing at Beula Spa (LMA SC/GL/NOB/C/OO1/1-12).*

by visiters [*sic*] for their own exclusive use'. Servants in livery were not admitted 'unless in waiting on visiters'[40]. 'Marshal Soult', of course, was Nicolas-Jean de Dieu Soult (1769-1851), Marshal of France, who was Wellington's adversary during the Peninsular War, declared himself a Royalist after Napoléon's first abdication, once more became a Bonapartist in 1815, then again a Royalist, and in 1830 he supported (or said he supported) Louis-Philippe. He was Ambassador Extraordinary to London for the Coronation of Queen Victoria in 1838, and it was after then that his marquee was acquired by *Beulah Spa*. In 1848, when Louis-Philippe was overthrown, Soult declared himself a Republican. The Vicar of Bray had nothing on Soult.

'Gipsy Parties', however, had nothing to do with Gipsies: in the 1830s the term referred to open-air meals, so was really another way of referring to picnics, although the word 'Gipsy' was used as an adjective, as in 'Gipsy breakfast', 'Gipsy dinner', 'Gipsy tent', and so on. Nevertheless, there was a 'Gypsy' fortune-teller available at *Beulah Spa (Plate 183)*, as is clear from some doggerel entitled *The Norwood Gipsey; or, Secrets worth knowing at Beula Spa*:

'Oh, thou well skill'd to tell our fate —
Meg Merrilies of Beula Spa!
What luck doth this sweet maid await?
What lay the lines across her paw?[41]

Tis yours her future lot to scan,
While the delightful damsel mute is:
To promise her a nice young man
And half a dozen little beauties.

Thou hair-lipp'd Sybil! thou canst show
How sweethearts may be won and lost;
And thou canst promise weal or woe,
According as thy palm is cross'd.

Now, Miss, what I'm about to tell,
Depend upon, it will not grieve you;

And if you'll only pay me well,
The Norwood Gipsey won't deceive you.

Of sorrows you will have but few
As surely as the stars I study;
And you have got a lover true,
With flaxen locks and visage ruddy.

With rosy lips and dark blue eyes,
And in the prime of manly vigour;
In form above the middle size,
And quite a fascinating figure'[42].

Various other entertainments were on offer, including 'Grotesque Dancers' (i.e. given to comic distortion or exaggeration in clowning, otherwise known as 'Merry-Andrews', entertainers by means of buffoonery), who performed such delights as 'Chinese Comic Dance', 'A Comic Bedouin', 'Old English May-pole Morris Dance', and other 'turns'. Ramo Samee (d. 1850)[43], the Indian Juggler, performed at *Beulah Spa*: he was an expert sword-swallower, and was mentioned by Thackeray and William Hazlitt (1778-1830). Among the 'celebrated Grotesque' dancers in 1836 were 'Misses Gibson, King, and Brown', assisted by 'Mrs Gibson, Miss Davies, and Miss Smithson'. One wonders if this 'Miss Smithson' could have been related to Harriet Constance Smithson (1800-54), who married Louis-Hector Berlioz (1803-69) in 1833.

From the large number of advertisements and articles concerning *Beulah Spa* it is clear the management attempted to keep the place in the public eye, appealing to those who wished to be associated with an establishment patronised by the upper echelons of society. A selection of advertisements is shown here, not only to demonstrate the entertainments and facilities on offer, but to display the splendidly robust typography typical of the 1840s and 1850s *(Plates 184-186)*. However, in spite of all these efforts to attract custom, there were several problems, not least the extension of the railway network so that the middle classes could travel further afield in search of their pleasures, and balloon ascents, firework-displays, and other familiar fare of pleasure-ground entertainments were no longer sufficient to draw custom in profitable numbers. Plaintive reports that the Spa had 'fallen into a languid and deserted condition'[44] tend to make melancholy reading, but the widow of the original proprietor regained possession of the grounds and tried to revive the fortunes of *Beulah Spa*. In 1852 a *Fête Villageoise* was held, but success was short-lived: in 1854 the Spa buildings were described as 'more or less decayed and neglected'[45]. The *Beulah Spa* closed in 1856, a victim of the growth of the railways, the spread of the Great Wen, and the rival attractions of the Crystal Palace and Sydenham[46] (improbably looming in *Plate 178*). John Corbet Anderson (1827-1907)[47], however, in 1898, noted that the 'charming grounds of Beulah Spa' remained 'comparatively intact. The old paths still wind through the shrubberies and woods; the octagonal-shaped rustic orchestra, overgrown with ivy, still stands not far from the once famous well. The well itself, as yet uninjured, is about 12 feet deep, and full of water'.

A. S. Foord visited the Spa in 1903, and found it in much the same state as described by Corbet Anderson. After 1856 development occurred along the Beulah Hill and Grange Road frontages: a bird's-eye view *(Plate 187)* of the proposal of *c*.1858 shows 14 large terrace-houses in spacious gardens with a vast mansion in the centre of the old Spa grounds which would enjoy agreeable views over the pretty lakes designed by Burton and Atkinson. As it happens, 21 rather fine houses went up on the main road, and the proprietor's house was erected (*c*.1860) on high ground near the entrance. This 'proprietor's house' was called 'The Lawns', and stood in some 20 acres of ground: it failed to sell for £7,000 in 1903, and was withdrawn from sale in 1904 when only £13,200 was offered[48]. 'The Lawns', at 37 Beulah Hill, became the All Nations Bible College, but was demolished in the 1960s after it 'went on fire'. The grounds were reclaimed for recreation purposes, and still command stunning views to the south. At the junction of Spa Hill and Beulah Hill the much-altered Burton lodge survives, though barely recognisable.

Foord referred to an advertisement in the *Athenæum*[49] for a hydropathic establishment not far from the Spa in 1862. This became the *Beulah Spa Hydro and Hotel* and had several Springs in the gardens[50]: it was still in existence when Sunderland published his book in 1915.

Plate 184: Advertisement for 'Royal Beulah Spa' of 1841 extolling the twenty-three-acre Gardens. From the Terrace Windsor Castle and the Hampshire hills could be seen, and the attractions of the new Archery-Ground were puffed. 'Pic-Nic and Gipsy Parties', bringing their own 'Provisions and Wines', were 'furnished with every table requisite', and 'Tents & Marquees' could be 'engaged'. A 'Brass and Quadrille Band' was in 'daily attendance during the Summer season', and 'Refreshments of Every Description', including 'Ices, &c.', 'Dejeuners', and 'Dinners' were also provided *(LMA SC/GL/NOB/C/001/1-12).*

Plate 185: Advertisement printed by C. M. Firth, 8 St Michael's Alley, Cornhill, of 1843, in which H. Dixon, Archery Manufacturer, of 10 Ball Alley, Lombard Street, London, informed 'the Nobility and Gentry' that he had taken 'a suitable Piece of Ground in the BEULAH SPA GARDENS' for 'the practice of that agreeable pastime ARCHERY'. Bows and arrows 'of best quality' were provided 'at very moderate charges' *(LMA SC/GL/NOB/C/001/1-12).*

BIGGIN HILL SPRING

Another Mineral-Spring, discovered in 1809, existed about half a mile north-west of *Beulah Spa* at Biggin Hill, producing about seven gallons each minute of 'mild aperient' water containing magnesium, sodium, and calcium sulphates as well as sodium chloride. It was supposed to be 'beneficial in scrofulous, rheumatic, and bilious complaints', and 'in cases of impaired constitution by long residence in hot climates, or the too free use of spirituous liquors' it was claimed to be 'more beneficial than any other spa in this kingdom'[51]. The *Biggin Hill Spring* does not seem to have acquired any great reputation, and only appears to have enjoyed the interest of local inhabitants. The waters were supposed to have

BEULAH SPA AND GARDENS,
NORWOOD.
1851
This Delightful Place will OPEN ON TUESDAY, the 3rd of JUNE, for every Day except Sundays.
AMONGST ITS MOST INTERESTING FEATURES ARE
THE GREAT LAWN,
THE ORNAMENTAL WATER,
THE FLORA PROMENADE,
THE
Saline Spring,
THE TERRACE,
ARCHERY GROUND, CAMERA OBSCURA,
REFRESHMENT ROOMS, &c.
BY SPECIAL PERMISSION,
The Juvenile Band of the Caledonian Asylum and the Pipers of that National Institution will be present, and perform under the Direction of
MR. ANGUS MACKAY, PIPER TO THE QUEEN.
AN EXTRA BAND IN ATTENDANCE.
A Ground and Marquees for Pic Nic Parties.
Admission, ONE SHILLING,
Except on Mondays & Fete Days: on MONDAYS, 6d.; FETE DAYS, Extra.

Plate 186: Advertisement of 1851 for *Beulah Spa* and *Gardens*, Norwood, mentioning the 'Great Lawn', the 'Ornamental Water', the 'Flora Promenade', the 'Saline Spring', 'The Terrace', the 'Archery Ground', the 'Camera Obscura', the 'Refreshment Rooms', the 'Juvenile Band of the Caledonian Asylum and the Pipers of that National Institution' to perform under 'Angus Mackay, Piper to the Queen', the 'Extra Band' in attendance, and the 'Ground and Marquees for Pic Nic Parties'. Admission was one shilling (except on Mondays [sixpence] and Fête Days [extra]), although 'Children, Societies, and Schools' were charged 'half-price' *(LMA SC/GL/NOB/C/001/1-12).*

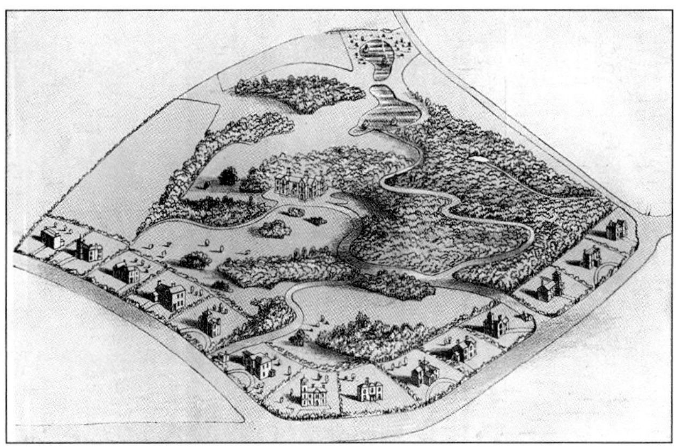

Plate 187: Bird's-Eye view of proposed villas to be erected at *Beulah Spa, c.*1858 *(LMA SC/GL/NOB/C/001/1-12).*

poisoned a domestic pet and the Spring was blocked off by the sanitary authorities in 1898.

A. S. Foord reported that water from a Well in the grounds of *White Lodge*, Biggin Hill, was analysed in 1907. This well 'undoubtedly' tapped the same Spring that used to issue forth at the bottom of Biggin Hill: the water was 'faintly yellow and turbid... containing a larger quantity of mineral matter that is often found in mineral springs', and its substance included magnesia, lime, sodium chloride, sodium nitrate, sodium sulphate, magnesium sulphate, calcium sulphate and carbonate, but organically was 'very impure... absolutely unfit for domestic purposes'[52].

Biggin Hill was ruined in the twentieth century by chaotic, sprawling, speculative housing over the sides of a long valley: if one ventures further into Surrey one can glean an inkling of 'what glorious country this once was'[53].

Chapter XIII References: Beulah and Biggin Hill

1 Sunderland (1915) 122. *See* also Warwick (1986) for a short history of the Spa.
2 Thornbury & Walford **vi** (1879-85) 315.
3 *ODNB* **lvii** (2004) 789.
4 Weatherhead (1832).
5 Foord (1910) 223, and Sunderland (1915) 123, for example.
6 A chloride, or combined with chlorine.
7 Scudamore (1833). Scudamore also published Analyses of the waters of Tunbridge Wells, Kent (1816), Buxton, Derbyshire (1820), and other Spas, including that at Gräfenberg (1843), near Kiedrich in the Rhineland. *See ODNB* **xlix** (2004) 576-7.
8 Maxfield (*c.*1840).

9 Wyld (1834). For the Wyld family *see ODNB* **lx** (2004) 642-3.

10 Coulter (1996) Plates 97 and 98. *See* also Warwick (1986).

11 In 1812 she had sung Cherubino in the first staging of part of *Figaro* (Acts I and II only).

12 Sadie (*Ed.*) **iv** (2002) 539-40.

13 *ODNB* **lii** (2004) 458-60. *See* Ledger (*Ed.*) (1888) 67.

14 Coulter (1996) 81, 84, for example.

15 William Lamb (1779-1848), 2nd Viscount Melbourne from 1828, Prime Minister 1834-1841, and Victoria's chief adviser and courtier 1837-41. *See ODNB* **lii** (2004) 460.

16 Foord (1910) 224.

17 Dance (1833).

18 *ODNB* **xv** (2004) 41-3.

19 I am grateful to my old friend and former colleague, John Earl, for making the music available to me and permitting me to have the vignettes photographed by Geremy Butler.

20 Unlawful because the Act of Settlement (12 & 13 Will. III *c.* 2) and Act of Union (6 Ann. *c.* 40) excluded any Prince or Princess married to a Roman Catholic (Mrs Fitzherbert was an R.C.) from ascending to the Throne, and there was a further prohibition to such a marriage in the Royal Marriages Act (12 Geo. III *c.* 11).

21 This was noted: the 'Beulah Spa, at Norwood, has become a favourite lounge with the Beau Monde. During the coming week a Military Band will attend every day – Mrs Fitzherbert and the Earl and Countess of Munster were among the visitors on Friday' (cutting, 9 June 1833, in LMA Beulah Spa C.01/12 T.1832).

22 'Mr Jordan' was entirely fictitious: her real name was Dorothy Phillips, the daughter of Captain Francis Bland of Derriquin, County Kerry, and Grace Phillips, daughter of a vicar, who was also an actress.

23 He married (1816) his first cousin, Princess Mary (1776-1857), daughter of King George III and Queen Charlotte.

24 Cutting in LMA Beulah Spa C. 01/12 T. 1832 dated 1832.

25 *ODNB* **lvii** (2004) 319-21.

26 Coulter (1996) 84.

27 Various cuttings in LMA Beulah Spa C.01/12 T.1832.

28 *Ibid.*

29 Cutting in LMA Beulah Spa C.01/12 T.1836 dated 23 May 1836.

30 *Ibid.* dated 18 June 1836.

31 *Ibid.* dated 28 June 1836.

32 Called 'Willaw' in Papworth (*Ed.*) **i** (1852-92) 119. Colvin (2008) 79 states that his middle name was 'Witlam' and that he designed, according to Papworth (*Ed.*) 'a crescent of terraced houses in Beulah Spa', but Papworth (*Ed.*) actually states that he designed a 'crescent for the terrace' in 1836, which is something rather different. In other words Atkinson designed the crescent-shaped wings attached to the octagonal building (which did not exist before 1835), but he also prepared designs for a 'Crescent' to stand on the 'Terrace'. This, illustrated in *Plate 181*, is sometimes wrongly attributed to Decimus Burton.

33 Cutting in LMA Beulah Spa C.01/12 T.1836 dated 5 July 1836.

34 *Ibid.* dated 23 May 1836.

35 The report does not seem to be able to decide between 'Miechel' and 'Meichel', a common problem among the English, who believe *Riesling* is pronounced 'Reisling'.

36 Cutting in LMA Beulah Spa C.01/12 T.1836 dated 5 July 1836.

37 Formerly Adelheid Luise Therese Caroline Amalie, Princess of Saxe-Meiningen (1792-1849).

38 George Cruikshank (1840): *Comic Almanack for 1840* (London: Charles Tilt).

39 Thornbury & Walford **vi** (1879-85) 315.

40 Cutting in LMA Beulah Spa C.01/12 T.1832 dated 1839.

41 Note that 'paw' is intended to rhyme with 'Spa'.

42 *Ibid.* undated, but probably 1832-3.

43 *Bell's Life in London, and Sporting Chronicle* (1 September 1850) 3a.

44 Foord (1910) 226.

45 Weale (1854).

46 Wroth (1907).

47 Anderson (1898).

48 *The Daily Telegraph* (4 July 1904).

49 13 December 1862

50 Foord (1910) 227. *See* also Warwick (1986).

51 Quoted by Sunderland (1915) 126.

52 Report signed by F. B. Burls A.I.C. 7 July 1894 quoted in Foord (1910) 228-9.

53 Cherry & Pevsner (1991) 165.

CHAPTER XIV

AN AFTERWORD

Georgian Pleasures; The Fashion for Gardens; The Assembly- or Long-Room; Conclusion

'Tell it not in Bath,
publish it not in the streets of Cheltenham...

I will be off to Tunbridge Wells,
or some different, less lugubrious Spa,
than tiresome, boring Bath,
or deadly soporific Cheltenham....'
JAMES STEVENS CURL (1937-) *Taking the Waters* (London: Swan Press 1978) 55.

GEORGIAN PLEASURES

Londoners always seem to have taken their pleasures with gusto, and Georgian Londoners were no exception. Although some of the songs performed in eighteenth-century Spas and Pleasure-Grounds often had vapid lyrics, with vague nods to Classical mythology, zephyrs, and so on, and the music does not seem to have always been of any great consequence (apart from works by Arne, Händel, and other masters which were sometimes performed), the merriment, fuelled by vast quantities of drink and food, must have been genuine enough, though at times perhaps offensively boisterous, especially when 'macaronis' got above themselves.

A trawl through some of the song-books of the period[1] reveals a great deal of flabby doggerel, with tiresomely predictable rhymes, empty sentiments, and thin allusions to pastoral landscapes, yet the Georgian period did produce its own poetic and literary giants: Alexander Pope (1688-1744), the Great Cham himself (Samuel Johnson [1709-84]), Johnson's biographer, James Boswell (1740-95), Oliver Goldsmith (*c*.1730-74), Thomas Gray (1716-71), Henry Fielding (1707-54), Samuel Richardson (1689-1761), and very many others attest to this. Boswell's London and other Journals are not only extremely amusing, but shed light on many aspects of the period that are otherwise sanitised and distorted. His *London Journal* (1762-1763), for example, is hilarious, with its accounts of Boswell's single-handed pursuit of venery, his adventures 'in armour'[2], his inevitable contraction of The Clap, and his self-disgust at his recurrent drunkenness and compulsive whoring: it is a masterpiece of observation, often extremely funny, and never tedious. The letters of Lady Mary Wortley Montagu (1689-1762) are always witty, congenial, and never dull, while the letters of Philip Dormer Stanhope, 4th Earl of Chesterfield (1694-1773), sent almost daily to his illegitimate son, and those of Horace Walpole, 4th Earl of Orford (1717-97), are utterly absorbing, often catty, beautifully written, and very useful as indicative of Georgian attitudes, concerns, and manners. Edmund Burke (1729-97), Fanny Burney (1752-1840), and her father, Charles Burney (1726-1814), all repay repeated reading. Dr Burney's accounts of his Continental travels, made in order to collect material for his great *History of Music* (1776-89), are essential texts to shed light on European musical taste of the time.

The Georgians (and it should be remembered that the Georgian Period stretched from 1714-1830) were certainly robust in their diversions, which were many and varied. Witty and intelligent conversation, learning, and scholarship were obviously much prized, and the Enlightenment brought an insatiable curiosity about the natural world. Discoveries concerning botany, Classical archaeology (think of Pompeii, Herculaneum, Stabia, Greece, and Egypt, for a start), the study of mediæval architecture, advances in science, exploration of the globe, the huge improvements in agriculture, and the immense importance of harnessing energy in what we now term the Industrial Revolution were all significant Georgian achievements. The first steam-engines, railways, the canal systems, and the development of factories were *Georgian* rather than Victorian inventions.

The Georgians produced an architecture that was very pleasing, and created landscapes that were as agreeable as anything in a painting (the so-called Picturesque aesthetic category), and their furniture, clocks, scientific instruments, and other artefacts were often beautifully designed, well-made, and useful. But the Georgians had their coarser sides, including public hangings (and enjoying the last speeches of the condemned), attending cock- and dog-fights, bear-baiting, pugilistic displays (without the soft gloves which were introduced later), horse-racing, and other spectacles, all of which involved betting (some of it extraordinarily profligate). But it should be recognised that their ancestors enjoyed the burnings at the stake of 'heretics' (i.e. those who held views unacceptable to what ever orthodoxy had the upper political hand at the time); hangings, drawings, and quarterings (which were extremely nasty, drawn-out, very bloody, and appallingly cruel); and other spectacles we *might* abhor today.

Travel in the Georgian Period was often dangerous, with the main roads the haunt of highwaymen (who were not always the chivalrous gentlemen of juvenile romantic fictions) and paths through open fields at the edges of towns infested with footpads who were not averse to extreme violence or even murder. Hygiene (except among the upper echelons of society) was rudimentary, and the dangers of infection imperfectly understood: many of the Wells around London must have been polluted long before, and, in the second half of the nineteenth century, it was proved scientifically that they were. One wonders how many 'aperient', 'catharic', 'purging', or 'emetic' waters had such properties *because* they were polluted. It was little wonder that alcohol was consumed in such vast quantities: water was dangerous.

Infant-mortality was very high, life-expectancy was not over-long (it got a lot shorter once the rural population flocked to the towns from the 1840s onwards), and the physicians killed more than they cured. A stay in hospital was often a death-sentence and the very poor and very old, if they were fortunate, had to rely on the charity of individuals or philanthropic institutions. Certainly there was much *noblesse oblige* that was to be destroyed in the twentieth century as the State took over (not always as humanely as at one time was imagined).

THE FASHION FOR GARDENS

The Georgians appreciated their great parks and gardens that surrounded their country houses. They often saw themselves as New Romans, with their Palladian houses from which carefully composed landscape gardens could be viewed and enjoyed, as though in a picture by Claude, Poussin, or Salvator Rosa. If there were a Gothic ruin in the grounds, well and good, but if not, one could be designed and built, suggesting a long-established link with the past, all part of the search for stability after years of religious strife, civil war, and so on[3]. It is difficult for many today to appreciate the huge sense of relief that pervaded the nation when the Jacobite attempts to place the Stuarts on the Throne failed in 1715 and 1745-6. The Georgian Period was one of immense strides in terms of national wealth, national security, national standing, and, above all, stability. The religious upheavals of the sixteenth century, the Civil War, Cromwellian 'Commonwealth', and the removal of Absolutist tendencies in Monarchs with the ejection of James II and VII had left deep scars, and repeats of such events were to be avoided (something that has been forgotten in recent years). The Georgian Period was one of the *construction* of a unified nation, and a wealthy and powerful one too, without Stuart ambitions (linked as they were with Continental despotisms) rocking the boat.

If one did not have one's own park, one's own *designed* and contrived landskip (and *all* country-house landskips were contrived), one could enjoy the public park or promenade, and flock to the Pleasure-Gardens which had their own walks, arbours, Long- or Assembly-Rooms, Orchestras, Breakfast- and Supper-Rooms, and so on, and if there were 'medicinal' waters as well as copious choices of drinks, varied food, and confectionery, then so much the better. These Spas, Wells, Gardens, and so on catered for an enormous number of persons in search of pleasure (and sometimes of health), and in such establishments the manners, customs, dress, and conversation of the *haut ton* would be aped, not always with success, but at least the Georgians looked up, not down.

In the foregoing Chapters something of the astonishing number of such Gardens has been suggested: some, like Vauxhall, were large, grand, and showy, embellished with exotic structures, and we know that *Ranelagh Gardens* had buildings designed by William Capon (1757-1827 – the theatre and some other buildings), William Jones (d.1757 – the Rotunda), and Sir John Soane (1753-1837 – the Summerhouse), but others seem to have acquired their trellised alcoves, arbours, walks, and various ornamental buildings of less substantial construction run up at great speed, and replaced as rapidly as taste and demand changed, designed by persons whose names have not always been recorded. Water, of course, played its part, either for the supposed medicinal properties, or as decorative elements such as fountains, ponds, or canals. There were more substantial ponds too, used for bathing. But the number of Georgian Gardens, attached to Taverns or not, which had Wells, was astonishing. And, as has been pointed out, if no water existed on the site, Wells were often sunk to find some as the provision of chalybeate, purging, or just drinkable water was regarded as important for the success of such places as Pleasure-Gardens. Even establishments which, rarely, had no Well, provided bottled water from another source. Timbs noted the large numbers of Wells that had been sunk or bored in various parts of the metropolis, and listed several of very great depth, often associated with breweries[4].

As Peter Borsay[5] and others[6] have pointed out, Georgian men and women enjoyed outdoor entertainments, and the whole business of seeing and being seen, dressing up, and promenading, was an essential part of eighteenth-century urban life, requiring suitable tree-lined walks, flower-beds, seating areas, and facilities for refreshments to be laid on. Even quite small Gardens had provision for walks, secluded seating where conversation could be enjoyed and refreshments consumed, and games such as bowls or skittles played. Some large part of the activities in such places of popular resort, of course, was dalliance.

That Pleasure-Grounds were also places of assignment and amorous intrigue (some of it commercial) cannot be doubted, and some of the written and graphic evidence proves this. Even a decorous observer such as Fanny Burney does not evade the subject. In addition, they were magnets for the unscrupulous rake, the practised thief, and, of course, those of both sexes on the look-out for adventures, amorous or financial, or both.

THE ASSEMBLY- OR LONG-ROOM

One is struck by the number of Taverns and Pleasure-Grounds which had such places. To judge from the surviving illustrations they were really utilitarian sheds, put up quickly, with any embellishments in the form of chandeliers, wall-lights, furnishings, and, in some cases, organs from which music would issue, sometimes of a reasonably edifying kind, but more often not. The Long-Rooms of *Bagnigge Wells* and *St George's Spaw*, for example, appear from the images reproduced above to have been of this type and even the Hampstead Assembly-Room, shown in the illustration entitled 'Made. Duval Dancing a Minuet at the Hampstead Assembly', of 1822, by William Heath (1794/5-1840), indicates that the interior was bare in the extreme *(see Plate 104)*. Bare, too, is the interior of the room shown in *WALTZING! Or a peep into the Royal Brothel Spring Gardens dedicated with propriety to the Lord Chamberlain* by Isaac Robert Cruikshank (1789-1856) *(Plate 188)*, and it was not only the room itself that was denuded.

WALTZING! or a peep into the Royal Brothel Spring Gardens dedicated with propriety to the Lord Chamberlain

Plate 188: *WALTZING! or a peep into the Royal Brothel Spring Gardens dedicated with propriety to the Lord Chamberlain* by Isaac Robert Cruikshank, published by J. Sidebotham, 96 The Strand, London, 1816. The Assembly-Room is bare except for the pictures showing three women 'NAKED, but not ashamed!!!', two men saluting each other, and 'Tobacco pipe imitations of Female Dress- or- Smoaking the Fashons [*sic*] for 1816', and a suspended gasolier or chandelier. The dancers are grotesque-caricatures oozing lewdness (one short-sighted dancer almost buries his nose in the capacious bosom of his partner), while a collection of unprepossessing spectators gazes on the proceedings as a band plays in the gallery. This appears to be a satire on the dress and conduct of those attending dances at *Vauxhall Gardens* in the Regency Period *(LMA SC/GL/SAT/1816/Ce18163/cat.no.p5386139).*

Such establishments, suitably caricatured, must nevertheless have had more than a whiff of the *louche* about them. To judge from the company shown by Heath, Cruikshank, and Carington Bowles (among others), the description 'Brothel' cannot have been all that far off the mark. Daniel Thomas Egerton (*c*.1800-42) gave a fair flavour of certain aspects of Regency London in his etchings, one of which, entitled *The Unpleasant Encounter*, published by Thomas McLean, of 26 Haymarket, in 1824, shows an event at the corner of Soho Square and Sutton Street (now Row): a young, well-dressed woman, accompanied by her smartly-attired black servant, spots her husband-to-be 'stealing out of the Temple of Venus', and therefore being 'fastidious', 'might cease to treat him' with her 'former cordiality'. Indeed, she might 'perhaps talk of postponing the happy day' *(Plate 189)*.

By the 1820s, indeed, the number of prostitutes plying for trade in London streets was enormous, and caused comment from visitors. That keen observer of the social scene, Prince Hermann Ludwig Heinrich von Pückler-Muskau (1785-1871), was genuinely shocked by the 'humiliating spectacle so openly exhibited': he referred to the throngs of harlots, many drunken, in the theatres and streets of London in the 1820s[7]. It was not long before servant-girls, shop-girls, and country-girls began to cater for a demand for instant sexual gratification, and as the Tea-Gardens, Spas, and Pleasure-Gardens declined

Plate 189: *The Unpleasant Encounter* by D. T. Egerton (1824), showing a fashionable young woman, accompanied by her impeccably accoutred black servant, finding her husband-to-be coming out of a brothel. A 'macaroni' with spy-glass finds the whole business vastly amusing, while two dogs, eagerly greeting each other, underscore the innuendo (as if the phallic cast-iron bollard were insufficient) *(LMA SC/GL/WAK/W2/PAU-YOR/Ce29821/cat.no.p7488594).*

in number so girls-on-the-make haunted the streets, theatres, and public-houses in search of customers. John Leech (1817-64) produced a celebrated cartoon for *Punch*[8] showing two girls meeting at midnight 'not a Hundred Miles from the Haymarket': they knew each other from another walk of life (perhaps as servants, shop-girls, etc.), and are surprised to meet in such circumstances. One ('Bella') says to the other 'Ah! Fanny! How long have you been Gay?' *(Plate 190).* The word clearly meant 'on-the-game', 'promiscuous', or 'engaged-in-prostitution', and not homosexual. On the wall behind one of the girls is a poster advertising the 'Great Success' of *La Traviata* ('The Fallen Woman' or 'The Corrupted Woman'), the opera by Giuseppe Fortunino Francesco Verdi (1813-1901) with libretto by Francesco Maria Piave (1810-76) after *La dame aux camélias*[9] by Alexandre Dumas (1824-95), which was first given at Her Majesty's Theatre in the Haymarket on 24 May 1856, so was very topical.

Robert Loudan (*fl.*1855-95) produced numerous wood-engravings, including a scene in Kate Hamilton's, a notorious 'Night-House', where higher classes of prostitutes would go to pick up clients. The establishment was in theatre-land, and was mentioned in Henry Mayhew's (1812-87) monumental study, *London Labour and the London Poor*[10], as a place where 'prima donna' prostitutes could enjoy the 'hospitality of Mrs Kate Hamilton extended to them after the fatigues of dancing'. Hamilton's 'Night-House' *(Plate 191)* was really a Victorian version of the Assembly-Rooms of an earlier period. Kate's was visited 'not only to dissipate ennui, but with a view to replenishing an exhausted exchequer', and her

Plate 190: *THE GREAT SOCIAL EVIL. Time: Midnight. A Sketch not a Hundred Miles from the Haymarket* by John Leech. *Punch* **xxxiii** (10 January 1857) 114. One girl ('Bella') says to the other: 'Ah! Fanny! How long have you been *Gay*?, meaning 'on the game', or promiscuous *(Collection JSC)*.

Supper-Rooms were frequented by a 'better set of men and women than perhaps any other in London'. Be that as it may, scenes in places like The Haymarket at midnight *(Plate 192)* have a flavour that is perhaps less attractive than was that of the elegant parades in Georgian Assembly-Rooms: the Exquisite Mob had been superseded by top-hatted, cigar- and pipe-smoking, moustachioed and side-whiskered Victorians. Somehow it was all less lighthearted, more serious (and seedy), and less stylish.

Many persons flocked to the *Argyll Rooms*, Windmill Street, the continuation of The Haymarket before Shaftesbury Avenue cut its swathe through the urban fabric, as crass a piece of urban 'planning' imaginable. These Rooms were open every evening for promenade concerts and dancing, and proved 'a source of great attraction for the habitués of the Haymarket and its immediate neighbourhood'[11]. They were 'vicious' but not as 'aristocratic' as an earlier establishment of the same name which once stood on the corner of Little Argyll Street and Regent Street. This latter concern had been built in 1818 to designs by John Nash (1752-1835) and George Stanley Repton (1786-1830), replacing an earlier structure enlarged (1806) by Henry Hakewill (1771-1830) for Colonel H. F. Greville, 'of sporting notoriety'[12] and was patronised by the *haut ton* until it burned down in 1830: it was pronounced 'aristocratic and bad'[13]. The Windmill Street Rooms were little more than a rendezvous where men with money to spare could pick up 'gay' women and then venture to some discreet hat-shop or milliner's near by where there were facilities upstairs for the women to entertain their clients. The *Argyll Rooms* presented a suitably blowsy façade to the street *(Plate 193)* as well as a glittering interior with gallery for the orchestra, the whole lit by gasoliers *(Plate 194)*, but it could not be regarded as stylish or sophisticated, even by architectural standards: it actually *looked* disreputable and even slightly repulsive, as many of the women must also have looked in the cold light of day, without their paint and finery.

CONCLUSION

To re-visit the eighteenth- and early-nineteenth-century London Spas, Wells, and Pleasure-Gardens has been a nostalgic, if melancholy experience, for it is extremely difficult today, when travelling through ugly, seedy, and often run-down parts of London, to imagine the fashionable crowds, the Beaux and Belles, the arbours, gazebos, pavilions, tree-lined walks, canals, ponds, fountains, Assembly-Rooms,

Plate 191: *(opposite,top) Kate Hamilton's Night-House*, off The Haymarket, engraved by Robert Loudan *(Collection JSC)*.

Plate 192: *(opposite, bottom) The Haymarket – Midnight* in the 1850s showing whores who were probably once servants, milliners, dress-makers, furriers, hat-binders, tambour-makers, shoe-binders, or worked for cigar-shops, bazaars, and so on, and who may also have maintained day-time jobs *(Collection JSC)*.

Plate 193: Exterior of the *Argyll Rooms* (later the *Trocadero Music-Hall*), Great Windmill Street, Westminster, with projecting over-sized gas-lights and an architectural treatment suitably blowsy. From a water-colour by John Philipps Emslie (1839-1913) of *c*.1865 *(WCA/D137(2J)*.

Plate 194: Interior of the *Argyll Rooms*, a favourite rendezvous of the *demi-monde*, with gallery, gasoliers, and plenty of mirrors. From a water-colour by John Philipps Emslie of *c*.1865 *(WCA/D137(1J)*.

skittle-grounds, bowling-greens, Tea-Gardens, and trellised, colonnaded, and arcaded alcoves hung with flowers: ephemeral they were, and ephemeral they proved to be. They have vanished, and with them the Exquisite Mobs, the quizzers and oglers, the pumps that raised the waters (medicinal or not), the pretty sopranos warbling their ballads and arias, the virtuoso organists entertaining the company with music by Händel, Arne, and others, and the 'consorts' of musicians who played for hours on end.

All of them, all the artefacts, personalities, arbiters of taste, wits, gulls, strumpets, and beauties have passed into the void: just as a bubble in a cup of chalybeate water slowly rises, bursts, and leaves no trace, so it has been with these remarkable, lively, often lovely, and rarely dull places of entertainment[14].

Chapter XIV References: An Afterword

1 Such as Bickham (1737-9) or Lampe (1739).

2 Condom made of animal gut.

3 Curl (2007) Ch. I.

4 Timbs (1867) 23-4.

5 Borsay (2006).

6 *See* especially Wroth & Wroth (1896).

7 Butler (*Ed.*) (1957) 84.

8 **xxxiii** (10 January 1857) 114.

9 It appeared first as a novel in 1848, then as a play in 1852 (Théâtre de Vaudeville): it was based on Dumas *fils*'s own affair (1844-5) with Alphonsine Plessis (1824-47), a noted *demi-mondaine*, known as Marie Duplessis.

10 London: Griffin, Bohn, & Co. 1862

11 Thornbury & Walford **iv** (1879-83) 237.

12 Timbs (1867) 22.

13 Thornbury & Walford **iv** (1879-83) 237.

14 *See* Curl (1971*a*, 1971*b*, 1976*a*, 1976*b*, 1979), Margetson (1963, 1964, 1965), and other writings listed in the Select Bibliography.

SELECT BIBLIOGRAPHY

'Books are sepulchres of thought'.
HENRY WORDSWORTH LONGFELLOW (1807-82): 'The Wind over the Chimney' *Tales of a Wayside Inn* (Boston MA: Ticknor & Fields 1863) 8.

This Select Bibliography does not have any spurious claims of comprehensiveness, so is exactly what its title suggests: it is intended to assist the reader with suggestions concerning further explorations of the background to the subject, and backs up the Chapter Notes. Although it is my own compilation, I acknowledge the help of John Harris, Ralph Hyde, Norma McCaw, John Richardson, and Jeremy Smith, all of whom drew my attention to works that might have escaped my notice: I thank them most sincerely.

ADDISON, WILLIAM WILKINSON (1951): *English Spas* (London: B. T. Batsford), Chapters 3 and 4 deal with London.

ALDERSON, FREDERICK (1973): *The Inland Resorts and Spas of Britain* (Newton Abbot: David & Charles).

ALLEN, BENJAMIN (1699): *The Natural History of the Chalybeat and Purging Waters of England: with their particular Essays and Uses. Among which are treated at large the Apoplexy and Hypochondriacism. To which are added, Some Observations on the Bath Waters of Somersetshire* (London: S. Smith & B. Walford).

——————— (1711): *The Natural History of the Mineral-Waters of Great-Britain* (London: William Innys for The Author).

ALLEN, BRIAN (1981): 'Jonathan Tyers's Other Garden' *Journal of Garden History* **i**/3 (July-September) 215-38.

ALLEN, THOMAS (1827-37): *The History and Antiquities of London, Westminster, Southwark, and Parts Adjacent, etc.* (London: George Virtue).

——————— (1827): *The History and Antiquities of the Parish of Lambeth* (London: T. Allen).

ALLPORT, DOUGLAS (1841): *Collections Illustrative of the Geology, History, Antiquities, and Associations, of Camberwell, and the Neighbourhood* (Camberwell: The Author).

ALTHAUS, JULIUS (1987): *The Spas of Europe* (Cambridge: Chadwyck-Healey Ltd.).

ALTICK, RICHARD DANIEL (1978): *The Shows of London* (Cambridge MA: Belknap Press).

AMES, RICHARD (1691): *Islington-Wells or The Threepenny Academy* (London: E. Richardson).

ANDERSON, ALAN BRUCE (1974): *Vanishing Spas* (Dorchester: Friary Press).

ANDERSON, JOHN CORBET (1898): *The Great North Wood: with a Geological, Topographical, and Historical Description of Upper, West, & South Norwood, in the County of Surrey* (London: Blades, East, & Blades).

ANDREWS, WILLIAM (*Ed.*) (1899): *Bygone Middlesex* (London: William Andrews & Co.).

ANGELO, HENRY CHARLES WILLIAM (1904): *The Reminiscences of Henry Angelo* with Introduction by LORD HOWARD DE WALDEN & Notes by H. LAVERS SMITH (London: K. Paul, Trench, Trübner & Co. Ltd.).

ANONYMOUS (1684*a*): *Islington Wells. A Song: Of all the Virtues of those Old Waters, newly found out*, etc. (London: James Dean).

——————— (1684*b*): *A Mornings Ramble, or, Islington Wells burlesq't* (London: Geogre [*sic*] Croom for the Author).

——————— (1726): *A New Guide to London: or, Directions to Strangers; shewing the chief things of Curiosity and Note in the City and Suburbs* (London: J. Smith, T. Bowles, & J. Bowles).

——————— (1733): *A Satyr on the New Tunbridge Wells: Being a Poetical Description of the Company's Behaviour to Each Other,... Occasion'd by a most Stupid Pamphlet... under the Title of Islington: or, the Humours of the New Tunbridge Wells,... To Which is Added, Advice to an aspiring Youn* (sic) *Lady*. The added poem is a reprint of *Advice to Lady* by GEORGE LYTTELTON (London: J. Iorns).

——————— (*c*.1750): *A Sketch of the Spring-Gardens, Vaux-hall. In a Letter to a Noble Lord* probably by JOHN LOCKMAN (London: G. Woodfall).

——————— (1751): *Experimental Observations on the Water of the Mineral Spring near Islington: commonly called New Tunbridge Wells: tending, as well as to explain and illustrate the General Nature of Chalybeat Waters; etc., To which is subjoined, An Account of its Medicinal Virtues and Uses* (London: J. Robinson).

——————— (1760): *The Analysis of Stretham Waters: with Experiments that lead to a New Theory of the Composition and Decomposition of Mineral Waters in General* (London: M. Kingman).

——————— (1764): *Low-Life: or one half of the world knows not how the other half lives... etc.* (London: J. Lever).

——————— (1774): *The Ambulator; or, The Stranger's Companion in a Tour round London* (London: Bew). Later edns. were also published: the eighth (1796), by Scatcherd, who may have edited it.

——————— (*c*.1776): *A Sunday Ramble: or, Modern Sabbath-Day Journey; in and about the Cities of London and Westminster. Describing, in an agreeable Manner, the various interesting Scenes which are Weekly to be met with at the Mineral Wells, Coffee-Houses, Places of Publick Worship, Taverns, Ordinaries, Publick Gardens, Parks, Sunday Routs, Bagnios, &c. of this metropolis and its environs. Exhibiting a true Account of the Manner in which that Day is generally employed by all Ranks and Degrees of People, from the common Beggar to the dignified Peer. The Whole illustrated with a great Variety of Original Characters, Anecdotes, and Memoirs, of Persons in real Life; with pleasing Remarks thereupon. Intended to shew, in their proper Light, the Follies of the Present Age; without the Severity of a Cynick, or the Indulgence of a Sensualist* (London: James Harrison for The Author). *See* also subsequent edns.

——————— (1779): *Bagnigge Wells: A Poem: In which are pourtrayed the characters of the most eminent filles-de-joye. With notes and illustrations* (London: Henry Hawkins *or* Haukins).

——————— (1797): *A Modern Sabbath; or, a Sunday Ramble and Sabbath-day Journey... in and about the Cities of London and Westminster,* &c. (London: ? B. Crosby).

——————— (1965): *Tea-Gardens and Spas of Old London* (from an original text of 1880) (London: Coptic Press).

ANVERS, CALEB D' (pseudonym of NICHOLAS AMHERST) *ET AL.* (*Eds.*) (1729-30): *The Country Journal: or, The Craftsman* (London: Richard Francklin etc.).

ARCHENHOLZ, JOHANN WILHELM VON (1789): *A Picture of England: Containing a Description of the Laws, Customs, and Manners of England* (London: Edward Jeffery).

ARCHER, JOHN WYKEHAM (1851): *Vestiges of Old London: A Series of Etchings from Original Drawings, Illustrative of the Monuments and Architecture of London* etc. (London: David Bogue).

ARNE, THOMAS AUGUSTINE (1751): *Vocal Melody. A favourite Collection of Songs and Dialogues sung at Marybon-Gardens by Master Arne and Miss Falkner...* (London: I. Walsh).

ARNOLD, FREDERICK (1886): *The History of Streatham: being an account of the ancient parish of Estreham, with the history of the manors of Tooting Bec, Leigham, and Balham, and a short sketch of the County of Surrey* (London: Elliot Stock).

ARUNDELL, DENNIS (1978): *The Story of Sadler's Wells, 1683-1977* (Newton Abbot: David & Charles).

ASHTON, JOHN (1889): *The Fleet: its river, prison, and marriages* (London: T. Fisher Unwin).

AUBREY, JOHN (1718-19): *The Natural History and Antiquities of Surrey: begun in the Year, 1673* (London: Edmund Curll). The Streatham section was reprinted (1989) (London: Local History Reprints).

BAINES, F. E. (*Ed.*) (1890): *Records of The Manor, Parish, and Borough of Hampstead, in the County of London, to December 31st, 1889* (London: Richard Clay & Sons).

BAINES, PAUL, & ROGERS, PAT (2007): *Edmund Curll, Bookseller* (Oxford: Clarendon Press).

BAKER, DAVID LIONEL ERSKINE (1782): *Biographia Dramatica, or, a Companion to the Playhouse* ISAAC REED (*Ed.*) (London: Rivingtons *et al.*).

BAKER, THOMAS (1706): *Hampstead Heath: A Comedy* (London: Bernard Lintott).

BAKER, THOMAS F. T. (*Ed.*) (1989): *Victoria County History; Middlesex* **ix** (Oxford: Oxford University Press for the Institute of Historical Research).

BALDWIN, MARGARET (1993): *Streatham Old and New* JOHN W. BROWN (*Ed.*) (Streatham: Local History Reprints), originally publ. (1910) (London: Neves & Biscoe).

BANKS, JOSEPH (1792): *see* SCHMEISSER, JOHANN GOTTFRIED.

BARING-GOULD, SABINE (1914): *The Lives of the Saints* (Edinburgh: John Grant).

BARRATT, THOMAS J. (1972): *The Annals of Hampstead* (London: Lionel Leventhal Ltd. in assn. with The Camden History Society). This three-volume work was originally published in 1912 by Adam & Charles Black Ltd., and the 1972 volumes are handsome facsimiles of that.

BARTON, NICHOLAS JAMES (1965): *The Lost Rivers of London: A Study of their effects upon London and Londoners and the effects of London and Londoners upon them* (London: Phoenix House).

BAYLEY, PETER (1821): *Sketches from St George's Fields* Series 2 (London: R. & M. Stodart).

BEAUMONT, FRANCIS, & FLETCHER, JOHN (1613): *The Knight of the Burning Pestle* (London: Walter Burre).

BEDWELL, WILLIAM (1718): *A Brief Description of the Towne of Tottenham Highcrosse in Middlesex* (London: reprint of the 1631 edn. by W. Mears, J. Browne, & F. Clay).

BELLAIGUE, GEOFFREY DE (1984): 'Huzza, the King is Well!' *Burlington Magazine* **cxxvi** 325-31.

BENEDICT, BARBARA (1995): 'Consumptive Communities: Commodifying Nature in Spa Society' *The Eighteenth Century. Theory and Interpretation* **xxxvi**/3 (Lubbock TX: Texas Tech Press) 203-19.

BENHAM, WILLIAM, & WELCH, CHARLES (1901): *Mediaeval London* (London: Seeley & Co. Ltd.; New York: Macmillan).

BENNETT, ENOCH ARNOLD: *Riceyman Steps: A Novel* (London & New York: Cassell & Co.).

BERMINGHAM, ANN, & BREWER, JOHN (*Eds.*) (1995): *The Consumption of Culture, 1600-1800: Image, Object, Text* (London: Routledge).

BESANT, WALTER (1899): *The Orange Girl* (London: Chatto & Windus).

BETTLEY, JAMES, & PEVSNER, NIKOLAUS (2007): *Essex* in *The Buildings of England* series (New Haven CT & London: Yale University Press).

BEVIS, JOHN (1760): *An Experimental Enquiry concerning the Contents, Qualities, and Medicinal Virtues, of the two Mineral Waters: lately discovered at Bagnigge Wells, near London; with Directions for drinking them, and Some Account of their Success in Obstinate Cases* (London: J. Clarke, J. Schuckburgh, & J. Walter). *See* also the second edn. (London: J. Newbery 1767).

BICKHAM, GEORGE (1737-9): *The Musical Entertainer*

(London: G. Bickham).

BIRCH, GEORGE HENRY (1903): *London on Thames in Bygone Days* (London: Seeley & Co.; New York: Macmillan).

BLACKMORE, SIR RICHARD (1708): *The Kit-Cats: A Poem* (London: E. Sanger & Edmund Curll).

BLANCH, WILLIAM HARNETT (1875): *Ye Parish of Camerwell: A Brief Account of the Parish of Camberwell* (London: E. W. Allen). *See* also facsimile reprint (1976) (London: Stephen Marks for The Camberwell Society).

BLISS, JOHN (1802): *Experiments and Observations on the Medicinal Waters of Hampstead and Kilburn* (London: s.n.).

BLOCH, HOWARD (1985): 'Extra everything and everything extraordinary': a history of the North Woolwich Pleasure Gardens *Theatrephile* **ii**/7 (Summer) 37-42.

BLOM, ERIC (*Ed.*) (1966): *see* GROVE, SIR GEORGE.

BONNEMAISON, SARAH, & MACY, CHRISTINE (*Eds.*) (2008): *Festival Architecture* (Abingdon: Routledge).

BORSAY, PETER (1989): *The English Urban Renaissance: Culture and Society in the Provincial Town 1660-1770* (Oxford: Clarendon Press).

——— (2006): *A History of Leisure: the British Experience since 1500* (Basingstoke & New York: Palgrave Macmillan).

BOSWELL, JAMES (1924): *The Life of Samuel Johnson* with *Preface* by CLEMENT K. SHORTER (London: The Navarre Society).

BOULTON, WILLIAM B. (1901): *The Amusements of Old London: Being a Survey of the Sports and Pastimes Tea Gardens and Parks, Playhouses and Other Diversions of the People of London from the 17th to the Beginning of the 19th Century* (London: John C. Nimmo).

BOWACK, JOHN (1705-6): *The Antiquities of Middlesex* (London: S. Keble, D. Browne, A. Roper, R. Smith, & F. Coggan).

BOYLE, ROBERT (1690): *Medicina Hydrostatica* (London: Samuel Smith).

BOYNE, WILLIAM (1889-91): *Trade Tokens issued in the Seventeenth Century in England, Wales, and Ireland, by Corporations, Merchants, Tradesmen* GEORGE CHARLES WILLIAMSON (*Ed.*) (London: Elliot Stock).

BRASBRIDGE, JOSEPH (1824): *The Fruits of Experience: or, Memoir of Joseph Brasbridge, written in his 80th Year* (London: The Author).

BRAY, WILLIAM (1804-14): *see* MANNING, OWEN.

BRAYLEY, EDWARD WEDLAKE (1829): *Londiniana, or Reminiscences of the British Metropolis* (London: Hurst, Chance, & Co.).

———, BREWER, JAMES NORRIS, & NIGHTINGALE, JOSEPH (1810-16): *London and Middlesex: or, A Historical, Commercial, & Descriptive Survey of the Metropolis of Great-Britain, including Sketches of its Environs, and a Topographical Account of the Most Remarkable Places in the above County* (London: Vernor, Hood, & Sharpe, etc.).

———, BRITTON, JOHN, BRAYLEY, E.W. JR., & MANTELL, GIDEON (1841-4): *The History of Surrey* (Dorking: R. B. Ede; London: Tilt & Bogue). *See* also the (1878-81) edn. EDWARD WALFORD (*Ed.*) (London: Virtue).

BREWER, JAMES NORRIS (1810-16): *see* BRAYLEY, EDWARD WEDLAKE.

BREWER, JOHN (*Ed.*) (1995): *see* BERMINGHAM, ANN

BRIDGES, JOSEPH (*Tr.*) (1697): *see* GREW, NEHEMIAH.

BRITTON, JOHN (1816): *The Beauties of England and Wales* **x** *Middlesex* (London: Vernor & Hood).

——— (1841-4): *see* BRAYLEY, EDWARD WEDLAKE.

BROADLEY, ALEXANDER MEYRICK (1913): 'The rariora of tea and the tea gardens' *Country Life* **xxxiii** 875-8.

BROCK, ALAN SAINT HILL (1922): *Pyrotechnics: The History and Art of Firework Making* (London: O'Connor).

——— (1949): *A History of Fireworks* (London: Harrap).

BROME, RICHARD (1658): *Five New Playes,...viz....The New Academy...*(London: A. Crook & R. Brome).

BROWN, JOHN W. (*Ed.*) (1993): *see* BALDWIN, MARGARET.

——— (1995): *see* GALER, ALLAN MAXCEY.

BROWN, THOMAS (1700): *Amusements, Serious and Comical* (London: John Nutt).

——— *ET AL.* (1702): *Letters from the Dead to the Living* (London: s.n.)

BUCKINGHAM, JOHN SHEFFIELD, DUKE OF (1726): *The Works of John Sheffield, Earl of Mulgrave, Marquis of Normanby, and Duke of Buckingham* (The Hague: Printed for John Barber).

BURNEY, FANNY (1778): *Evelina: or, A Young Lady's Entrance into the World* (London: T. Lowndes). See also the 1822 edn., entitled Evelina: or, Female Life in London: Being the History of a Young Lady's Introduction to Fashionable Life... embellished and illustrated with a series of humorous coloured engravings... (London: Jones).

BURNIM, KALMAN A. (1973-93): *see* HIGHFILL, PHILIP H.

BUTLER, ELIZA MARIAN (*Ed.*) (1957): *A Regency Visitor: The English Tour of Prince Pückler-Muskau described in his letters, 1826-1828* (London: Collins).

BUTTS, ROBERT (1878): *Butts's Historical Guide to Lewisham* (Lewisham: Robert Butts).

BYFIELD, TIMOTHY (1684): *The Artificial Spaw, or Mineral-waters to drink: imitating the German Spaw-Water* (London: James Rawlins for The Author).

——— (1687): *A Short and Plain Account of the late-found Balsamick Wells at Hoxdon: and of their Excellent Virtues above other Mineral Waters; which make 'em effectually cure most Diseases, both Inward and Outward* (London: Christopher Wilkinson).

BYNUM, W. F., & PORTER, ROY SYDNEY (*Eds.*) (1987): *Medical Fringe and Medical Orthodoxy 1750-1850* (London, etc.: Croom Helm).

——— (1993): *Companion Encyclopedia of the History of Medicine* (London & New York: Routledge Taylor & Francis Group).

CAMBRIDGE, RICHARD OWEN (1752): *A Dialogue between a Member of Parliament and his Servant. In Imitation of the Seventh Satire of the Second Book of Horace* (London: R. Dodsley).

CAREY, GEORGE SAVILLE (1799): *The Balnea: or, an impartial Description of all the popular Watering Places in*

England (London: W. West, C. Chapple, R.H. Westley, & T. Bellamy). An enlarged edn. came out in 1801 (London: West & Hughes).

CASSELL & COMPANY (1913): *Cassell's Guide to London* (London: Cassell & Co.).

CASTRO, JAMES DE (1824): *The Memoirs* (London: Sherwood, Jones).

CHALMERS, ALEXANDER (*Ed.*) (1816): *see* JOHNSON, SAMUEL.

CHAMBERS, ROBERT (*Ed.*) (1862-4): *The Book of Days: A Miscellany of Popular Antiquities* (London: W. & R. Chambers).

CHANCELLOR, EDWIN BERESFORD (1928): *Vauxhall and its Memories, with a short account of the area around its famous gardens* (London: Anglo-American Oil Co.).

——————— (1931): 'Ranelagh' *Architectural Review* **lxix** 191-5.

CHAPPELL, WILLIAM (1855-9): *Popular Music of the Olden Time; a Collection of Ancient Songs...* etc. (London: Cramer, Beale, & Chappell).

CHARKE, CHARLOTTE (1755): *A Narrative of the Life of Mrs Charlotte Charke, Written by Herself* (London: W. Reeve, A. Dodd, & E. Cook).

CHATELAIN, JEAN-BAPTISTE-CLAUDE (1750): *Fifty Small Original, and Elegant Views of the Most splendid Churches, Villages, Rural Prospects...adjacent to London* engraved by J. ROBERTS (London: Henry Roberts).

CHAUNCY, SIR HENRY (1700): *The Historical Antiquities of Hertfordshire* (London: Ben. Griffin *et al.*).

CHERRY, BRIDGET, & PEVSNER, NIKOLAUS (1983): *London 2 South* in *The Buildings of England* Series (Harmondsworth: Penguin Group).

——————— (1991): *London 3 North West* in *The Buildings of England* Series (London: Penguin Group).

CHILDREY, JOSHUA (1661): *Britannia Baconica; or, The Natural Rarities of England, Scotland, and Wales* (London: The Author).

CHRISTIE, MILLER (*Ed.*) (1915): *see* TRINDER, WILLIAM MARTIN.

CHURCHILL, CHARLES (1769): Poems,...Containing the Rosciad, the Apology, etc. (London: The Author).

CLARKE, BENJAMIN (1894): *Glimpses of ancient Hackney and Stoke Newington: Being a Reprint of a series of articles appearing in the Hackney Mercury...* by F.R.C.S. (London: London Borough of Hackney in assn. with The Hackney Society).

CLARKE, WILLIAM (1827): *Every Night Book, or Life after Dark* (London: T. Richardson; Sherwood & Co.).

CLINCH, GEORGE (1890): *Marylebone and St Pancras: their History, Celebrities, Buildings, and Institutions* (London: Truslove & Shirley).

CLIPPINGDALE, SAMUEL DODD (1914): *London as a Health Resort and as a Sanitary City* (London: Royal Society of Medicine). Reprint from *Proceedings* (Balneological and Climatological Section) **vii**/4 (February) 33-44.

COLMAN, GEORGE (1775): *see* GARRICK, DAVID.

COLSONI, FRANÇOIS (1951): *Le Guide de Londres, 1693* WALTER H. GODFREY (*Ed.*) (London: London Topographical Society).

COLVIN, HOWARD MONTAGU (2008): *A Biographical Dictionary of British Architects 1600-1840* (New Haven CT & London: Yale University Press for The Paul Mellon Centre for Studies in British Art).

COMBE, WILLIAM (1808-10): *see* PYNE, WILLIAM HENRY.

COMPTON-RICKETT, ARTHUR (1909): *The London Life of Yesterday* (London: Constable).

COOK, EMILY CONSTANCE (1897-8): *Darlington's London and Environs* (Llangollen: Darlington & Co.; London: Simpkin, Marshall, Hamilton, Kent, & Co.).

COOPER, T. (1735): *A Seasonable Examination of the Pleas and Pretensions of, the Proprietors of, and Subscribers to, Play-Houses, Erected in Defiance of the Royal Licence* (London: T. Cooper).

COPYWELL, J. (1760): *see* WOTY, WILLIAM

CORBETT, CHARLES (1755): *London in Miniature: being a concise and comprehensive description...*(London: the Author).

COSH, MARY (2005): *A History of Islington* (London: Historical Publications Ltd.).

COSSIC, ANNICK, & GALLIOU, PATRICK (*Eds.*) (2006): *Spas in Britain and in France in the Eighteenth and Nineteenth Centuries* (Newcastle: Cambridge Scholars Press).

COULL, THOMAS (1861): *The History and Traditions of St Pancras* (London: T. & W. Coull).

——————— (1864): *The History and Traditions of Islington* (London: Miles).

COULTER, JOHN (1996): *Norwood Past* (London: Historical Publications Ltd.).

COWELL, RONALD (2001): *Essex Spas and Mineral Waters* (Romford: Ian Henry).

COWIE, EVELYN ELIZABETH (*Ed.*) (1997): *see* COWIE, LEONARD WALLACE.

COWIE, LEONARD WALLACE, & COWIE, EVELYN ELIZABETH (*Eds.*) (1997): *British Spas from 1815 to the Present Day: A Social History* (London: Athlone Press). *See* also HEMBRY, PHYLLIS MAY.

COX, THOMAS (1724): *Magna Britannia et Hibernia, Antiqua et Nova* **iii** (London: E.& R. Nutt).

COXE, EDWARD (1805): *Miscellaneous Poetry* (Bath: R. Cruttwell; London: White, Hatchard, & Ginger).

CRACE, FREDERICK (1878): *A Catalogue of Maps, Plans, and Views of London* JOHN GREGORY GRACE (*Ed.*) (London: Spottiswoode & Co.).

CRISP, RICHARD (1866): *Richmond and its inhabitants from the Olden Time. With Memoirs and Notes* (Richmond: Sampson, Low, Son, & Marston).

CROFT-MURRAY, EDWARD (1974): 'Cremorne Gardens' *Chelsea Society Report* 30-40.

CROMWELL, THOMAS KITSON (1828): *History and Description of the Parish of Clerkenwell* with engravings by J. & H. S. STORER (London: Orme, Rees, Orme, Brown, & Green, etc.).

——————— (1835): *Walks Through Islington: Comprising an Historical and Descriptive Account of that Extensive and Important District* etc. with engravings by J. & H. S. STORER (London: Sherwood, Gilbert, & Piper).

CRUCHLEY, GEORGE FREDERICK (1829): *Cruchley's Picture of London, or Visitor's Assistant* (London: G. F. Cruchley) with subsequent edns. *See* especially the edn. (1831) containing *A New Map of London containing the latest improvements.*

CRUICKSHANK, DAN (2009): *The Secret History of Georgian London: How the Wages of Sin Shaped the Capital* (New York & London: Random House Books).

CUNNINGHAM, PETER (1850): *Hand-Book of London, Past and Present* (London: John Murray).

CURL, JAMES STEVENS (1971*a*): 'Taking the Waters in London I: Old Spas North of the Thames' *Country Life* **cl** (2 December) 1534-8.

——————— (1971*b*): 'Taking the Waters in London II: In Search of Health and Pleasure. Old Spas South of the Thames' *Country Life* **cl** (9 December) 1669-73.

——————— (1976*a*): 'Taking the Waters in London: Old Spas, Wells, and Baths' *Country Life* **clx** (11 November) 1386-90.

——————— (1976*b*): 'Spas on the City's Fringes' *Country Life* **clx** (18 November) 1499-1502.

——————— (1979): 'Spas and Pleasure Grounds of London, from the Seventeenth to the Nineteenth Century' *Garden History. The Journal of the Garden History Society* **vii**/2 (Summer) 27-68.

——————— (2000): *The Honourable The Irish Society and the Plantation of Ulster, 1608-2000. The City of London and the Colonisation of County Londonderry in the Province of Ulster in Ireland. A History and Critique* (Chichester: Phillimore & Co. Ltd.).

——————— (2004): *The Victorian Celebration of Death* (Thrupp, Stroud: Sutton Publishing Ltd.).

——————— (2005): *The Egyptian Revival: Ancient Egypt as the Inspiration for Design Motifs in the the West* (London & New York: Routledge Taylor & Francis Group).

——————— (2007): *Victorian Architecture: Diversity & Invention* (Reading: Spire Books Ltd.).

CURTIS BROS (*c*.1895): *Streatham Mineral Wells, Valley Road, Streatham, S.W.* (Streatham: Curtis Bros.).

CURTIS, JOHN HARRISON (1842): *Observations on the Preservation of Health in Infancy, Youth, Manhood, and Age. With a Brief Account of the Principal British and Continental Spas and Watering Places* (London: J. Churchill).

CURTIS, WILLIAM (1805): *Lectures in Botany, as delivered in the Botanic Garden at Lambeth* (London: H. D. Symonds & Samuel Curtis).

DANCE, CHARLES (1833): *The Beulah Spa: A Burletta* (London: John Miller).

DANIEL, GEORGE (1842): *Merrie England in the Olden Time* (London: Richard Bentley).

DAVIES, ARTHUR MORLEY (1911-13): 'London's First Conduit System: A Topographical Study' *London and Middlesex Archaeological Transactions* N. S. **ii** 9-59. *See* also the paper of 1904 (1907) (London: Blades).

DAVIES, GEORGE MACDONALD (1939): *Geology of London and South-East England* (London: Thomas Murby & Co.).

DAVIS, CHARLES (*Ed.*) (1859) *see* DAVIS, HENRY GEORGE.

DAVIS, HENRY GEORGE (1859): *The Memorials of the Hamlet of Knightsbridge* CHARLES DAVIS (*Ed.*) (London: J. Russell Smith).

DEANE, EDMUND (1626): *Spadacrene Anglica; Or, the English Spaw-Fountaine. Being a Brief Treatise of the Acide, or Tart Fountaine in the Forest of Knaresborow...etc. As also a relation of other Medicinall Waters in the Said Forest* (London: John Grismand).

DEFOE, DANIEL (1742): *A Tour thro' the Whole Island of Great Britain* (London: J. Osborn *et al.*).

DELANY, MARY (1862): *The Autobiography and Correspondence of Mary Granville, Mrs Delany: with Interesting Reminiscences of King George III and Queen Charlotte* LADY LLANOVER (*Ed.*) (London: Richard Bentley).

DENBIGH, KATHLEEN (1981): *A Hundred British Spas: A Pictorial History* (London: Spa Publications).

DIBDIN, CHARLES (1807): *Songs, duets, trios, chorusses, &c., in the new grand aquatic romance, called the Ocean fiend, or, The infant's peril. Performing at the Aquatic Theatre, Sadler's Wells* (London: W. Glendinning).

DIPROSE, JOHN (1868-76): *Some Account of the Parish of Saint Clement Danes (Westminster) Past and Present* (London: Diprose & Bateman).

DITCHBURN, JONATHAN (1982): *see* JENKINS, SIMON.

DIXON, ANNE CAMPBELL (1987): 'Pyrotechnical Passion' *Country Life* **clxxxi**/45 86-8.

DODSLEY, ROBERT (1761): *London and its Environs Described* (London: R. & J. Dodsley).

DORAN, JOHN (1864): *Their Majesties' Servants: Annals of the English Stage from Thomas Betterton to Edmund Kean* (London: W. H. Allen).

DRAKE, JAMES (*pseud.* for LOCKMAN, JOHN) (1734): *The Humours of New Tunbridge Wells at Islington* etc. (London: J. Roberts). *See* also BICKHAM, GEORGE (1737-8).

DUNKLING, LESLIE, & WRIGHT, GORDON (1994): *The Wordsworth Dictionary of Pub Names* (Ware: Wordsworth). Originally publ. (1987) (London: Routledge & Kegan Paul).

DYCE, ALEXANDER (*Ed.*) (1856): *see* ROGERS, SAMUEL.

EDELSTEIN, T. J. (1983): *Vauxhall Gardens* (New Haven CT: Yale Center for British Art).

ELLIOTT, WILLIAM (1821): *Some Account of Kentish Town, shewing its ancient condition, progressive improvement, and present state: in which is comprised a brief view of the River Fleet, or the River of Wells, &c.* (Kentish Town: J. Bennett).

ERA ALMANACK, THE (1868-92): *see* LEDGER, EDWARD (*Ed.*).

ESSER, RAINGARD, & FUCHS, THOMAS (*Eds.*) (2003): *Bäder und Kuren in der Aufklärung: Medizinaldiskurs und Freizeitvergnügen* (Berlin: Berliner Wissenschafts-Verlag).

EVANS, JOHN (1825): *Richmond, and its Vicinity: with a Glance at Twickenham, Strawberry Hill, and Hampton Court* (Richmond: J. Darnill).

FARMER, DAVID HUGH (1992): *The Oxford Dictionary of Saints* (Oxford: Oxford University Press).

FAULKNER, THOMAS (1820): *History and Antiquities of Kensington, interspersed with Biographical Anecdotes* (London: T. Egerton, Payne & Foss, and Nichols & Son).

——————— (1829): *An Historical and Topographical Description of Chelsea and its Environs* (Chelsea: T. Faulkner). This was an expanded version of the original edn. of 1810.

FAUSSETT, WILLIAM (1867): *Observations on the Mineral*

Springs of Lisdoonvarna, County of Clare, with Suggestions for Rendering the Chalybeate and Sulphureous Spas of Ireland more Nationally Useful (Dublin: s.n.).

FEDERATION OF BRITISH SPAS (1920): *British Spas and Health Resorts* (London: Pitman). Another version, *The Spas of Britain*, was published in 1925.

FELTHAM, JOHN (1802): *The Picture of London for 1802* (London: Phillips). *See* also the same author (1829): *The Original Picture of London* (London: Longman, Rees, Orme, Brown, & Green).

FENNELL, CHARLES AUGUSTUS MAUDE (*Tr.*) *see* MICHAELIS, ADOLF THEODOR FRIEDRICH.

F. G., F.R.S. (1733): *Islington: or, the Humours of New Tunbridge Wells, entertaining and useful, adapted to the taste of both Sexes and all Ages: or, the Blazing Star in the World of the Moon; Being a True Description of the Company, Character, Manners, and Conversation of the Various Inhabitants, with Some Poetical Embellishments, useful Speculations, Serious and Comical Puns, Crotchets and Conclusions* &c.. It was 'address'd' to Mrs Reason and 'Humbly Dedicated' to the Princess Royal (London: W. Webb).

FIELD, JOHN (1652): *A Perfect Diurnal of Some Passages and Proceedings* (London: John Field).

FITZGERALD, PERCY HETHERINGTON (1890): *Picturesque London* (London: Ward & Downey).

FITZSTEPHEN, WILLIAM (1772): *Fitz-Stephen's Description of the City of London* (London: B. White).

FLOYER, JOHN (1697): *An Enquiry into the Right Uses and Abuses of the Hot, Cold, and Temperate Baths in England* (London: R. Clavel).

FOORD, ALFRED STANLEY (1909): 'The Hampstead Assembly Rooms in Weatherall Place' *Home Counties Magazine* **xi** 7-15.

——— (1910): *Springs, Streams, and Spas of London: History and Associations* (London & Leipzig: T. Fisher Unwin, & New York: F. A. Stokes Co.).

FORES, S. W. (1789): *Fores's New Guide for Foreigners* (London: Fores).

FORSTER, JOHN (1848): *The Life and Adventures of Oliver Goldsmith: A Biography in Four Books* (London: Bradbury & Evans).

F.R.C.S. (1892-3): Series of articles in *The Hackney Mercury* (23 April 1892-25 November 1893). *See* CLARKE, BENJAMIN.

FROST, THOMAS (1899): 'The tea-gardens of the 18th century' in ANDREWS, WILLIAM *(Ed.)* (1899) 164-74.

FUCHS, THOMAS (*Ed.*) (2003): *see* ESSER, RAINGARD (*Ed.*).

FULLER, THOMAS (1662): *The History of the Worthies of England* (London: John Grismond, William Leybourne, & William Godbid for Thomas Williams).

GALER, ALLAN MAXCEY (1890): *Norwood & Dulwich: Past and Present, with Historical and Descriptive Notes* (London: Truslove & Shirley). *See* also the reprint JOHN WILLIAM BROWN (*Ed.*) (1995): (London: Local History Reprints).

GALLIOU, PATRICK (*Ed.*) (2006): *see* COSSIC, ANNICK (*Ed.*).

GARBOTT, WILLIAM (1728): *New-River, A Poem* (London: The Author & J. Hooke).

GARDINER, SAMUEL RAWSON (*Ed.*) (1865-8): *Letters...* etc. *illustrating the relations between England and Germany at the commencement of the Thirty Years' War* (London: Camden Society) **xc xcviii**.

GARRICK, DAVID (1775): *Bon Ton, or, High Life above Stairs* with Prologue by GEORGE COLMAN (London: T. Becket).

——— (1777): *Epilogue* to *The Maid of the Oaks* (London: T. Becket).

GARTH, SAMUEL (1699): *The Dispensary. A Poem* (London: J. Nutt).

GASPEY, WILLIAM (*Ed.*) (1851-2): *Tallis's Illustrated London... forming a Complete Guide to the British Metropolis and its Environs* (London: J. Tallis & Co.).

GAY, JOHN (1716): *Trivia: or, the Art of Walking the Streets of London* (London: Bernard Lintott).

GEORGE, HARRIET & PETER (1982): *see* JENKINS, SIMON.

GILBERT, SUSIE (2009): *Opera for Everybody: The Story of English National Opera* (London: Faber & Faber).

GLOVER, ROBERT MORTIMER (1857): *On Mineral Waters: Their Physical and Medicinal Properties* (London: Henry Renshaw).

GODFREY, WALTER HINDES (*Ed.*) (1951*a*): *see* COLSONI, FRANÇOIS.

——— (1951*b*): *see* ROBERTS, SIR HOWARD (*Ed.*).

GOODRICK, A.T.S. (*Tr.*) (1962): *see* GRIMMELSHAUSEN, H.J.C. VON.

GOODWIN, THOMAS (1804): *An Account of the Neutral Saline Waters recently discovered at Hampstead* (London: J. Murray and J. & J. Richardson).

GOVER, JOHN ERIC BRUCE, MAWER, ALLEN, & STENTON, SIR FRANK MERRY, with the collaboration of SIDNEY JOSEPH MADGE (1942): *The Place-Names of Middlesex apart from the City of London* (London: Cambridge University Press).

GRANVILLE, AUGUSTUS BOZZI (1841): *The Spas of England and Principal Sea-Bathing Places* (London: Henry Colburn). A new edn. GEOFFREY MARTIN (*Ed.*) was published in 1971 (Bath: Adams & Dart).

GRAY, VALERIE (2006): *Charles Knight: Educator, Publisher, Writer* (Aldershot: Ashgate Publishing Ltd.).

GREGO, JOSEPH (1880): *Rowlandson the Caricaturist: A Selection from his Works, with Anecdotal Descriptions of his Famous Caricatures and a Sketch of his Life, Times, and Contemporaries* (London: Chatto & Windus).

GREW, NEHEMIAH (1695): *Tractatus de salis cathartici amari in aquis Ebeshamensibus...* etc. (London: S. Smith & B. Walford).

——— (1697): *A Treatise of the Nature and Use of the Bitter Purging Salt: Easily known from all Counterfeits by its Bitter Taste... now published in English, by JOSEPH BRIDGES... With Animadversions on a late corrupt Translation published by FRANCIS MOULT, Chymist* (London: Walter Kettilby).

GRIMMELSHAUSEN, H. J. C. VON (1962): *The Adventurous Simplicissimus: Being the Description of the Life of a Strange Vagabond named Melchoir Sternfels von Fuchshaim* A.T.S. GOODRICK (*Tr.*) (Lincoln NE: University of Nebraska Press).

GROVE, SIR GEORGE (1966): *Grove's Dictionary of Music and Musicians* ERIC BLOM (*Ed.*) (London: Macmillan &

Co. Ltd.).

GUEDALLA, PHILIP (1929): *The Missing Muse: and Other Essays* (London: Hodder& Stoughton).

GUIDOTT, THOMAS (1694): *A True and Exact Account of Sadler's Well: or, The New Mineral-Waters lately found at Islington* (London: Thomas Malthus).

HALL, WILIAM HENRY (1789-91): *The New Royal Encyclopedia, or, Complete Modern Universal Dictionary of Arts and Sciences* (London: C. Cooke).

HAMLIN, CHRISTOPHER (1990): *Chemistry, Medicine, and the Legitimization of English Spas, 1740-1840* in *The Medical History of Waters and Spas* 67-81 (London: Wellcome Institute for the History of Medicine).

HARCUP, JOHN WINSOR (1992): *The Malvern Water Cure or Victims for Weeks in Wet Sheets* (Marlvern: Winsor Fox Photos).

HARDWICKE, HERBERT JUNIUS (1883): *Health Resorts and Spas, or, Climatic and Hygienic Treatment of Disease* (London: W. H. Allen & Co.).

HARDY, WILLIAM JOHN, & PAGE, WILLIAM (*Eds.*) (1892): *A Calendar to the Feet of Fines for London and Middlesex [from the Reign of Richard I]* (London: Hardy & Page).

HARRIS, THOMAS (1887): *A Historical and Descriptive Sketch of Marylebone Gardens collated from various Sources* (London: Chiswick Press).

HASSALL, WILLIAM OWEN (1938): 'Plays at Clerkenwell' *Modern Language Review* **xxxiii** (Jan.-Oct.) 564-7.

——— (1939): *The Conventual Buildings of St Mary Clerkenwell* reprint from *Transactions* of the London and Middlesex Archaeological Society N.S. **viii**/II 234-82.

——— (*Ed.*) (1949): *The Cartulary of St Mary Clerkenwell* (London: Royal Historical Society).

HATTON, EDWARD (1708): *A New View of London: or, an Ample Account of the City* (London: John Nicholson & Robert Knaplock).

HASTED, EDWARD (1778-99): *The History and Topographical Survey of the County of Kent...* etc. (Canterbury: Simmons & Kirkby for The Author).

HAUGHTON, EDWARD (1858): 'Hot Air Baths' *Dublin Hospital Gazette* **v**

——— (1861): *The Uses and Abuses of the Turkish Bath* (London: Simpkin, Marshall).

HAWKINS, WILLIAM (1776): *The Shrubs of Parnassus, or Juvinile Muse. A Collection of Songs and Poems, Chiefly Pastoral* (London: J. Rozea for The Author).

HAZLITT, WILLIAM CAREW (1892): *Tales and Legends of National Origin or Widely Current in England from Early Times* (London: Macmillan & Co.).

HECKETHORN, CHARLES WILLIAM (1899): *London Souvenirs* (London: Chatto & Windus).

——— (1900): *London Memories: Social, Historical, and Topographical* (London: Chatto & Windus; Philadelphia PA: Lippincott).

HEMBRY, PHYLLIS MAY (1990): *The English Spa, 1560-1815: A Social History* (London: Athlone Press; Rutherford NJ: Farleigh Dickinson UP).

——— (1997): *British Spas from 1815 to the Present Day* completed by LEONARD WALLACE COWIE & EVELYN ELIZABETH COWIE (*Eds.*) (London: Athlone Press).

HENCHY, PATRICK (1958): *A Bibliography of Irish Spas* (Dublin: At the Sign of the Three Candles).

HIGHFILL, PHILIP H., BURNIM, KALMAN A., & LANGHANS, EDWARD A. (1973-93): *A Biographical Dictionary of Actors, Actresses, Musicians, Dancers, Managers, and Other Stage Personnel in London, 1660-1800* (Carbondale; Edwardsville IL: Southern Illinois University Press).

HIND, ARTHUR MAYGER (1922): *Wenceslaus Hollar and his Views of London and Windsor in the Seventeenth Century* (London: John Lane).

HOFMANN, AUGUST WILHELM VON (1854): *Harrogate and its resources: chemical analysis of its medicinal waters* (London: S. Galon).

HOLMES, MRS BASIL ISABELLA (1896): *The London Burial Grounds: Notes on their History from the Earliest Times to the Present Day* (London: T. Fisher Unwin).

HOME, GORDON COCHRANE (1901): *Epsom, its History and Surroundings* (Epsom: Homeland Library).

HOME COUNTIES MAGAZINE, THE (1899-12): *Subtitled Devoted to the Topography of London, Middlesex, Essex, Berkshire, Surrey, Kent, & Sussex* (London: G. Bell & Sons Ltd., & F. E. Robinson & Co.).

HONE, WILLIAM (1832-5): *The Every-Day Book and Table Book* (London: Thomas Tegg & Son).

HOOPER, S. (1762): *A Description of Vaux-Hall Gardens: Being a Proper Companion and Guide for All who Visit That Place* (London: S. Hooper).

HOTTEN, JOHN CAMDEN (1868): *see* LARWOOD, JACOB.

HOWITT, WILLIAM (1869): *The Northern Heights of London; or, Historical Associations of Hampstead, Highgate, Muswell Hill, Hornsey, and Islington* (London: Longmans, Green, & Co.).

HUGHSON, DAVID (i.e. DAVID PUGH [d.1813]) (1805-9): *London: Being an Accurate History and Description of the British Metropolis and its Neighbourhood* (London: J. Stratford). *See* also edn. (1806-13) (London: J. Stratford and J. Robins).

HUMPHREYS, R. (*Ed.*) (1824): *The Memoirs of J. De Castro* (London: Sherwood, Jones, & Co.).

HUNT, JOHN DIXON (1985): *Vauxhall and London's Garden Theatres* (Cambridge: Chadwyck-Healey).

HUNTER, HENRY (1811): *The History of London, and its Environs* (London: S. Gosnell for J. Stockdale).

HUNTER, MICHAEL (2009): *Boyle: Between God and Science* (New Haven CT & London: Yale University Press).

HYDE, RALPH NIGEL (1980): 'A London Panorama, c.1800, Resurrected' *London Topographical Record* **xxiv** 211-16.

INGRAM, DALE (1767): *An Enquiry into the Origin and Nature of Magnesia Alba, and the Properties of Epsom Waters* (London: W. Owen).

JAMESON, ANNA BROWNELL (1848): *Sacred and Legendary Art* (London: Longman, Brown, Green, & Longmans).

——— (1907): *Legends of the Madonna as represented in the Fine Arts* (London: Hutchinson & Co.).

JEFFERY, J. (1906): 'Ranelagh Gardens, Chelsea' *Home Counties Magazine* **viii** 52-4.

JENKINS, SIMON (1982): *Images of Hampstead* with

Catalogue by JONATHAN DITCHBURN & *Gallery of Prints* by HARRIET & PETER GEORGE (Richmond-upon-Thames: Ackermann).

JOHNSON, JAMES (1841): *Pilgrimages to the Spas in Pursuit of Health and Recreation, with an Inquiry into the Comparative Merits of Different Mineral Waters* (London: S. Highley). *See* also 1987 edn. (Cambridge: Chadwyck-Healey Ltd.).

JOHNSON, SAMUEL (1816): *The Works of Samuel Johnson* with an Essay by ARTHUR MURPHY. ALEXANDER CHALMERS (*Ed.*) (London: J. Johnson *et al.*).

KAHRL, GEORGE MORROW (*Ed.*) (1963): *see* LITTLE, DAVID MASON (*Ed.*).

KEARSLEY, CATHARINE (1791): *Kearsley's Strangers' Guide: or Companion through London and Westminster, and the Country Around* (London: C. & G. Kearsley).

KEELING, CLINTON HARRY (1984): *Where the Lion Trod: A Study of Forgotten Zoological Gardens* (Guildford: Clam Publications).

——— (1985): *Where the Crane Danced: More About Zoological Gardens of the Past* (Guildford: Clam Publications).

KEYSE, FRANK (1986): *Thomas Keyse and the Bermondsey Spa* (Aberystwyth: F. Keyse).

KILBURNE, RICHARD (1659): *A Topographie, or Survey of the County of Kent...* etc. (London: Thomas Mabb).

KING, ERASMUS (1741): *A Catalogue of the Experiments made by Mr King, in his Course of Natural Philosophy* (London: s.n.).

KING, WILLIAM (1708): *The Art of Cookery: A Poem, in Imitation of Horace's Art of Poetry, by the Author of A Tale of a Tub* (but not, in fact, by Swift) (London: Printed and Sold by the Booksellers of London & Westminster).

KINGMAN, M. (1760): probable author of *The Analysis of Stretham Waters* (*see* ANONYMOUS [1760]).

KINGSFORD, CHARLES LETHBRIDGE (*Ed.*) (1905): *Chronicles of London* (Oxford: Clarendon Press).

——— (1908): *see* STOW, JOHN.

KITCHIN, THOMAS (1743): *see UNIVERSAL HARMONY.*

KNIGHT, CHARLES (*Ed.*) (1878): *London* revised by EDWARD WALFORD (London: Virtue & Co.).

LAMBERT, B. (1806): *The History and Survey of London and its Environs. From the Earliest Period to the Present Time* (London: T. Hughes & M. Jones).

LAMPE, JOHN FREDERICK (1739): *The British Melody: or, the Musical Magazine* (London: Benjamin Cole).

LANGHANS, EDWARD A. (1973-93): *see* HIGHFILL, PHILIP H.

LARWOOD, JACOB (*pseudo.* for SCHEVICHAVEN, HERMAN DIEDERIK JOHAN VAN), & HOTTEN, JOHN CAMDEN (1868): *The History of Signboards, from the Earliest Times to the Present Day* (London: John Camden Hotten). Hotten brought out the First Edn. in 1866, and Chatto & Windus published a new Edn. in 1898.

LEAMINGTON SPA (1954): *The English Spas: An Exhibition of Pictures, Books, Pamphlets, Maps, and Plans* (Leamington Spa: Royal Leamington Spa Library, Art Gallery, & Museum).

LEDGER, EDWARD (*Ed.*) (1868-92): *The Era Almanack* (London: s.n.).

LELAND, JOHN (1744-5): *The Itinerary of John Leland the Antiquary* (Oxford: James Fletcher).

LEWIS, SAMUEL (1842): *The History and Topography of the Parish of St Mary, Islington* (London: J. H. Jackson).

——— (1854): *Islington as it was and is* (London: J. H. Jackson).

LIGUORI, ST ALFONSO MARIA DE' (1837): *Les Gloires de Marie* (Paris: Gaume Frères).

LINDEN, DIEDERICK WESSEL (1749): *Directions for the use of that Extraordinary Mineral-Water, Commonly called Berry's Shadwell-Spaw: in Sun-Tavern Fields, Shadwell, near London. More especially, in the several Distempers wherein it has proved by Experience, of the Greatest Efficacy and Success: Such as Colds, lax, or weak Fibres, and affected Nerves; the Palsy, Rheumatism, and Gout; the Yaws, Venereal Distempers, Gleets, and Fluor Albus; the Leprosy, King's-Evil, Scurvy, and Consumption; the Dropsy, Jaundice, Fistulas, and Ulcers; Fluxes, and Inward-Bleedings; Broken Constitutions by Intemperance, or otherwise; the Diabetes, Sore-Eyes, Catarrhs, and other Defluxions of Humours, &c.* (London: Printed for the Proprietor; and to be had at the Shadwell-Spaw, in Sun-Tavern-Fields, Shadwell; and F. Jones, Mineral Water Purveyor to His Royal Highness the Duke of Cumberland, in Tavistock-Street, Covent-Garden).

LITTLE, DAVID MASON, & KAHRL, GEORGE MORROW (*Eds.*) (1963): *Letters of David Garrick* PHOEBE DE K. WILSON (*Ass.Ed.*) (London: Oxford University Press).

LLANOVER, LADY (*Ed.*) (1862): *see* DELANY, MARY.

LLOYD, JOHN HARRY (1888): *The History, Topography, and Antiquities of Highgate, in the County of Middlesex, with Notes on Hornsey, Crouch End, Muswell Hill, &c.* (Highgate: Highgate Library & Scientific Association).

LOCKMAN, JOHN (also known as JAMES DRAKE) (1734): *The Humours of New Tunbridge-Wells at Islington* (London: John Roberts). *See* BICKHAM, GEORGE (1737-8).

——— (*c.* 1750): *see* ANONYMOUS (*c.*1750). Lockman was probably responsible for *A Sketch of the Spring Gardens, Vaux-Hall.*

LOFTIE, WILLIAM JOHN (1875): *In and Out of London, or, the Half-Holidays of a Town Clerk* (London: SPCK). *See* new edn. (2004) (Cambridge: Chadwyck-Healey Ltd.).

——— (1888): *Kensington: Picturesque and Historical with upwards of three hundred illustrations (some in colour) by William Luker Jun... engraved by Chs. Guillaume et Cie., Paris* (London: Field & Tuer, The Leadenhall Press, etc.).

——— (1892): *London* (London: Longmans, Green, &. Co.). The 1887 edn. was reprinted (2004): (Cambridge: Chadwyck-Healey Ltd.).

LONDON COUNTY COUNCIL (1901): *Sydenham Wells Park: Ceremony of dedicating to Public Use For Ever* (London: Jas. Truscott).

LUCAS, EDWARD VERRALL (1926): *E. V. Lucas's London* (London: Methuen & Co. Ltd.).

LUKE, THOMAS (1919): *Spas and Health Resorts of the British Isles* (London: A. & C. Black).

LYSONS, DANIEL (1792-6): *The Environs of London: being an Historical Account of the Towns, Villages, and Hamlets, within Twelve Miles of that Capital* etc. (London: T. Cadell & W. Davies). *See* especially **i** *County of Surrey* (1792) and **iii** *County of Middlesex* (1795). *See* also Second edn.

(1811), known as the *Supplement* to the First edn.

LYTTELTON, GEORGE (1733): *see* ANONYMOUS.

MAAS, JEREMY (1988): *Victorian Painters* (London: Barrie & Jenkins).

MACKENZIE, EDWARD MONTAGUE COMPTON (1911): *The Passionate Elopement* (London: Martin Secker).

MACKY, JOHN (1724): *A Journey through England: In familiar Letters from a Gentlemam* [sic] *here, to his friend abroad* (London: John Hooke & J. Pemberton).

MACPHERSON, JOHN (1871): *Our Baths and Wells: The Mineral Waters of the British Islands* (London: Macmillan).

——————(1888): *The Baths and Wells of Europe; With a Sketch of Hydrotherapy, and Hints on Climate, Sea-Bathing, and Popular Cures* (London: Edward Stanford).

MAC-STURDY, HERCULES (*pseudonym*, supposedly 'of the County of Tipperary, Esq.') (1737): *A Trip to Vaux-Hall: or, a Genteel Satyr on the Times. With some Explanatory Notes* (London: A. Moore).

MACY, CHRISTINE (*Ed.*) (2008): *see* BONNEMAISON, SARAH (*Ed.*).

MADGE, SIDNEY JOSEPH (1942): *see* GOVER, JOHN ERIC BRUCE.

MAITLAND, WILLIAM (1756): *The History and Survey of London* (London: T. Osborne & J. Shipton).

MALCOLM, JAMES PELLER (1802-7): *Londinium Redivivum, or, an Ancient History and Modern Description of London*, etc. (London: Rivington).

MANDER, DAVID (*Ed.*) (1986): *see* CLARKE, BENJAMIN (1894).

MANLEY, BILL (1990): *Islington Entertained: or, a Pictorial History of Pleasure Gardens, Music Halls, Spas, Theatres, and Places of Entertainment* (London: Islington).

MANNING, OWEN, & BRAY, WILLIAM (1809-14): *The History and Antiquities of the County of Surrey* (London: J. White).

MANTELL, GIDEON (1841-4): *see* BRAYLEY, EDWARD WEDLAKE.

MARGETSON, STELLA (1963): 'The Vanished Gardens of London' *Country Life* **cxxxiv** 1259-63.

——————(1964): 'London's Lost Pleasure Gardens' *Country Life* **cxxxv** 490-2.

——————(1965): 'Taking the London Waters' *Country Life* **cxxxvii** 714-6.

MARTIN, GEOFFREY (*Ed.*) (1971): *see* GRANVILLE, AUGUSTUS BOZZI.

MARTYN, JOHN, FRS (1741): 'An Account of a new Purging Spring discovered at Dulwich in Surrey' *Philosophical Transactions* of the Royal Society **xli**/461 xxii 835-8.

MATHER, WILLIAM (1727): *The Young Man's Companion* (London: S. Clarke).

MAWER, ALLEN (1942): *see* GOVER, JOHN ERIC BRUCE.

MAY-DAY: OR, THE ORIGINAL OF GARLANDS. A POEM (1720): (London: J. Roberts). Recounts the origins of the 'London Spaw'.

MAXFIELD, ARCHIBALD (*c.*1840): *Practical Observations on the Medicinal Virtues of the Beulah Saline Spa, Norwood, and on the Disorders in which it is most efficacious, especially those connected with derangements of the digestive organs* (London: s.n.).

MELVIN, JULIA (1980): *see* NELSON, JOHN.

MICHAELIS, ADOLF THEODOR FRIEDRICH (1882): *Ancient Marbles in Great Britain* CHARLES AUGUSTUS MAUDE FENNELL (*Tr.*) (Cambridge: Cambridge University Press).

MILLER, FREDERICK (1874): *St Pancras Past and Present: Being Historical, Traditional, and General Notes of the Parish, etc.* (London: A. Heywood & Son).

MISSON, HENRI (1719): *M. Misson's Memoirs and Observations in his Travels over England* JOHN OZELL (*Tr.*) (London: D. Browne etc.).

MONRO, DONALD (1770): *A Treatise on Mineral Waters* (London: D. Wilson & G. Nichol).

MONTAGU, LADY MARY WORTLEY (1861): *The Letters and Works of Lady Mary Wortley Montagu* LORD WHARNCLIFFE (*Ed.*) (London: Henry G. Bohn).

MORANT, PHILIP (1768): *The History and Antiquities of the County of Essex* (London: T. Osborne, J. Whiston, S. Baker, *et al.*).

MOTTLEY, JOHN (1753): *The History and Survey of the Cities of London and Westminster...* The Whole being an Improvement on Mr Stow's and Other... Surveys... by Robert Seymour Esq. (i.e. John Mottley) (London: M. Cooper, W. Reeve, & C. Sympson).

MOULT, FRANCIS (1697): *A Treatise of the Nature and Use of the Bitter Purging Salt contain'd in Epsom and such other Waters* (London: Francis Moult).

MUNK, WILLIAM (1878): *The Roll of the Royal College of Physicians of London* **i** (1518-1700) **ii** (1701-1800) **iii** (1801-25) (London: The College).

MURPHY, ARTHUR (1816): *see* JOHNSON, SAMUEL.

MURRAY, JOHN FISHER (1845): *The World of London* (London: R. Bentley).

NELSON, JOHN (1823): *The History and Antiquities of the Parish of Islington; in the County of Middlesex* (London: T. Lester). *See* also the facsimile (1980), of the first edn. (1811) with Introduction by JULIA MELVIN (London: Philip Wilson).

NEVILLE HAVINS, PETER J. (1976): *The Spas of England* (London: Hale).

NICHOLS, JOHN (1786): *The History and Antiquities of the Parish of Lambeth, in the County of Surrey* (London: J. Nichols).

——————(1788): *The History and Antiquities of Canonbury-house, at Islington* (London: J. Nichols).

NIGHTINGALE, JOSEPH (1810-16): *see* BRAYLEY, EDWARD WEDLAKE.

NOAKES, AUBREY (1970): 'From ale-house to pleasure garden: the story of White Conduit House, Islington' *Country Life* **cxlvii** 14-15.

NOORTHOUCK, JOHN (1773): *A New History of London: including Westminster and Southwark. To which is added, a general Survey of the Whole...* etc. (London: R. Baldwin).

NORDEN, JOHN (1723): *Speculum Britanniae: An Historical and Chorographical Description of Middlesex and Hartfordshire* (London: David Browne Sr. & Jr., & James Woodman). Originally published (1593) (London: Eliot's Court Press).

NORMAN, PHILIP (1888): *see* RENDLE, WILLIAM.

O'BYRNE, ALISON F. (2003-4): '"A Place of General Resort": Bagnigge Wells in the Eighteenth Century' *The*

London Gardener or The Gardener's Intelligencer **ix** 22-29.

——————— (2003): *Walking, Rambling, and Promenading in Eighteenth-Century London* (York: University of York PhD).

OETTERMANN, STEPHAN (1980): *Das Panorama: die Geschichte eines Massenmediums* (Frankfurt-am-Main: Syndikat).

OGBORNE, ELIZABETH (1814): *The History of Essex, from the Earliest Period to the Present Time* (London: Longman *et al.*).

OGILVY, JAMES S. (1914): *A Pilgrimage in Surrey* (London: George Routledge; New York: E.P. Dutton).

OSBORNE, BRUCE (1996): *Aquae Britannica. Rediscovering 17th-Century Springs and Spas in the Footsteps of Celia Fiennes* (Malvern: Cora Weaver).

OZELL, JOHN (*Tr.*) (1719): *see* MISSON, HENRI.

PAGE, WILLIAM (*Ed.*) (1892): *see* HARDY, WILLIAM JOHN (*Ed.*).

PALMER, SAMUEL (1870): *St Pancras: being antiquarian, topographical, and biographical memoranda, relating to the extensive Metropolitan Parish of St Pancras, Middlesex* (London: S. Palmer etc.).

PAPWORTH, WYATT ANGELICUS VAN SANDAU (1852-92): *Dictionary of Architecture* (London: Architectural Publication Society).

PARISH, R. B. (1997): *Kent's Other Spas: A Discussion of Other Mineral Spas that hoped to capitalise on Tunbridge Wells. Bygone Kent* **xviii**/1 (January) 14-22

PARK, A. J. (1895): *see* STUART, CHARLES DOUGLAS.

PARK, JOHN JAMES (1814): *The Topography and Natural History of Hampstead, in the County of Middlesex* (London: Nichols, Son, & Bentley).

PARREAUX, ANDRÉ, & PLAISANT, MICHÈLE (*Eds.*) (1977): *Jardins et Paysages: Le Style Anglais* (Villeneuve-d'Ascq: Publications de l'Université de Lille III).

PARTON, JOHN (1822): *Some Account of the Hospital and Parish of St Giles in the Fields, Middlesex* (London: Luke Hansard & Sons).

PASMORE, H. STEPHEN (1988): 'Admirable landscape: the Bayswater Tea Gardens' *Country Life* **clxxxii** 212.

PENNANT, THOMAS (1793): *Some Account of London* (London: Robert Faulder).

PEPYS, SAMUEL (1953): *The Diary of Samuel Pepys* JOHN WARRINGTON (*Ed.*) (London: Dent; New York: Dutton).

PETER, JOHN (*c.*1680) *Dr Peter's Judgement, or Dullidge or Lewisham Water* (London: Samuel Tidmarsh).

PETER, JOSIAH (1701): *Truth in Opposition to Ignorant and Malicious Falsehood: or, a Discourse written to vindicate the Honour, and to assert the Right, of Dr Nehemiah Grew... with Respect to his Invention for making the Salt of the Purging Waters...* etc. (London: The Author).

PEVSNER, NIKOLAUS (1983): *see* CHERRY, BRIDGET.

——————— (1991): *see* CHERRY, BRIDGET.

——————— (2007): *see* BETTLEY, JAMES.

PHILLIPS, GEORGE W. (1841): *History and Antiquities of the Parish of Bermondsey* (London: J. Unwin).

PHILLIPS, HENRY (1823): *Sylva Florifera: the Shrubbery historically and botanically treated: with Observations on the Formation of Ornamental Plantations, and Picturesque Scenery* (London: Longmans, Hurst, Rees, Orme, & Brown).

PHILLIPS, SIR RICHARD (1805): *Modern London: being the History and Present State of the British Metropolis* (London: R. Phillips).

PHILLIPS, RICHARD, FRS (1842): *A Brief Account of Hockley Spa near Southend, Essex,... with an Analysis of the Water* (London: Phillips).

PINKS, WILLIAM JOHN (1880): *The History of Clerkenwell* EDWARD J. WOOD (*Ed.*) (London: Charles Herbert).

PLAISANT, MICHÈLE (*Ed.*) (1977): *see* PARREAUX, ANDRÉ (*Ed.*).

POOR ROBIN: AN ALMANACK (1664-1776): (London: Company of Stationers).

POPE, ALEXANDER (1876): *The Poetical Works of Alexander Pope, with Memoir, Explanatory Notes, &c.* (London & New York: Frederick Warne & Co.).

PORTER, ROY SYDNEY (*Ed.*) (1987, 1993): *see* BYNUM, W. F. (*Ed.*).

——————— (1990): *The Medical History of Waters and Spas. Medical History* **x** *Supplement* (London: Wellcome Institute for the History of Medicine).

POTTER, GEORGE WILLIAM (1904): *Hampstead Wells: A Short History of Their Rise and Decline* (London: George Bell). *See* also the reprint with additional material (London: Carlile House Press; Camden History Society 1978).

——————— (1907): *Random Recollections of Hampstead* (London: Eyre & Spottiswoode).

POWNALL, HENRY (1825): *Some Particulars relating to the History of Epsom... with an Account of the Mineral Waters,* etc. (Epsom: W. Dorling; London: J. Hearne).

PRICKETT, FREDERICK (1842): *The History and Antiquities of Highgate, Middlesex* (Highgate: The Author).

PUGH, DAVID (1805-9): *see* HUGHSON, DAVID

PUGIN, AUGUSTUS CHARLES (1808-10): *see* PYNE, WILLIAM HENRY.

PYNE, WILLIAM HENRY, & COMBE, WILLIAM (1808-10): *The Microcosm of London* with plates by AUGUSTUS CHARLES PUGIN & THOMAS ROWLANDSON (London: R. Ackermann's Repository of Arts).

READ, JOAN (1977): *Read about Sydenham Wells* (London: The Author).

REEVE, WILLIAM (1807): *The Favourite Overture, to the Grand melo dramatic romance called the Ocean-Fiend, or the Infant's Peril; as performed... at the Aquatic Theatre...* (London: Skillern & Challoner).

RENDLE, WILLIAM, & NORMAN, PHILIP (1888): *The Inns of Old Southwark and Their Associations* (London: Longmans & Co.).

RICHARDSON, JOSEPH (1788): *The Album of Streatham, or Ministerial Amusements* (London: J. Ridgway).

RICHARDSON, SAMUEL (1735): *A Seasonable Examination of the Pleas and Pretensions of the Proprietors of, and Subscribers to, Play-Houses, erected in Defiance of the Royal Licence* (London: T. Cooper).

RITCHIE, JAMES EWING (1858): *The Night Side of London* (London: W. Tweedie).

ROBERTS, SIR HOWARD, & GODFREY, WALTER HINDES (*Eds.*) (1951): *Survey of London* **xxiii** *South Bank & Vauxhall: The Parish of St Mary Lambeth, Part I* (London: London County Council).

ROBINSON, WILLIAM (1840): *History and Antiquities of the Parish of Tottenham High Cross* (London: J. B. Nichols & Son etc.).

——— (1842-3): *The History and Antiquities of the Parish of Hackney, in the County of Middlesex* (London: John Bowyer Nichols & Son, W. Pickering, & Caleb Turner).

ROCQUE, JOHN (1746): *A Plan of the Cities of London and Westminster...* engraved by JOHN PINE (London: John Pine & John Tinney).

RODWELL, JOHN (1828): *On Water, with Considerations upon the Supply of Water to the Inhabitants of the Metropolis... containing a List of the Pure Soft Spring Water Wells already in Use* (London: John Rodwell).

ROFFE, EDWIN (1865): *Pancredge: A Perambulating Survey, or Topographical & Historical Account of the Parish of St Pancras* (London: E. Roffe).

ROGERS, H. A. (1896): *Views of Some of the Most Celebrated By-Gone Pleasure Gardens of London* (London: H. A. Rogers).

ROGERS, SAMUEL (1856): *Recollections of the Table-Talk of Samuel Rogers* ALEXANDER DYCE (*Ed.*) (London: E. Moxon).

ROSE, MILLICENT (1951): *The East End of London* (London: Cresset Press).

ROWLANDSON, THOMAS (1808-10): *see* PYNE, WILLIAM HENRY.

RUDOLPH, KARL ASMUND (1862): *Numismata* (Danzig: s.n.).

RUSSELL, RICHARD (1753): *A Dissertation concerning the Use of Sea Water in Diseases of the Glands,* &c. (Oxford: James Fletcher; London: J. & J. Rivington).

RUTTY, JOHN (1757): *A Methodical Synopsis of Mineral Waters,* etc. (London: William Johnston).

SADIE, STANLEY (*Ed.*) (2002): *The New Grove Dictionary of Opera* (London: Macmillan).

SAINT, ANDREW (*Gen. Ed.*) (2008*a*): *Survey of London* **xlvi** *South and East Clerkenwell* PHILIP TEMPLE (*Ed.*) (New Haven CT & London: Yale University Press for English Heritage).

——— (2008*b*): *Survey of London* **xlvii** *Northern Clerkenwell and Pentonville* PHILIP TEMPLE (*Ed.*) (New Haven CT & London: Yale University Press for English Heritage).

SALMON, NATHANIEL (1736): *Antiquities of Surrey: Collected from the Most Antient Records. With Some Account of the Present State and Natural History of the County* (London: The Author).

SANDERS, JOHN (1772): *The Bread and Butter Manufactory, or, the Humors of Bagnigge Wells* (London: Carington Bowles).

SANDS, MOLLIE (1946): *Invitation to Ranelagh, 1742-1803* (London: John Westhouse).

——— (1987): *The eighteenth-century pleasure gardens of Marylebone, 1737-1777* (London: Soc. For Theatre Research).

SCHEVICHAVEN, HERMAN DIEDERIK JOHAN VAN (*pseud.*) (1866): *see* LARWOOD, JACOB.

SCHMEISSER, JOHANN GOTTFRIED, & BANKS, JOSEPH (1792): 'Description of Kilburn Wells, and Analysis of Their Water' *Philosophical Transactions of The Royal Society* **lxxxii** (1 January 1792) 115-127.

SCOTT, GEORGE GILBERT (1879): *Proposed Destruction of the Well Walk, Hampstead* (London: The Author).

SCOTT, WALTER SIDNEY (1948): *Bygone Pleasures of London* (London: Marsland).

——— (1955): *Green Retreats: the Story of Vauxhall Gardens, 1661-1859* (London: Oldhams).

SCUDAMORE, CHARLES (1833): *A Treatise on the Composition and Medical Properties of the Mineral Waters of Buxton, Matlock, Tunbridge Wells,... and the Beulah Spa, Norwood* (London: Longman, Rees, Orme, Brown, Green, & Longman).

SCULL, ANDREW T. (1993): *The Most Solitary of Afflictions: Madness and Society in Britain, 1700-1900* (New Haven CT & London: Yale UP).

SEARLE, MURIEL VIVIENNE (1977): *Spas and Watering Places* (Tunbridge Wells: Midas Books).

SERIOUS PERSON OF QUALITY, A (1722): *Belsize-house: A Satyr, exposing the Fops and Beaux who daily frequent that Academy,* etc. (London: T. Warner).

SHEPPARD, FRANCIS H. W. (2000): *London: A History* (Oxford: Oxford UP).

——— (*Gen Ed.*) (1957): *Survey of London* **xxvii** *Spitalfields and Mile End New Town* (London: Athlone Press for the London County Council).

——— (*Gen Ed.*) (1973): *Survey of London* **xxxvii** *Northern Kensington* (London: Athlone Press for the Greater London Council).

——— (*Gen Ed.*) (1983): *Survey of London* **xli** *Southern Kensington: Brompton* (London: Athlone Press for the Greater London Council).

SHERIDAN, RICHARD BRINSLEY BUTLER (1789): *St Patrick's Day: or, the Scheming Lieutenant* (Dublin: P. Byrne).

SHORTER, CLEMENT K. (1924): *see* BOSWELL, JAMES.

SIGERIST, HENRY ERNEST (1946-7): *European Spas Through the Centuries. Ciba Symposia* **viii**/1/2 (April-May) 302-312.

SLEIGH, W. WILLCOCKS (1842): *The Dorton Spas, Bucks. Chalybeate, Sulphurous, and Saline. A Treatise on the Effects produced by the Use of the Waters of Dorton, etc.* (London: J. Ollivier).

SMITH, JOHN THOMAS (1828): *Nollekens and his Times; comprehending a Life of that celebrated Sculptor; and Memoirs of several contemporary Artists* (London: Henry Colburn).

——— (1861): *A Book for a Rainy Day: or, Recollections of the Events of the Years 1766-1833* (London: R. Bentley).

SMITH, THOMAS (1833): *A Topographical and Historical Account of the Parish of St Mary-le-bone* &c. (London: John Smith).

SNODIN, MICHAEL (*Ed.*) (1984): *Rococo: Art and Design in Hogarth's England* (London: Trefoil Books in assn. with the Victoria & Albert Museum).

SOAME, JOHN (1734): *Hampstead-Wells: or, Directions for the drinking of those Waters...With an Appendix, relating to the Original of Springs in General; with some Experiments of the Hampstead Waters, and Histories of Cures* (London: The Author).

SOUTHGATE, THOMAS LEA (1911): *English Music 1604 to 1904* (London: Walter Scott).

——— (1911-12): 'Music at the Public Pleasure Gardens of the Eighteenth Century' *Proceedings of the Royal Musical Association* **xviii** (London: The Association).

SOUTHWORTH, JAMES GRANVILLE (1941): *Vauxhall Gardens: A Chapter in the Social History of England* (New York: Columbia UP).

SPEAIGHT, GEORGE (*Ed.*) (1956): *Professional and Literary Memoirs of Charles Dibdin, the Younger* (London: Society for Theatre Research).

SPENCER, RAINE (1983): *Spencers on Spas* (London: Weidenfeld & Nicolson).

STENTON, SIR FRANK MERRY (1942): *see* GOVER, JOHN ERIC BRUCE.

STONE, ELIZABETH (1845): *Chronicles of Fashion: from the Time of Elizabeth to the early part of the Nineteenth Century, in Manners, Amusements, Banquets, Costume,* &c. (London: Richard Bentley).

STORER, J. & H. S. (1828): *see* CROMWELL, THOMAS KITSON (1828 & 1835).

STOTT, ANDREW MCCONNELL (2009): *The Pantomime Life of Joseph Grimaldi: Laughter, Madness, and the Story of Britain's Greatest Comedian* (Edinburgh: Canongate).

STOW, JOHN (1633): *A Survey of London* etc. (London: John Windet). It contains Fitzstephen's earlier work on London. *See* also the revised edn. of JOHN STRYPE (1754-5): (London: Innys & Richardson, J. & P. Kempton, etc.). The edition used here is that with Introduction and Notes by CHARLES LETHBRIDGE KINGSFORD (1908): *A Survey of London by John Stow. Reprinted from the text of 1603* (Oxford: Clarendon Press).

STOW, WILLIAM (1722): *Remarks on London: Being an Exact Survey of the Cities of London and Westminster, Borough of Southwark, and the Suburbs and Liberties contiguous to them*...etc. (London: T. Norris & H. Tracy).

STRAUS, RALPH (1927): *The Unspeakable Curll: Being Some Account of Edmund Curll, Bookseller; to which is added a Full List of his Books* (London: Chapman & Hall Ltd.).

STRYPE, JOHN (1754-5): *see* STOW, JOHN.

STUART, CHARLES DOUGLAS, & PARK, A. J. (1895): *The Variety Stage: A History of the Music Halls from the Earliest Period to the Present Time* (London: Fisher Unwin).

SUNDERLAND, SEPTIMUS PHILIP (1915): *Old London's Spas, Baths, and Wells* (London: John Bale, Sons, & Danielson).

——————— (1924): 'The Spas of Old London and its Vicinity' *London Society Journal* **lxxxii** 5-12.

SUREL, JEANNINE (1977): 'Un jardin pour les Londoniens: Vauxhall Gardens' in PARREAUX & PLAISANT (*Eds.*) 215-27.

SYMES, MICHAEL (2005): *The English Rococo Garden* (Princes Risborough: Shire Publications).

TAVERNER, JAMES (1737): *An Essay upon the Witham Spa: Or, a Brief Enquiry into the Nature, Virtues, and Uses of a Mineral Chalybeate Water at Witham, Essex* (London: B. Motte & C. Bathurst).

TEMPLE, PHILIP (*Ed.*) (2008*a* and *b*): *see* SAINT, ANDREW (*Gen. Ed.*).

THOMSON, WILLIAM ARCHIBALD ROBSON (1978): *Spas that Heal* (London: A. & C. Black).

THORNBURY, WALTER, & WALFORD, EDWARD (1879-85): *Old and New London: A Narrative of its History, its People, and its Places* (London, Paris, & New York: Cassell, Petter, & Galpin).

THORNE, JAMES (1876): *Hand-Book to the Environs of London* (London: J. Murray).

TIEBEL, H. C. (1896): *Dr Tiebel's Official Handbook of Spas, Watering Places, and Health Resorts* (London: C. Letts & Co.).

TIMBS, JOHN (1865): *The Romance of London: Strange Stories, Scenes, and Remarkable Persons of the Great Town* (London: R. Bentley).

——————— (1867): *Curiosities of London exhibiting the Most Rare and Remarkable Objects of Interest in the Metropolis* (London: Virtue & Co.).

TINSLEY'S MAGAZINE (1870): 'The Chelsea Bowers' **vii** 429-32. Describes aspects of Cremorne Gardens in decline.

TOLAND, JOHN (1711): *The Description of Epsom: With the Humors and Politicks of the Place* (London: A. Baldwin).

TOMLINS, THOMAS EDLYNE (1858): *Yseldon: A Perambulation of Islington* (London: S. Hodson).

TRINDER, WILLIAM MARTIN (1783): *An Enquiry, by Experiments, into the Properties and Effects of the Medicinal Waters in the County of Essex* (London: J. F. & C. Rivington).

——————— (1800): *Chymical Experiments on the Barnet Well Water* (London: Mrs Aldridge). This material also appears in a later work (1812): *The English Olive-Tree;... to which are subjoined chymical experiments on the Barnet Well Water, Harts.* (London: T. Underwood).

——————— (1915): *The Chigwell Row Medicinal Springs: a late-eighteenth-century account of them* MILLER CHRISTIE (*Ed.*) reprinted from *The Essex Naturalist* **xvii** (Stratford).

TRUSLER, JOHN (1786): *The London Adviser and Guide: containing every instruction and information useful and necessary to persons living in London and coming to reside there... Together with an abstract of all those laws which regard their protection against the frauds, impositions, insults, and accidents to which they are liable* (London: The Author).

——————— (1806): *Memoirs of the Rev. Dr. Trusler: with his Opinions on a Variety of Interesting Subjects, through a Long Life, on Men and Manners...Written by Himself. Replete with Humour, Useful Information, and Entertaining Anecdote* (Bath: John Browne).

UNIVERSAL HARMONY; OR, THE GENTLEMAN AND LADIE'S SOCIAL COMPANION: CONSISTING OF A GREAT VARIETY OF THE BEST AND MOST FAVOURITE ENGLISH AND SCOTS SONGS, &c., &c., (1743): Contains an engraved plate by THOMAS KITCHIN (London: J. Newbery).

VICKERY, AMANDA (2009): *Behind Closed Doors: At Home in Georgian England* (New Haven CT & London: Yale University Press).

VINCENT, WILLIAM THOMAS (1888-90): *The Records of the Woolwich District* (Woolwich: J. P. Jackson & London: J. S. Virtue & Co.).

WAKEFIELD, PRISCILLA (1809): *Perambulations in London, and its Environs: comprehending an historical sketch... and a short account of the surrounding villages* (London: Darton & Harvey). A second edn. came out in 1814.

WALFORD, EDWARD (1878): *see* KNIGHT, CHARLES (*Ed.*).

——————— (1879-85): *see* THORNBURY, WALTER.

——————— (1884): *Greater London: A Narrative of its*

History, its People, and its Places (London: Cassell & Co.).

——— (*Ed.*) (1878-81): *A Topographical History of Surrey* by EDWARD WEDLAKE BRAYLEY *revised* and *edited* by EDWARD WALFORD (London: J. S. Virtue & Co.).

WALKER, ANTHONY (1685): *Fax fonte accensa...; or, An endeavour to kindle devotion, from the consideration of the fountains God hath made... Designed for the benefit of those who use the waters of Tunbridg-Wells, the Bath, Epsom, Scarborough, Chigwell, &c.* (London: Nathaniel Ranew).

WALKER, GEORGE ALFRED (1839): *Gatherings from Grave-Yards, Particularly those of London*, etc. (London: Longman &c.).

——— (1843): *Interment and Disinterment* (London: Longman &c.).

WALLER, JOHN GREEN (1875): 'The Hole-Bourne' *London and Middlesex Archaeological Society Transactions* Series I **iv** 97-123.

WARD, EDWARD (1699): *A Walk to Islington: with a New Description of New-Tunbridge-Wells and Sadler's Musick-House* (London: s.n.).

——— (1709): *Miscellaneous Writings* (London: A. Bettesworth).

——— (1714): *The Field-Spy: or, the Walking Observator* (London: J. Woodward & J. Morphew).

WARNER, HENRY (1810): *Survey and Admeasurement of all the Public Roads, Lanes and Footpaths in the Parish of St Mary, Islington, in the County of Middlesex. Measured in May, 1735, by H. Warner* (London: s.n.).

WARRINGTON, JOHN (*Ed.*) (1953): *see* PEPYS, SAMUEL.

WARWICK, JOAN (1986): *Down at Beulah: A Short History of the Royal Beulah Spa and Gardens* (London: Norwood Society).

WEALE, JOHN (1854): *Pictorial Handbook of London, comprising its Antiquities...* etc... *together with some account of the principal Suburbs and Most Attractive Localities* (London: Bohn).

WEATHERHEAD, GEORGE HUME (1832): *An Account of the Beulah Saline Spa at Norwood, Surrey, containing a Description of its Medicinal Properties and Effects, of the Diseases in which it is remedial, and Directions for its Use* (London: J. Hatchard &Son; W. Joy, & S. Highley).

WEBER, FREDERICK PARKES, & WEBER, HERMANN (1898): *The Mineral Waters and Health Resorts of Europe: Treatment of Chronic Diseases by Spas and Climates, with Hints as to the Simultaneous Employment of Various Physical and Dietetic Methods* (London: Smith, Elder). Another edn. subtitled *Climatotherapy and Balneotherapy* came out from the same publisher in 1907. *See* also 1997 edn. (Cambridge: Chadwyck-Healey Ltd.).

WEBER, HERMANN (1898): *see* WEBER, FREDERICK PARKES.

WECHSBERG, JOSEPH (1979): *The Lost World of the Great Spas* (New York & London: Harper & Row).

WEINSTEIN, ROSEMARY (1976): 'An Amazing Flow of Spirits' *Camden History Review* **iv** 32-3.

WELCH, CHARLES (1901): *see* BENHAM, WILLIAM.

WELLCOME INSTITUTE FOR THE HISTORY OF MEDICINE (1988): *Taking the Waters: An Exhibition to Celebrate the Symposium entitled 'The Medical History of Waters and Spas' held on Friday 22 April 1988* (London: Wellcome Institute).

WELSTED, LEONARD (1732): *Of False Fame. An Epistle to the... Earl of Pembroke* (London: T. Cooper).

WHARNCLIFFE, LORD (*Ed.*) (1861): *See* MONTAGU, LADY MARY WORTLEY.

WHEATLEY, HENRY BENJAMIN (1870): *Round About Piccadilly and Pall Mall* (London: Smith, Elder).

——— (1891) *London Past and Present: its History, Associations, and Traditions* (London: John Murray).

WILKINSON, ROBERT (1819-25): *Londina Illustrata: Graphic and Historic Memorials of....Places of Early Amusement....*etc. (London: R. Wilkinson).

WILLIAMS, JOHN, *ET AL.* (1772-3): *The Macaroni and Theatrical Magazine: or, Monthly Register of the Fashions and Diversions of the Times* (London: John Williams).

WILLIAMS, JOHN (1883): *Some London Theatres, Past and Present* (London: Sampson Low, Marston, Searle, & Rivington).

WILLIAMSON, GEORGE CHARLES (*Ed.*) (1889-91): *see* BOYNE, WILLIAM.

WILSON, PHOEBE DE K. (*Ass. Ed.*) (1963): *see* LITTLE, DAVID MASON (*Ed.*).

WITHER, GEORGE (1628): *Britain's Remembrancer...*etc. (London: John Grismond).

WITT, REGINALD ELDRED (1971): *Isis in the Graeco-Roman World* (London: Thames & Hudson).

WITTY, ROBERT (1660): *Scarborough Spaw: or, A Description of the Nature and Vertues of the Spaw... To which is added, a Short Discourse concerning Mineral Waters, especially that of the Spaw* (London: Charles Tyus).

WOOD, EDWARD J. (*Ed.*) (1880): *see* PINKS, WILLIAM JOHN.

WOODWARD, GEORGE MOUTARD (1796): *Eccentric Excursions, or, Literary & Pictorial Sketches of Countenance, Character, & Country in Different parts of England and Wales* (London: Allen & West).

WOODWARD, HORACE BOLINGBROKE (1906): *Soils and Subsoils from a Sanitary Point of View: with especial reference to London and its Neighbourhood* (London: H.M. Stationery Office).

WORSLEY, GILES (1986): '"I thought myself in Paradise": Ranelagh Gardens and its Rotunda' *Country Life* **clxxxix** 1380-4.

WOTY, WILLIAM (1760): *The Shrubs of Parnassus: Consisting of a Variety of Poetical Essays, Moral and Comic, by J. Copywell of Lincoln's Inn, esq.* (London: sold by J. Newbery for The Author).

WRIGHT, GORDON (1994): *see* DUNKLING, LESLIE.

WROTH, WARWICK WILLIAM (1898): 'Tickets of Vauxhall Gardens' *Numismatic Chronicle* 3 ser. **xviii** (London: Royal Numismatic Society) 73-92.

——— (1907): *Cremorne and the Later London Gardens* (London: Elliot Stock).

———, & WROTH, ARTHUR EDGAR (1896): *The London Pleasure Gardens of the Eighteenth Century* (London & New York: Macmillan).

WYLD, JAMES (1834): *A Guide to the Beulah Spa, Norwood, with a descriptive Account of the Surrounding Villages* (London: J. Wyld).

INDEX

Compiled by Auriol Griffith-Jones

'...the best book in the world would owe most to a good index, and the worst...., if it had but a single good thought..., might be kept alive by it...'
HORACE BINNEY (1780-1875): *Letter to Samuel Austin Allibone* (8 April 1868).

Note: Principal Places of Resort are indicated in ***bold italics***. Page numbers in **bold** refer to illustrations; those in *italic* refer to chapter headings